4TH NATIONAL EDITION

LEGAL RESEARCH

How to Find and Understand the Law

BY ATTORNEYS STEPHEN ELIAS
AND SUSAN LEVINKIND

Edited by Janet Portman

NOLO PRESS BERKELEY

YOUR RESPONSIBILITY WHEN USING A SELF-HELP LAW BOOK

We've done our best to give you useful and accurate information in this book. But laws and procedures change frequently and are subject to differing interpretations. If you want legal advice backed by a guarantee, see a lawyer. If you use this book, it's your responsibility to make sure that the facts and general advice contained in it are applicable to your situation.

KEEPING UP TO DATE

To keep its books up to date, Nolo Press issues new printings and new editions periodically. New printings reflect minor legal changes and technical corrections. New editions contain major legal changes, major text additions or major reorganizations. To find out if a later printing or edition of any Nolo book is available, call Nolo Press at (510) 549-1976 or check the catalog in the *Nolo News*, our quarterly newspaper.

To stay current, follow the "Update" service in the *Nolo News*. You can get a two-year subscription to the paper free by sending us the registration card in the back of the book. In another effort to help you use Nolo's latest materials, we offer a 25% discount off the purchase of any new Nolo book if you turn in any earlier printing or edition. (See the "Recycle Offer" in the back of the book.) This book was last printed in **June 1995**.

Fourth Edition	June 1995
Editor	JANET PORTMAN
Production	STEPHANIE HAROLDE
Illustrations	MARI STEIN
Book Design	JACKIE MANCUSO
	EDDIE WARNER
Cover Design	SUSAN WIGHT
Index	SAYRE VAN YOUNG
Proofreading	ELY NEWMAN
Printing	DELTA LITHOGRAPH

Elias, Stephen.
Legal research : how to find and understand the law / by Stephen Elias and Susan Levinkind. -- 4th national ed.
p. cm.
Includes index.
ISBN 0-87337-301-4
1. Legal research--United States--Popular works. I. Levinkind, Susan, 1942- . II. Title.
KF240.E35 1995
349.73'072--dc20
[347.30072]

95-110
CIP

Printed on paper with recycled content.

DEDICATION

To Catherine and Megan
Whose special gifts
Ease these troubled times
And Illuminate my future

—SE

To Elana
my heart's companion
To Andrea
my delightful daughter
To my Mom and Dad
For the art of critical discourse

—SL

ACKNOWLEDGMENTS

Without the contributions of many wonderful people this book would not exist. Our profuse thanks to:

Ralph "Jake" Warner, publisher of Nolo Press, for his unflagging vision of universal access to the law and for turning Nolo's considerable resources loose to make this book the best that it could be.

Mary Randolph and Janet Portman for their editorial genius in pushing an already good book into an infinitely better one.

Jackie Clark Mancuso, Eddie Warner and Stephanie Harolde for turning our caterpillar text into a monarch butterfly.

Ely Newman, copy editor extraordinaire, for being a perfectionist.

Diana Vincent-Daviss, Yale law librarian and Shirley Hart-David, Sacramento County law librarian, for reviewing the manuscript and contributing their considerable professional expertise.

Nolen Barrett and Brigitte Davila for their helpful research assistance.

The staffs of the San Francisco and Alameda County Law Libraries for being invariably helpful and patient when we relied on their skills to develop our materials.

Robert Berring, University of California, Berkeley, Law Librarian, for pioneering the concept that legal research really can be fun.

Terri Hearsh for her Friday photography.

Our legal research students for their insight and suggestions.

Our many wonderful friends at Nolo, each of whom is indispensable to the ultimate success of this book

TABLE OF CONTENTS

LIBRARY EXERCISES

CHAPTER 1

How to Use This Book

Legal research comes in many forms. Legal researchers have a myriad of faces. Recognizing these two obvious facts, we have designed this book to be a flexible tool, of use to researchers of various levels of sophistication.

If you are new to legal research, start with Chapter 2 and work your way through the book. Chapter 2 will introduce you to an efficient and sensible method for approaching most any legal research project. Chapter 3 provides an overview of our legal system. Chapters 4 through 11 show you how to:

- identify your research problem according to recognized legal categories
- locate books that will give you an overview of the law that affects your particular issues
- find, read and understand the law itself: statutes (laws passed by legislatures), regulations (rules issued by government agencies) and cases (decisions by courts)
- use the tools found in all law libraries—*Shepard's Case Citations* and *Case Digests*—that let you find court opinions that address the issues you're interested in
- organize the results of your research into a legal memorandum.

Chapter 12 provides a real-life example that puts all the steps together and gives you a clear picture of how to solve a legal research problem. Chapter 13 provides a brief overview of computer-assisted legal research—what it is and how to use it.

The Appendix contains a set of legal research problems and answers that lets you test your skills in a law library. Selected library exercises to enhance your skills in certain key areas are also contained in several of the chapters. Finally, Chapters 2 through 10 have review questions and answers at the end.

If you already have some general legal research skills but want guidance on a particular aspect or phase, turn to the appropriate chapters and sections for a thorough explanation of a particular strategy.

If you want a quick refresher on the specific steps involved in a particular research task—for example, how to find a particular state statute you've heard about—use our "Summing Up" feature. These are boxed and identified by a symbol. There is also a list of the Summaries directly following the table of contents in the front of the book.

The primary purpose of this book is to show you the "how to do it" of legal research in a regular law library. As mentioned, review questions following Chapters 2 through 10 help you focus on the important points you should know before going on. To the extent you need more in-depth information about a particular research tool or resource, your newly acquired skills will help you find it in the law library itself.

One last word. The best place to read this book is in a law library. Getting your hands on the books will make much of this book come alive in a way that our words, no matter how carefully chosen, can not. You will especially benefit by actually doing—one step at a time—the research examples set out in some of the chapters and by completing the research problems set out in the Appendix.

We'd Like to Hear From You

The Registration Card at the back of the book allows us to notify you of current product information and is our way of hearing from our readers about how they liked (or didn't like!) this book. We use your comments when we prepare for new printings and editions. But we have found that people tend to fill the card out right away, before they have used the book and can tell us specifically what worked and what didn't. Please use the copy of the card printed below as a working sheet to note your thoughts as you use the book, then fill-in the tear-out card and mail it to us. Thanks!

REGISTRATION CARD

NAME ______ DATE ______

ADDRESS ______

______ PHONE NUMBER ______

CITY ______ STATE ______ ZIP ______

WHERE DID YOU HEAR ABOUT THIS BOOK? ______

WHERE DID YOU PURCHASE THIS PRODUCT? ______

DID YOU CONSULT A LAWYER? (PLEASE CIRCLE ONE) YES NO NOT APPLICABLE

DID YOU FIND THIS BOOK HELPFUL? (VERY) 5 4 3 2 1 (NOT AT ALL)

SUGGESTIONS FOR IMPROVING THIS PRODUCT ______

______

WAS IT EASY TO USE? (VERY EASY) 5 4 3 2 1 (VERY DIFFICULT)

DO YOU OWN A COMPUTER? IF SO, WHICH FORMAT? (PLEASE CIRCLE ONE) WINDOWS DOS MAC

YOUR PRIVACY IS IMPORTANT TO US. WE PROMISE NOT TO SELL, RENT OR LEND YOUR NAME AND ADDRESS TO ANY OTHER BUSINESS OR ORGANIZATION.

LRES 4.0

CHAPTER 2

An Overview of Legal Research

This chapter has two purposes: to give you some basic rules for efficient use of the law library and a basic legal research approach good for virtually any legal task. This is nothing we invented; rather, it is the almost-universal method of experienced legal researchers. Once you understand how this overall approach works, any research task will be greatly simplified. Although some of what we say is fairly conventional (for example, keep accurate notes), much of it isn't. For example, we suggest that achieving the highest quality of legal research requires a commitment to perseverance and patience, and a belief in yourself.

A. Patience and Perspective

A certain type of attitude and approach are required to efficiently find the information you need among the billions of other legal facts and opinions in the law library. Probably the most important quality to cultivate is patience—a willingness to follow the basic legal research method diligently, even though it's a time-consuming process. (See Section D, below.)

Unfortunately, many legal researchers are impatient, preferring to make a quick stab at finding the particular piece of information they think they need. While a quest for immediate gratification is sometimes appropriate when attempted by a master researcher, it most often results in no satisfaction at all when attempted by the less experienced.

Perhaps it will be easier to understand how legal research is best approached if we take an analogy from another field.

Seeking and finding information in a law library is a lot like learning how to cook a gourmet dish. To cook the dish you first need to settle on a broad category of cuisine—Japanese, French, Nouvelle California, etc. Next, you would find one or two good cookbooks that provide an overview of the techniques common to that specific cuisine. From there you would get more specific. You would find a recipe to your liking, learn the meaning of unfamiliar cooking terms and make a list of the ingredients. Finally, you would assemble the ingredients and carefully follow the instructions in the recipe.

Legal research also involves identifying a broad category before you search for more specific information. Once you know the general direction in which you're headed, you are prepared to find an appropriate background resource—an encyclopedia, law journal, treatise—to educate yourself about the general issues involved in your research. Armed with this overview, you can then delve into the law itself—cases, statutes, regulations—to find definitive answers to your questions. And, when your research is through, you can pull your work together into a coherent written statement. (We explain in Section E, below, that writing up your research is crucial to knowing whether you're done.)

Of course, in the legal research process there are lots of opportunities for dead ends, misunderstandings and even mental gridlock. Answers that seemed in your hand five minutes ago evaporate when you read a later case or statutory amendment. Issues that seemed crystal clear become muddy with continued reading. And authoritative experts in a field often contradict each other.

Take heart. Even experienced legal researchers often thrash around some before they get on the right track. And the truth is, most legal issues are confused and confusing—that's what makes them legal issues. Just remember that the main difference between the expert and novice researcher is that the expert has faith that sooner or later the research will pan out, while the novice too easily becomes convinced that the whole thing is hopeless. Fortunately, this book and many law librarians are there to help the struggling legal researcher.

B. How to Find (and Feel at Home in) a Law Library

Before you can do legal research, you need access to good research tools. Not surprisingly, these are found primarily in law libraries, although sometimes legal research involves government document and social science collections. Many law libraries are open to the public and can be found in most federal, state and county courthouses.

Law school libraries in public universities also routinely grant access to members of the public, although hours of access may be somewhat restricted depending on the security needs of the school. It is also often possible to gain access to private law libraries maintained by local bar associations, large law firms, state agencies or large corporations if you know a local attorney or are willing to be persistent in seeking permission from the powers that be.

Law libraries can be intimidating at first. The walls are lined with thick and formally bound books that tend to look exactly alike. Then too, for the layperson and beginning student, it is easy to feel that you are treading on some sacred reserve, especially in courthouse libraries where the average user is a formally attired lawyer and where, on occasion, a judge is present. You might even have the secret fear that if it is discovered that you're not a lawyer, you'll either be asked in a loud voice to leave or at best be treated as a second-class citizen.

If you remember that public funds (often court filing fees) probably help buy the books in the library and pay the people running it, any initial unease should disappear. It may also help you to know that most librarians have a sincere interest in helping anyone who desires to use their library. While they won't answer your legal questions for you, they will often put your hands on the materials that will give you a good start on your research or help you get to the next phase.

Another way to deal with any feelings of intimidation is to recall your early experiences with the public library. Remember how the strangeness of all the book shelves, the card catalog and the reference desk rather quickly gave way to an easy familiarity with how they all fit together? Your experience with law libraries will similarly pass from fear to mastery in a very short time.

Helping you understand the cataloging, cross-reference and indexing systems law libraries use is the most important function of this book. As you proceed, we hope you will see that learning to break the code of the law library can be fun.

C. A Basic Approach to Legal Research

The diagram below depicts the usual flow of legal research when you start from scratch. Take a good look at it, but don't worry too much about the details. They are covered in later chapters.

As you can see, the diagram is shaped a bit like an hourglass. You start with a universe of possibilities, then narrow your search until you find one or two relevant cases. In turn, those cases, with the assistance of certain cross-reference tools, allow you to rapidly locate many additional relevant cases.

Your most fervent hope when you start a basic legal research task is to find at least one case that perfectly—and favorably—answers your specific research question in an identical factual context. Of course, this goal is seldom if ever met in reality. But the more cases you can locate that are relevant to your question, the better your chances of nailing down a firm answer.

While this method depicted in the diagram is appropriate for the type of research that involves an open-ended question about the law, it may be overkill for someone who has a very specific research need—find a specific case, read a specific statute, find out whether a specific case is still good law and so on.

Also, we don't intend the diagram as a lockstep approach to legal research. For example, it may be most efficient in certain circumstances to start your research in a *West Digest* (a tool that summarizes cases by the legal topics they address) instead of using a background resource or code for this purpose. It all depends on such variables as the amount of information you already bring to your quest, the time you have to spend and the level of certainty you are after. Your goal, after all, is to arrive at the best possible answer to your question in the least possible time, not to mechanically complete a laborious research process.

Here, then, is the diagram and a discussion of each research step portrayed in it.

Step 1: Formulate Your Legal Questions

The top box, "Your Research Topic," represents the first step in legal research: formulating the questions you wish to answer. This is not easy as you may think. Often we think we have a question in mind but when we try to answer it, we find that we don't quite know what we're looking for. The best bet here is to make sure that your question has a logical answer. For instance, if you have been bitten by a dog and are looking for information about dog bites, break your search down into some specific answerable questions, such as:

- Who is responsible for injury caused by a biting dog?
- What facts do I have to prove to sue and win compensation for the dog bite?
- Is there a statute or ordinance that covers dog bites?
- Does it make any difference if the dog has or has not ever bitten anyone before?

Keep in mind that the first articulation of your research questions will probably change as your research progresses. In this example, you may start out thinking that your issue involves dogs, only to find out that it really involves the duties of a landowner to prevent harm from dangerous conditions on the land.

Step 2: Categorize Your Research Questions

The next box down represents the classification stage. Because of the way legal materials are organized, it is usually necessary to place your research topic into a category described by using the three variables shown in this box. Exactly how this is accomplished is the primary subject of Chapter 4, *Putting Your Questions Into Legal Categories*.

Also covered in Chapter 4 is the next stage in the chart, when you break down your question into many words and phrases. That enables you to use legal indexes to find a background discussion of your topic.

BASIC LEGAL RESEARCH METHOD CHART

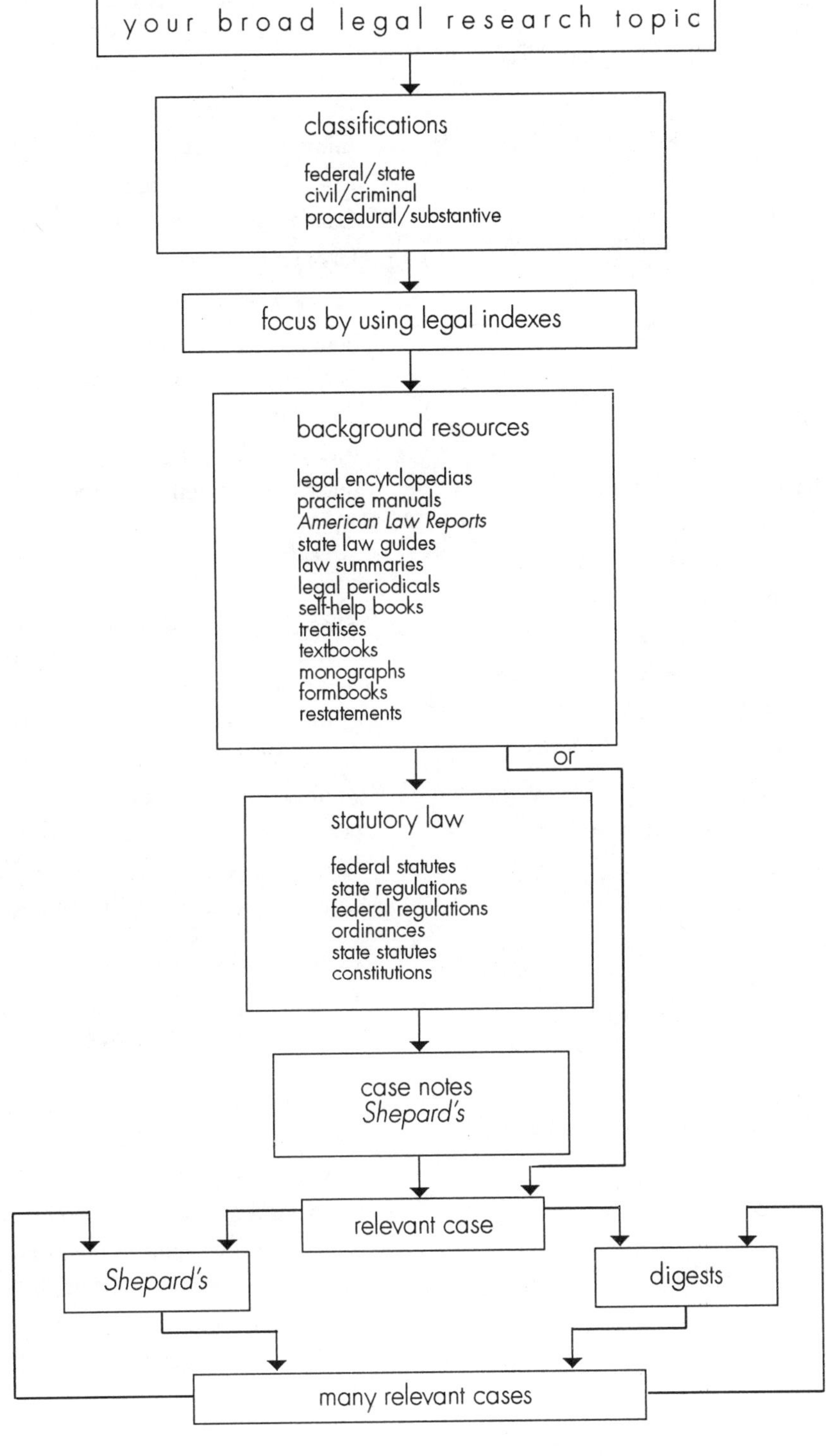

Step 3: Find Appropriate Background Resources

When starting a legal research task, you need an overview of the legal issues connected with your questions and an idea of how your questions fit into the larger legal fabric. This background information can normally best be obtained from books and articles, written by experts, that summarize and explain the subject. How to identify and use these background resources is covered in Chapter 5, *Getting Some Background Information*.

Step 4: Look for Statutes

After you review background resources, you will want to proceed to the law itself. Usually, you should hunt for statutory law first. In most instances, the law starts with legislative or administrative enactments—statutes and rules—and ends with court decisions that interpret them. You too should usually deal with the statutory material first and the cases second. We show you how to research statutes in Chapter 6, *Constitutions, Statutes, Regulations and Ordinances*.

However, some important areas of the law are developed primarily in the courts—the law of torts (personal injuries) is a good example. If you have a tort problem, and the background resource provides you with appropriate references, you might wish to start with cases first, and then come back and research statutory law if and when it is indicated. This alternative path is shown on the chart by the line that goes directly from "Background Resources" to "Relevant Case."

Step 5: Find a Relevant Case

After finding one or more relevant statutes or rules, you will want to see how they have been interpreted by the courts. To pinpoint cases that discuss the statute (or rule, regulation or ordinance) you are interested in, use the tools listed in the next box: case notes, key words and phrases, and *Shepard's Citations for Statutes*. These tools are addressed in Chapter 9, *Finding Cases*.

As soon as you find a case that speaks directly to your research question, you are almost home. This is because two major research tools cross-reference all cases by the issues decided in them. So if you find one case discussing your question, you can often quickly find a bunch of others discussing the same question.

Step 6: Use *Shepard's* and Digests to Find More Cases

Once you find a relevant case, *Shepard's Citations for Cases* and the West digest system allow you to rapidly go from that case to any other cases that have some bearing on your precise questions. These tools are covered in detail in Chapter 10, *Shepard's and Digests: Expand and Update Your Research*.

Step 7: Use *Shepard's* to Update Your Cases

Once you have found cases that pertain to your issue, you need to find out whether the principles stated in these cases are still valid law. To do this, you need to understand the factual context of each case, analyze each case for its value as precedent and use the digests and *Shepard's Citations for Cases* to locate the most recent cases that bear on your issue. We show you how to do all of this in Chapters 7 through 10.

D. Six Time-Saving Research Tips

The research method just outlined, and the techniques explained in the rest of this book, work only if you proceed with method rather than madness. Otherwise, even though you know how to accomplish many legal research tasks, you are still likely to end up sifting through the law library book-by-book, spending many hours more than are necessary. In this context, here are six tips for more efficient legal research.

1. Take Careful Notes

Beginning any legal research effort involves a certain amount of guesswork. You may make several false starts before adopting an approach that works. And what may seem like a wrong approach at first may turn out to be the best one after all. Unfortunately, it is human nature not to carefully keep track of your preliminary work, which means that you may find yourself repeating it.

To avoid this, teach yourself to take complete notes from the beginning on all the materials you're using, including the location and substance of any possibly relevant statute, case or comment mentioned in the materials. It may seem like a burden at first, but it will soon become second nature as you see how often it saves you time in the long run. A good article entitled *How to Look Up Law and Write Legal Memoranda Revisited*, by F. Trowbridge Vom Baur, that provides some still-sound, structured methods for documenting your research, appears in a law journal called *The Practical Lawyer* (May 1965), and is located in most law libraries.

2. Check Out the Law Library

Law libraries are always organized according to some plan. When first using a law library, it is helpful to take a brief self-guided tour, carefully noting where the major groupings of materials are located, so you'll know where to go for your books instead of repeatedly searching from wall-to-wall. This book introduces you to such legal research materials and tools as codes, case reports, digests, encyclopedias and *Shepard's Citations*. Knowing where they are before you dig into your research will make your efforts more efficient. Although many libraries have maps at the reference counter that show where materials are located, they don't replace the walk-around method.

LIBRARY PAPER CHASE

This PAPER CHASE will lead you to many of the legal research resources that you will be learning to use in this book. Follow the instructions, and when you are finished you will have a profound and witty quotation as well as the knowledge of where things are in your law library.

Here is the quotation, with blanks to be filled in according to the instructions for each word:

"________ (1) is ________ (2) ly ________ (3) and ________ (4) ________ (5) ." ________ (6) ________ (7) , ________ (8) - ________ (9)

A. Find the *Unites States Code Annotated (U.S.C.A.)*. Find the volumes for Title 42 Public Health and Welfare. Find the volume containing Title 42 §§ 1771-1982. Turn to page 26. Halfway down the page starts the first section of Chapter 16, Section B. What is the number of the §? Write the number in blank (9).

B. Find the *Supreme Court Reporter*. Find Volume 80A and turn to page 900. What is the last name of the plaintiff in the case starting on page 900, Victor Donald ________? Write the name in blank (7).

C. Find *Federal Reports, 2d series*. Find Volume 939 and turn to page 808. What is the last name of the first named plaintiff in the case starting on page 808, Ruth E. ________? Write the name in blank (6).

D. Find *Federal Supplement*. Find Volume 616 and turn to page 1528. What is the first word of the name of the plaintiff in the case that starts on page 1528, ______ Blue Music, Inc.? Write the word in blank (2).

E. Find the *Federal Practice Digest 4th*. Find the volumes covering Criminal Law. Select Volume 35 and turn to page 725. Find the case in the right-hand column under "C.A. 10 (N.M.) 1985. Eighth Amendment does not apply until after adjudication of guilt." What is the third word of the name of the defendant? Write the word in blank (1).

F. Find *U.S. Code Congressional and Administrative News*. Find the volumes for 103rd Congress First Session 1993, and select Volume 2. The pages in the first part of the book are numbered 107 STAT 1485, then 107 STAT 1486, etc. Go to the Act that starts on page 107 STAT 1547 (NATIONAL DEFENSE AUTHORIZATION ACT FOR FISCAL YEAR 1994). Find § 1702 of the Act (Consolidation of Chemical and Biological Defense Training Activities). What page is it on? 107 STAT ______. Write the page number in blank (8).

G. Find *Corpus Juris Secundum (C.J.S.)*. Find the article on Negligence, and find § 21 that defines mere accident or Act of God. The definition of *Unavoidable accident* starts on page 647. At the end of the first paragraph of this definition is the phrase "and in this sense the term is held to be equivalent to or synonymous with, 'mere accident or ________ accident.'" Write the left-out word in blank (3).

H. Find *American Jurisprudence 2d (Am. Jur. 2d)*. Find the article on Interest and Usury. The article begins with "I. In General; § Definitions and distinctions." The second sentence of Definitions and distinctions starts with the phrase : "________ interest is interest computed on the principal only." Write the left-out word in blank (5)

I. Find *Words and Phrases* (the large 40+ volume set). Find the definition for "Neutral Spirits" in Volume 28A. What is the next word defined? Write the word in blank (4).

Answer: "Truth is rarely pure and never simple." Oscar Wilde, 1854-1900.

3. Collect Your Materials in Advance

As you check different cases and statutes for relevant material, you may find yourself reading only a few lines in many different books. So it is a good idea to make a list of all the books involved in the next phase of your research task and gather them in one place before you start reading. This allows you to find everything you need at once rather than continually popping up and down. While this advice may seem obvious, apparently it isn't; you can observe the "jump up and scurry" approach to legal research on any visit to the library.

4. Find Special Tools and Resources Unique to Your State

This book focuses on the legal research resource tools that are common to the 50 states and are found in the great majority of law libraries. We also discuss some of the resources particular to the more populous states. There are, however, a number of special state-specific tools and resources that we don't mention. So in addition to using the major legal research materials and tools discussed here, check with your law librarian about other state-specific materials.

For instance, where we discuss legal encyclopedias in Chapter 5, we provide the titles of the two main national legal encyclopedias and 15 state-specific encyclopedias. If you are interested in the law of one of the states for which we have not specified an encyclopedia, don't turn to one of the national ones without first checking to see whether the subject you are interested in has been dealt with in a resource designed specifically for your state. If you can find such local materials (perhaps a law review article or a state bar publication), you stand a good chance of finding the answer to your question a lot faster than if you use general or national materials.

5. Get Yourself a Good Law Dictionary

Your legal research will constantly introduce you to new and strange terminology that has developed over hundreds of years. When doing research in the law library, it is extremely helpful to have a good law dictionary at your finger tips.

The most well known law dictionary is *Black's Law Dictionary*. Unfortunately, many of the entries are hard to decipher and are not sufficiently context-sensitive—that is, they are too abstract to fit real-life situations. More user-friendly dictionaries that should serve you well are:

- *Law Dictionary*, Gifis (2d ed. Barron's 1984)
- *Dictionary of Legal Terms: A Simplified Guide to the Language of Law*, Gifis (Barron's 1983)
- *Law Dictionary for Non-Lawyers*, Oran (2d ed. West 1985)
- *Legal Thesaurus/Dictionary*, Statsky (West 1985).

6. Use the Card Catalog

Each law library has a card catalog that lists by author and subject all of the books and periodicals in the library. Sometimes the catalog is computerized and sometimes on cards, but they both work in pretty much the same way. The call number on the upper left-hand portion of the card or on the screens tells where the item is located in that library. If an unaided search seems a bit intimidating at first, the law librarian will be happy to show you where to find your materials.

It is important to remember that many important legal research materials—such as articles, statutes and cases—are collected and published in large books. The card catalog will tell you where the books are located, but it doesn't tell you where a specific article, case or statute is. For example, if you want to do your own divorce and there is no good self-help find such helpful background materials as a law school textbook on divorce law, the *Family Law Reporter* (a loose-leaf publication) and any practice manuals or form books on divorce that have been published for your state. However, you couldn't use it to locate the statutes of your state concerning divorce; nor would the catalog help you find any cases on a particular point. To do that, you would have to use legal indexes and other research tools that we discuss later in the book.

E. Know When You're Done

Legal research rarely produces an absolutely certain answer to a complicated question. Indeed, unless you are searching for a simple bit of information, such as the maximum jail sentence for arson in Texas, trying to find the definitive answer to a legal research problem is often impossible.

There is a reason for this legal "uncertainty principle." Under the American justice system, any dispute that ends up in court is subject to the adversary process, where two or more parties fight it out and a judge or jury decides who wins. Of course, the fact that statutes are constantly cranked out and amended by legislatures and then subjected to judicial definition and redefinition substantially adds to the total confusion.

What all this means is that defining the "law" that governs any set of facts almost by definition involves predicting how the courts would rule if presented with the question. If a prediction is based on clear statutes and court decisions, the level of uncertainty will be fairly low. However, if statutes and case law are themselves subject to conflicting interpretations, as many are, then even the best legal research may amount to little more than a sophisticated form of fortune-telling. Put another way, while in some instances you may believe you have found out "what the law is," a person with a different set of preconceptions will probably arrive at a different result.

Why do we mention the legal uncertainty principle? Simply to warn you against trying to nail down an absolute answer to most legal questions. Often, the best you can hope for is to understand the legal issues involved in a particular problem well enough to convince those who need to be convinced that your view is correct.

Once you understand your search for the truth will necessarily come up short of absolute certainty, how can you tell when it's time to quit? To answer this question when the time comes, it's essential to develop a good sense of proportion and priorities.

Here are some questions to answer as part of trying to conscientiously answer the big question, "Are you done?"

- *Have you logically answered the question you wanted answered when you began?* To test your answer, buttonhole a friend, pose your question and then answer it on the basis of what your research disclosed. You will soon discover whether your logic holds up.
- *Are the laws and facts in the cases you have found pertinent to the facts of your situation?* To test your answer, decide whether the difference between the facts of your situation and the facts of any cases you've found (or those addressed by the statute you've located) could possibly make a difference in the answer to your question.
- *Are the materials you've found to support your answer as up-to-date as you can get?* Because law changes so rapidly, a case or statute that is only a year old may already be obsolete. You haven't finished your research until you've checked all information to be sure it's current.
- *Have you used all major research resources that might improve your understanding or make your answer*

more certain? If there are four different resources that might bear on a tax problem (for example, books that interpret Internal Service Revenue regulations), it is wise to check all four rather than presuming any one to be correct.

- *Can you explain your reasoning in writing?* If your research is reasonably complete, you should be able to express in writing the question you researched, your answer to it and the basis for your answer. It is common to think you've finished a research task, only to discover when you try to write it up that there are gaping holes. Chapter 11 suggests some guidelines for putting your research results into written form, and the answers to the research problems in Appendix 2 contain sample memoranda as examples.

If your answer to all the questions posed above is a resounding or even qualified "yes," then you've probably done about as much as makes sense. If you feel, however, that any of these questions deserves an honest "no" or a waffling "maybe," you have more work to do.

REVIEW

Questions

1. *Where can law libraries be found?*
2. *Give six examples of legal research.*
3. *What is your most fervent hope when you begin a basic legal research task?*
4. *What are the seven basic steps to legal research?*
5. *What are some ways to know when you're done with your research?*

Answers

1. Most federal, state and county courthouses.

   Law schools.

   Privately maintained law libraries (local bar associations, large law firms, state agencies and large corporations).
2. A police officer looks in her manual to decide what charges to hold a criminal suspect for.

   A social security recipient calls up his regional office to ask about the agency's eligibility policies.

   Looking up a specific statute.

   Reading a newly-decided U.S. Supreme Court case.

   Studying a new federal regulation published in the *Federal Register*.

   Obtaining documents from a state or federal government.
3. To find at least one case that perfectly—and favorably—answers your specific research question in an identical factual context.
4. Formulate your research questions.

   Categorize your research questions.

   Find appropriate background resources.

   Look for statutes.

   Find a relevant case.

   Use *Shepard's* and Digests to find more cases.

   Use *Shepard's* to update your cases.
5. You have logically answered the question you wanted answered when you began.

   The laws and facts in the cases you've found are pertinent to the particular facts of your situation.

   The materials you've found to support your answers are as up-to-date as you can get.

   You have utilized all major research resources that might improve your understanding or make your answer more certain.

CHAPTER 3

An Overview of the Law

A. What Is the Law?

In this book we generally think of "law" as the sum total of the rules governing individual and group behavior that are enforceable in court. Primarily, as you will see, this means state and federal statutes, agency regulations, local ordinances and court decisions. However, this is not the only possible definition of law.

It's important to view law in a more practical way, focusing not only on the law as it is written down in statutes and casebooks, but also on what happens in the real world. For example, if the Social Security Administration terminates the disability benefits of eligible recipients despite the repeated rulings of federal courts that such terminations violate federal law, the fact that the federal law exists appears of little value to the people affected. Similarly, if police and prosecutors are reluctant to prosecute certain types of crimes, such as those involving domestic violence, law as it exists in the community will be far different than what is written in the books. Finally, suppose a Supreme Court justice votes to reverse a murder conviction on the basis of previous court decisions. If the other eight vote to uphold the conviction, the "law" will appear vastly different to the one justice and the condemned person than to the eight-justice majority.

At the very least, we recommend cross-checking information from library research with what goes on in the particular legal area on a day-to-day basis. Probably the best way is to check your conclusions with lawyers or other people familiar with local court, agency or police practices.

Another important view of law is that our Constitution is ultimately subject to a higher law. Some people believe that this law exists in nature and applies to everyone whether they ascribe to it or not; others believe that ethics are many sets of rules developed by various philosophers over the ages and either chosen or imposed on society. Those who believe that ethics are derived from one true source are often the ones who want only judges who will rule a particular way on such issues as abortion, capital punishment and prayer in schools reflects this approach to law. When Supreme Court nominees come before the Senate for confirmation, they usually are asked whether they believe that written law—constitution, statutes, cases—is all there is, or whether natural law should be used to "inform" or guide their interpretations of the Constitution.

CHANGING THE LAW

A number of groups who feel that the American legal system is no longer designed to produce justice are engaged in an effort to examine and replace many of the system's legal underpinnings. This effort is not dealt with in this book. If you believe things should be different than they are, and you find no support for your view in existing statutory or case law, you may wish to study some of the books you will find cataloged under the heading "jurisprudence" in any good-sized law library. Legal reform, ethics, philosophy and religion are other likely headings.

Also, there are an increasing number of groups dedicated to changing the law in a specific area. One is MADD (Mothers Against Drunk Driving), a group that is generally credited with pushing judges and legislatures into imposing substantial punishment on drunk drivers. Another national group is HALT (Americans for Legal Reform), which is working to increase access to the courts and cut the lawyer monopoly down to size. For a number of suggestions on how our legal system might be changed for the better, see *Fed Up With the Legal System* (Nolo Press).

B. Foundations of American Law

Because we draw our cultural heritage from so many different traditions, our legal system is a bit like a jigsaw puzzle. There are big pieces of English law (itself drawn from Norman, German, Saxon, Scandinavian and Roman societies) side-by-side with smaller bits from Spanish, French, Native American and ancient biblical sources. These have all been modified by our peculiar North American experience.

Until the 12th century, law in the western world operated on several primary levels. Collections of written laws, such as the *Augustinian Code* or the *Code of Charlemagne* (both traceable to Roman law) created a broad written legal framework. This basic system still prevails in many countries (and in Louisiana in this country) and is known as the "civil" law. In addition, the Catholic Church governed many activities under a large body of ecclesiastical law. Finally, all kinds of rules and regulations, many of which were never written down, were enforced by kings, local lords and courts, both ecclesiastical and secular.

A legal tradition called the "common" law, quite different from that of the civil law, developed in England after the Norman conquest in 1066. At least since the reign of the great legal reformer Henry II in the 1100s, decisions by English grand juries, kings, magistrates and (slightly later) trial juries were written down and eventually catalogued according to the type of case. When the courts were called on to decide similar issues in subsequent cases, they reviewed the earlier decisions and, if one was found that logically covered the contemporary case, they applied the principle of the earlier decision. This doctrine is called *stare decisis*—Latin for "let the decision stand." The common law thus consists of court opinions in specific disputes that state legal principles and must be followed in subsequent court cases about the same type of dispute.

This does not mean that every judge's decisions stand forever. Courts, however imperfectly, reflect society's values, and old case law is rejected as society changes. The principle of *stare decisis* is a strong one, however; judges are reluctant to discard well-established rules and take pains to explain (or deny) a significant departure from precedent.

Large areas of law developed in England in this case-by-case common law tradition. Eventually, two basic types of courts evolved: the law courts and special "chancery" courts established by the king to handle types of cases and provide types of relief that tradition did not allow the regular courts to entertain. The principles developed in the law courts were called "legal" or "law," while the principles developed in the king's chancery courts were called "equitable" or "equity." This distinction still exists in modern American law, although there are usually no longer two separate kinds of courts.

England also, beginning hesitantly with the Magna Carta in 1215, developed a parliamentary system under which statutes proposed by the king or his ministers were enacted by Parliament. These statutes were gathered together in books not too different from civil law codes.

During America's colonial period, most of the English common law tradition and many of the English statutes became firmly entrenched, though modified to some extent in accordance with the religious and cultural beliefs of the colonists. At independence, the basic legal system did not change. For the most part, the new country simply continued to follow English law.

There was, of course, one big difference. The U.S. Constitution was ratified in 1789, and neither the laws of Parliament nor the edicts of King George III had any further power in the new United States. The Constitution became the foundation on which our legal house was built. Both the law inherited from England and that enacted by Congress and state legislatures eventually had to either find support in this foundation or be discarded.

C. The Increasing Importance of Statutes and Regulations

In the 200-plus years of American history, the English common law (case-by-case) tradition has been modified. Statutes and administrative regulations have become more important, both to make new law and codify (put into a written, prescriptive form) broad principles developed by the case law. Especially since the New Deal of the 1930s, federal and state agencies have been created at a rapid rate. Most of these agencies have the authority, within certain prescribed limits, to make rules that have the force of statutes passed by Congress and state legislatures. Many of them also have the power to judge disputes that arise under these rules. For example, Congress passed a statute—the Social Security Act of 1935—that created the Social Security Administration (SSA). The Social Security Act also authorizes the SSA to write rules, and to set up its own forums to decide disputes that arise under the rules.

D. The Development of American Common Law

Despite the increasing importance of statutes and regulations, many areas of our law still consist almost entirely of court decisions—but now by American courts. Also, the courts of this country are empowered to interpret statutes when a dispute arises as to their meaning. As well as using other interpretative techniques, a judge will look at earlier cases to see how they have interpreted the statute and will apply the prevailing interpretation unless she feels it is wrong or clearly doesn't apply to the current dispute. In other words, court opinions in America, as in England, serve as authority or "precedent," which is often binding and always important to subsequent court decisions.

The courts whose decisions are published and thus become part of the common law are almost always appellate courts, not trial courts. Trials are for determining facts. In other words, it's usually a jury that decides who did it, while the legal consequences of the act are left to the judge. If a question that involves the law, or the way the law was applied in the trial, is appealed to an appellate court, the appellate judges (there is no jury) generally issue a written opinion that decides the legal questions presented in the appeal. Only in very rare instances will an appellate court agree to review the factual findings of the judge or jury. (Appeals are discussed in more detail in Section F2, below.)

So far we have talked about America as if it were one political unit. For many reasons, it often seems like this is true. However, it is important to remember that we have a federal system under which 50 sovereign political states voluntarily banded together and agreed to give the federal government certain powers spelled out in the U.S. Constitution. All powers not expressly granted to the federal government are reserved to the states. The states in turn have divvied up some of their power among counties, cities and special districts.

E. Where Modern American Law Comes From

Laws are made at three basic levels: federal, state and local. Operating at each of these levels are three sources of law: legislatures, judges and executive officers (usually acting through government agencies). See the list set out below. The next chapter provides some tips on deciding which source of law controls your issue.

SOURCES OF LAW

- The U.S. and state constitutions and cases that interpret them produce constitutional law.
- Congress passes laws called "statutes," which constitute federal statutory law.
- Federal courts decide cases and write opinions that constitute federal case law.
- Federal courts decide cases and write opinions about state statutes when the parties before the court are from different states.
- Federal administrative agencies created by Congress and staffed by the executive branch issue regulations that constitute the federal administrative law.
- Sovereign Indian tribes have their own courts and laws, which constitute tribal law.
- State legislatures pass statutes, which constitute state statutory law.
- State courts decide state cases and write opinions, which constitute state case law.
- State administrative agencies (created by state legislatures and staffed by governors' office appointees) write regulations, which constitute state administrative law.
- Local governments pass ordinances that become police codes, building codes, planning codes, health codes, etc.

F. About Going to Court

When someone new to the law, whether law student, paralegal or citizen interested in her own case, thinks of "going to court," the images that come to mind are often movie-like scenes with argumentative attorneys, stern judges and courtrooms filled with spectators and the press. The complexity of it all can seem too much to deal with. As one judge put it:

> *The lay litigant enters a temple of mysteries whose ceremonies are dark, complex and unfathomable. Pretrial procedures are the cabalistic rituals of the lawyers and judges who serve as priests and high priests. The layman knows nothing of their tactical significance. He knows only that his case remains in limbo while the priests and high priests chant their lengthy and arcane pretrial rites.*[1]

In fact, the great majority of court matters are handled in a quite straightforward manner, without fanfare, argument or stress. Typical are cases that ask a judge to appoint a guardian or conservator, approve an adoption or name change, allow the probate of a simple estate, grant an uncontested divorce or seal a criminal record. On the other hand, criminal cases are usually no picnic, and *any* case can get messy when a real dispute exists or lawyers have a financial incentive to string the matter out, as can often be the case in complicated business disputes for which attorneys bill by the hour.

SMALL CLAIMS COURT

All states have a small claims court or procedure with simplified rules and procedures that are usually fairly easy to follow. Small claims court clerks are usually required by statute to help people with all procedural details. If you can squeeze the amount of your monetary claim within the small claim limits for your state (usually about $2,000 to $5,000), you may find that small claims court is an excellent alternative to the formal legal system. One of the nicest aspects of small claims court is that in many states litigants are not allowed to be represented by lawyers. By learning to do your own research and writing, you can present a solid case and not run the risk of being overwhelmed by an experienced hired gun on the other side. Unfortunately, most small claims courts are not designed to handle problems other than those where one person has a monetary claim against the other. (For more information, see *Everybody's Guide to Small Claims Court,* by Warner (National and California editions, Nolo Press).)

[1] *Daley v. County of Butte*, 227 Cal. App. 2d 380, 392 (1964).

But whatever the matter, filing a case and pushing it through court always involves carefully following a number of technical court rules. The trick is knowing these procedural rules in minute detail. Among the highest of compliments a lawyer can be paid is, "she sure knows her way around the courthouse"—that is, she has mastered the rules of the game. Fortunately, these rules are, for the most part, available to all.

For example, suppose you want court protection against someone in your household who is abusing you. You must understand not only the law that governs such a situation (what protection is available), but also the actual steps that you must follow to properly get your request before a judge. You may have the best case in the world, but a lack of knowledge about court procedures will prevent anyone from knowing about it.

This is not a practice guide This section talks in general terms about the steps in civil litigation, and it is not intended as a guide for the aspiring lawyer or paralegal, or for the reader who intends to represent herself in court. To find out in more detail about civil *and* criminal procedure, start with a good background resource (as discussed in Chapter 5). You can get information about how to represent yourself in a civil court proceeding in *Represent Yourself in Court,* by Paul Bergman and Sara J. Berman-Barrett (Nolo Press).

1. How a Court Case Works: Steps in Litigation

Court procedures and rules are substantially similar in all state and federal courts. Details vary, however, and similar procedures are often referred to by different names. For example, an eviction action is called "unlawful detainer" in California and "summary process" in Massachusetts. Yet, both types of proceedings are basically quite similar.

If your case is uncontested—that is, there's no dispute and it's simply a matter of getting the papers right—a lot of this section won't apply. The discussion here is intended primarily for people who are involved in a civil dispute that the court is being asked to resolve. It looks at how a typical contested case develops and proceeds through the courts.

a. The Pretrial Process

The first phase of a contested civil case is called the pre-trial phase.

■ The plaintiff files a complaint

A case begins when a document called a "complaint" is filed with the court by the plaintiff (the party who sues). This document tells what happened and what the plaintiff wants done about it—that is, a monetary award, court order or other remedy.

■ The defendant responds

The defendant (the party who is sued) is given (served with) a copy of the complaint and has a certain time to respond in writing—usually 30 days. If no response is made, a "default" judgment may be obtained by the plaintiff, which means the plaintiff wins without having to fully prove the case.

There are a variety of ways the defendant may respond. Together, the plaintiff's complaint and the defendant's responsive papers are commonly referred to as the "pleadings" in the case.

The Answer Most commonly, the defendant files an "answer," a statement setting out which parts of the complaint the defendant agrees and disagrees with. Under the procedural rules of most states, the defendant's answer can also contain affirmative defenses (factual statements of the reasons or excuses for the defendant's actions) and counterclaims (claims that the plaintiff in fact owes the defendant money). The defendant can also state that she doesn't have enough information about the allegations and denies the complaint on that basis.

Motion to Dismiss for Failure to State a Claim This document—also called a "demurrer" in some states—asks the court to dismiss the suit in lieu of requiring an answer from the defendant. Usually, the basis for this request boils down to this: even if the facts in the plaintiff's complaint are true, so what? Or to put the same thing a little more formally, the defendant is saying that the plaintiff has no legal theory (given the facts as the plaintiff has alleged them) upon which to properly base a lawsuit. The defendant is requesting the court to stop the plaintiff from wasting everyone's time and to end the matter then and there.

The court does not decide any facts as part of a hearing on a motion to dismiss. Strictly for the purpose of deciding the motion, the judge assumes that the factual allegations in the complaint are true and then decides whether the law supports the claim for relief. If the judge grants the motion, but allows the plaintiff a chance to fix the problem ("granted with leave to amend"), the plaintiff simply re-writes the Complaint and the process starts all over again. If the judge grants the motion without leave to amend, the case is ended unless the plaintiff appeals the decision. On the other hand, if the judge overrules (denies) the demurrer, the defendant must file an answer. The defendant can ask the appellate court to review the denial (called asking for a "writ of mandamus"), but this remedy is rarely granted.

■ Both sides engage in discovery

From the time that the pleadings in a case are filed (and rarely, before), each party has the right to engage in an activity termed "discovery." Discovery involves a number of specific procedures by which the parties seek information from each other both to bolster their case and prevent Perry Mason-type surprises at trial.

Discovery often adds considerably to the time and expense of litigation. Because each side usually attempts to avoid giving information to the other, disputes constantly arise over what information must be turned over. These disputes are resolved by the trial court in "discovery motion" proceedings. If a party does not like the result, it is usually possible to take the matter to a higher court before the underlying case proceeds further. Accordingly, discovery often results in cases going into a holding pattern.

Normally, discovery consists of the following devices:

Depositions Witnesses or parties are required to go to the office of one of the attorneys and answer questions, under oath, about their knowledge of the dispute. The testimony is taken down by a stenographer or, increasingly, by a tape recorder. Usually the attorney for the side of the case on which the witness will testify is also present.

Interrogatories One party sends another written questions to be answered under oath by a certain date. Interrogatories are also used to ask the other party to identify the source and validity of documents that may be introduced as evidence at trial.

Admissions of Facts Factual statements are set out that the other side must admit or deny. Anything that isn't denied is considered admitted.

Production of Documents One party asks another to produce specified documents. In a complicated case, one side may ask the other for file cabinets full of material. There are often arguments (motions heard by a judge) about how much fishing one side can do in the other's records.

■ Summary judgment is requested

Once the pleadings are on file, either side may ask the court to rule in their favor without trial. To get a summary judgment, the party must show the absence of a dispute about any important facts in the case (called "triable issues of material fact"). This showing is made in the form of written statements under oath, termed "declarations" or "affidavits." Trials serve to determine facts, so if there are no disputed facts, there's no reason to have a trial. The judge can go ahead and apply the relevant law to the undisputed facts.

DIFFERENT SIDES OF THE COIN: THE DIFFERENCE BETWEEN A DEMURRER AND SUMMARY JUDGMENT

A demurrer and a motion for summary judgment are both motions that may be made by the defense in an attempt to get rid of the case before it goes further. (The plaintiff may also move for summary judgment, in an attempt to secure a quick victory without the expense of a trial.) A demurrer argues to the judge "All the factual claims are true, but there's no legal issue here"; a motion for summary judgment says "In spite of the claims, there's no *real* factual dispute that would merit a full trial." In federal court, a demurrer is brought as a motion to dismiss.

Example 1 Peter is a woodworker who lives on United States government land (a federal Air Force base) and sells wooden toys to the toy store on the base. The written agreement with the store specifies the price the store will pay for each toy, when Peter is to deliver the toys, and what materials he is to use. The contract says nothing about the store buying a minimum number of toys each month. Peter has increased his production and would like the store to buy his entire line, and he sues them in federal court for breach of contract when they refuse. The toy store files a "motion to dismiss," pointing out that since the contract does not have an "output" clause they cannot legally be forced to buy all of Peter's toys.

Example 2 Peter's sales to the toy store continue and one of his toys, a rocking horse, is sold to a family with a two-year old. The child develops a rash that the parents believe is caused by the finish on the rocking horse. Peter discovers that all of the children in the youngster's day care center on the base have identical rashes, which have been traced to the use of a harsh cleanser on the center's furniture. Armed with an affidavit from the center's Director, Peter moves for "summary judgment." The parents are unable to offer factual support for their theory that the toy's finish caused the rash, so the court grants Peter's motion.

■ One or more sides files motions

At any time after the pleadings have been filed, but before trial, the plaintiff or defendant may ask the court to order the other side to do something or to refrain from doing something. Sometimes these requests, called motions, are used to preserve the status quo until the case can come to trial. For example, if the circumstances are truly urgent, a party can request the court to issue a "temporary restraining order" (TRO) or "preliminary injunction" stopping the defendant from taking some action before trial. As mentioned, motions may also be filed to enforce discovery (that is, to require a party to answer questions or produce documents when appropriate) or to protect a party against abusive discovery (for example, requiring attendance at a week-long deposition).

■ One side requests a trial date

In some court systems, a case is never set for trial unless one of the parties requests it. Accordingly, a party who feels adequately prepared can file a document with the court requesting a trial and specifying whether it should be held in front of a jury. These documents are called by a wide variety of names in different courts, including "memorandum to set," "at-issue memorandum" and "motion to set for trial." Whatever their names, they may either be opposed by the other party, for a variety of reasons, or agreed to.

■ A pre-trial conference is held

Usually, once a case is set for trial, a pre-trial conference between the parties, their lawyers and the judge is scheduled. At the pre-trial conference, the judge makes sure that everyone understands what the remaining issues are in the case and gets an idea of how long the trial will take. Many judges use these conferences—often quite successfully—to pressure the parties to settle the case. If no settlement is reached, the trial date is fixed.

b. The Trial

Most lawsuits never go to trial. Instead, the parties settle their dispute or simply drop the case. If a case does go to trial, it's usually because the parties disagree so much about the underlying facts that they need a judge to decide whose version is correct.

Trials involve a set of rituals that are supposed to ferret out the truth. No one trial is like any other—they all are a function of who the parties are, what type of legal issues are involved, the personalities of the attorneys and the demeanor of the judge. But the biggest determinant of what happens in a trial is whether it is a trial by jury or a trial by judge. Many of the rules governing trial procedure are aimed at producing an impartial jury and making sure that the jury doesn't receive evidence that is unreliable in some fundamental way. Judges on the other hand are presumed to be able to act impartially and tell reliable evidence from unreliable evidence.

■ Jury trials

Jury trials begin with the selection of the jury. The judge and lawyers for both sides question potential jurors about their knowledge of the case and possible biases relating to their clients and the important issues in the case. This process is called "voir dire."

MOTIONS IN LIMINE

From the first moment of the trial to the last, one or both parties may want the judge to run some aspect of the trial in a certain way. For instance, the plaintiff may want to prevent the defendant from even trying to prove a certain point, believing that to do so would hopelessly prejudice the jury against the plaintiff. These types of requests are called "motions in limine" (that is, motion on the verge of trial). They are considered by the judge in a meeting outside the hearing of the jury, usually in the judge's office.

Once a jury is selected, the attorneys address the jury in opening statements that outline what they expect to show in the upcoming trial. Then the plaintiff begins, offering testimony from witnesses and information in documents to establish a version of events. The testimony and documents are then subject to challenge by the defendant through a process called "cross-examination."

Once the plaintiff's case is presented, the defendant has the opportunity to present a defense, subject to the plaintiff's cross-examination. Commonly, the plaintiff gets the last shot (called a "rebuttal") in an opportunity to answer the defendant's case .

RESEARCHING THE RULES OF EVIDENCE

Any source of information that a party offers as proof of a fact is called "evidence." There is admissible evidence and inadmissible evidence, and the rules that determine which is which are quite complex. But they almost always revolve around two issues:

- whether a particular source of information is too unreliable to let a jury consider
- whether an out-of-court conversation that someone is trying to introduce may be kept out of evidence.

Many of the disputes during a trial revolve around what evidence is admissible and what isn't, and the many bench conferences (when the attorneys and the judge huddle and whisper out of the jury's hearing) that occur during the typical trial involve whether a bit of testimony or a particular document should or should not be allowed "into evidence." Decisions by the judge on these disputes are often the subject of severe Monday-morning quarterbacking by the losing party in an appeal.

The rules of evidence for each state are usually published as part of that state's statutes. Most states also have background resources that devote themselves to analyzing the rules of evidence in excruciating detail. Although evidence is clearly related to court procedure, it is often considered a "substantive law" field of its own. (See Chapter 5, *Getting Some Background Information*.)

When the parties are through presenting their cases, each side gets to make a closing argument, summarizing what they think they've proved and imploring the jury to see it their way. Then the judge explains to the jurors that it is their job to decide what the facts are in the case and that they should follow certain legal principles in deciding whether those facts warrant a decision for the plaintiff or the defendant. Collectively, these explanations are called "jury instructions."

Although it is the judge's responsibility to give the instructions, the plaintiff and defendant are first invited to give the judge their proposed instructions. Because the jury instructions in a case often determine who will win and who will lose, both sides spend a considerable amount of time drafting instructions that will be most favorable to their side. A meeting between the judge and the parties is held to iron out discrepancies, the judge being the final decision maker. Then the judge assembles the instructions that are to be given in a final written version and reads from it verbatim.

RESEARCHING JURY INSTRUCTIONS

Compilations of acceptable jury instructions are available in most states for common types of cases—for instance, auto accident cases. In California, jury instructions are published in a series called B.A.J.I. (*Book of Approved Jury Instructions*) (West Publishing Co.). Federal jury instructions can be found in *Modern Federal Jury Instructions,* by Sand (Matthew Bender).

If the losing party appeals, the instructions that were offered by that party but rejected by the judge often form an important part of the appeal, since the decision by the judge is considered a "legal decision" that is an appropriate subject for an appeals court. (See subsection 2, below.)

Once the jury has heard the instructions, they retire to a room to decide the case. In civil cases the plaintiff must prove its case by a "preponderance of evidence"—that is, it must be more probable than not that the plaintiff is right. The jury need not be unanimous; the normal requirement is a 3/4 vote in favor of the either the plaintiff. Most civil juries consist of twelve jurors, but some states are experimenting with six-member juries.

When the jury has reached a verdict, they report it to the judge, who announces it in open court with the parties present.

If either party is dissatisfied with the verdict, they can ask the judge to set it aside or modify it. But usually the judge upholds the verdict and issues a judgment for the winner.

■ Judge trials

Judge trials are a lot easier than jury trials. There are far fewer squabbles about evidence, since there is no jury to be concerned about, and no jury instructions to prepare. When all the evidence is in and parties have made final arguments to the judge, the judge decides the case and issues a judgment, usually accompanied by a document termed "Findings of Facts and Conclusions of Law." This document lets the parties know why the judge reached the decision and gives them a basis for deciding whether or not to appeal.

2. Appeals

Any party who is dissatisfied with the judgment may appeal the issue to a higher court. Appeals are almost always about the legal decisions made in a trial—in jury trials decisions about evidence and the jury instructions, and in judge trials decisions about the judge's conclusions of law. They are seldom about the decision by the judge or jury as to whether certain facts were true or false. However, some appeals successfully argue that the judge's or jury's decision was not properly based on the evidence introduced in the case.

Appeals are usually allowed from final decisions in a case, such as a judgment of dismissal, summary judgment or judgment after trial. However, sometimes decisions by the court before final judgment is entered can also be reviewed by an appellate court before the trial continues. These are termed "interlocutory appeals."

For example, as discussed in subsection 1, above, parties are usually subjected to a pre-trial process called "discovery." This requires each side to disclose to the other the evidence and testimony that will be presented at trial so that the element of surprise is reduced. Should one party refuse to disclose information, the other party can seek an order from the court requiring disclosure. If the non-disclosing party wants to contest the court order, an appellate court can be asked to immediately step in and decide whether the order was improper. These interim interlocutory appeals are the exception to the rule; appellate courts much prefer to refrain from reviewing lower court decisions until the trial is over and they can decide all questions at once.

In some states, seeking help from a higher court in these situations is termed an appeal, while in others it is termed a request for a "writ of mandate" or "writ of prohibition." Writs are orders directed at officials by courts, or at lower courts by higher ones. When immediate relief from a higher court is necessary, the relief often involves a "petition for a writ" rather than the "filing of an appeal."

As mentioned, sometimes the basis of an appeal is a disagreement with the trial court's determination of the facts. This might happen, for instance, when there is clear and overwhelming evidence on behalf of one party, but the judge or jury ignores the evidence and finds for the other side. Generally speaking, however, appellate courts don't disturb a trial court's determination of the facts unless it was completely unsupported by the evidence.

In an appeal, "briefs"—typewritten statements of the parties' view of the facts and law— are submitted to the appellate court. The appellate court also has a copy of the entire written "record" of the trial court. This record usually consists of all documents submitted by the parties to the trial court, exhibits and documents introduced in the trial, a transcript of exactly what was said at the trial (produced by a court reporter or a tape recorder), and all judgments and orders entered by the trial court.

In addition to considering the briefs and the trial court record, the appellate court usually hears oral argument from the attorneys on each side. After the oral argument, the justices (judges on courts of appeal are usually called "justices") discuss the case and arrive at a decision. A justice representing the majority (sometimes the justices who hear the case will not agree on how it should be decided) is assigned to write the opinion.

If a party disagrees with the outcome of an appeal in the appellate court, another appeal can usually be made—to a state supreme court or the U.S. Supreme Court. (See Chapter 7, Section B, for which courts appeals are filed in.) That requires filing a "Petition for Hearing" (in a state court), or a "Petition for Writ of Certiorari," or, as it is usually called, "Petition for Cert," asking the U.S. Supreme Court to consider the case. If the Court grants a hearing or issues a Writ of Certiorari to the court that decided the case being appealed, it will consider the case. If it denies a hearing or cert, then it won't.

Supreme courts grant hearings or cert only in a very small percentage of cases presented to them. They usually choose cases that present interesting or important questions of law or an issue that two or more lower appellate courts have disagreed on. For example, if the federal Court of Appeals for the 6th Circuit decides that the military registration system is unconstitutional because it doesn't include women, and the Court of Appeals for the 7th Circuit decides that the system is constitutional, the U.S. Supreme Court might grant cert in these cases and resolve the conflict.

FILING CASES DIRECTLY IN APPELLATE AND SUPREME COURTS

Occasionally, cases can be brought directly in the intermediate appellate courts or supreme courts, but only when there are extremely important issues of law in the case and little factual dispute. Also, under federal and state constitutions, certain types of disputes go directly to the supreme courts; this is called "original jurisdiction," as opposed to their usual appellate jurisdiction. For example, if one state sues another, the suit is brought in the U.S. Supreme Court, not a U.S. district court.

When the U.S. Supreme Court or a state supreme court decides a case, it almost always issues a published opinion. U.S. Supreme Court cases serve as precedent and binding authority for all courts, and state supreme court cases serve as precedent and authority for all courts in the state. Supreme Court decisions are very important sources of law. (See Chapter 7, *Understanding Case Law*, for more on precedent and authority.)

3. Introduction to Reported Cases

Decisions by appellate courts (and some trial courts) are printed in books called "Reporters." Each set of Reporters contains opinions from a particular court or group of courts. For example, there are regional reporters (these contain opinions from the appellate courts of a group of neighboring states), state reporters (these contain only one state's appellate decisions), and subject matter reporters (these contain decisions affecting a certain area of law). For instance, "P." is the reporter series that collects the appellate decisions from the western states, Hawaii and Alaska; "Cal. App." contains appellate (but not Supreme Court) "cases" from California; and "BK" contains federal bankruptcy opinions. In addition, federal cases are reported in their own sets, one for trial level decisions (called "F. Supp"), and one for appellate opinions from the Circuit courts of appeal (abbreviated as "F."). When the editors of the Reporters decide that their sets have become too long, they begin a new series and identify the new one as "2d" or "3d", and so on. In Chapter 9, we provide more information on how to use and interpret case citations.

LIBRARY EXERCISE

Using Citations to Find Cases

A case citation is like a street address: it tells you where you can find the case among the many sets of reported cases (called "Reporters") in the library. For example, the citation "26 F.2d 234" tells you that the case is found in the "Federal 2d" set of reporters, in volume 26, on page 234. Most citations end with information in parentheses, which tells you what court decided the case and the year of the decision, but you do not need to use that information when you are simply trying to locate a case in the library.

Questions

1. *Find the case at 766 F. Supp. 662. What is the name of the case? What opinions are contained in the reporter series?*
2. *Find the case at 792 P.2d 18. What is the name of the case? What opinions are collected in the reporter abbreviated "P."?*
3. *Find the case at 830 F.2d 11. What is the name of the case, and what is contained in the reporter series that printed it?*
4. *Find the case at 461 N.W.2d 884. What is the name of the case? What decisions are included in the "N.W." reporters?*
5. *Find the case at 476 A.2d 1236. What is the name of the case, and which reporter series contains it?*

Answers

1. The case is *Johnson v. Johnson*. "F. Supp." contains trial level cases from the federal district courts.
2. The case is *Petersen v. Bruen*. The Pacific Reporter contains appellate and supreme court decisions from the Western states, Hawaii and Alaska.
3. The case is *Smith v. Smith*. All of the decisions from the federal Circuit courts are printed in the "F." series of reporters, which has gone beyond "2nd" and now is in its "3rd" series.
4. The case is *People v. Jamieson*. The "N.W." (Northwest) reporter is in its second series, and contains opinions from the appellate and supreme courts of the northwest states.
5. The case is called *State v. Medina*. The "A." (Atlantic) reporter, second series, contains opinions from the appellate and supreme courts of the Atlantic states.

REVIEW

Questions

1. *What is the "law" that people research in the law library?*
2. *What does the common law consist of?*
3. *What does stare decisis mean?*
4. *How is power shared between the federal, state and local governments?*
5. *What are the three major phases in civil litigation?*
6. *What are pleadings?*
7. *What is summary judgment?*
8. *What's the difference between summary judgment and a trial?*
9. *What aspects of a trial court's decision are reviewable on appeal?*

Answers

1. The "law" is the sum total of the rules governing individual and group behavior that are enforceable in court. Primarily, as you will see, this means state and federal statutes, agency regulations, local ordinances and court decisions.
2. The common law consists of court opinions in specific disputes that state legal principles and must be followed in subsequent court cases about the same type of dispute.
3. *Stare decisis* is Latin for "let the decision stand." When the courts were called on to decide similar issues in subsequent cases, they reviewed the earlier decisions and, if one was found that logically covered the contemporary case, they applied the principle of the earlier decision. This is how the common law developed.
4. Fifty sovereign political entities (states) have voluntarily banded together in a union and agreed to give the federal government certain defined powers spelled out in the U.S. Constitution. All powers not expressly granted to the federal government are reserved to the states. The states in turn have divided up some of their power among counties, cities and special districts.
5. Pre-trial, trial and appellate.
6. Together, the plaintiff's complaint and the defendant's responsive papers are referred to as the "pleadings" in the case. Pleadings articulate the issues in the case—the actual dispute between plaintiff and defendant.
7. To get a summary judgment, the party must show the absence of a dispute about any important facts in the case (called "triable issues of material fact"). This showing is made in the form of written statements under oath, termed "declarations" or "affidavits." If they show a lack of basic factual disagreement between the parties, as is often the case, the judge will then proceed to apply the law to the facts and decide the case.
8. Trials are held to determine the facts when they are disputed by the parties, and involve a formal procedure designed to control just which evidence will be considered. Summary judgment is premised on the idea that there are no factual disputes, and therefore no need for a trial. The judge can go ahead and apply the relevant law to the undisputed facts.
9. Normally, appellate courts only are interested in whether the law was correctly followed and won't disturb a trial court's determination of the facts—unless it was completely unsupported by the evidence.

CHAPTER 4

Putting Your Questions Into Legal Categories

This chapter helps you accomplish Step 2 of the legal research method (described in Chapter 2). First, it shows how to organize your legal question into the conceptual categories used by law book publishers, a necessary and preliminary step to finding appropriate background resources (which are covered in the next chapter). Second, this chapter introduces you to some techniques for using legal indexes. Legal indexes are most commonly used to find:

- relevant discussions in the background resources you select
- statutes in annotated codes (Chapter 6), and
- cases through the case digest system (Chapter 9).

A. The Land of the Law

GUARD:	*Sir, we have interrogated the prisoner for three hours but can't get any information.*
SUPERVISOR:	*Does the prisoner refuse to speak?*
GUARD:	*Oh no, sir, he talks constantly, it's just that we can't understand a word of it.*
SUPERVISOR:	*Oh, what nationality is he?*
GUARD:	*Lawyer.*[1]

If "lawyer" is a nationality, the judicial system itself is certainly a foreign country complete with its own rules, logic, customs, values, benefits, penalties and linguistic peculiarities. Fortunately, the gulf between the "land of the law" and the "land of normal life," which seems extremely broad at times, can be bridged without great difficulty.

Two basic facts, once firmly understood, will greatly help you cope when you visit the Land of the Law. The first is obvious: the Land of the Law is run almost exclusively by lawyers. Laws are drafted by lawyers for legislatures, which are also often heavily influenced by or made up of lawyers. Laws are interpreted by lawyers who have become judges. Laws are enforced by lawyers who are district attorneys and attorneys general. Disputes are commonly arbitrated and decided by lawyers acting as referees. Agency regulations are drafted by the agency's legal department. Presidents, governors and corporate executives all have lawyers at their sides. In short, the lawyers are in firm control of the law business.

The second important fact is that lawyers tend to think very much alike. It is no wonder. Lawyers gain entrance to their profession by going to law school, where they are taught by law professors who are lawyers. As part of this training, law students are taught subtly and not so subtly to think like lawyers, act like lawyers, talk like lawyers, dress like lawyers, breathe like lawyers and so on. In addition:

- Most law schools teach the same subjects.
- Most law schools use the same teaching method.
- Most law schools attempt to produce the same type of product.
- Most law schools succeed.

How does this uniformity help you find your way around the Land of the Law? It simply means that you only need come to terms with one foreign dialect and culture. A lawyer from California can speak to a lawyer in North Dakota using one set of terms and concepts, and you can too once you learn the lingo.

Obviously, you won't be able to do this all at once, but if you spend any amount of time in the Land of the Law, you'll be surprised at how fast your

---

[1]This is a paraphrase of the words which accompanied a cartoon in the popular "Crock" cartoon series.

vocabulary grows. Indeed, you'll soon realize that what seemed like a foreign language is really only a collection of terms (jargon) containing very few verbs, and most of the nouns are only new terms for concepts you already know. (This is why we advise you to arm yourself with a good law dictionary.)

That lawyers think alike as well as talk alike is extremely helpful to the lay legal researcher. Lawyers are great reductionists. The system they use to classify legal knowledge involves carving it all into successively smaller categories. If you think of the set of Chinese boxes you had as a kid, which always seemed to have yet another small box inside, you will have a pretty good idea of how this works.

The background materials you will use in your research also are organized this way, dividing their contents into smaller and smaller subject categories. As a first step in performing effective legal research, then, you need to be able to think of your problem in terms of these categories. Then you'll be able to find relevant background materials and really get going on your legal research. Section B introduces you to the main legal classifications and suggests how to go about applying them to your problem.

B. Find the Broad Legal Category for Your Problem

Assume that you seek a lawyer's advice because you injured your back when you slipped on a banana peel at the supermarket. An experienced lawyer will go through a thought process that if verbalized might sound something like this:

"Ah, let's see, this person slipped, fell and injured herself, possibly badly. Back injuries cause a lot of pain—that means high damages. Definitely it is a personal injury case, a civil matter, negligence. Let's see, in order to recover for negligence, some action or inaction on the part of the supermarket must have been wrongful. In this situation it probably wasn't an intentional tort, but more likely carelessness, or negligence. Hmm, whether the market was negligent probably depends on how long employees let the peel remain on the floor before the accident. Hmm, wonder if there were any prior occurrences like this?"

This exercise in stream-of-consciousness writing demonstrates how lawyers love to reduce problems to smaller parts and to classify the parts according to familiar—to them—legal jargon. While this process may seem a little intimidating if you are unfamiliar with the law, don't worry. Anybody can learn to break big questions down into little ones and to cast a legal research problem into its appropriate topics and subtopics. And as we mentioned, once you are able to hang the proper labels on various factual situations, your ability to perform meaningful legal research will be almost assured. You may be surprised at how easy the classification game really is.

There are four main questions to answer when classifying your legal question:

- Does it involve federal law, state law or both?
- Does it involve criminal law or civil law?
- Does it involve the substance of the law or legal procedure?
- What legal category does it belong in?

When you have answered each of these questions, you will find it much easier to choose the background resources to look in first. If your question involves the substance of the federal criminal law, you will be interested in one group of books; if it involves state civil law, you will be looking for others. Narrowing your search further, placing your question in the right category will tell you which specific books—and parts of the books—you need. For instance, if your federal law problem involves the federal drug laws, you will probably use a different book than if it involves securities fraud.

1. Does the Situation Involve Federal Law or State Law?

Probably the single most important classification is whether your issue involves state law, federal law or both. This is because discussions of state law and federal law are commonly found in completely different books. The chart below lists topics usually covered by state law, federal law or both.

a. State Law

For constitutional and historical reasons, most legal research involves state rather than federal law. The U.S. Constitution restricts Congress's power to regulate to a few specific areas and leaves most law-making power to state governments.

b. Federal Law

For most our country's history, federal law was limited to court interpretations of the U.S. Constitution and the bill of rights, and the topics that Congress is specifically authorized to address under the Constitution, such as the regulation of commerce and immigration. Social welfare was not high on the government's agenda. Now, however, federal law commonly affects a broad range of social welfare, health and environmental issues.

c. Both State and Federal Law

A large number of legal areas now involve both state and federal law. Federal and state governments both are concerned about such topics as environmental law, consumer protection and the enforcement of child support statutes, and both have written laws on these subjects. And a good general rule is that whenever federal funds are involved, at least an element of federal law is involved.

One reason for the increasing overlap of federal and state law is that Congress is authorized by the Constitution to spend money for the general welfare, and it creates programs under which federal funds are offered to state governments under certain conditions. Typically, the state must match the funds in whole or in part and administer the program in strict conformity with requirements established by Congress. While no state must participate in this type of program, few states are able to resist. Since the 1930s (the New Deal), hundreds of these cost-sharing programs have been created and continue to operate.

When states participate in these programs, typically they are given some latitude by the federal laws in how the program is conducted. This means that state statutes and regulations must be passed to govern the state operation. And courts end up interpreting these statutes and regulations when disputes arise under them. In short, federal cost-sharing programs created by federal law stimulate the creation of state law as well.

If you have a problem that is affected by both federal and state law, you may have to look to both state and federal law background resources to get a firm handle on your problem.

A PARTIAL LISTING OF FEDERAL, STATE AND MIXED CATEGORIES

State Law Child custody, conservatorships, contracts, corporations, crimes (in most cases), divorce, durable powers of attorney for health care and financial management, guardianships, landlord-tenant relationships, licensing (businesses and professions), living wills, motor vehicles, partnerships, paternity, personal injuries, probate, property taxation, real estate, trusts, wills, worker's compensation and zoning.

Federal Law Admiralty, agriculture, bankruptcy, cases that interpret and reinterpret the U.S. Constitution and civil rights laws, copyright, crimes involving the movement of people or substances across state lines for illegal purposes, customs, federal tax, food and drug regulation, immigration, interstate commerce, maritime, Native Americans, patent, postal, social security and trademark.

Both State and Federal Law Consumer protection, employment, environmental protection, health law, labor law, occupational safety, subsidized housing, transportation, unemployment insurance, veteran's benefits and welfare law.

2. Does the Situation Involve Criminal Law or Civil Law?

Another important classification to make before beginning your research is whether you are dealing with "criminal" or "civil" law. This classification is also necessary to determine which background resources to use first.

a. Criminal Law

Generally, if a certain type of behavior is punishable by imprisonment, then criminal law is involved. For example, legislatures have generally chosen to treat shoplifting as a crime, and convicted shoplifters can end up in jail. On the other hand, most legislatures have chosen not to criminalize shady business practices. Instead they have designated them as matters for which victims can sue for monetary compensation—that is, civil offenses.

Criminal charges are usually initiated in court by a government prosecutor, though some states allow minor criminal charges to be brought by a victim. The government is always involved, however, because crimes are considered "offenses against the people." Accordingly, if you are involved in a legal dispute with an non-governmental individual or corporation, then the matter is not criminal. But because both the state and federal governments are often involved in civil as well as criminal matters, it is impossible to tell whether you are dealing with a criminal or civil situation just because a government entity is one of the parties.

b. Civil Law

All legal questions that don't involve crimes are matters of the civil law. When a suit is filed in court over a broken contract, deliberate or negligent injury, withheld government benefit, failed marriage (divorce), or any other dispute, a civil action has been brought and civil law is involved. In a civil action, the court may be asked to issue orders, award monetary damages or dissolve a marriage, but imprisonment is almost never a possibility. An exception is when a court orders a parent to pay child support and the parent willfully refuses.

3. Is the Problem Substantive or Procedural?

Primarily for legal analysis and classification, the law has been divided into two large subgroups. One of these includes all law that establishes the rights we enjoy and the duties we owe to the government and to other people and entities. This type of law is often referred to as the "substantive law." The other major subgroup includes all law that governs the way the justice system works. This law is termed "procedural." Once you pigeonhole your issue into one of these two categories you are much closer to jumping into your research. To see how this classification works, let's apply it to the criminal and civil areas of the law.

a. Criminal Law

"Criminal law" and "criminal procedure" are treated separately by most legal resources.

THE DIFFERENCE BETWEEN CRIMINAL LAW AND CRIMINAL PROCEDURE

The difference between substantive criminal law and criminal procedure is well-illustrated in cases where a person is found guilty of a particular crime but escapes punishment because the proper procedures weren't used and her rights were violated. For example, if the police search a house without a search warrant and they find an illegal drug, the possessor of the drug may go free because there was no warrant. The fact that the possession of the drug is defined as a crime is a substantive criminal law matter while the results of engaging in a warrantless search is a matter of criminal procedure.

Substantive Criminal Law Substantive criminal law concerns the definition and punishment of crimes. For example, the substantive criminal law tells us the difference between burglary (breaking and entering into the premises of another with the intent to commit a theft or felony) and larceny (taking personal property rightfully in the possession of another with intent to steal). It also specifies how each of these crimes is to be punished. Below is a list of common criminal substantive law categories.

Criminal Law Substantive Categories

Assault and battery
Breaking and entering
Burglary
Conspiracy
Disorderly conduct
Drug and narcotics offenses
Drunk driving
Juvenile offenses
Kidnapping
Larceny
Lewd and lascivious behavior
Malicious mischief
Marijuana cultivation
Murder
Rape
Robbery
Shoplifting
Smuggling
Tax evasion
Trespass
Weapons offenses

Criminal Procedure Criminal procedure concerns the way people accused of crimes are treated by the criminal justice system. For example, criminal procedure involves such things as what kinds of evidence can be used in a criminal trial, when an accused must be brought to trial, when a person can be released on bail and so on. Below is a list of common criminal procedure categories.

Criminal Procedure Topics

Arraignments
Arrests
Confessions
Cross-examination
Extradition
Grand jury
Indictments
Jury selection
Jury verdicts
Miranda warnings
Plea bargaining
Pleas
Preliminary hearings
Probation
Probation reports
Right to counsel
Search and seizure
Sentencing
Speedy trial
Suppression of evidence
Trials
Witnesses

b. Civil Law

Substantive Civil Law Substantive civil law consists of numerous sets of principles that determine the rights, duties and obligations that exist between individuals and institutions such as corporations and governments. Each set of principles is covered by a separate civil law category, developed by the courts and legislatures over a long time. For example, when a car accident damages property and injures people, a set of principles labeled "tort law" that has been formulated over a 600-year period determines who is liable to whom and for what.

Most legal research involves the substantive civil law. To help you fit your problem into the correct category we have provided a large list of categories with definitions for each. These are found in Section 4, below.

Civil Procedure The rules that govern how our civil justice system works are often termed "rules of civil procedure." They control such matters as which courts have authority to decide different kinds of lawsuits, what papers need to be filed, when they need to filed, who can be sued, what kinds of proof can be offered in court and how to appeal.

In the past, civil procedure varied considerably from state to state and court to court. Now, many states have procedures that are very similar to the Federal Rules of Civil Procedure that are used in all federal courts. However, although the trend is definitely toward national uniformity, courts' procedures still vary from one location to the next.

Rather than provide a list of civil procedure categories here, we refer you back to Chapter 3, Section F, for a close reading of court procedures. That material will provide some categories to start your research. Also, see Chapter 6, Section P, for pointers on researching procedure.

4. Substantive Civil Law Categories

The list set out below contains some of the more common substantive civil law categories utilized by the law books. While some of these areas overlap and may be used interchangeably by book titles and indexes, if you can assign one or more of the categories to your problem, it will be much easier for you to find what you're looking for. If you can't get your problem to fit within one of these categories, don't despair. Go on to the discussion in Section C of this chapter on how to use legal indexes, and then proceed with your research.

Administrative Law The law governing how administrative agencies function. This includes: the procedures used by agencies when they issue regulations, the way agencies conduct hearings, the scope of authority granted agencies by the legislature, and how agencies enforce their policies, decisions and regulations.

Bankruptcy Who can use the bankruptcy courts and under what circumstances, the rules and procedures used by the bankruptcy courts when a person or business files a bankruptcy petition to cancel debts or restructure them so as to continue operations, which debts are subject to cancellation or restructuring and how any remaining assets of the person declaring bankruptcy are distributed.

Business and Professions Law Restrictions and license requirements placed on professionals (for example, doctors and lawyers) and other occupational groups, such as building contractors and undertakers.

Civil Rights Law Statutes and constitutional provisions that apply to discrimination on the basis of such characteristics as race, sex, ethnic or national background, or color. (See also Housing Law and Prison Law.)

Commercial Law The federal and state regulations governing commercial relations between borrowers and lenders, banks and their customers, wholesalers and retailers, and mortgagors and mortgagees. Generally, this area involves disputes between businesspeople rather than between a businessperson and a consumer. (See Consumer Law.)

Computer Law The various issues that are especially relevant to the manufacture, use and sale of computers and computer software. This area includes such topics as copyrighting and patenting of computer software, warranties connected with computer sales, use of computer-generated documents in court, access to computerized files, privacy in connection with computer databases, computer-related crimes and trade secret protection in the computer industry.

Constitutional Law All situations where the constitutionality of governmental action is called into question. A few representative examples of constitutional law issues are: state laws that conflict with federal laws, the imposition of prison discipline on prisoners without adequate regard for fairness, federal laws that give Congress veto power over subsequent administrative regulations and a school board permitting prayer to occur in its schools. There are hundreds of other constitutional law questions. Many of these are also found under the other substantive law labels, such as housing law, civil rights, prison law and media law.

Consumer Law Federal and state statutory requirements governing transactions between a seller and a buyer of personal property in a commercial setting. This field typically involves situations where persons buy items on time—such as cars, household furniture or electronic equipment—and a dispute arises as to whether the transaction was fair, whether the buyer was provided with sufficient notice of what the transaction actually involved or if the goods didn't work, whether the seller is responsible under a warranty or guarantee.

Contracts Written and oral agreements, when such agreements are enforceable, when they may be broken, and what happens if they're broken or cancelled. Contract law is primarily concerned with general questions of contract law rather than with specific types of contracts. For specific types of contracts, see Consumer Law, Commercial Law, Insurance Law, Real Estate Law, Landlord-Tenant Law, Intellectual Property Law and Labor Law.

Corporation Law How corporations are formed, the requirements for corporate structure, the rights of shareholders, the rights and duties of corporate officers and directors, the relationship between a corporation and outside parties who commercially interact with it, procedures for elections of officers, how stock is issued, and similar matters.

Education Law The rights of students and the restrictions placed on them by schools, school funding formulas, educational standards, competency testing, remedial programs for the developmentally disabled and educationally handicapped, financial assistance to students, student political affairs, teachers' rights and responsibilities, business and labor matters peculiar to schools (for example, teachers' unions, tenure, placement) and similar matters.

Employment Law The rights of employees and the restrictions placed on employers by law. This area is also concerned with employment discrimination against minorities (also see Civil Rights), wrongful discharge of employees (also see Torts) and management-labor relations (also see Labor Law).

Energy Law The state and federal laws governing the production, distribution and utilization of coal, natural gas, oil, electrical and nuclear power, and with such alternative sources of energy as solar power, wind power and co-generation. What rates energy companies are entitled to charge consumers, the process for obtaining rate changes, the licensing of energy production plants and consumer service requirements are also covered by this field.

Environmental Law The numerous state and federal statutes, regulations and cases that govern the uses of the environment by business, government and individuals. Issues of air and water pollution, the environmental impact of new projects, the uses of national forests and parks, the preservation of endangered species, toxic and nuclear wastes and similar matters are covered under this topic.

Estate Planning How people arrange for the distribution of their property after they're dead, and how they can avoid paying taxes and probate fees by taking certain actions while they're living. Includes such subjects as living trusts, joint tenancies, wills, testamentary trusts and gifts.

Evidence What kinds of items and testimony can be introduced as proof in a trial or hearing, the methods used to introduce such proof, who has the responsibility to introduce what types of proof on what types of issues and how much weight the trier of fact (judge or jury) should give different types of proof.

Family Law, Divorce Law, Domestic Relations Law All matters relating to annulment, marriage, separation, divorce, taxation upon divorce, child support, child custody, child visitation, marital property, community property, guardianships, adoptions and durable powers of attorney. Many of the principles governing living-together situations are taken from this area of the law. (Also see Juvenile Law.)

Health Law The type and quality of medical treatment received from hospitals, health facility regulation and planning, occupational health and safety requirements, rural and neighborhood health clinics, the management of epidemics, the control of pesticide use and other issues related to health.

Housing Law The numerous programs financed in whole or in part by the federal government that involve housing subsidies for construction and rental assistance, public housing, state and local planning requirements related to the type and amount of housing in different areas and discriminatory housing practices. (Also see Civil Rights Law.)

Insurance Law The problems arising under any kind of insurance contract, such as life insurance, car insurance, homeowners' insurance, fire insurance and disability insurance. (See Unemployment Insurance law for a separate treatment of that topic.) This area is also concerned with the duty of insurance companies to exercise good faith when dealing with insureds and beneficiaries. (Also see Tort Law.)

Intellectual Property Law The laws and procedures governing copyrights, trademarks, trade secrets and patents.

Juvenile Law Juvenile delinquency (when a child commits an act that would be a crime if he were an adult), child neglect and abuse by parents, juvenile-status offenses (acts that are not crimes but that are juvenile offenses, like running away from home or being truant from school) and juvenile court procedures.

Labor Law Issues surrounding unionization, union actions and actions by employers towards workers, whether organized or not, that are considered unfair labor practices, collective bargaining agreements, strikes, labor negotiations and arbitration under a collective bargaining agreement.

Landlord/Tenant Law Concerned with all issues arising out of the landlord-tenant relationship, such as evictions, responsibility for repairs, cleaning deposits, leases and rental agreements, inspections, entries by the landlord, liability for injuries, rent control, and similar matters

Media Law The laws and requirements that pertain to the print and broadcast media, and includes such items as libel, privacy, censorship, open meeting laws, access to government information and court records, licensing of radio and television stations and restrictions on television and radio programming.

Military Law All matters under the authority (jurisdiction) of the military, including discharges, enlistment contracts, mandatory registration laws, court martials, pay and pension benefits.

Municipal Law Zoning, ordinances, land-use planning, condemnation of property, incorporation of cities, contracting for public improvements, and other matters of local concern.

Prison Law Prison conditions, prison disciplinary procedures, parole, constitutional rights of prisoners and adequate access to legal information and medical treatment. (These issues are also often found under the Civil Rights, Civil Procedure, Criminal Procedure and Constitutional Law categories.)

Property Law The purchase, maintenance and sale of real estate, easements, adverse possession, landowner's liability, mortgages and deeds of trust, homesteads, subdivision and construction requirements, and issues arising from land use regulation. (See also Municipal Law.)

Public Utilities Law The duties, responsibilities and rights of public utilities that provide water telephone service, sewage and garbage disposal, and gas and electricity.

Tax Law All issues related to federal and state taxation of such items as income, property left in an estate, personal property, business profits, real estate, and sales transactions.

Tort Law (personal injury law—"tort" is the French word for wrong): Any injury to a person or business that is directly caused by the intentional or negligent actions of another. Examples of commonly known intentional torts, where the person intends the act and knew or should have known that it would result in someone being injured, are:

- assault (putting another in reasonable fear of being struck)
- battery (the objectionable touching of another without his or her consent)
- intentional infliction of emotional distress (outrageous actions affecting another person that the actor knows or should know will result in extreme emotional discomfort)
- libel and slander (a false statement made to someone about a third person that has the

capacity to harm the third person's reputation or business)

- trespass (entering onto another's property without consent or legal justification)
- false imprisonment (restricting a person's freedom of movement without legal justification)
- invasion of privacy (substantially interfering with the right of a person to be left alone)
- malicious prosecution (suing a person without just cause for ulterior motives)
- wrongful discharge from employment (under certain circumstances, terminating an employee for improper reasons)
- breach of covenant of good faith and fair dealing (the bad faith refusal of a party to a contract to perform its obligations under the contract, usually under circumstances where the other party is left personally vulnerable, as in insurance and employment situations).

The most common tort of all is called "negligence." This involves behavior that is considered unreasonably careless under the circumstances and that directly results in injury to another. In deciding whether a given activity is unreasonably careless, the courts must determine whether it was reasonably foreseeable that the kind of injury suffered by the plaintiff would result from the act alleged to be negligent. Medical malpractice, legal malpractice and most automobile accidents are examples of negligence.

Finally, some persons are held liable under tort law for acts that weren't intentional or negligent. Usually some kind of inherently dangerous activity is involved. The legal classifications are:

- Strict liability (holding certain classes of service providers, such as residential landlords and common carriers, or persons who operate dangerous businesses, such as explosives manufacturers, strictly liable for injuries to persons partaking of the services)
- Product liability (a kind of strict liability that holds a manufacturer liable for injuries caused by unsafe products).

Unemployment Insurance All matters relating to unemployment insurance benefits.

Vehicle Law All matters related to the registration, use and transfer of motor vehicles, driver's licenses and non-criminal traffic offenses (legally most traffic offenses are "infractions," not crimes; however, driving while intoxicated, reckless driving and hit-and-run are usually considered crimes).

Veterans' Law The treatment of veterans under various federal programs dealing with education, health, disability and insurance benefits. Also concerned with the upgrading of less-than-honorable discharges.

Warranties The obligations of sellers of goods and services to stand behind their products. The law of warranties comes from state and federal statutes and from common law contract principles. (See Contract Law and Consumer Law.)

Welfare Law, Social Welfare Law Two phrases for the laws concerned with Aid to Families with Dependent Children (AFDC), general assistance (county relief), social security, food stamps, Supplemental Security Income (SSI), school lunches, foster homes, Medicaid (see Health Law as well), Medicare and state disability.

Wills How wills are interpreted and the requirements for making a valid will that will effectively allow a person to carry out her desires after her death in respect to her property, her family and any other person or institution to whom she wishes to leave property. (See Estate Planning.)

Worker's Compensation Rights of workers who are injured or killed in work-related accidents.

5. Classification Overview

If you have roughly classified your problem as suggested above, you will have one of the following types of problems:

- Federal—Criminal—Substantive
- Federal—Criminal—Procedural
- Federal—Civil—Substantive
- Federal—Civil—Procedural
- State—Criminal—Substantive
- State—Criminal—Procedural
- State—Civil—Substantive
- State—Civil—Procedural

Once you categorize your research question in this manner you will be prepared to find the most appropriate background resource to start your research. The next chapter shows you how to find a good source of background information. First, however, we introduce you to legal indexes. Whether you are using background resources, looking for statutes or finding cases in a legal digest, you will be well served by the information in the following section.

C. Identify Specific Terms for Your Problem

Most law books contain indexes organized by subject. These indexes are usually quite specific, and you almost always have to use them to strike pay dirt in your legal research. You have gotten off to a good start by putting your problem into a broad legal category. But you must now get more specific.

There are no hard and fast rules for how indexes are set up and what headings are used. How well an individual index is organized depends so much upon the knowledge and thoroughness of the person making it that indexing is recognized as an art form. One index might refer to divorces under the "domestic relations" category, while another might use the term "family law" to designate the broad category. Still a third index might use only the word "divorce."

Most people—especially those unfamiliar with the law—experience difficulty when first faced with a legal index. This, of course, is because the indexes themselves often use legal jargon. For instance, the law on the subject of whether more than one person can be sued in one lawsuit is typically indexed under "Joinder of Parties." Who would think of looking there unless he was already familiar with the term?

MORTGAGES **INDEX TO TITLE 2A**

General Index:
New Jersey Statutes

Also, indexes can be quite unpredictable when it comes to more specific matters. For example, suppose you wanted to find out who is responsible for the back injury that resulted from your slip and fall at the supermarket. After some cross-referencing by using the list of civil topics in Section B4 of this chapter, you might figure out that you were dealing with a "tort." Where would you go next, however? Under this general category, would you look under "slip," "fall," "back injury," "liability," "carelessness," "negligence" or "supermarket"? Unfortunately, there is no clear answer to this question.

You must be prepared to use all of these words, as well as a number of others, to get to the specific material you desire. The trick in using an index well mostly involves being able to come up with many alternative words that describe or relate to your research topic. Simply put, the more words you can think of, the better your chances of finding what you're looking for.

If you're feeling a bit overwhelmed at this point, here's some good news. Many legal indexes use ordinary as well as legal words for their headings, and contain elaborate cross-indexing systems so that even if you don't choose the right word to begin with, you will finally get to it through cross-reference entries. Good indexes cross-reference every significant term so that if the primary information is carried under "family law," for example, the word "divorce" would have "see family law" under it.

Several legal research experts have constructed methods for breaking a legal research problem down into words and phrases that can be looked up in a legal index. Probably the most complete method is that employed by law professor William Statsky.

1. The Statsky "Cartwheel" Approach

The Statsky approach uses a diagram—called a cartwheel—which prompts the reader for different categories of words.

For example, suppose that the research problem involved, among other things, who is authorized to perform a wedding and what ceremony, if any, need be conducted. The structure of the Cartwheel is shown below:

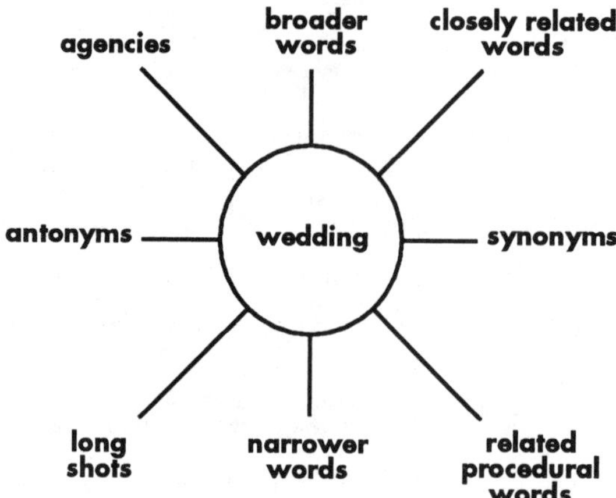

The Research Cartwheel

Reproduced by permission from *Domestic Relations,* by William P. Statsky, copyright © 1978 by West Publishing Company. All Rights Reserved.

The first step in using the index and table of contents in any law book is to look up the key word—"wedding" in this case—in that index and table. If that's not successful, either because the word is not in the index or table or because the page or section references after the word in the index and table do not lead to relevant material in the book, the next step is to think of as many different phrasings and contexts of the word "wedding" as possible.

The Cartwheel method has 18 steps to help you come up with terms to look up in an index or table of contents. It is, in effect, a word association game that should become second nature to you with practice.

1. Identify all the major words from the facts of the research problem. Place each word or small set of words in the center of the Cartwheel.
2. In the index and table of contents, look up all of these words.
3. Identify the broader categories of these major words.
4. In the index and the table of contents, look up all of these broader categories.
5. Identify the narrower categories of these words.
6. In the index and table of contents, look up all of the narrower categories.
7. Identify all of the synonyms of the words.
8. In the index and table of contents, look up all of these synonyms.
9. Identify all of the antonyms of these words.
10. In the index and table of contents, look up all of these antonyms.
11. Identify all closely related words.
12. In the index and table of contents, look up all of these closely related words.
13. Identify all procedural terms related to these words.
14. In the index and table of contents, look up all of these procedural terms.
15. Identify all agencies, if any, which might have some connection to these words.
16. In the index and table of contents, look up all of these agencies.
17. Identify all long shots.
18. In the index and table of contents, look up all of these long shots.

If we were to apply these 18 steps of the Cartwheel to the word "wedding," here are some of the words and phrases that you would check in the index and table of contents of every law book that deals with family law.

Broader Words celebration, ceremony, rite, ritual, formality, festivity

Narrower Words civil wedding, church wedding, proxy wedding, sham wedding, shotgun marriage

Synonyms marriage, nuptial

Antonyms alienation, annulment, dissolution, divorce, separation

Loosely Related Words matrimony, marital, domestic, husband, wife, bride, anniversary, custom, children, blood test, premarital, spouse, relationship, family, home, consummation, cohabitation, sexual relations, betrothal, minister, wedlock, oath, contract, name change, domicile, residence

Procedural Terms application, petition, authorization

Agencies Bureau of Vital Statistics, county clerk, License Bureau, Secretary of State, Justice of the Peace

Long Shots dowry, common law, single, blood relationship, fraud, religion, license, illegitimate, remarriage, antenuptial, alimony, bigamy, pregnancy, gifts, chastity, community property, impotence, incest, virginity, support, custody, consent, paternity

Perhaps you might think that some of the word selections in the above categories are a bit farfetched. But you simply will not know for sure whether or not a word will be fruitful until you try it. To be successful, you must be imaginative.

An excellent aid for coming up with lots of related legal words is the *Legal Thesaurus/Dictionary* by William Statsky (West Publishing Co.). By simply finding one related term or phrase, you will open up a cornucopia of additional leads. Also, a regular thesaurus can be helpful in stimulating your imagination.

UNDERSTANDING INDEX JARGON

Indexes themselves use jargon that may be quite confusing if you're not used to it. Here are some definitions of some of the more commonly used indexing terms of art:

Generally, this index When a term is followed by a "Generally, this index," it means that the term can be located as a main entry in its alphabetical place in the index. For instance, if you find "child support" under the larger heading of "Minors," and it is followed by "Generally, this index," look for it as a main entry.

See also The terms following the "see also" may produce related subject matter.

See The material you are seeking will be found directly under the term following the "see" rather than under the original term.

See ___ *infra* The entry is found under the same main entry but further down alphabetically. Basically, it's Latin for "below."

See ___ *supra* The entry is found under the same main entry, but further up alphabetically. Latin for "above."

2. An Informal Approach

If you don't want to follow the Cartwheel method, there are other ways to approach legal indexes. The one that we use most of the time has six steps:

Step 1: Select several key plain-English terms that define the research problem, and several alternatives to these terms.

Step 2: Use these words to select one or more probable legal categories.

Step 3: Search the index for a main entry relevant to your problem and be prepared to follow up cross-references.

Step 4: Search for relevant sub-entries under the main entry.

Step 5: Bounce back to another main entry if your first choice doesn't pan out.

Step 6: Once you find a good main entry and sub-entry, think even smaller and more detailed.

For instance, suppose your research question is whether a drunk driving conviction results in the loss of a driver's license. The first step is to determine some key terms. You might start with drunk driving and such variations as "operating a motor vehicle under the influence of intoxicating beverages" or "driving while intoxicated." The same process would hold true for "driver's license." Possible alternative terms for driver's license are "operator's permit" or "operator's license."

The second step is to determine whether these terms logically fit under one of the general civil or criminal law substantive categories. Vehicle law would be the most appropriate category, so you would probably start with vehicles.

The third step is to search the index and be prepared to follow up cross-references. For instance, in this example, if you started with vehicles, you would probably be referred to "motor vehicles."

The fourth step is to search for sub-entries under an appropriate main entry. For instance, if you looked for drunk driving under motor vehicles, you might find an alternative term, such as "operating under the influence."

The fifth step is to go back to another main entry if your first choice doesn't pan out. For example, if you found no reference to drunk driving or its equivalent under motor vehicles, consider looking under "alcohol," "traffic offenses," "alcoholic beverages" or "automobiles." You also might come up with some more variations of your specific terms.

The sixth step is to conceptualize even more detailed entries that are likely to refer you to material on your specific question. For instance, once you find an entry that covers drunk driving under the main entry motor vehicles, you might consider looking for such specific terms as "license," "suspension," "revocation," "restriction" and "forfeiture."

If you run up against a brick wall, take a deep breath and start over. Reconceptualize your question, come up with new terms, find a different substantive category. We can't emphasize strongly enough that the reason most research fails is that the researcher runs out of patience at the index searching stage.

Below are three examples from index listings for this example to demonstrate the different ways indexes can be organized. The one thing they all have in common is that they are organized from general terms in the main entry to specific sub-entries. The samples show the different ways that indexes can treat the topic of license revocation for drunk driving.

Pennsylvania Index

MOTOR VEHICLES

Vermont Index

TRAFFIC

330

Oklahoma Index

REVIEW

Questions

1. *Why is it necessary to fit your research problem within certain legal categories?*
2. *What are the four main questions to answer when categorizing your legal question?*
3. *What are some legal categories that usually are a matter of state law?*
4. *What are some legal categories that involve federal law?*
5. *What are some categories that involve both state and federal law?*
6. *What's the main way you can tell whether a research issue involves criminal or civil law?*
7. *What's the difference between civil substantive law and civil procedure?*
8. *What's the first step to using the informal index-searching method?*

Answers

1. The books that you start your research with are organized according to these categories.
2. Does it involve federal law, state law, or both?
   Does it involve criminal law, civil law or both?
   Does it involve the substance of the law, or legal procedure?
   If it involves the substance of the law, what is its appropriate subtopic?
3. Real estate, zoning, divorce, guardianship, paternity, child custody, conservatorships, living wills, durable powers of attorney for health care and financial management, contracts, testamentary wills, probate, personal injuries, trusts, the licensing of businesses and professions, landlord-tenant relationships, partnerships and small corporations, motor vehicles and most, but not all, crimes
4. Admiralty, agriculture, bankruptcy, copyright, federal tax, food and drug regulation, immigration, interstate commerce, maritime, patent, postal, trademark, customs, Native Americans and crimes involving the movement of people or substances across state lines for illegal purposes. Also a matter of federal law are the many cases that interpret and reinterpret the U.S. Constitution and the civil rights laws that have been passed by Congress since 1964.
5. Environmental protection, labor law, consumer protection, veteran's benefits, health law, welfare law, occupational safety, subsidized housing, transportation, employment, unemployment insurance, child support enforcement,
6. If the research issue involves behavior that is punishable by imprisonment, then criminal law is involved. Civil law is involved in cases of a broken contract, personal injury, withheld government benefit, divorce, or other dispute where the court is asked to issue orders, award money damages or dissolve a marriage.
7. Substantive civil law consists of numerous sets of principles that determine the rights, duties and obligations that exist between individuals and institutions such as corporations and governments. Civil procedure involves how our civil justice system works—that is, such matters as which courts are appropriate for which kinds of lawsuits, what papers need to be filed, when they need to filed, who can be sued, what kinds of proof can be offered in court and how to appeal.
8. Select several key plain-English terms that define the research problem, and several alternatives to these terms.

CHAPTER 5

Getting Some Background Information

Once you've tentatively classified your problem (Chapter 4), you are on much the same footing as any law school graduate who undertakes legal research. You have squeezed your issue (often a somewhat square peg) into its proper legal niche (the proverbial round hole) and are now ready to find some answers. First you will find the appropriate resources to answer your questions. Then you will use your legal index skills to find helpful discussions within the resources themselves.

A. How Background Resources Can Help

Especially if you're unfamiliar with the area of law you're going to be researching, it makes great sense to start with broader introductory materials rather than plunging directly into the primary sources of the law (statutes, cases and regulations). Fortunately, nearly every major area of the law has been discussed and summarized by experts, in many different kinds of books and periodicals.

Starting with background materials (often called "secondary sources") is the same technique you used when you did research for high school or college papers. For example, if you wanted to teach yourself something about computers, you would probably start by reading a broad introduction to computers such as that found in many popular encyclopedias. This might lead to a book that presented more detail. Next you would probably be ready to dive into materials dealing with the specific areas you were interested in, perhaps semiconductors, multi-media, programming or database management.

Getting a general understanding of an area before looking for the answer to a narrow question is particularly important when it comes to legal research. The answers to almost all specific legal questions depend on a number of variables that the background resource can alert you to. Then, when you go on to read the actual laws—statutes, cases and regulations—you'll know what to look for.

For instance, consider this question: Can an unmarried tenant be evicted for having overnight guests? The answer depends on such variables as:

- What does the lease or rental agreement say?
- How long do the guests stay?
- Are the guests lovers, and is this a factor in the landlord's decision to evict?
- Does the state or city have a statute or ordinance making it illegal to discriminate in the renting of housing against people based on their marital status or sexual orientation?
- Is overcrowding a factor?
- Does the city or county have a rent control ordinance?
- Is the eviction really for some other reason not permitted by law?

Reading a background resource's discussion of guests and eviction would tell you that these are the questions you need to answer to resolve your original question. In his excellent videotape on basic legal research, *Legal Research Made Easy* (Nolo Press), Professor Robert Berring calls this "scouting the terrain."

Legal background materials are usually directed at one of three audiences: non-lawyers, law students or lawyers. But don't let these labels scare you off—non-lawyers often find useful information in materials that were written with lawyers in mind, and vice versa. Many books, articles and, increasingly, computer programs and data bases can be of immense help to all users.

AN ENCYCLOPEDIA OF BACKGROUND RESOURCES: WEST'S LEGAL DESK REFERENCE

West's Legal Desk Reference, by Statsky, Hussey, Diamond and Nakamura lists background (secondary) resources both by state and by legal topic. For instance, if you are in Illinois this resource tells you what background materials have been published specifically for that state. And if your research question involves drunk driving, you can find many pertinent articles, books and encyclopedia entries under "Alcohol". Additionally, the *West Legal Desk Reference,* provides key words and phrases that will help you use the indexes to other resources that you encounter in the course of your research.

B. Background Resources for Non-Lawyers

In recent years many law books aimed at non-lawyers have been published. Some of these books impart an overall understanding of one or more legal topics; others are more in the "how to do it" spirit. The publisher of this book, Nolo Press, has the longest list. Nolo has titles ranging from *How to File for Bankruptcy* and *How to Form a Nonprofit Corporation* (both nationwide) to *How to Buy a House in California.* A complete list of Nolo publiations is in the back of this book.

Another popular series of books written for non-lawyers is sponsored by the American Civil Liberties Union and published by Bantam books. A partial list of titles includes:

Norwick, *The Rights of Authors and Artists*
Stark, *The Rights of Crime Victims*
Outten, *The Rights of Employees*
Stoddard, *The Rights of Gay People*
Pevar, *The Rights of Indians and Tribes*
Rudovsky, *The Rights of Prisoners*
Bernard, *The Rights of Single People*
Rubin, *The Rights of Teachers*
Robertson, *The Rights of the Critically Ill*
Ross, *The Rights of Women*
Guggenheim, *The Rights of Young People*
Marwick, *The Right to Government Information*

Look first for self-help law materials in a law library or large public library. Many of them carry complete sets of Nolo Press books as well as self-help books by other publishers. If you want to buy a self-help book, check out the business, reference or law sections of a larger book store (or call Nolo Press).

We suggest that before buying a book or computer program, you take a moment to do a little reading to see whether the language is understandable and the concepts useful and specific. And if you are planning on using the book to accomplish a legal task, rather than simply to obtain a general overview of the subject, check whether the material actually leads you step by step through the entire process, gives you the necessary forms for doing it yourself and is sufficiently sensitive to differences in state laws. Otherwise the book or program may turn out to be useless for your purpose.

A BIBLIOGRAPHY OF SELF-HELP LAW PUBLICATIONS

Law For The Layman: Annotated Bibliography of Self-Help Law Books by Frank G. Houdek (Fred B. Rothman & Co.) provides a selected list of self-help law resources by topic, state, title, author and publisher. It is often the case that law libraries don't stock self-help titles (there are many reasons for this) but if your law library has this publication, you may discover the perfect resource for beginning your research. Of course you may have to search out the publication in a book store or even order it directly from the publisher.

C. Background Resources for Law Students

Many books published as textbooks for law students (sometimes called "hornbooks") offer an excellent point of departure for legal research. Most of these textbooks are published by the West Publishing Company or Foundation Press. These books, which are conceptual in nature, are excellent if you want a basic understanding of the variables in any specific area of concern. They are not very helpful when it comes to finding specific answers to specific questions or providing accurate, up-to-date information about the state of the law when you need it.

You can find most of these books in any law bookstore (usually near law schools) or law library.[1] Below is a partial list of some commonly used and relatively up-to-date legal textbooks.

[1]For a catalog of materials published by the West Publishing Co., write to 50 W. Kellogg Blvd., St. Paul, MN 55102. The University Textbook series is published by Foundation Press, 170 Old Country Road, Mineola, NY 11501.

SELECTED TEXTBOOKS

Administrative Law
Davis, *Administrative Law and Government* (2d Ed., West 1975)

Agency and Partnership
Reuschlein and Gregory, *Law of Agency and Partnership* (2d Ed., West 1990)

Commercial Law
White and Summers, *Uniform Commercial Code* (3d Ed., West 1988)

Constitutional Law
Nowak, Rotunda and Young, *Constitutional Law* (4th Ed., West 1991)

Contracts
Calamari and Perillo, *Contracts* (3d Ed., West 1987)

Corporations
Henn and Alexander, *Corporations* (3d Ed., West 1983)

Environmental Law
Rodger, *Environmental Law* (West 1977)

Evidence
McCormick, *Evidence* (3rd Ed., West 1984)

Legal Research
Cohen and Berring, *How to Find the Law* (9th Ed., West 1989)

Legislation
Statsky, *Legislative Analysis: How to Use Statutes and Regulations* (3d Ed., West 1988)

Municipal Law
Reynolds, *Local Government Law* (West 1982)

Property Law
Cunningham, Whitman and Stoebuck, *Law of Property* (West 1984)

Torts
Prosser and Keeton, *Torts* (5th Ed., West 1984)

Other good background resources are the concise law summaries intended primarily as study guides for law students. Titles such as *Gilbert's Law Summaries*, *Black Letter Series*, *Emmanuel Law Outlines*, *Legalines* and *Law in a Nutshell* can be found in law bookstores and libraries. All provide an up-to-date framework or overview of a legal subject area, making it easier to understand the law you are researching. Look through a few first to see which best meets your research needs; some will be more useful than others. They are often written in a dense conceptual shorthand and are more helpful as a review once you already have a grasp of a particular area.

D. Background Resources for Lawyers

There are lots of books designed to educate lawyers about the ins and outs of various legal subjects. They are usually very specific—sometimes to a fault—and usually provide a truckload of references (citations) to the primary law sources (cases, statutes and regulations) on which the discussion is based. Simply put, these background resources provide not only a conceptual overview of your research problem, but also an excellent bridge from your background reading to the next phase of your research—the law itself. The most common of these background resources are discussed in this section.

1. Legal Encyclopedias

Legal encyclopedias contain detailed discussions of virtually every area of the law. These encyclopedias are organized alphabetically by subject matter like regular encyclopedias, but with broader main entries and a lot more sub-entries. In addition, they contain thorough indexes at the end of the entire set of volumes and detailed tables of contents at the beginning of each topic. The discussions are footnoted with references to cases and statutes that provide the primary-law foundation for the statements in the text. Keep in mind that legal encyclopedia articles discuss and describe the law—they aren't part of the law. Judges and legislatures write "the law," as discussed in Chapter 3.

Legal encyclopedias are often a good place to start your research. Because they cover the entire range of law and their entries are broken into small segments, you are very likely to find material relevant to your research problem. Each entry provides a solid treatment of the particular topic, gives you a good idea of the all-important variables associated with your issue, and refers you to specific statutes and cases (the stuff the law is made of) to help you get to the next research phase.

Also, most law libraries—even small ones—have encyclopedias, but may not have some of the other resources described in this chapter.

a. National Legal Encyclopedias

Two encyclopedias, *American Jurisprudence* and *Corpus Juris*, provide a national overview of American law. The entries are generalized and don't necessarily provide state-specific information. However, they do contain footnoted references to court decisions from many different states and from federal courts, where relevant. *American Jurisprudence* is commonly known as *Am. Jur.* The current edition of *American Jurisprudence* is abbreviated *Am. Jur. 2d.* The current edition of *Corpus Juris* is abbreviated *C.J.S.* (*Corpus Juris Secundum*—they love Latin). Always use the most recent series—law libraries usually shelve only the most recent—unless you are looking for something that you believe was carried in the earlier series but dropped in the later.

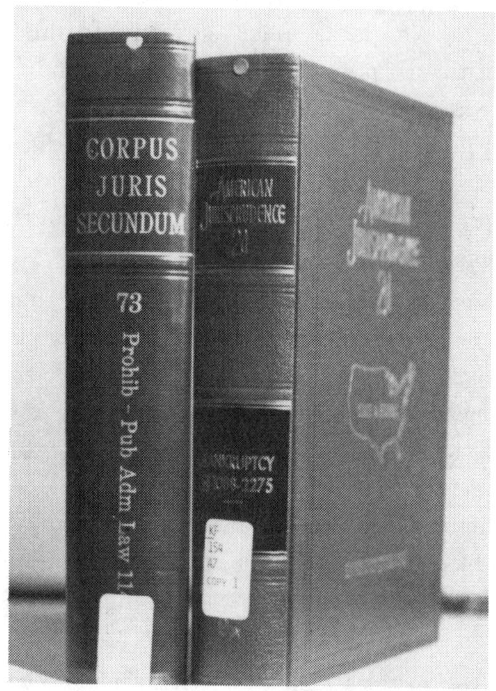

American Jurisprudence & Corpus Juris Secondum

To give you an idea of how these books are set up, the Table of Contents and discussion employed by *Am. Jur.* on the law concerning firearms are shown below.

Which legal encyclopedia should you use if your law library has both? Many researchers favor *Am. Jur. 2d* over *C.J.S.* because they feel that *C.J.S.* tends to have too much unnecessary information. However, to fully answer this question, it is necessary to make a brief detour into the world of law book publishing. Bear with us, please; you'll find this information valuable in other phases of your legal research.

There are two primary publishers of American law library resources and tools: West Publishing Co. and Bancroft-Whitney/Lawyers Coop. West publishes *C.J.S.* while Bancroft-Whitney/Lawyers Coop publishes *Am. Jur. 2d.* Each publisher has also produced a great many other legal titles. More important, each has attempted to structure its family of books into a complete, internally cross-referenced research system. To some extent both have been successful. Thus it is often possible to complete a legal research task by only using West publications. The same is somewhat less true with Bancroft Whitney/Lawyers Coop resources.

If you prefer the West system of research (called the "key number system," discussed in detail in Chapter 11), you may want to use *C.J.S.*, which uses this system by providing cross-references after each article, even though you might feel that *Am. Jur. 2d* has some advantages. Likewise, if you are a Bancroft-Whitney/Lawyers Coop fan, *Am. Jur. 2d* may be your cup of tea despite the fact that *C.J.S.* has some excellent features.

As a general rule, the West publishing philosophy is to provide all the information and let you, the researcher, choose what you wish to use. The Bancroft-Whitney/Lawyer's Coop philosophy is to exercise a little editorial discretion and present you only with what it thinks is likely to be of use. So if you are worried about information overload, veer towards *Am. Jur. 2d.* If you want all possibly relevant material, go with *C.J.S.*

Am. Jur. 2d Part of Table of Contents for Topic "Weapons and Firearms"

79 Am Jur 2d WEAPONS AND FIREARMS § 3

§ 3. —Unloaded firearm.

Generally, it is held that an unloaded gun, used as a firearm and not as bludgeon, is not a dangerous weapon within the contemplation of statutes punishing assaults made with dangerous or deadly weapons, although there is substantial authority to the contrary.[36] It is generally, but not universally, considered to be a matter of defense to show that the weapon was unloaded, rather than a substantive part of the state's case to aver and prove that it was loaded.[37] There also is authority that an unloaded revolver or gun merely pointed at the person is not a dangerous weapon within the meaning of statutes defining assault and robbery while armed with a dangerous weapon, although many courts hold that an unloaded gun or pistol is a dangerous weapon within the meaning of such statutes;[38] and generally, an unloaded pistol or revolver is regarded as within the meaning of statutes against carrying concealed "dangerous or deadly weapons"[39] or denouncing the carrying "of any concealed and dangerous weapon."[40] It has been held that a statute prohibiting the carrying of a weapon capable of inflicting bodily harm, concealed on or about the person, did not apply to an unloaded pistol found in the glove compartment of the defendant's automobile, no ammunition having been found on or about the defendant's person or in the vehicle.[41] In a few cases the courts have recognized that if the gun was unloaded, that fact would have a bearing on the determination as to whether it was carried as a weapon.[42]

Generally an unloaded gun or pistol used to strike with is not necessarily a dangerous weapon, but is such, or not, according to its size, weight, and the manner of using it.[43] Accordingly, to resolve the factual question whether a

36. See 6 Am Jur 2d, ASSAULT AND BATTERY § 54.

As to whether a simple criminal assault may be committed with an unloaded firearm, see 6 Am Jur 2d, ASSAULT AND BATTERY § 34.

As to civil action for damages for an assault by pointing unloaded firearm, see 6 Am Jur 2d, ASSAULT AND BATTERY §§ 109, 123.

37. See 6 Am Jur 2d, ASSAULT AND BATTERY § 93.

As to presumption as to whether gun was loaded, see 6 Am Jur 2d, ASSAULT AND BATTERY § 94.

38. See 67 Am Jur 2d, ROBBERY § 5.

39. Asocar v State, 252 **Ind** 326, 247 NE2d 679; Mularkey v State, 201 **Wis** 429, 230 NW 76.

Annotation: 79 ALR2d 1430, § 8.

40. Mularkey v State, 201 **Wis** 429, 230 NW 76.

A pistol mechanically capable of being fired is a deadly weapon within the meaning of the statute prohibiting the carrying of a concealed "deadly weapon," even though it was unloaded and no ammunition was on the carrier's person or was readily available. Commonwealth v Harris (**Ky**) 344 SW2d 820.

41. State v Haugabrook, 31 **Ohio** Misc 157, 57 Ohio Ops 2d 322, 272 NE2d 213.

42. State v Larkin, 24 **Mo** App 410.

Annotation: 79 ALR2d 1432, § 8.

In Carr v State, 34 **Ark** 448, in reversing a conviction under a statute making it a misdemeanor to wear any pistol concealed as a weapon unless upon a journey, the evidence being that defendant was carrying two unloaded pistols, the court said that it must be shown that the pistols were carried as weapons, for the purpose of convenience in a fight, and that in the instant case the pistols were useless for that purpose.

43. State v Mays, 7 **Ariz** App 90, 436 P2d 482; State v Jaramillo (App) 82 **NM** 548, 484 P2d 768; Hilliard v State, 87 **Tex** Crim 15, 218 SW 1052, 8 ALR 1316.

Annotation: 79 ALR2d 1423, § 6[a]; 8 ALR 1319.

Am. Jur. 2d, "Weapons and Firearms"

LIBRARY EXERCISE

Using Am. Jur.

You are on a team researching the question whether a parent in Indiana may educate her children at home because she believes she can do a better job of educating them than can the teachers in the local school. The school district superintendent has demanded that the children enroll in school. If home schooling is an option in Indiana, what is the standard by which the quality of the home education is measured?

You are assigned to use American Jurisprudence 2d ("Am. Jur.") to find Indiana home schooling cases. Give the full citation, including the date, for each case. Do not go beyond Am. Jur. except to obtain information needed for full citations.

Questions

1. *Go first to the General Index to Am. Jur. 2d. What will you look under? Think of at least two subject headings to try.*
2. *Look under these headings. What do you find regarding home schooling?*
3. *Is there a statement in the Article regarding the parent's inquiry? What is the law in Indiana? What citations to cases do you find?*
4. *Don't give up! Are there any references to Indiana cases?*
5. *From your research thus far, what can you tell the parent?*

Answers

1. Probable headings might be: Home Schooling, Education, Schools.
2. Under Home Schooling there is nothing listed in the index. Under Education, it says "see Schools" (the article entitled Schools). Under "Schools," there is a subheading "Home Instruction" with a sub-subheading "by parents," which sends you to the article entitled Schools, sections 229-231.
3. We are told that some states allow home schooling provided the home education is "substantially equivalent" or "simply equivalent" to that offered by the public schools. There is no reference to Indiana in the main text, however.
4. Yes, in footnote 20 we are referred to *Mazanec v. North Judson-San Pierre School Corp* (N.D. Ind. 1985), 614 F. Supp 1152, aff'd (C.A.7 Ind. 1986) 798 F.2d 230. This footnote amplifies a discussion in the text regarding the standards of some states that do allow home schooling. We can conclude that, since *Manzanec* is cited, Indiana does allow home schooling, but we don't know what standard the parent will have to meet.
5. Indiana does allow home schooling, but we will have to read *Mazanec* in order to tell her by what standard her home schooling will be measured.

b. State Encyclopedias

In addition to national encyclopedias, there are 15 state-specific encyclopedias. State-specific encyclopedias are organized the same way as the national ones. When researching a question that deals with the law of your particular state, it is almost always best to start with the state-specific encyclopedia, if one exists. That way you can avoid sifting through a discussion on the law in all the states to find the law of your state.

State-Specific Legal Encyclopedias
(alphabetized by state)

California Jurisprudence 3d (Bancroft Whitney/ Lawyers Coop)

Florida Jurisprudence 2d (Bancroft Whitney/Lawyers Coop)

Encyclopedia of Georgia Law (Harrison)

Illinois Law and Practice (West)

Indiana Law Encyclopedia (West)

Maryland Law and Practice (West)

Michigan Civil Jurisprudence (Callaghan)

Michigan Law and Practice (West)

Strong's *North Carolina Index 3d* (Bancroft Whitney/ Lawyers Coop)

New York Jurisprudence 2d (Bancroft-Whitney/ Lawyers Coop)

Ohio Jurisprudence 3d (Bancroft-Whitney/ Lawyers Coop)

Pennsylvania Law Encyclopedia (West)

Tennessee Jurisprudence (Michie)

Texas Jurisprudence (Bancroft-Whitney/Lawyers Coop)

Michie's *Jurisprudence of Virginia and West Virginia* (Michie)

2. American Law Reports

This series of books has two titles: *American Law Reports* (*A.L.R.*) and *American Law Reports, Federal* (*A.L.R. Fed.*). *A.L.R.* covers issues primarily arising under state statutes and in state cases, as well as federally oriented issues that arose before 1969, the year *A.L.R. Fed.* was first published. *A.L.R. Fed.* covers issues that arise primarily under federal statutes or in federal cases. One of these titles is an excellent place to begin.

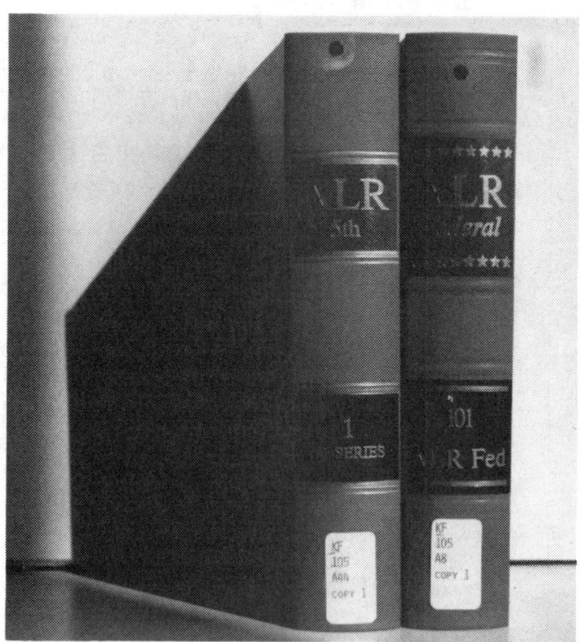

American Law Reports

Both publications are multi-volume sets that contain discussions of narrow issues that have been suggested by newly-decided court cases. Each discussion comments on the case itself and then discusses other cases that have considered the same or similar issues.

A.L.R. and *A.L.R. Fed.* are different from encyclopedias in that they don't attempt to cover every subject. This, of course, means some bad news and some good. You may not find what you're looking for, but if you do you'll be well rewarded. Fortunately, *A.L.R.* has an excellent index that allows you to very quickly find out whether the news is good or bad for you.

EXAMPLES OF THE KINDS OF ISSUES COVERED BY *A.L.R.*

- Circumstances justifying grant or denial of a petition to change an adult's name
- Visitation rights of the father of a child born out of wedlock
- Whether a public utility is responsible for dam ages for interruption, failure, or inadequacy of electric power.

A.L.R. comes in five series (*A.L.R.*, *A.L.R. 2d*, *A.L.R. 3d*. *A.L.R. 4th* and *A.L.R. 5th*) according to the date of the articles. Unlike the legal encyclopedias, the newest series does not replace previous ones. *A.L.R. 5th* may contain an almost entirely new set of topics not covered in *A.L.R. 4th*, for example. The older series are kept up to date with "pocket parts" (inserts in the back of each hardcover volume) and hardbound volumes called the *Later Case Service*. *A.L.R. Federal* is still in its first series.

PHONE UPDATES

The publisher of A.L.R. now offers a telephone hotline that provides up-to-date information about cases that have been decided but not yet published. The number is 1-800-225-7488.

EXAMPLES OF WHAT THE *A.L.R. FED.* SERIES COVERS ARE:

- What constitutes violation of § 134 of the Consumer Credit Protection Act prohibiting fraudulent use of credit cards
- The seizure and forfeiture under 19 U.S.C.S. ¶ 1526(e) of imported merchandise bearing a counterfeit trademark
- Employer's right under § 8(a)(1) of the National Labor Relations Act to ask an employee whether the employee intends to participate in a strike.

A.L.R. is published by Bancroft-Whitney/Lawyers Coop. This means that each article contains cross-references to other Bancroft-Whitney/Lawyers Coop publications on the same issue, which is of great assistance. And starting with *A.L.R. 5th*, the articles cross-refer to non-Bancroft-Whitney/Lawyer's Coop sources as well. Because of its good index, *A.L.R.* is usually easy to use. If you need more help, Bancroft-Whitney/Lawyers Coop publishes a book called *The Living Law* that gives you detailed instructions on how to use *A.L.R.*

Here is a detailed example of how *A.L.R.* works. Any topic can be similarly researched through *A.L.R* if a relevant article can be located.

Facts Jeff is obligated to pay child support to his ex-wife, Tracy, as a result of a Virginia court order. Tracy tells Jeff he can stop paying support if he gives Tracy his relatively new car. But before Jeff signs over title to the car, he wants to be sure that Tracy can't later sue for child support.

Jeff turns to the *American Law Reports* for an answer. While each *A.L.R.* series has its own index, Jeff starts with the *Index to Annotations*, a five-volume set that includes the annotations to *A.L.R. 2d, 3d* and *4th* as well as *A.L.R. Fed.* and *Supreme Court Reports, Lawyers' Edition (L. Ed.)* (the Bancroft-Whitney collection of U.S. Supreme Court decisions). First Jeff studies the Explanatory Illustration page at the beginning of the volume. This page explains how the entries are organized and coded; one is shown below.

EXPLANATORY ILLUSTRATION

ABORTION ←	Main topic heading
For digest treatment, see title **Abortion in ALR Digest** ←	ALR Digest reference
Accomplices (this index) ←	Cross-reference to other main topic
Consent ←	Group heading
—judicial consent to minor's abortion, 23 ALR4th 1061 ←	Reference to ALR4th
—malpractice, see group Malpractice in this topic ←	Internal reference to group within same topic
—parental consent, right of minor to have abortion without, 42 ALR3d 1406 ←	Reference to ALR3d
Constitutionality of abortion laws, 35 L Ed 2d 735 ←	Reference to L Ed 2d
Long-arm statute, medical malpractice action, 25 ALR4th 706, §§ 5, 9[a] ←	Reference to sections within annotation
Public Health Service Act, family planning services, 71 ALR Fed 961, §§ 3, 7 ←	Reference to ALR Fed

Jeff next turns to the Index to Annotations and finds a major entry for "Custody and Support of Children." Since Jeff is concerned about the validity of an agreement, he looks under the "Contracts" subheading. There he finds two entries that look promising: "modification" and "release." (They are shown below as they appear in the index).

INDEX TO ANNOTATIONS

CUSTODY AND SUPPORT OF CHILDREN —Cont'd

Conflict of laws—Cont'd

- legitimacy of children, law governing enforceability and validity of contract made for support of illegitimate child, 87 ALR2d 1306
- third person's or child's right against parent for support of child, 34 ALR2d 1460

Consent

- constitutional principles applicable to award or modification of custody of child—Supreme Court cases, 80 L Ed 2d 886
- interference with noncustodial parent's visitation rights as ground for custody change, 28 ALR4th 9, § 6[b]
- laches or acquiescence as defense, so as to recovery of arrearages, 5 ALR4th 1015
- limitation of actions, 70 ALR2d 1250
- regaining custody after temporary conditional relinquishment, 35 ALR4th 61, §§ 3, 4[a], 6, 7
- stepparent's post divorce duty to stepchild, 44 ALR4th 520, §§ 4[b], 5[b]
- termination of support obligation, what voluntary acts of child, other than marriage or entry into military service, terminate parent's obligation, 32 ALR3d 1055, §§ 4[a], 5[a], 6, 7[b]

Contempt

- arrearages, power of divorce court, after

CUSTODY AND SUPPORT OF CHILDREN —Cont'd

Contracts—Cont'd

- modification of decree for support of child which was based on agreement of parties, 61 ALR3d 657
- putative father, validity and construction of putative father's promise to support or provide for illegitimate child, 20 ALR3d 500
- release, validity and effect, as between former spouses, of agreement releasing parent from payment of child support provided for in an earlier divorce decree, 100 ALR3d 1129
- religion as factor in custody, 22 ALR4th 971, §§ 15, 16
- separation or property settlement agreement of parent, child's right to enforce provisions of, 34 ALR3d 1357
- statute of frauds, contract to support, maintain, or educate a child as within provision of statute of frauds relating to contracts not to be performed within a year, 49 ALR2d 1293
- statutory family allowance to minor children as affected by previous agreement or judgment for their support, 6 ALR3d 1387
- stepparent's postdivorce duty to support stepchild, 44 ALR4th 520, §§ 3, 4[b], 6

Index to Annotations, "Support and Custody of Children"

Although these summaries of the articles are written in typical legalese, the "release" article appears relevant to Jeff's question.

At the end of the index summary, a citation appears. To find this article, Jeff locates volume 100 of A.L.R.*3d* and turns to page 1129.

TOTAL CLIENT-SERVICE LIBRARY® REFERENCES

24 Am Jur 2d, Divorce and Separation § 871; 59 Am Jur 2d, Parent and Child § 70

8 Am Jur Pl & Pr Forms (Rev), Desertion and Nonsupport, Forms 1 et seq.; 8 Am Jur Pl & Pr Forms (Rev), Divorce and Separation, Forms 623, 624, 626, 627; 19 Am Jur Pl & Pr Forms (Rev), Parent and Child, Forms 43, 45, 46, 50

1 Am Jur Legal Forms 2d, Alimony and Separation Agreements §§ 17:35, 17:104, 17:105; 7 Am Jur Legal Forms 2d, Desertion and Nonsupport §§ 89:6, 89:12; 13 Am Jur Legal Forms 2d, Parent and Child § 191:127; 17 Am Jur Legal Forms 2d, Support of Persons §§ 243:1 et seq.

1 Am Jur Proof of Facts 2d 1, Change in Circumstances Justifying Modification of Child Support Order; 15 Am Jur Proof of Facts 1, Child Custody §§ 21–24

17 Am Jur Trials 721, Defenses Against Wife's Action for Support

US L Ed Digest, Divorce and Separation § 9.5

ALR Digests, Divorce and Separation § 127

L Ed Index to Annos, Children and Minors; Contracts; Divorce and Separation; Release

ALR Quick Index, Children; Contracts; Custody and Support of Children; Divorce and Separation; Parent and Child, Release or Discharge; Support and Maintenance

Federal Quick Index, Children and Minors; Contracts; Custody of Children; Divorce and Separation; Release; Support and Maintenance

Total Client Service Box

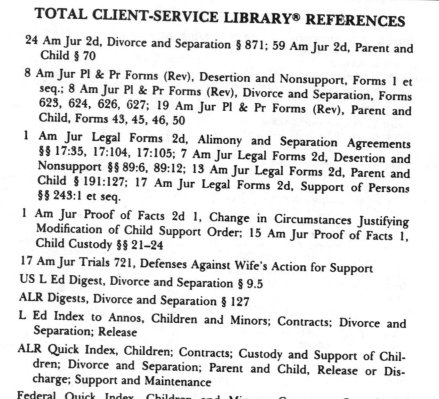

The first page (shown above) contains the Total Client Service Box, which refers to other materials published by Bancroft-Whitney/Lawyer's Coop that contain information on the same or similar issue to that covered in the *A.L.R.* annotation. In other words, just by finding this article in *A.L.R. 3d*, Jeff has obtained citations to a number of other Bancroft-Whitney/Lawyer's Coop resources that may help answer his question.

After reading the article in the hardcover part of the book, Jeff checks the pocket part (usually in the front of the volume) to see whether *A.L.R.* has noted any new developments on the topic.

Shown below are four pages taken from the beginning of the annotation. The first page demonstrates how the article is indexed. The second page shows a breakdown of states that are referred to in the article. If Jeff's state is not among them, he at least knows that he will not find any specific discussion in the article about his state's laws or cases. The third page shows the scope of the article, so that a researcher who is looking for something different won't waste time. Also, the third and fourth pages show the list of other *A.L.R.* articles on related topics.

VALIDITY OF RELEASE FROM CHILD SUPPORT 100 ALR3d
100 ALR3d 1129

INDEX

1130

Annotation from A.L.R 3d

100 ALR3d VALIDITY OF RELEASE FROM CHILD SUPPORT
100 ALR3d 1129

TABLE OF JURISDICTIONS REPRESENTED
Consult POCKET PART in this volume for later cases

US: §§ 3[b], 4[c], 6[b]
Ala: §§ 4[c]
Ariz: §§ 4[a], 5[a]
Ark: §§ 3[a], 4[a], 5[b]
Cal: §§ 2[b], 3[a, b], 4[a], 5[a, b]
Colo: §§ 3[a], 4[a], 5[a]
DC: §§ 3[b], 4[c], 6[b]
Fla: §§ 4[a], 5[b]
Ga: §§ 2[b], 4[a, c], 5[c], 6[b]
Hawaii: §§ 4[c], 6[b]
Idaho: §§ 3[a], 4[a, b], 5[a]
Ill: §§ 3[a, b], 4[a, c], 5[a, b], 6[a]
Ind: §§ 4[c], 6[b]
Iowa: §§ 3[a, b], 4[a, c], 5[a]
Kan: §§ 3[a], 4[a, c]
Ky: §§ 3[a, b], 4[a], 5[b], 6[a, b]
La: §§ 4[a]
Md: §§ 4[c]
Mich: §§ 5[a]
Mo: §§ 3[a, b], 4[a, b], 5[a], 6[b]
Neb: §§ 3[b]
NH: §§ 5[a, b]
NJ: §§ 5[b]
NY: §§ 3[a, b], 4[a], 6[a, b]
ND: §§ 5[b]
Ohio: §§ 3[a, b], 4[a], 5[a]

Annotation from A.L.R 3d

Okla: §§ 5[c]
Or: §§ 3[a, b], 4[a], 5[a]
Pa: §§ 3[a], 4[a]
RI: §§ 5[b]
Tex: §§ 6[b]
Utah: §§ 4[a-c], 5[a]
Wash: §§ 3[b], 4[c]
Wyo: §§ 3[a], 4[a, b], 5[a]

§ 1. Introduction

[a] Generally

This annotation[1] collects and analyzes the cases determining the validity and effect, as between divorced spouses, agreements[2] between such divorced spouses, made subsequent to the entry of their divorce decree, to a release of the child support obligation provided in the decree. Agreements between divorced spouses for the reduction of child support awarded in the divorce decree are included to the extent they have been treated as releases pro tanto.[3]

The reader is reminded that the annotation does not purport to represent the statutory law of any jurisdiction except to the extent that it is reflected in the reported cases within the scope of the annotation, so that the latest enactments of the jurisdiction of interest should be consulted.

[b] Related matters

Delay by divorced wife in seeking enforcement of permanent alimony or child support award as constituting laches or acquiescence, so as to bar recovery of arrearages. — ALR3d —.

Divorced wife's duty to pay child support. — ALR3d —.

Father's liability for support of child furnished after divorce decree which awarded custody to mother but made no provision for support. 91 ALR3d 530.

Right to credit on child support payments for social security or other government dependency payments for benefit of child. 77 ALR3d 1315.

Divorce: power of court to modify decree for support of child which was based on agreement of parties. 61 ALR3d 657.

Divorce: withholding or denying visitation rights for failure to make alimony or support payments. 51 ALR3d 520.

Right to credit on accrued support

---

1. This annotation supersedes the annotation at 57 ALR2d 1139, entitled "Validity and effect, as between former spouses, of agreement releasing father from further payment of child support provided for in an earlier divorce decree."

2. The annotation assumes that the agreement is in the required form, if such a form is required, and is not vitiated by duress, fraud, or mistake.

The annotation does not include the question whether a custodial parent's conduct may preclude enforcement of decretal child support provisions unless the court clearly construes such conduct as an agreement. In this regard see the annotation at 70 ALR2d 1250, entitled "Statute of limitations, laches, or acquiescence as defense to action or proceeding for alimony or support of child allowed by court order or decree."

3. As to whether a child may maintain a suit against a parent for support, see the annotation at 13 ALR2d 1142, entitled "Maintenance of suit by child, independently of statute, against parent for support."

To be distinguished is the question whether a parent may, prior to the entry of a divorce decree, release the other parent from the duty to make payments for child support. In this connection see the annotation at 61 ALR3d 657, entitled "Divorce: power of court to modify decree for support of child which was based on agreement of parties."

Annotation from A.L.R 3d

payments for time child is in father's custody or for other voluntary expenditures. 47 ALR3d 1031.

Income of child from other source as excusing parent's compliance with support provisions of divorce decree. 39 ALR3d 1292.

What voluntary acts of child, other than marriage or entry into military service, terminate parent's obligation to support. 32 ALR3d 1055.

Power of divorce court, after child attained majority, to enforce by contempt proceedings, payment of arrears of child support. 32 ALR3d 888.

Spouse's acceptance of payments under alimony or property settlement or child support provisions of divorce judgment as precluding appeal therefrom. 29 ALR3d 1184.

Father's criminal liability for desertion of or failure to support child where divorce decree awards custody to another. 73 ALR2d 960.

Statute of limitations, laches, or acquiescence as defense to action or proceeding for alimony or support of child allowed by court order or decree. 70 ALR2d 1250.

Pleading and burden of proof, in contempt proceedings, as to ability to comply with order for payment of alimony or child support. 53 ALR2d 591.

Maintenance of suit by child, independently of statute, against parent for support. 13 ALR2d 1142.

◆

Validity of parental agreement to reduce decretory child support payments. 46 Iowa L Rev 675 (1961).

§ 2. Summary and comment

[a] Generally

In determining the validity and effect, as between divorced spouses, of an agreement by which the custodial parent releases the noncustodial parent from his or her obligations under the provisions of the divorce decree to pay child support, the first question to be considered is whether the agreement meets the tests of validity applicable to all releases. Thus, while it has been generally held that such agreements must be supported by valid consideration, as the courts found present in particular agreements, one court held that, although the agreement lacked consideration, it was supported by the requisite donative intent.[4] Some courts have held that particular agreements lacked consideration where, for instance, there was no evidence of a bargain and exchange, or that either party gave up anything or gained anything, or where it was held that the custodial parent's agreement to take less than the amount of a liquidated debt was not a valid consideration.[5] On the other hand, some courts have held such agreements invalid and have expressly indicated that an executory agreement can not be pleaded as an accord and satisfaction.[6]

It has also been held, generally, that such agreements between former spouses are valid so long as the interests of the child are not adversely affected, and also in particular cases, that such agreements were valid.[7] And some courts have expressly held that such agreements are valid despite the absence of court sanction.[8]

In some cases the courts have distinguished between past-due and fu-

4. § 3[a], infra.

5. § 3[b], infra.

6. § 3[b], infra.

7. § 4[a], infra.

8. § 6[a], infra.

Annotation from A.L.R 3d

Jeff finds the discussion he seeks in Section 5. The California case of *Allen v. Allen* seems to say that an agreement such as the one Jeff was considering making with Tracy cannot take the place of court-ordered support payments. Jeff will now want to find out what the law is in Virginia, but he is well on his way to doing so. (See Chapter 10 on using one case to find additional relevant cases.)

§ 5[a] VALIDITY OF RELEASE FROM CHILD SUPPORT 100 ALR3d
100 ALR3d 1129

of a divorce decree in exchange for interests in real property which serve only to enhance the financial interests of the parties themselves and completely disregard the welfare of the children. The court said that this did not mean that the trial court, in determining whether custody or support provisions of a decree should be modified, could not take into account the wishes of the divorced parents, but that it meant that the court could not be bound by such an agreement. Accordingly, the court affirmed the trial court's dismissal of the father's petition to modify the divorce decree in accordance with the parties' agreement.

→ In Allen v Allen (1956, 1st Dist) 138 **Cal** App 2d 706, 292 P2d 581, the court held that its authority to make necessary orders for the support of minor children of divorced parents could not be limited or abridged by any agreement between the parents, even if it had been incorporated into a modified divorce decree and even though it was valid and binding as between the former spouses. The court thus affirmed the trial court's order that the father pay a monthly sum for the support of his children, despite the parents' agreement that the mother would waive all claims for the support of the minor children and would assume the sole responsibility of providing for their support, in consideration of the father's paying a lump sum to her and giving his consent to the adoption of the children by the wife's future husband.

For somewhat different reasons, the court in Singer v Singer (1970, 2d Dist) 7 **Cal** App 3d 807, 87 Cal Rptr 42, held that a stipulation between former spouses that the provisions of their divorce decree would be modified so that the wife's decretal support allowance would be reduced by whatever increase might be granted her for additional child support (all medical and dental expenses as opposed to extraordinary ones, and reasonable allowances for the children), was not binding upon the trial court, even though it had modified the decree in accordance with the stipulation, because the decree was modified without the presentation of any evidence. Accordingly the court remanded the cause to the trial court with directions that it allow the wife, the custodial parent, to present evidence respecting her increased costs of supporting the children over the entire period from the entry of the original decree, instead of restricting her to introducing evidence only since the date of the stipulation 8 years later.

To the effect that such an agreement does not prevent the court from ordering child support in amounts greater than the parties agreed to, see Innes v McColgan (1941) 47 **Cal** App 2d 781, 118 P2d 855, motion den 52 Cal App 2d 698, 126 P2d 930, infra § 5[b]; Hunter v Hunter (1959, 2d Dist) 170 **Cal** App 2d 576, 339 P2d 247, supra § 4[a]; and Potts v Superior Court of Los Angeles County (1964, 2d Dist) 229 **Cal** App 2d 692, 40 Cal Rptr 521, supra § 4[a].

Also to similar effect see, Hill v Hill (1940) 106 **Colo** 492, 107 P2d 597, supra § 4[a].

Similarly see Andersen v Andersen (1965) 89 **Idaho** 551, 407 P2d 304, supra § 4[b].

In Page v Page (1975) 30 **Ill** App 3d 514, 334 NE2d 212, the court held that although the former spouses had agreed to reduce the noncustodial parent's decretal child support obligations from $60 to $40 per week in consideration of the noncustodial par-

1154

Section 5

LIBRARY EXERCISE

Using A.L.R.

Paula was a quiet woman who lived in Michigan, and was known on her job as a "straight arrow" and honest worker. When her husband died suddenly, she was left with many debts and an infant daughter. She considered bankruptcy, but was ashamed to be known as a "deadbeat."

She poured out her heart to Dave, a co-worker who was also a good friend. Dave was actually a police officer on an undercover assignment to ferret-out suspected on-going drug traffic within Paula's company. He told Paula that, as her good friend, she could count on him. He knew of a way that she could make big money fast. All she had to do was to take a package once a week to the office of a friend of his, where she would be given an envelope containing $5,000, of which she could keep $1,000. She was suspicious but, with creditors getting more insistent, she eventually agreed to the plan.

After the first week, when Paula had begun to pay off her creditors, Dave told her that the packages contained drugs. Paula was shocked, but Dave told her that they were in this together and they had nothing to fear. Paula considered quitting, but she saw it as the only way out of financial ruin, and she did not want to abandon Dave. She told Dave she'd continue to deliver the packages, but only for a few more weeks until her debts were paid off. Dave increased the deliveries to $10,000 each. On the third delivery, Paula was arrested.

Your friend Paula tells you the story above. She admits that she carried the drugs and money, but thinks that, in view of her recent bereavement and vulnerability, the police acted despicably. She feels that she was entrapped and wants to know what she will have to prove in order for that defense to be successful.

Questions

1. *Use the A.L.R. index to find a recent A.L.R. article on entrapment. Where do you look?*
2. *As you look through the entries under ENTRAPMENT, do you find a recent article relevant to entrapment in a drug case?*
3. *Using the Volume 9 of the A.L.R.5th Series, find the Article. Turn to the Index, which appears near the beginning of the Article. Find entries that deal with outrageous police conduct.*
4. *Remember, you are looking for Michigan law on these issues. How can you quickly determine whether this Article cites Michigan case law?*
5. *Looking at the cases listed under* **Michigan***, are there any cases whose section numbers correspond to those we found for "outrageous conduct" (§§ 5[b], 8[b], and 10[b])?*
6. *Now that you know which Article section cites a Michigan case for your question, how do you find the Michigan case within the section?*
7. *Having read the analysis of Michigan law in the Article, what will you tell Paula about her chances of establishing a defense of entrapment?*
8. *Check the Pocket Part in the back of 9 A.L.R.5th. (Remember, these inserts sometimes are known as "Supplements.") Do you find an entry for our Article?*
9. *Pull down volume 18 of A.L.R.5th and find the Article on page 1. How can you find out if there are any Michigan cases in this Article?*
10. *Turn to these sections, read the section titles, and find the discussion of* Williams*, which is preceded by the* **Mich** *abbreviation. From the description of the facts in* Williams*, what is the difference between that case and Paula's situation?*

Answers

1. In the series of A.L.R. Indices, the third Volume ("E - H") includes a heading entitled "ENTRAPMENT." Several entries are listed. There are also recent entries in the Pocket Part under ENTRAPMENT.
2. Yes, in the Pocket Part there is a listing for an article entitled "Drugs and narcotics, entrapment as defense to charge of selling or supplying narcotics where government agents supplied narcotics to defendant and purchased them from him, 9 A.L.R.5th 464."
3. "Outrageous government conduct" is discussed in the Article in §§ 5[b], 8[b], and 10[b].
4. After the Index, there is a section entitled "Jurisdictional Table of Cited Statutes and Cases." States are listed alphabetically. The cases from Michigan that are cited in the Article are listed, followed by the Article sections in which that case is cited.
5. Yes, *People v Jamieson* and *People v Roy* are cited in section 8[b].
6. Search through section 8[b] for the bold-faced abbreviations of state names. (The section begins with federal law and goes through the states alphabetically.) The discussion of **Mich** law and cases (*Jamieson* and *Roy*) begins on page 530.
7. The judge will consider whether the average person (in a situation similar to Paula's) who was *not* ready and willing to commit crime would have been induced to do so by the police conduct. If Paula can convince the judge that any law-abiding person in her position would have been overwhelmed by Dave's misuse of their friendship and sly escalation of her involvement, she may be able to establish the defense of entrapment.
8. Yes, a reference to "9 A.L.R.5th 464 - 552" is found on page 7. Under §1[b], **Introduction - Related annotations,"** the reader is referred to an article about a state official's "outrageous conduct" in 18 A.L.R.5th 1.
9. As we did in the answer to Question 4, we go to the Jurisdictional Table and find **Michigan.** *People v Williams* is cited in sections 4[a] and 20[a].
10. In *Williams*, undercover cops stood passively on street corners, ready to sell drugs if approached. Since they did not initiate contacts with the buyers and made no initial offers to sell the drugs, the court held that they merely furnished an opportunity to commit crime and therefore had not entrapped the defendants. Paula can use the case by arguing that, by contrast, Dave "initiated" her drug selling as the solution to her problems, thereby entrapping her.

LIBRARY EXERCISE

Using A.L.R. & C.J.S.

You are researching the case of the Minnesota landlord whose storefront was rented by a couple whom he thought planned to run a respectable grocery store. In fact, the renters were the police, who used the grocery for two months as a front for a sting operation designed to catch drug traffickers. The police paid the rent and left the place in good shape, but the community continues to associate the site with drug activity. As a result, the landlord cannot find any new renters. He wants to know if he can sue the government because he is now unable to use the premises as rental property.

Questions

1. *One of your co-workers has pointed you toward an A.L.R. article entitled "RIGHT TO COMPENSATION FOR REAL PROPERTY DAMAGED BY LAW ENFORCEMENT PERSONNEL IN COURSE OF APPREHENDING SUSPECT" in 23 A.L.R.5th. How do you find it?*
2. *After you find the Article, read the synopsis at the beginning. How do the facts of the Minnesota case resemble your client's situation, and how do they differ?*
3. *You need to find a Minnesota case that discusses non-physical damage, since there are none cited in the Article. In the beginning of the Article there are several tables and lists. Which of them will give you a reference to other research sources that might discuss non-physical damage?*
4. *Take down volume 29A from the* Corpus Juris Secundum *(C.J.S.) set, and turn to §82 in the Eminent Domain article. How will you find out whether there are Minnesota cases dealing with a governmental taking that is non-physical?*
5. *What would a careful researcher do with the cases referred to in the footnotes?*

Answers

1. Take down volume 23 of A.L.R.5th and open to the Contents at the beginning of the Volume. The Article is listed last and starts on page 836.
2. In *Wegner v Milwaukee Mutual Insurance Company,* the police threw hand-grenades into a house where a suspect was hiding. The house was wrecked and the owner sued. The court held that the owner could collect money damages for a governmental "taking" of his home. Our client's premises, however, sustained no *physical* damage.
3. Under RESEARCH SOURCES near the beginning of the Article, there is a reference to 29A C.J.S. Eminent Domain §82.
4. The footnotes of the Article can be skimmed to look for Minnesota cases. *State v Bentley* (fn. 61) and *Johnson v City of Plymouth* (fn. 78) are cited to support the statements of the law, in the text, that a governmental diminution in the rights of ownership is compensible; and that actual physical invasion or appropriation of the property is not required.
5. It would be important to read *Bentley*, *Johnson*, and *Wegner*. You should not assume that the cases actually stand for the statements of law they are said to support. Sometimes the editors of the secondary materials make mistakes!

3. Form Books

Form books are pretty much what their name suggests: collections of legal documents. Practicing attorneys copy and use the forms, so they don't have to reinvent the wheel every time they need a new document.

Form books can be of great help if your research question involves either state or federal procedure, whether civil or criminal. Judicial and administrative procedures inevitably involve the preparation and filing of forms: there are forms for almost every possible legal action, from petitioning for a divorce to changing your name, to evicting a tenant or to petitioning the United States Supreme Court. Court rules invariably require specific documents to be filed in very specific formats, depending on the type of case. You can copy the format from the examples.

The documents are usually presented in a fill-in-the-blanks format. To accomplish a specific procedural task, the user need only choose the correct document, modify the language a little to fit the needs of the particular case, fill in the information where indicated and file the finished document in court.

Leaving nothing to chance, form books usually discuss the procedural rules that are relevant to the use of each form. In other words, when you find the form you need, chances are you'll also find an overview of the procedure itself and instructions on how to make the most common modifications.

It's important to understand that these form books may not contain certain forms required by state law. For instance, many California court procedures require forms prepared by the California Judicial Council. These California forms can be obtained free or at a nominal price from the courts that use them, and also are collected in a special book called the *California Judicial Council Forms Manual*, published by an organization called the Continuing Education of the Bar (CEB) and available in most law libraries.

A typical form book entry, taken from *American Jurisprudence Legal Forms, Second Series*, is shown below. We show the form as well as the accompanying material provided about the law governing the procedure. Pay attention to the paragraph labeled "Annotation References," which is taken directly from the book's pocket part (update). It refers to an article on name changes in the *American Law Reports* (*A.L.R.*, covered in the preceding section), which illustrates how one Bancroft-Whitney/Lawyers Coop publication can lead directly to others.

Form Books

The forms in *Am. Jur. Legal Forms* are national in scope and often lack the specificity found in a form book prepared specifically for your state. When looking for an appropriate form or the procedure that goes with it, it is best to start with a publication that is specific to your state or topic, if there is one. As in the case of state encyclopedias, form books have been published only in the more populous states.

Finding Forms If you are looking for a particular form used in your state, you can often obtain it from a store specializing in legal forms. Call your local stationery store and ask. If they don't carry forms, they'll tell you who does.

The following is a partial list of form books and their publishers. After each title is an abbreviation that conforms to the classification system set out in Chapter 4. For example, *California Practice With Forms* carries the code S/C/P for State/Civil/Procedural. The entire list of abbreviations follows the list of form books.

If your state is not represented in the list, ask your law librarian to help you find a form book for your state. Also, read the next section on Practice Manuals; you might find some help there.

of __18______, State of __19______, and since such time has resided with her husband at the above address.

4. Applicant desires to change her name to __20______, her maiden surname, for the following reasons: __21______ *[specify reasons, such as* to continue her professional or business use of her maiden name *or* to avoid confusion between her professional or business relations with those of her husband *or* to assert her equal partnership with her husband in the marital relation *or* to assert her ethnic heritage, of which she is proud, *or other legally permissible reason].*

5. __22______ *[State information as to publication of notice of intent to change name, if required by statute.]*

Dated: __23______, 19_24_.

[Signature]

[Jurat]

☑ **Notes on Use:**

See also Notes on Use following § 182:43.

Annotations: Right of married woman to use maiden surname. 67 ALR3d 1266.

Circumstance justifying grant or denial of petition to change adult's name. 79 ALR3d 562.

Cross references: For other change of name forms, see § 182:54 et seq.

V. CHANGE OF NAME

§ 182:51 Scope of division

Material in this division consists of forms related to change of name. Included are such matters as application to a court of record for change of name and relevant affidavits and notices.

§ 182:52 Introductory comments

Unless applicable statutes provide otherwise, a person may change such person's name at will, without any legal proceedings, merely by adopting another name. In most states, however, statutes set forth specific procedures and requirements for change of name; such procedure usually includes filing a petition or application with a court of record. The court hearing a petition or application for change of name has discretion to either grant or deny it, the general rule being that there must exist some substantial reason for the change.[8]

8. *Text references:* Change of name, generally. 57 Am Jur 2d, Name §§ 10–16.

Annotations: Circumstances justifying grant or denial of petition to change adult's name. 79 ALR3d 562.

(For Tax Notes and Notes on use, see end of form)

Form and Explanation from Am. Jur. Legal Forms, 2nd Series

§ 182:53 Annotation references

ALR annotations treating the subject of change of name by an individual are set forth below.

ALR annotations:

Circumstance justifying grant or denial of petition to change adult's name. 79 ALR3d 562.

Change of child's name in adoption proceeding. 53 ALR2d 927.

§ 182:54 Application for change of name

To: __1__ *[court of record]*

APPLICATION FOR CHANGE OF NAME

Applicant states:

1. Applicant resides at __2__ *[address]*, City of __3__, County of __4__, State of __5__, __6__ *[ZIP]*, and has resided there for more than __7__ *[number of months or years]* prior to filing this application.

2. Applicant was born __8__ [in the City of __9__, County of __10__, State of __11__ *or set forth foreign address]* on __12__, 19__13__. Applicant was named __14__ and has always been known by that name.

3. The name of applicant's father is __15__, and the name of applicant's mother is __16__. They reside at __17__ [__18__ *(address)*, City of __19__, County of __20__, State of __21__, __22__ *(ZIP) or set forth foreign address]*.

4. Applicant __23__ [is *or* is not] married. __24__ *[If married, give information as to date and place of marriage, spouse's name, and date and place of spouse's birth.]*

5. Applicant desires to change applicant's name to __25__ for the following reasons: __26__.

6. __27__ *[State information as to publication of notice of intent to change name, if required by statute.]*

7. __28__ *[State information required by statute as to financial matters, any criminal records, and pending actions or other proceedings in which the applicant may be a party.]*

Dated: __29__, 19__30__.

[Jurat] *[Signature]*

☑ **Notes on Use:**

Text references: Statutory regulation of change of name, generally. 57 AM JUR 2d, Name §§ 11–16.

(For Tax Notes and Notes on use, see end of form)

Form and Explanation from Am. Jur. Legal Forms, 2nd Series

Form Books (Partial List)

Bender's Forms for Pleading (Matthew Bender) S/C/P

California Forms of Pleading and Practice (Matthew Bender) S/C/P

California Practice With Forms (Bancroft-Whitney/Lawyers Coop) S/C/P

California Forms—Legal and Business (Bancroft-Whitney/Lawyers Coop) S/C/Su

Commencing Civil Actions in California (Continuing Education of the Bar) S/C/P

Federal Procedural Forms, L. Ed. (Bancroft-Whitney/Lawyers Coop) F/C/Cr/P

Florida Jur. Forms Business and Practice (Bancroft-Whitney/Lawyers Coop) S/C/Su

Florida Criminal Procedure (Bancroft-Whitney/Lawyers Coop) S/Cr/P

Bender's Florida Form—Pleadings (Matthew Bender) S/C/P

Illinois Forms Business and Practice (Bancroft-Whitney/Lawyers Coop) S/C/Su

Indiana Forms of Pleading and Practice (Matthew Bender) S/C/P

Massachusetts Pleading and Practice, Forms and Commentary (Matthew Bender) S/C/P

New Jersey Forms—Legal and Business (Bancroft-Whitney/Lawyers Coop) S/C/Su

New Jersey Criminal Procedure (Bancroft-Whitney/Lawyers Coop) S/Cr/P

New Jersey Law with Forms (Matthew Bender) S/C/Su

New York Forms—Legal and Business (Bancroft-Whitney/Lawyers Coop) S/C/Su

Bender's Forms for the Consolidated Laws of New York (Matthew Bender) S/C/Su/P

Criminal Law of New York (Bancroft-Whitney/Lawyers Coop) S/Cr/Su

Carmody-Wait New York Encyclopedia of Practice 2d (Bancroft-Whitney/Lawyers Co-op) S/C/Su/P

Ohio Forms—Legal And Business (Bancroft-Whitney/Lawyers Coop) S/C/Su

Ohio Forms of Pleading and Practice (Matthew Bender) S/C/P

Pennsylvania Forms (Matthew Bender) S/C/Su/P

Standard Pennsylvania Practice 2d (Bancroft-Whitney/Lawyers Coop) S/C/Cr/Su

Texas Criminal Practice Guide (Matthew Bender) S/Cr/Su/P

Texas Forms—Legal and Business (Bancroft-Whitney/Lawyers Coop) S/C/Su

Texas Litigation Guide (Matthew Bender) S/C/Su/P

Texas Jurisprudence Pleading & Practice Forms 2d (Bancroft-Whitney/Lawyers Coop) S/C/P

S = State
F = Federal
C = Civil
Cr = Criminal
Su = Substantive
P = Procedural

4. Practice Manuals

Practice manuals, like form books, contain lots of forms and instructions for how to use them. However, form books tend to cover the entire spectrum of legal practice; practice manuals usually cover a specialized area of practice.

For example, a publication called *Defense of Drunk Driving Cases*, by Richard Erwin and Marilyn Minzer, tells you everything you need to know when handling a drunk driving offense. For attorneys who frequently handle this type of case, this book is the bible. There are practice manuals for torts, contracts, family law, real estate transactions, search and seizure questions and a myriad of other issues. Some are state-specific while others are national in scope.

Many of these books are well-written and organized. They can give you a good understanding of the procedural and substantive law, as well as the hands-on instructions necessary to file and prosecute your own case. These resources are generally available in law libraries. You can find them by looking up your subject in the electronic or manual card catalog (Section 9, below) or by asking the librarian. Below is a partial list to get you started.

LIBRARY EXERCISE

Using A.L.R.5th and Form Books

You are about to buy property that you fear may have been used to store hazardous waste and may thus be contaminated. You need to find a clause to use in your purchase agreement that makes the seller's disclosure of hazardous waste problems a necessary prerequisite for the sale of the property.

Use A.L.R.5th to find a recent article on the duty of a seller to disclose hazardous waste problems to the buyer.

Questions

1. *In which Volume of the set of A.L.R.5th do you start?*
2. *A quick perusal of the alphabetized subheadings in the main part of the volume shows nothing obviously on point. Be sure to consult the Pocket Part of the Index for more relevant articles and for the most recent articles. What do you find?*
3. *Find the A.L.R.5th article and, on page 631, fine the section headed "Research References" and the sub-heading "Practice Aids." In Practice Aids, find a listing for Am. Jur. Legal Forms. What form is listed?*
4. *How do you find the form in Am. Jur. Legal Forms?*
5. *Is the form at this section about hazardous waste disclosure or cleanup?*
6. *Where should you look now?*
7. *Among the many form descriptions in bold-face type, are there any which appear to deal with disclosures of environmental problems?*
8. *Are there words or phrases in the form which suggest that further research is needed?*

Answers

1. Choose the third A.L.R. Index volume and look under "Hazardous Substances."
2. Under "Hazardous Substances and Wastes" in the Pocket Part, under the subhead "Sale of property" you find "disclosure, vendors obligation to disclose...12 A.L.R.5th 630."
3. 16 Am. Jur. Legal Forms 2d, Real Estate Sales §219:874.
4. Find the set of books entitled "Am. Jur. Legal Forms." Choose Volume 16 and go to §219:874.
5. Although it is about an environmental issue (conditioning a sale on a successful Environmental Impact Report), it is not about hazardous waste.
6. Check the Pocket Part for forms with similar numbers—for example, §219.8_ _.
7. Yes, "§219.862.4 Condition for Sale-Environmental Concerns." This form makes the sale a conditional one: it will not go through unless the seller can show the buyer that the property has not been used for the handling, treatment, storage or disposal of hazardous or toxic substances.
8. Yes. The careful buyer would want to know what the "analogous laws and regulations of the State of ___" are for his or her state.

Practice Manuals (Partial List)

Arizona Probate (Bancroft-Whitney/Lawyer's Coop)

Bender's Forms of Discovery (Matthew Bender)

Connecticut Estates Practice (Bancroft-Whitney/Lawyer's Coop)

Defense of Drunk Driving Cases (Matthew Bender)

Defense of Narcotics Cases (Matthew Bender)

Florida Corporations (Bancroft-Whitney/Lawyer's Coop)

Georgia Divorce (Bancroft-Whitney/Lawyer's Coop)

Georgia Probate (Bancroft-Whitney/Lawyer's Coop)

Handling Accident Cases (Matthew Bender)

Illinois Tort Law and Practice (Bancroft-Whitney/Lawyer's Coop)

Immigration and Procedure Law (Matthew Bender)

Kentucky Probate (Bancroft-Whitney/Lawyer's Coop)

Law and the Family—New York (Bancroft-Whitney/Lawyer's Coop)

Massachusetts Corporations (Bancroft-Whitney/Lawyer's Coop)

Michigan Divorce (Bancroft-Whitney/Lawyer's Coop)

Michigan Probate (Bancroft-Whitney/Lawyer's Coop)

Minnesota Dissolution (Bancroft-Whitney/Lawyer's Coop)

Minnesota Probate (Bancroft-Whitney/Lawyer's Coop)

New York Estates Practice Guide, 3d Ed. (Bancroft-Whitney/Lawyer's Coop)

New York Law and Practice of Real Property (Bancroft-Whitney/Lawyer's Coop)

New York Zoning Law and Practice (Bancroft-Whitney/Lawyer's Coop)

Ohio Corporations (Bancroft-Whitney/Lawyer's Coop)

Ohio Probate (Bancroft-Whitney/Lawyer's Coop)

Ohio Real Estate (Bancroft-Whitney/Lawyer's Coop)

Pennsylvania Estates Practice (Bancroft-Whitney/Lawyer's Coop)

Prosecution and Defense of Criminal Conspiracy Cases (Matthew Bender)

Settlement of Estates and Fiduciary Law in Massachusetts, 4th (Bancroft-Whitney/Lawyer's Coop)

Tennessee Corporations (Bancroft-Whitney/Lawyer's Coop)

Tennessee Probate (Bancroft-Whitney/Lawyer's Coop)

Texas Family Law With Forms (Bancroft-Whitney/Lawyer's Coop)

Trademark Registration Practice (Clark Boardman Callaghan)

Wisconsin Corporations (Bancroft-Whitney/Lawyer's Coop)

Wisconsin Divorce (Bancroft-Whitney/Lawyer's Coop)

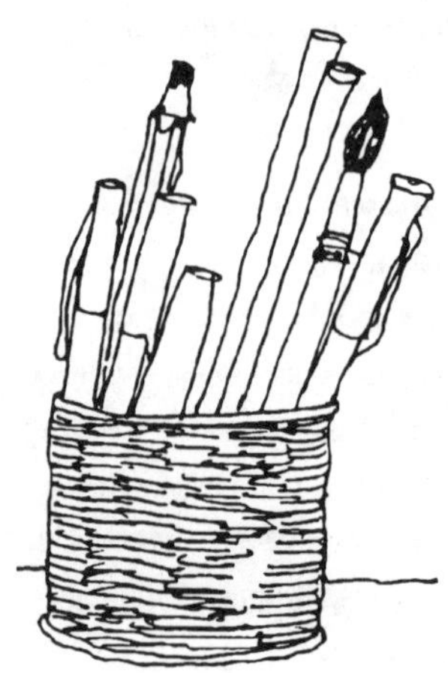

CONTINUING LEGAL EDUCATION PUBLICATIONS

Some publishers are dedicated to providing practicing lawyers with continuing education. Two of these—the Continuing Education of the Bar (CEB) and The Rutter Group—direct their materials towards California lawyers and one, the Practising Law Institute (PLI) focuses on New York lawyers. Publishers in some other states produce analogous resources, often called "CLE" (Continuing Legal Education) books.

Continuing legal education publishers produce detailed practice guidelines, instructions and forms for many different areas of law and practice, both state and federal. They also publish written materials used in continuing legal education seminars that they sponsor. Continuing education materials are usually available in the law libraries in the states for which they are published.

CEB (Partial List): *Advising California Employers, Advising California Partnerships, Debt Collection Practice in California, Tax Planning for Real Property Transactions, California Eviction Defense Manual, California Zoning Practice, California Tort Guide, California Automobile Insurance Law Guide,* and *California Administrative Hearing Practice.*

Rutter Group (Partial List): *Civil Procedure Before Trial, Personal Injury, Family Law, Landlord-Tenant.*

PLI (Partial List): Evidence in Negligence Cases, A Guide for Legal Assistants, Henn on Copyright Law: A Practitioner's Guide, Advertising Compliance Handbook, Friedman on Leases, How to Handle an Appeal, Bankruptcy Deskbook, How to Prepare an Initial Public Offering, Farm and Ranch Law, Litigating Copyright, Trademark and Unfair Competition Cases, Creative Real Estate Financing, Understanding the Securities Laws.

5. Proof of Facts

The publication known as *American Jurisprudence Proof of Facts* (Bancroft-Whitney/Lawyer's Coop) provides detailed discussions of what must be proved in virtually every kind of civil and criminal case. By using the subject index, you can find an excellent overview of the variables associated with your situation.

For example, suppose you want to open up a law clinic that will help people prepare their own simple wills. You want to use the slogan "Don't leave earth without one" in your advertising matter, but you wonder whether the slogan already used in advertising for American Express travelers' checks ("Don't leave home without them") precludes you from doing so. If you picked the term "trademark" and searched the index of *Proof of Facts*, you would find the entry shown below.

TRADE LIBEL PROOF OF FACTS 2d

TRADE LIBEL

Generally, 19 Am Jur Trials 499

TRADEMARKS AND TRADENAMES

Appropriation of competitor's advertising matter, methods or slogan, 18 POF2d 265

Cancellation of registration of trademark that has become generic term, 37 POF2d 67

Franchise tying agreements, 20 POF2d 197; 22 POF2d 267; 21 Am Jur Trials 453

Infringement
generally, 8 Am Jur Trials 359
– opinion survey, admissibility, 18 POF2d 305

Opinion surveys, admissiblity of, 18 POF2d 305, §§ 1, 2

Trade dress simulation, 3 POF2d 577

TRAFFIC EXPERTS

Signal, testimony as to unsafeness of, 6 POF2d 683, §§ 21, 22

TRAFFIC SIGNALS

Defective design or setting, 6 POF2d 683

TRAILERS

Mobile Home Defects (this index)

Photographs in civil cases, preparing and using, 3 Am Jur Trials 1

TRAILER TRUCKS

Taillights and reflectors, use or defect as factor in collision, 22 POF2d 225, §§ 18-21

TRAILS

Skiing accident litigation, 15 Am Jur Trials 147

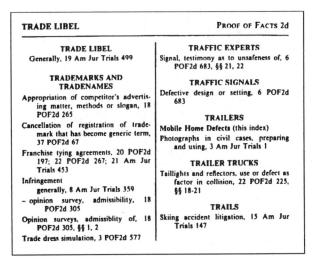

Index of Am. Jur. Proof of Facts

The first item in this entry appears to be relevant. Finding Volume 18 of *Proof of Facts* and turning to page 265, you find the entry shown below:

UNFAIR COMPETITION— APPROPRIATION OF COMPETITOR'S ADVERTISING MATTER, METHODS, OR SLOGAN

*BILL WISHARD, LL.B.**

Fact in Issue: Whether defendant advertised his goods in such a manner that there was an express or implied representation that the goods were those of a competitor, thereby deceiving the public as to the origin or identity of the goods.

This fact question may arise in an unfair competition action by the manufacturer or seller of goods for monetary and/or injunctive relief against another's use of particular advertising matter or methods, or other deceptive trade practices involving the "passing off" of the latter's goods as those of the plaintiff.

Related Proofs: Doing Business, 4 POF 483; Good Will, 5 POF 505; Trade Dress (Packaging) Simulation, 3 POF2d 577

I. BACKGROUND

* Senior Editor, Bancroft-Whitney Company.

18 POF 2d 265

Entry from Am. Jur. Proof of Facts

The first page of the article provides a succinct summary of the issue. The article then gives you an outline of its contents. Section I provides you with a background of the issue, while Section II tells you what American Express would have to prove to nail you for infringing on its advertising slogan.

After the outline, the article provides other references ("collateral references") that bear on the issue.

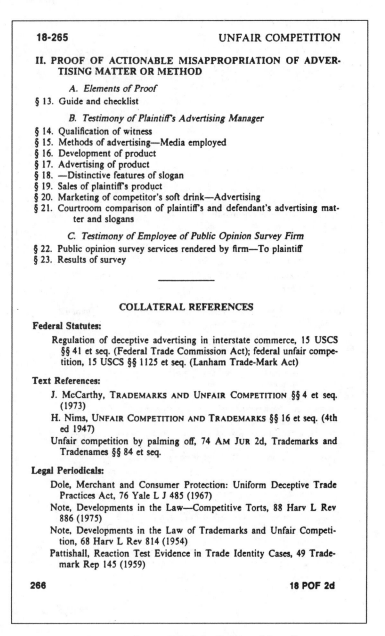

18-265 UNFAIR COMPETITION

II. PROOF OF ACTIONABLE MISAPPROPRIATION OF ADVERTISING MATTER OR METHOD

A. Elements of Proof

§ 13. Guide and checklist

B. Testimony of Plaintiff's Advertising Manager

§ 14. Qualification of witness
§ 15. Methods of advertising—Media employed
§ 16. Development of product
§ 17. Advertising of product
§ 18. —Distinctive features of slogan
§ 19. Sales of plaintiff's product
§ 20. Marketing of competitor's soft drink—Advertising
§ 21. Courtroom comparison of plaintiff's and defendant's advertising matter and slogans

C. Testimony of Employee of Public Opinion Survey Firm

§ 22. Public opinion survey services rendered by firm—To plaintiff
§ 23. Results of survey

COLLATERAL REFERENCES

Federal Statutes:

Regulation of deceptive advertising in interstate commerce, 15 USCS §§ 41 et seq. (Federal Trade Commission Act); federal unfair competition, 15 USCS §§ 1125 et seq. (Lanham Trade-Mark Act)

Text References:

J. McCarthy, TRADEMARKS AND UNFAIR COMPETITION §§ 4 et seq. (1973)

H. Nims, UNFAIR COMPETITION AND TRADEMARKS §§ 16 et seq. (4th ed 1947)

Unfair competition by palming off, 74 AM JUR 2d, Trademarks and Tradenames §§ 84 et seq.

Legal Periodicals:

Dole, Merchant and Consumer Protection: Uniform Deceptive Trade Practices Act, 76 Yale L J 485 (1967)

Note, Developments in the Law—Competitive Torts, 88 Harv L Rev 886 (1975)

Note, Developments in the Law of Trademarks and Unfair Competition, 68 Harv L Rev 814 (1954)

Pattishall, Reaction Test Evidence in Trade Identity Cases, 49 Trademark Rep 145 (1959)

266 18 POF 2d

Excerpt from "Unfair Competition," Am. Jur. Proof of Facts

After these references is a mini-index of the specific topics covered in the article. When doing legal research you will often be searching for one specific point and don't want to plow through 50 pages of irrelevant text to find it. This mini-index—common to most legal materials—gives you direct access to relevant material within the article. For example, since you want to find out whether there is any basis for your being liable to American Express, you would skim the index entry shown below.

18-265 **UNFAIR COMPETITION**

competition, including the area of conflict between federal and state law. 148 ALR 139.

Corporation's right to prevent use of its own or similar name by another corporation where they do business in different localities. 66 ALR 948, 962; 115 ALR 1241, 1245.

INDEX

268 18 POF 2d

Index to Entry from Am. Jur. Proof of Facts

When you came to the "Basis of Liability" entry, you could then proceed directly to Section 2 of the article. It is shown below.

§ 2. Basis of liability

Broadly, where the rights or privileges of a business competitor may conflict with those of another, each party must conduct his own business so as not to unnecessarily or unfairly injure that of the other.[8] Under this principle, where no valid trademark, copyright, or patent exists in a particular name or design, one producer or manufacturer may freely copy the goods, or the name or design used in connection with the goods, of another, or use the same name in his advertising, provided no deception is involved.[9] Thus, the mere appropriation by one of another's advertising matter, methods, slogan, or even his trademark or tradename, does not, of itself, constitute unfair competition.[10] However, if the goods or services in question are known to the buying public by such name, design, or physical appearance, any advertising by an imitator that deceives buyers as to the origin or identity of the goods or services is an actionable tort and may be enjoined as unfair competition.[11] That is, although competitive manufacturers or tradespersons may lawfully compete for the patronage of the public, they may not, by fraudulent imitative advertising devices or other unfair means, beguile or mislead prospective purchasers into buying their products under the impression that the purchasers are buying those of their competitors.[12]

☐ **Note:** The plaintiff is not required to show actual deception of

---

8. International News Service v Associated Press, 248 US 215, 63 L Ed 211, 39 S Ct 68, 2 ALR 293.

9. International Heating Co. v Oliver Oil Gas Burner & Machine Co. (CA8 Mo) 288 F 708, 30 ALR 611, cert den 263 US 714, 68 L Ed 521, 44 S Ct 135.

10. See §§ 3 et seq., infra.

11. Note, Developments in the Law of Trademarks and Unfair Competition, 68 Harv L Rev 814, 851 et seq.

☐ **Note:** The existence of an exclusive right to the use of the name or mark, whether a trademark or a tradename, is not essential to a right of action for unfair competition. 74 Am Jur 2d, Trademarks and Tradenames § 88. Nevertheless, because of the virtual identity of the facts that establish statutory trademark infringement and those that establish common-law unfair competition, counsel for the plaintiff ordinarily should allege a single cause of action on those two distinct grounds. Trademark Infringement and Unfair Competition Litigation, 8 Am Jur Trials 359, § 19.

Annotation: 15 ALR Fed 368, at pages 373–374.

12. American Steel Foundries v Robertson, 269 US 372, 70 L Ed 317, 46 S Ct 160.

Annotation: Rights and remedies with respect to another's use of a deceptively similar advertising slogan. 2 ALR3d 748.

18 POF 2d 271

Entry from Am. Jur. Proof of Facts

After reading the background material, you would probably want to skip to the section explaining what American Express has to prove. This section, shown below, provides a checklist of the type of evidence American Express would need to introduce and then provides some sample testimony.

UNFAIR COMPETITION 18-265 § 14

II. PROOF OF ACTIONABLE MISAPPROPRIATION OF ADVERTISING MATTER OR METHOD

A. Elements of Proof

§ 13. Guide and checklist

The following facts and circumstances, among others, tend to establish that the defendant intentionally appropriated plaintiff's advertising slogan, and that the consuming public associates plaintiff's slogan with a single source and is likely to be misled as to the source of defendant's similarly advertised product:

- ☐ Plaintiff's product development [§ 16]
- ☐ Promotion of plaintiff's product [§§ 16–19]
- ☐ Plaintiff's advertising methods and slogans—
  Media employed [§ 15]
  Slogan and pictorial representation used [§ 18]
- ☐ Entry of plaintiff's product in market [§ 19]
- ☐ Sales of plaintiff's product [§ 19]
- ☐ Development and marketing of defendant's product [§ 20]
- ☐ Adoption and use by defendant of plaintiff's advertising slogan [§ 20]
- ☐ Comparison of plaintiff's and defendant's advertising method or slogans [§ 21]
- ☐ Expert testimony by public opinion survey employee as to confusion of source by consumers [§§ 22, 23]

B. Testimony of Plaintiff's Advertising Manager

§ 14. Qualification of witness

[Plaintiff's advertising manager should be qualified to testify as to the history, development, and marketing objectives of plaintiff's product and its advertising.]

[After introduction and identification of witness]

Q. Please tell us your present position and business address.

A. I am vice-president in charge of advertising at the .... *[plaintiff]* Company, and our offices are at .... *[address]*, in ....*[city]*.

Q. What are the chief products developed and sold by that company?

18 POF 2d 289

Checklist from Am. Jur. Proof of Facts

LIBRARY EXERCISE

Using Proof of Facts

On Valentine's Day the Murphys ate dinner at Joe's World Famous Diner. Mr. Murphy ordered lasagna and Mrs. Murphy, a vegetarian, ordered a medley of sautéed vegetables. Their food came right away, but Mr. Murphy was disappointed to find his lasagna dry and tough, with lukewarm sauce congealed on the plate. Mrs. Murphy's veggies were crisp, bright, and fresh.

The Murphys finished their meal, went home and went to bed. A few hours later Mr. Murphy fell violently ill with nausea and diarrhea. Mrs. Murphy slept blissfully on. In the morning, he felt somewhat better, but was pale and weak. He went to the doctor, who took a stool sample. A few days later, the doctor called to say that the lab tests showed the presence of the bacteria *staphylococcus*.

Mrs. Murphy would like to know what Mr. Murphy would have to prove in order to hold Joe's liable for food poisoning. She has decided to consult the set of books entitled "Proof of Facts," because she knows that the articles in these books contain checklists of required facts and suggested lines of questioning of key witnesses.

Questions

1. *Three softbound volumes constitute the General Index for Am. Jur. Proof of Facts. What will she look under in the Index?*
2. *What is listed under STAPHYLOCOCCUS FOOD POISONING?*
3. *What does the article at 31 POF2d 81 tell Mrs. Murphy about the cause of staphylococcus food poisoning?*
4. *Does the reading suggest to Mrs. Murphy that Mr. Murphy might have a case?*
5. *Is there a helpful checklist for Mrs. Murphy to use as she plans her husband's direct testimony in court?*
6. *What questions could the attorney ask Mr. Murphy in Court to establish when the food was eaten?*

Answers

1. She should start with the most specific: staphylococcus food poisoning.
2. There is a "General" discussion at 31 POF2d 81, § 3, 19 - 34. (We ignore for now the reference to 5 POF 156, since this first edition is quite old. However, since there are pocket parts to even old articles, we may want to check it out later if the more recent article is not helpful.)
3. In section 3, the article says that this illness is the result of eating food that has been infected by the staphylococcus bacteria, which is produced when food is handled carelessly, such as being kept on a warming table for several hours at a temperature between 60 to 115 degrees F.
4. Yes. The rapidity with which he got his food, combined with its old and tired appearance, point towards a long wait on a not-so-hot steam table. His symptoms, Mrs. Murphy's avoidance of the problem, and the lab report all point to staphylococcus food poisoning.
5. Yes, the second part of the Article is entitled "PROOF OF STAPHYLOCOCCUS FOOD POISONING" and includes questions dealing with chronology, symptoms of the illness, the likely cause of the food poisoning, the diagnosis by a doctor, and identifying the unsafe food handling procedure and the source of contamination.
6. The following questions are suggested:

   Q. Did you and your wife have the occasion to eat dinner at Joe's World Famous Diner on the evening of February 14th?

   Q. Have you ever been there before?

   Q. How did you happen to select that restaurant?

   Q. At approximately what time did you arrive at the restaurant?

   Q. Are you sure of that time?

   Q. Did you have to wait to get your food?

   Q. Did you eat anything while you were waiting?

   Q. Do you know what time you actually started eating?

6. Law Reviews and Other Legal Periodicals

Because the law is always developing and changing, legal professionals are constantly analyzing its evolution. You can find articles about new legislation, current legal theories and viewpoints, and important cases in law journals published by law schools, commercial publishers, and professional legal societies, such as bar associations.

The articles in journals produced by law schools are written by law students, professors and even practicing attorneys, and sometimes present a whole new view of an area of the law. They tend to focus on where the law is going as opposed to where it is or where it's been, although they may provide some history to set the stage for the discussion.

On the other hand, journals produced by bar associations and other professional groups tend to be much more practical, with an emphasis on recent developments. Many law reviews and journals are general, covering subjects across the legal spectrum. But increasingly, legal periodicals are starting to specialize in such fields as taxation, environmental law, labor, entertainment and communications and women's studies.

Law reviews and journals are almost always published in paperback pamphlets, usually on a quarterly basis. At the end of the year, libraries bind the issues into a hardcover version.

Law Reviews

Even if articles are more academic than practical, they still may contain valuable descriptions of the state of the law in the specific area being discussed, and can provide you with research leads.

EXAMPLES OF TOPICS COVERED BY LEGAL PERIODICALS

- A father going through a divorce wants to find up-to-date information on how child support is handled in joint custody situations.
- A gay person wants to find out his remedies for employment discrimination.
- A computer programmer wants to find out the extent of patent protection for software.
- An estate planner wants to find out the trends in state legislation affecting revocable living trusts.
- A surrogate parent wants to know how the courts are handling custody and visitation requests.

Below is the cover of a recent issue of the *Harvard Journal on Legislation.*

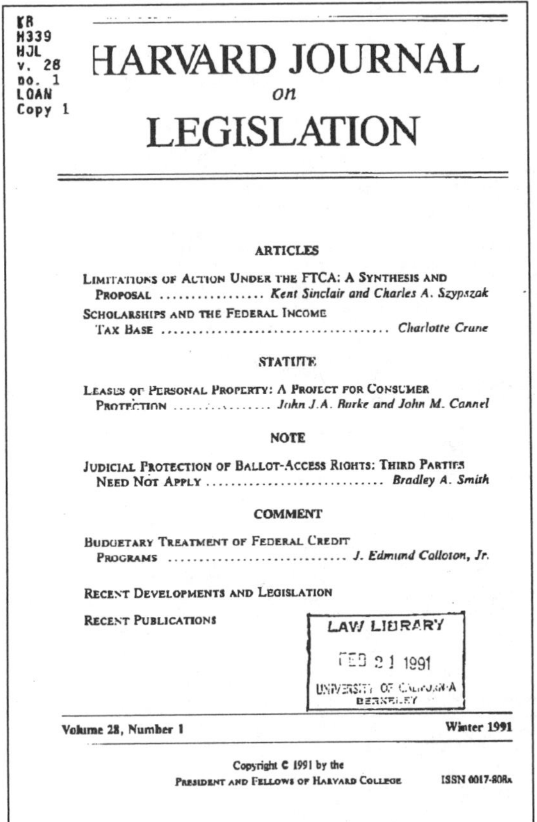

HARVARD JOURNAL
on
LEGISLATION

ARTICLES

LIMITATIONS OF ACTION UNDER THE FTCA: A SYNTHESIS AND PROPOSAL .... *Kent Sinclair and Charles A. Szypszak*

SCHOLARSHIPS AND THE FEDERAL INCOME TAX BASE .... *Charlotte Crane*

STATUTE

LEASES OF PERSONAL PROPERTY: A PROJECT FOR CONSUMER PROTECTION .... *John J.A. Burke and John M. Cannel*

NOTE

JUDICIAL PROTECTION OF BALLOT-ACCESS RIGHTS: THIRD PARTIES NEED NOT APPLY .... *Bradley A. Smith*

COMMENT

BUDGETARY TREATMENT OF FEDERAL CREDIT PROGRAMS .... *J. Edmund Colloton, Jr.*

RECENT DEVELOPMENTS AND LEGISLATION

RECENT PUBLICATIONS

Volume 28, Number 1 Winter 1991

 ISSN 0017-808x

Harvard Journal on Legislation

Most law libraries contain the more influential of these journals and law reviews, and some libraries (especially in large law schools) have virtually a complete set. You can find articles by using an electronic index, called LEGALTRAC, or either of two printed indexes, the *Index to Legal Periodicals* (tan cover) or the *Current Law Index* (red and black cover).

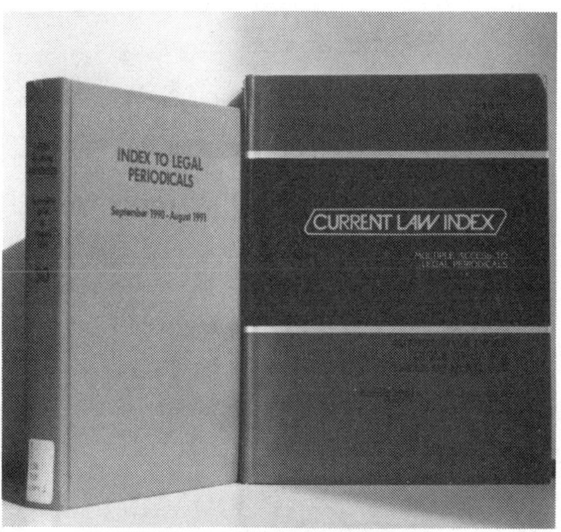

Index to Legal Periodicals and Current Law Index

All indexes are organized by subject, author and title, and contain an abbreviated reference to the review or journal in which the article is located. The printed indexes contain numerous volumes, which are organized according to the years in which the contents were published. The electronic index provides a cumulative listing and is thus easier to use than the printed indexes. Below is an excerpt from the *Index to Legal Periodicals* that lists, by subject, the article titled "Leases of Personal Property: A Project for Consumer Protection," which appears in the issue of the *Harvard Journal on Legislation* shown above.

18 INDEX TO LEGAL PERIODICALS

Constitutional theory—United States—*cont.*
Twentieth century Jeffersonian: Brandeis, freedom of speech, and the republican revival. H. Garfield. 69 *Or. L. Rev.* 527-88 '90
Construction industry
See also
Architects and engineers
The Kentucky no action statute: down for the count?. 79 *Ky. L.J.* 159-75 '90/'91
The qualification of arbitrators for construction disputes. M. F. Hoellering. 45 *Arb. J.* 34-41+ D '90
Construction of statutes *See* Statutory interpretation
Constructive trusts *See* Implied trusts
Consumer credit *See* Credit
Consumer protection
See also
Advertising
Credit
Health
Loans
Prices
Products liability
Unfair insurance settlement practices
Advanced Hair Studio Pty Ltd. & Anor v. TVW Enterprises Limited [[1987] 77 A.L.R. 615]. 17 *Melb. U.L. Rev.* 527-32 Je '90
Consumer problems and ADR: an analysis of the Federal Trade Commission-ordered General Motors mediation and arbitration program. A. Best. 1990 *J. Dis. Res.* 267-92 '90
→ Leases of personal property: a project for consumer protection. J. J. A. Burke, J. M. Cannel. 28 *Harv. J. on Legis.* 115-66 Wint '91
Shysters, sharks, and ambulance chasers beware: attorney liability under CUTPA. 11 *U. Bridgeport L. Rev.* 97-125 '90
Contempt
Current problems in the law of contempt. J. Laws. 43 *Current Legal Probs.* 99-114 '90
A new perspective on the judicial contempt power: recommendations for reform. L. Raveson. 18 *Hastings Const. L.Q.* 1-65 Fall '90
Continental shelf
See also
Exclusive economic zone
Territorial waters
The EEC's continental shelf: a "terra incognita". J. E. Harders. 8 *J. Energy & Nat. Resources L.* 263-79 '90
Secured transactions affecting the federal outer continental shelf. M. C. Maloney. 34 *Inst. on Min. L.* 47-78 '87
Contracts
See also
Conflict of laws—Contracts
Government contracts
Sales
Contract versus contractarianism: the regulatory role of contract law. J. Braucher. 47 *Wash. & Lee L. Rev.* 697-739 Fall '90
Contractual concerns for hospitals and other health care organizations. M. L. Malone, R. C. Beasley. 32 *S. Tex. L. Rev.* 77-104 D '90
The myth that promisees prefer supracompensatory remedies: an analysis of contracting for damage measures. A. Schwartz. 100 *Yale L.J.* 369-407 N '90
Reconsidering the reliance rules: the Restatement of Contracts and promissory estoppel in North Dakota. T. C. Folsom. 66 *N.D.L. Rev.* 317-447 '90
Strategic bargaining and the economic theory of contract default rules. J. S. Johnston. 100 *Yale L.J.* 615-64 D '90
Unconscionable conduct and small business: possible extension of section 52A of the Trade Practices Act 1974. G. Q. Taperell. 18 *Austl. Bus. L. Rev.* 370-88 D '90

Acceptance
See Contracts—Offer and acceptance

Consideration
La opcion de compra en Puerto Rico. M. J. Godreau. 53 *Rev. Jur. U.P.R.* 563-608 '84

Covenants
Flats: mutual enforceability of covenants. Two views. J. E. Adams, S. Baughen. 134 *Solic. J.* 1504-5 D 14 '90

Offer and acceptance
See also
Options
Liability for mistake in contract formation. M. P. Gergen. 64 *S. Cal. L. Rev.* 1-49 N '90
The strategic structure of offer and acceptance: game theory and the law of contract formation. A. Katz. 89 *Mich. L. Rev.* 215-95 N '90

Performance
La clausula penal. P. F. Silva-Ruiz. 54 *Rev. Jur. U.P.R.* 89-112 '85
Expectations, loss distribution and commercial impracticability. S. Walt. 24 *Ind. L. Rev.* 65-109 '91
Punitive damages for breach of contract—a principled approach. F. J. Cavico, Jr. 22 *St. Mary's L.J.* 357-453 '90
Contributory negligence
See also
Comparative negligence
Controlled substances *See* Narcotics
Conversion
Commercialization of human tissues: has biotechnology created the need for an expanded scope of informed consent?. 27 *Cal. W.L. Rev.* 209-30 '90/'91
Moore v. The Regents of the University of California: balancing the need for biotechnology innovation against the right of informed consent. M. S. Dorney. 5 *High Tech. L.J.* 333-69 Fall '90
Tort law—informed consent—California Supreme Court recognizes patient's cause of action for physician's nondisclosure of excised tissue's commercial value.—Moore v. Regents of the University of California, 793 P.2d 479 (Cal.). 104 *Harv. L. Rev.* 808-15 Ja '91
Conveyancing *See* Title to land
Convicts *See* Prisons and prisoners
Cook, Rebecca J.
International human rights law concerning women: case notes and comments. 23 *Vand. J. Transnat'l L.* 779-818 '90
Cooperative federalism
See also
Federalism
States' rights
Cooperatives
See also
Condominium and cooperative buildings
IRS expands availability of patronage dividend deductions and tax-exempt status for cooperatives but restricts benefit of package design expenditures. D. W. Butwill. 12 *J. Agric. Tax'n & L.* 342-51 Wint '91
Copyright
See also
Authors and publishers
The 101st Congress: a review of amendments to the Copyright Act. 37 *J. Copyright Soc'y U.S.A.* 462-98 '90
Accounting for profits gained by infringement of copyright: when does it end?. L. Bently. 13 *Eur. Intell. Prop. Rev.* 5-15 Ja '91
Applying the merger doctrine to the copyright of computer software. 37 *Copyright L. Symp. (ASCAP)* 173-214 '90
Computer protection against foreign competition in the United States. 10 *Computer L.J.* 393-412 O '90
The continuing battle over music performance rights in television programming. 36 *Copyright L. Symp. (ASCAP)* 167-91 '89
Contribution of the Bar to the development of copyright law. S. Rothenberg. 37 *J. Copyright Soc'y U.S.A.* 453-61 '90
Copyright and computer databases: is traditional compilation law adequate?. 37 *Copyright L. Symp. (ASCAP)* 85-125 '90
Copyright law—Fifth Circuit interprets Copyright Act to allow copying of software for any legitimate reason—Vault Corp. v. Quaid Software Ltd., 847 F.2d 255. 23 *Suffolk U.L. Rev.* 905-12 Fall '89
Copyright ownership of commissioned computer software in light of current developments in the work made for hire doctrine. 24 *Ind. L. Rev.* 135-59 '91
Copyright protection of computer "interfaces" in Japan. O. Hirakawa, K. Nakano. 7 *Computer Law.* 1-16 D '90
Copyright wrong: the United States' failure to provide copyright protection for works of architecture. 47 *Wash. & Lee L. Rev.* 1103-27 Fall '90
Copyrighted software and tying arrangements: a fresh appreciation for per se illegality. 10 *Computer L.J.* 413-52 O '90
Copyrighting "look and feel": Manufacturers Technologies v. CAMS [706 F. Supp. 984]. 3 *Harv. J.L. & Tech.* 195-208 Spr '90
Copyrights and copyremedies: unfair use and injunctions. J. L. Oakes. 18 *Hofstra L. Rev.* 983-1003 Summ '90

Listings in the Index to Legal Periodicals

"Harv. J. on Legis." is an abbreviation for "Harvard Journal on Legislation." The numbers indicate that the article is in Volume 28, pages 115-161, and that Volume 28 was published in the winter of 1991.

If you look at some other listings, you will see other strange abbreviations for law reviews, like *Ky. L. J.* and *Ark. J.* You are not expected to magically guess what these abbreviations mean. Lawyers don't carry this information around with them either. When you become mystified by an entry, simply consult the table of abbreviations at the front of the volume. An excerpt from the table is shown below.

The *Current Law Index* is used in the same way; you go from the index to the table of abbreviations to the actual article.

The LEGALTRAC computerized index to legal periodicals is part of a larger database called INFOTRAC, which contains information on a number of additional resources such as business and general periodicals. Larger law libraries may offer the complete INFOTRAC database. Most, however, have only the LEGALTRAC index. Instructions for using LEGALTRAC are shown on the screen and are very easy to follow. If you get confused, ask a law librarian for help. Incidentally, LEGALTRAC may be connected to a printer so that you can print out the information instead of copying it longhand.

ABBREVIATIONS OF PERIODICALS INDEXED

For full information consult the list of Periodicals Indexed

A

A.B.A. J. — American Bar Association Journal
A.F.L. Rev. — The Air Force Law Review
Adel. L. Rev. — Adelaide Law Review
Adelphia L.J. — The Adelphia Law Journal
Admin. L.J. — Administrative Law Journal (Washington, D.C.)
Admin. L. Rev. — Administrative Law Review
Advoc. Q. — The Advocates' Quarterly
AIPLA Q.J. — AIPLA Quarterly Journal
Akron L. Rev. — Akron Law Review
Akron Tax J. — Akron Tax Journal
Ala. L. Rev. — Alabama Law Review
Ala. Law. — The Alabama Lawyer
Alaska L. Rev. — Alaska Law Review
Alb. L. Rev. — Albany Law Review
Alta. L. Rev. — Alberta Law Review
Am. Bankr. L.J. — The American Bankruptcy Law Journal
Am. Bus. L.J. — American Business Law Journal
Am. Crim. L. Rev. — American Criminal Law Review
Am. Indian L. Rev. — American Indian Law Review
Am. J. Comp. L. — The American Journal of Comparative Law
Am. J. Crim. L. — American Journal of Criminal Law
Am. J. Fam. L. — American Journal of Family Law
Am. J. Int'l L. — American Journal of International Law
Am. J. Juris. — The American Journal of Jurisprudence
Am. J.L. & Med. — American Journal of Law & Medicine
Am. J. Legal Hist. — The American Journal of Legal History
Am. J. Tax Pol'y — The American Journal of Tax Policy
Am. J. Trial Advoc. — The American Journal of Trial Advocacy
Am. Soc'y Int'l L. Proc. — American Society of International Law Proceedings
Am. U.J. Int'l L. & Pol'y — The American University Journal of International Law and Policy
Am. U.L. Rev. — The American University Law Review
Anglo-Am. L. Rev. — The Anglo-American Law Review
Ann. Conf. on Intell. Prop. — Annual Conference on Intellectual Property
Ann. Rev. Banking L. — Annual Review of Banking Law
Ann. Surv. Am. L. — Annual Survey of American Law
Ann. Surv. Austl. L. — Annual Survey of Australian Law
Annals Air & Space L. — Annals of Air and Space Law
Antitrust Bull. — The Antitrust Bulletin
Antitrust L.J. — Antitrust Law Journal
Arb. J. — The Arbitration Journal
Ariz. J. Int'l & Comp. L. — Arizona Journal of International and Comparative Law
Ariz. L. Rev. — Arizona Law Review
Ariz. St. L.J. — Arizona State Law Journal
Ark. L. Notes — Arkansas Law Notes
Ark. L. Rev. — Arkansas Law Review
Army Law. — The Army Lawyer
Auckland U.L. Rev. — Auckland University Law Review
Austl. B. Rev. — Australian Bar Review
Austl. Bus. L. Rev. — Australian Business Law Review
Austl. J. Fam. L. — Australian Journal of Family Law
Austl. J.L. & Soc'y — Australian Journal of Law and Society
Austl. J. Lab. L. — Australian Journal of Labour Law
Austl. L.J. — Australian Law Journal
Austl. Tax Rev. — Australian Tax Review
Austl. Y.B. Int'l L. — Australian Yearbook of International Law

B

B.C. Envtl. Aff. L. Rev. — Boston College Environmental Affairs Law Review
B.C. Int'l & Comp. L. Rev. — Boston College International and Comparative Law Review
B.C.L. Rev. — Boston College Law Review
B.C. Third World L.J. — Boston College Third World Law Journal
B.U. Int'l L.J. — Boston University International Law Journal
B.U.J. Tax L. — Boston University Journal of Tax Law
B.U.L. Rev. — Boston University Law Review
B.Y.U. J. Pub. L. — BYU Journal of Public Law
B.Y.U. L. Rev. — Brigham Young University Law Review
Banking L.J. — The Banking Law Journal
Bankr. Dev. J. — Bankruptcy Developments Journal
Baylor L. Rev. — Baylor Law Review
Berkeley Women's L.J. — Berkeley Women's Law Journal
Bldg. & Constr. L. — Building and Construction Law
Bond L. Rev. — Bond Law Review
Bracton L.J. — Bracton Law Journal
Brit. Tax Rev. — British Tax Review
Brit. Y.B. Int'l L. — The British Year Book of International Law
Brooklyn J. Int'l L. — Brooklyn Journal of International Law
Brooklyn L. Rev. — Brooklyn Law Review
Buffalo L. Rev. — Buffalo Law Review
Bus. Law. — The Business Lawyer

C

C. de D. — Les Cahiers de Droit
Cal. Law. — California Lawyer
Cal. Real Prop. J. — California Real Property Journal
Cal. W. Int'l L.J. — California Western International Law Journal
Cal. W.L. Rev. — California Western Law Review
Calif. L. Rev. — California Law Review
Cambrian L. Rev. — The Cambrian Law Review
Cambridge L.J. — The Cambridge Law Journal
Campbell L. Rev. — Campbell Law Review
Can. B. Rev. — The Canadian Bar Review
Can. Bus. L.J. — Canadian Business Law Journal
Can. J. Fam. L. — Canadian Journal of Family Law
Can. J.L. Juris. — Canadian Journal of Law and Jurisprudence
Can. J. Women & L. — Canadian Journal of Women and the Law
Can. Tax J. — Canadian Tax Journal
Can.-U.S. L.J. — Canada-United States Law Journal
Can. Y.B. Int'l L. — The Canadian Yearbook of International Law
Canterbury L. Rev. — The Canterbury Law Review
Cap. U.L. Rev. — Capital University Law Review
Cardozo Arts & Ent. L.J. — Cardozo Arts & Entertainment Law Journal
Cardozo L. Rev. — Cardozo Law Review
Cardozo Stud. L. & Lit. — Cardozo Studies in Law and Literature
Case W. Res. J. Int'l L. — Case Western Reserve Journal of International Law
Case W. Res. L. Rev. — Case Western Reserve Law Review
Cath. Law. — The Catholic Lawyer
Cath. U.L. Rev. — Catholic University Law Review
Chi.-Kent L. Rev. — Chicago Kent Law Review
China L. Rep. — China Law Reporter
Civ. Just. Q. — Civil Justice Quarterly
Clearinghouse Rev. — Clearinghouse Review
Clev. St. L. Rev. — Cleveland State Law Review
Colo. Law. — The Colorado Lawyer
Colum. Bus. L. Rev. — Columbia Business Law Review
Colum. Hum. Rts. L. Rev. — Columbia Human Rights Law Review
Colum. J. Envtl. L. — Columbia Journal of Environmental Law
Colum. J.L. & Soc. Probs. — Columbia Journal of Law and Social Problems

Periodical Abbreviations

LIBRARY EXERCISE

Using Law Reviews: Exercise One

You have a friend who was sexually abused as a child. She had apparently repressed the memory completely until a recent incident, when she was 35 years old, brought floods of vivid and painful memories. Your friend asks you to help her do some legal research on whether she can sue the abuser after all this time. You want to learn how courts have dealt with the statute of limitations in such cases. You are part of a research team that is searching the literature for relevant law review articles, and you have been assigned to find articles published in 1990.

1. *What is the most direct way to find law review articles on a specific subject?*
2. *What subject headings could you look under? Think of three.*

3a. *Find six to ten relevant articles in the indexes for your time frame, and locate two or three of the articles. (When scanning lists of articles in the indexes, look for catchwords such as childhood, incest, sexual abuse. Don't select articles about statutes of limitation in general, or on related issues.) Which years of the indexes should you look in?*

3b. *What did you find under the topics you consulted in Current Law Index?*

3c. *What did you find under the topics you consulted in ILP?*

4. *What 1990 articles did you find?*
5. *It is also possible to do on-line research of this topic. Check with your librarian to see what services, if any, are available to you.*

Answers

1. Use the two major printed indexes to law reviews. They are the *Current Law Index* and the *Index to Legal Periodicals*.
2. Statute of Limitations; Child abuse; Sexual abuse.

3a. You are looking for articles published in 1990. Because these might not be in the index until the year after publication, use Current Law Index 1990 and 1991 (Subject Indexes) and Index to Legal Periodicals 89-90 and 90-91.

3b. In Current Law Index, under Statutes of Limitations, it says "see Limitation of Actions." Under Child Abuse, there were many subtopics, and among them, Adult Child Abuse Victims. Under Sexual Abuse of Children, it says see Child Molesting; there the articles seem to be all about situations in which the abused children are still children. Therefore, the topics to look under are: Limitation of Actions and Adult Child Abuse Victims.

3c. In the Index to Legal Periodicals, following what we found in the Current Law Index, look under Limitation of Action. The Index to Legal Periodicals uses this heading also. Under Adult Child Abuse Victims, Sexual Abuse of Children and Child Molesting there is nothing relevant.

4. The following articles were listed:

   Child Sexual Abuse and Criminal Statutes of Limitation: A Model for Reform, 65 Washington Law Review 189-207 (January 1990)

   Civil Incest Suits: getting beyond the statute of limitations, 68 Washington U. Law Quarterly 995-1020 (1990)

   The Statute of Limitations: a procedural stumbling block in civil incestuous abuse suits, 14 Law and Psychology Review 153-166 (Spring 1990)

   Use of the Discovery Rule in Cases of Alleged Child Abuse: does the statute of limitations ever run? 28 Duquesne Law Review 777-783 (Summer 1990)

   Use of the Massachusetts Discovery Rule by Adult Survivors of Father-Daughter Incest, 24 New England Law Review 1243-1281 (Summer 1990)

   (If you found others, congratulations!)
5. InfoTrac, a general periodical on-line indexing service, is subscribed to by many public libraries (as well as county law libraries). LegalTrac, a service within InfoTrac, indexes legal periodicals. If your library has InfoTrac, it may also have purchased LegalTrac.

LIBRARY EXERCISE

Using Law Review: Exercise Two

You are on a team researching the question whether a parent in Indiana may educate her children at home, over the objections of the school district, because she believes she can do a better job of educating them than can the teachers in her local school. You are assigned to use American Jurisprudence 2d (Am. Jur.) to find references to law review articles on the topic.

Questions

1. *Look in the five-volume softback set of the Am. Jur. 2d General Index under "Schools." Do you find an appropriate subheading?*
2. *Find the section on schools in Volume 68 of the set ("Sales and Use Taxes" to "Searches and Seizures"). What citations to law review articles do you find?*

Answers

1. Yes. Under Schools, there is a subheading "Home Instruction" with a subsub heading "by parents" which sends you to the article entitled Schools, sections 229-231.
2. Burges, *The Constitutionality of Home Education Statutes*, 55 U. Mo. KC Law Review 69 (Fall 1986).

7. Specialized Loose-leaf Materials

Most practicing lawyers and many others who work in the legal system, such as teachers, paralegals, legal research specialists and even some law librarians, find it necessary to specialize. There's just too much information generated by the courts and legislatures to keep up on everything. Specialization typically means not only mastering a particular body of knowledge—for example, tax, zoning, bankruptcy or personal injury—but maniacally keeping on top of it.

Several publications cater to this need by offering an exhaustive loose-leaf compilation of recent developments in a certain field and weekly or monthly loose-leaf supplements. These materials provide information about new laws, regulations, and judicial and administrative decisions that might affect the field of law covered by the publication.

For anyone who must maintain an up-to-the-minute grasp on what's going on in a particular legal area, these services can prove invaluable. However, they may be too specialized for your purposes unless your research topic falls squarely within one of these special categories. If it does, locate the appropriate service, read the instructions on how to use it at the front of the first volume and check the index. You may solve your problem almost immediately. All the loose-leaf services listed below can be found in a good law library.

SELECTED LOOSE-LEAF SERVICES

Commerce Clearing House (CCH)
- Bankruptcy Law Reporter
- Consumer Credit Guide
- Consumer Product Safety Guide
- Employment Safety and Health Guide
- Labor Law Reporter
- Medicare-Medicaid Guide
- Standard Federal Tax Reports
- State Tax Reports
- Unemployment Insurance Reports
- Worker's Compensation Law Reports

Bureau of National Affairs (BNA)
- Environment Reporter
- Fair Employment Practices
- The Family Law Reporter
- Labor Relations Reporter
- Occupational Safety and Health Reporter
- Product Safety and Health Reporter
- United States Law Week (U.S. Supreme Court decisions)

Prentice-Hall Law and Business (P-H)
- Labor Relations
- Social Security and Unemployment Compensation
- State and Local Tax Service

LIBRARY EXERCISE

Using a Loose-leaf Service

You are researching the issue of whether an author's royalties constitute "self-employment earnings" and are thus subject to the self-employment tax. You have been assigned to find cases on this issue in CCH *Standard Federal Tax Reporter*, a loose-leaf service.

Questions

1. *Find the Volumes entitled "CCH Standard Federal Tax Reporter." (Do not confuse them with the look-alike "State Tax Reporter" or the "Tax Court Reporter.") What Volume do you choose?*
2. *To find information by its topic (or subject) in which section of the Index volume do you look?*
3. *Under which tab heading do you look?*
4. *Is there an entry and subheading regarding the issue?*
5. *To what does the "§33,888.124" refer?*
6. *How do you find "¶ 33,888.124"?*
7. *When you go to that volume and find ¶33,888.124 (¶ numbers are at the bottom of each page), what do you find there?*
8. *What are the names and citations of the cases?*
9. *Where would you look to find out what the abbreviations in the citations [TCM, TC Memo, Dec.] mean?*

Answers

1. The most recent Index volume.
2. Topical Index.
3. First, behind the tab "Topical Index," we find "Authors." The "Rapid Finder Index" (an index of broad subjects) yields nothing, so we look under "Authors" in the thick Topical Index.
4. Yes. Under "Authors," there is a subheading entitled "Self Employment Tax...§33,888.124."
5. At the top of each page in the Topical Index it says "references are to Paragraph (¶) numbers."
6. Each volume of the 16 or so volume set shows the code sections and ¶ numbers included in it. Volume 11 includes ¶¶ 32,151 - 34,210.
7. Short descriptions of the facts and holdings of two cases about authors, royalties and self employment tax.
8. *W.R. Langford*, 55 TCM 1267, Dec. 44,891(M), TC Memo 1988-300. *R.L. Hittleman*, 59 TCM 1028, Dec. 46,683(M), TC Memo, 1990-325. Aff'd CA9 (unpublished opinion 10/8/91).
9. The Index volume begins with a red-tabbed section entitled "How to Use This Reporter." At the end of this section is a list entitled "ABBREVIATIONS AND REFERENCES."

8. Treatises and Monographs

Like experts in every field, legal experts publish books. When a book attempts to cover an entire area of the law, it is called a treatise. Typically, law treatises have titles like *Prosser on Torts*, *Powell on Real Property* and *Corbin on Contracts*. When a book covers just a small portion of a general legal field, or introduces a new concept into the legal realm, it is called a monograph. Whatever they are called, hundreds of these books can be found in the stacks of the normal law library, and can often be very helpful in providing an overview of a subject.

There is a big difference between these resources and the textbooks discussed earlier in this chapter (Section C). While textbooks cover entire legal topics with the intent to teach, treatises and monographs exist to provide in-depth reference materials. Generally, they delve much deeper into an area than you would care to go. They also become dated more quickly despite periodic supplementation. However, if you really want to amass expertise on a topic and have the patience to put up with the ultimate in hairsplitting, give these resources a try. Some of the more useful and up-to-date ones are listed below.

Treatises (Partial List)

The American Law of Mining (2d Ed. Rocky Mountain Mineral Law Foundation, Matthew Bender)

Anderson, *American Law of Zoning* (3rd Ed. Clark Boardman)

Business Organizations With Tax Planning (Matthew Bender)

Collier on Bankruptcy (Matthew Bender)

Rohan, *Condominium Law and Practice* (Matthew Bender)

Rohan, *Cooperative Housing Law and Practice Forms* (Matthew Bender)

Couch on Insurance (Clark Boardman)

Larson, *Employment Discrimination* (Matthew Bender)

Gorden and Rosenfield, *Immigration Law and Procedure* (Matthew Bender)

Kheel, *Labor Law* (Matthew Bender)

Long, *Law of Liability* (Matthew Bender)

Antieau, *Local Government Law* (Matthew Bender)

McQuillen, *Municipal Corporations* (Callaghan)

Nimmer on Copyrights (Matthew Bender)

Rohrlich, *Organizing Corporate and Other Business Enterprises* (Matthew Bender)

Rosenberg, *Patent Law Fundamentals* (Clark Boardman)

Powell on Real Property (Matthew Bender)

Frumer, *Products Liability* (Matthew Bender)

Securities and Federal Corporate Law (Clark Boardman)

McCarthy, *Trademarks and Unfair Competition* (2d Ed. Clark Boardman)

Feller, *U.S. Customs and International Trade Guide* (Matthew Bender)

Will Forms & Clauses (Anderson Co.)

Williston on Contracts (3rd Ed. Bancroft Whitney/Lawyers Coop)

Larson, *Workers Compensation Law* (Matthew Bender)

LIBRARY EXERCISE

Using Treatises

You are on a team researching the issue of whether a person who was arrested on a charge of selling drugs to an undercover police officer may use the defense of entrapment. The officers supplied the drugs to the person they eventually arrested, and also purchased them from him. You are assigned to find helpful treatises.

You have used the A.L.R. index to find a recent A.L.R. article on the specific situation of the defendant's arrest: Entrapment as a Defense to a Charge of Supplying Narcotics Where Government Agents Supplied the Narcotics to Defendant and Purchased Narcotics From Defendant, 9 A.L.R. 5th 464.

Questions

1. *Find the A.L.R. article and find one of the two treatises listed under "Helpful Sources" at the beginning of the article. What are the two treatises?*
2. *In one of these two treatises, find a 1987 New Mexico case which said that "where the government was both the supplier and the purchaser of the contraband, and the defendant was recruited as a 'mere conduit,'" the defendant may claim entrapment as a defense.*

Answers

1. Bailey and Rothblatt, *Handling Narcotic and Drug Cases*, 1972, Lawyers' Coop; and 1 LaFave and Israel, *Criminal Procedure*.
2. *Baca v. State*, 106 N.M. 338, 742 P.2d 1043 (1987).

9. Restatements of the Law

Legal scholars are always trying to pinpoint exactly what the law "is" on a particular subject. In some cases, groups of scholars have convened under the auspices of an organization called the American Law Institute (ALI) for the purpose of putting into writing definitive statements of the law in various areas. These statements are termed "Restatements of the Law" and have been produced for such topics as contracts, torts and property.

While these tomes cover their subjects exhaustively, they do not in any way constitute the law itself (although they may prove persuasive to courts considering a particular issue). They are usually of little help to the beginning researcher looking for a good background resource. To begin with, they are not in a narrative form but rather consist of very terse summations of legal principles and longer comments explaining them. The language in these comments is generally arcane, and the various restatements are not well indexed or organized for efficient retrieval of information. Because these publications are trying to reconcile often unreconcilable contradictions in the law, they tend to produce more confusion than enlightenment.[1]

You are most likely to encounter a Restatement when a case refers to a particular section or speaks of adopting the "Restatement view" on some issue. After you read the section and accompanying comments, you can see how other courts have interpreted it by using a book called *Restatement in the Courts*, found with the other volumes of the *Restatement*.

[1] In one case where one of the authors represented a group of people in a court action for nuisance damages against an airport for excessive noise, both the author's side and the airport relied on the same passages of the Restatement of Torts in arguing their clearly opposite positions.

REVIEW

Questions

1. *What is the primary reason for using background resources to start your research?*
2. *What are some tips to remember when purchasing a self-help law book?*
3. *What are law student study texts (Hornbooks) most useful for?*
4. *What are the advantages of starting your legal research in a legal encyclopedia?*
5. *What are the names of the two major national encyclopedias?*
6. *Who are the two primary publishers of legal reference materials in the United States and what are their publishing philosophies?*
7. *For what types of research issues is American Law Reports a good background resource to use to start your research?*
8. *When can legal periodicals be of most help in legal research?*
9. *How can you find articles of interest in legal periodicals?*

Answers

1. To get a general understanding of the relevant legal area before looking for the specific answer to a narrow question. The answers to almost all specific legal questions depend on a number of variables that the background resource can alert you to.
2. Do a little reading to see whether the language is understandable and the concepts useful and specific.

   Check whether the material actually leads you step-by-step through the entire process.

   Check whether the book gives you the necessary forms for doing it yourself.

   Check whether the book pays attention to differences in state laws.
3. These books, which are conceptual in nature, are excellent if you want a basic understanding of the variables in any specific area of concern.
4. Legal encyclopedias cover the entire range of law. Their entries are broken into small segments and you are very likely to find material relevant to your research problem. Each entry provides a solid treatment of the particular topic, gives you a good idea of the all-important variables associated with your issue, and refers you to specific statutes and cases (the stuff the law is made of) to help you get to the next research phase.
5. *Corpus Juris Secundum (C.J.S)* and *American Jurisprudence (Am. Jur)*.
6. West Publishing Co. and Bancroft/Whitney-Lawyer's Coop. As a general rule, the West publishing philosophy is to provide all the information and let you, the researcher, choose what you wish to use. The Bancroft-Whitney/Lawyer's Coop philosophy is to exercise a little editorial discretion and only present you with what it thinks is most important to researchers.
7. A.L.R. is an excellent place to begin when you have determined that your problem falls within the state/civil/substantive or federal/civil/substantive categories.
8. When you are interested in new legislation, current and innovative legal theories and the meaning of important cases.
9. There are three subject indexes to legal periodicals: LEGALTRAC, an electronic index and two printed indexes—the *Index to Legal Periodicals* (tan cover) and the *Current Law Index* (red and black cover).

CHAPTER 6

Constitutions, Statutes, Regulations and Ordinances

When people speak of the "law," they usually mean statutes—enactments by Congress and state legislatures. Statutes set out the rules that we all must live by. Reflecting this, most of this chapter tells you how to find and understand statutes.

We also address two other important research tasks: how to research constitutional issues and how to locate regulations issued by government agencies. Constitutions are important because they set the guidelines within which legislatures must operate when passing statutes. And agency regulations are important because they are the rules used to implement statutes in the real world.

A. Constitutional Research

The U.S. Constitution is the supreme law of the land. All laws, state and federal, must comply with it. Both state and federal courts use the U.S. constitution to decide whether a statute or regulation is proper and enforceable. Especially in areas dealing with civil rights and civil liberties, court decisions that interpret the U.S. Constitution affect everybody throughout the United States.

There are also state constitutions. These documents provide the same guidance at the state level that the U.S. Constitution does at the federal level. However, state constitutions are subject to the provisions of the U.S. Constitution in certain areas and even must bow to federal statutes in some contexts. As a general rule, state constitutions can add to a state citizen's rights but can't take rights away that are provided for in the U.S. Constitution. In other areas, conflicts between a state constitution and the U.S. Constitution are generally resolved in favor of the latter. And decisions by state courts that interpret state constitutions affect only the citizens of those states.

Most research into what the law is on a particular topic does not involve constitutional research. This is because statutes and regulations define the law in most instances. However, you may find yourself doing constitutional research if you suspect a statute or regulation is unconstitutional. For example, if a state statute barred anyone but a lawyer from holding estate planning seminars, non-lawyer estate planners would probably want to know whether this law violated the First Amendment's freedom of speech provision.

Constitutional research can be very time-consuming. Most constitutions use extremely broad language that creates the possibility of differing interpretations. And even if the language appears precise, many judges are willing to reach beyond the literal words to figure out what the constitution's framers really intended. These factors mean that you can't understand how a constitutional provision might affect your situation unless:

- you are already familiar with the constitution and how it has been applied to similar fact situations; or
- you engage in some first class constitutional research.

Below we provide some guidelines for doing constitutional research. An example of how this type of research proceeds is in Chapter 12, Section K.

1. The U.S. Constitution

Most constitutional research involves the U.S. Constitution. There are several basic steps to doing sound constitutional research.

Step 1: Find a good constitutional law textbook The federal Constitution and most state constitutions have been around a long time, and to really zero in on what the constitution will mean in your situation, you have to be aware of how each word and phrase in the relevant provision has been interpreted by the courts over the years (and centuries). There is nothing like a good textbook to bring you up to speed. Some of them are listed in Chapter 4.

Skim the table of contents until you find some subject listings that speak to your general issue. If that doesn't work, use the index. (Chapter 3, *An Overview of the Law*, explains how to come up with a list of terms to look up in a legal index.)

Most people undertaking constitutional research are concerned with the Bill of Rights (the first ten amendments). The Fourteenth Amendment is also a frequent subject of research, since it prohibits the states from denying their citizens due process of law and the equal protection of the law.

THE BILL OF RIGHTS

First Amendment: freedom of speech, freedom of religion, freedom of association, separation of church and state

Second Amendment: right to bear arms

Third Amendment: right not to have soldiers quartered in home

Fourth Amendment: right of privacy, right against unreasonable searches and seizures, right to confront adverse witnesses

Fifth Amendment: right to trial by jury, right to due process of law (life, liberty, property), right against self-incrimination, freedom from double jeopardy

Sixth Amendment: speedy and public trial, right to representation by counsel, right to confront witnesses (cross-examination), right to subpena witnesses

Seventh Amendment: right to trial in civil cases

Eighth Amendment: right to reasonable bail, ban on cruel and unusual punishment

Ninth Amendment: people retain rights in addition to those granted in the Constitution

Tenth Amendment: Everything not prohibited is allowed

Step 2: Find a good case When using a textbook to research constitutional issues, remember that—like most textbooks—constitutional textbooks are only intended to lay out some general principles and then pass you on to the actual court cases that have done the interpreting. So, when you read the textbook, be on the lookout for a citation to a case that might be relevant.

If the textbook doesn't do the job, use the subject indexes to the *Supreme Court Digest* or *Federal*

Practice Digest. We tell you how to do this in Section B4 of Chapter 9, *Finding Cases*.

If neither the textbook nor the digests get you started on the right track, use one of the annotated federal codes (discussed in Section B, below) to locate the actual constitutional provision. Then, use the case notes to locate one or more relevant cases (See Chapter 9, Section B2, where we explain how to do this)

Step 3: Find other relevant cases Once you find a case that appears to address your precise issues, you are in luck. You can use the techniques we describe in Chapter 10, *Shepard's and Digests: Expand and Update Your Research*, for skipping from that case to other similar cases until you find one or more that really nails down the answer you're seeking.

Two words of advice about federal constitutional research:

1. Judges often interpret a constitutional provision to achieve the result they want, not the result that might seem to naturally flow from past decisions or the plain language of the constitution. Be prepared to encounter court cases that contradict one another, that are shockingly illogical and that are flat out wrong. But remember, if it's the U.S. Supreme Court speaking, the case is the law of the land until another Supreme Court case says it isn't.
2. Constitutional research often is the art of getting around a case that appears to be squarely against your position. Even if you find one or a number of cases that seem to apply to your situation, there are almost always ways to argue that your situation is different and not governed by the cases. As an example, see the research story in Chapter 12, Section K, where we suggest some ways to get around a particular Supreme Court issue.

2. State Constitutions

State constitutions are a little easier to research than the U.S. Constitution, because they haven't gotten nearly as much judicial play over the years as the U.S. Constitution. However, as the U.S. Supreme Court continues to experience profound changes in its personnel, many advocacy groups may begin turning to state constitutions as a source of individual rights and liberties.

The best approach to researching your state's constitution is to find a state-specific encyclopedia (see the list in Chapter 4) and read a background discussion of the provision that relates to your situation. Then locate the actual constitutional provision and read the case notes that follow it. (We tell you how to do this in Chapter 9, Section B2, below.)

B. Introduction to Federal Statutes

Federal statutes are enactments by Congress, either signed by the President or passed over a veto. They are organized by subject, indexed and published under a specific title number in a series of books called the *United States Code*. We describe the *United States Code* in more detail in Section C, below.

But sometimes the statute you are looking for will not be in the code. It may have been passed too recently, or it may have been repealed and taken out of the code. Finding recent statutes is covered in Section D, and finding repealed statutes is covered in Section E.

Federal statutes start out as "bills" introduced in a session of Congress. They are assigned labels and numbers depending on which side of Congress they originate in. For example, a bill introduced in the U.S. Senate might be referred to as Senate Bill 2 (S. 2). A bill that originated in the U.S. House of

Representatives might be known as House of Representatives Bill 250 (H.R. 250).

Few of the many bills introduced in Congress become law. To do so they have to be passed by both houses and signed by the President, or passed over his veto. Once a bill becomes law, it is called a statute, assigned a new label and given a new number. The basic label is Public Law (Pub. L.). Following the Pub. L., the statute will have one number that corresponds with the number of the Congress (for example, 94th) that passed it, followed by a second number that is simply the number assigned to that specific bill by the Congress. So Pub. L. No. 94-586, for example, refers to Public Law 586 passed by the 94th Congress.

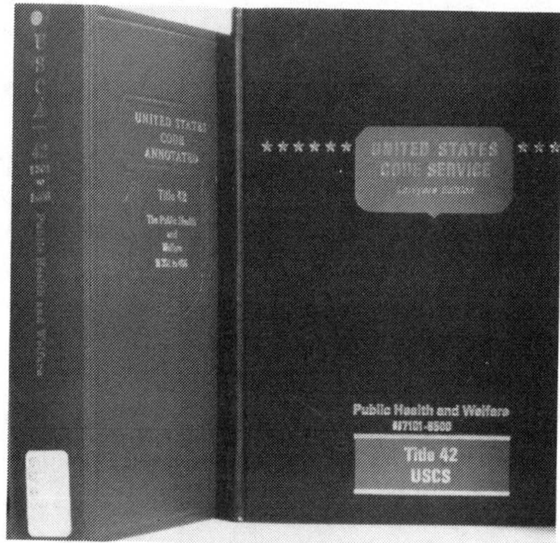

United States Code

In addition to all the federal statutes, these extremely useful sets of annotated books contain information pertaining to each statute, including:

- one-sentence summaries of court cases that have interpreted the statute (discussed in Chapter 8, *How Cases Are Published*)
- notes about the statute's history (such as amendments)
- cross-references to other relevant statutes
- cross-references to administrative regulations that may be helpful in interpreting the statute (see Section O, below)
- citations to the legislative history of the statute (see Section M, below)
- research guides (references to relevant materials by the same publisher)

Because of all this helpful information, these annotated codes are almost always used in place of the bare *U.S. Code* when doing research on federal statutes. Throughout this book, when we refer to "the federal code" or to the *U.S.C.* (*United States Code*), we mean an annotated edition (*U.S.C.A.* or *U.S.C.S.*).

C. How to Find Statutes in the United States Code

The U.S. Code is the starting place for most federal statutory research. It consists of fifty separate numbered titles. Each title covers a specific subject matter. For instance, Title 37 contains the statutes governing patent law, Title 11 contains the bankruptcy statutes and Title 10 contains most of the statutes governing federal crimes. Some titles are published in only one book—for instance, Title 17, which covers the law of copyright. Others have many volumes—Title 26, the tax code, currently has 16 hardcover volumes and a separate paperback index.

Two versions of the U.S. Code are published in annotated form: The *United States Code Annotated*, or *U.S.C.A.* (West Publishing Co.), and the *United States Code Service*, or *U.S.C.S.* (Bancroft-Whitney/Lawyer's Coop). Most law libraries carry both, but smaller libraries may only have one (usually the *U.S.C.A.*).

1. Getting Started

There are several approaches to finding statutes in the annotated U.S. codes:

- If you know the citation to the statute, select either *U.S.C.A.* or *U.S.C.S.*, find the title number given in the citation and turn to the indicated section. (See subsection 2, below.)
- If you know the common or popular name of the statute but don't have the citation, consult the *Shepard's* or *U.S.C.A. Popular Names Index*. (See subsection 3, below.)
- If you don't know the citation and don't know what the statute is called, but can figure out from its subject which title the statute will be found in, consult the subject index for the specific title, found in the last volume of the title. (See subsection 4, below.)
- If you don't find what you're looking for in the specific title index, or you don't know what title to start with, consult the general subject index at the end of the entire series. (See subsection 4, below.)

When you search for a statute it is crucial to get the most current version. Although the annotated codes are published in hardcover, each book has a paper supplement—called a pocket part—inserted in the back of the book. The pocket part updates the hardcover book annually. Always search the pocket part when you are trying to find a statute. See subsection 6, below, for more on this.

2. Using Citations to Find Federal Statutes

The reference to any primary law source—including federal statutes—is termed a "citation." The citation, which is always written in a standard form, tells you precisely where the law is located. Citations to federal statutes contain the title of the U.S. Code where the statute is found and the section number.

Example: The citation for the Civil Rights Act of 1964 is:

Sample Federal Statute

Finding this statute in the law library is easy. Locate the set of books labeled *U.S.C.A.* (maroon) or *U.S.C.S.* (black and blue). Look at the spine of the volumes marked 42 to find the one that includes § 2000a-h.

LIBRARY EXERCISE

Finding a Statute From Citation: Exercise One

You are reading a case about embezzlement of pension funds and the opinion refers to "Title 18 § 1961 et seq." The judge has overturned the defendant's conviction because the evidence showed that he stole only once. You decide to read the statute.

Questions

1. *Where do you look to find the statute?*
2. *Find the volumes covering Title 18. Select the volume covering §§ 1951 through 2310. Open the volume and find § 1961. What sections are included in this statutory scheme?*
3. *What is the title of this statutory scheme?*
4. *Read § 1961. Is embezzlement from pension and welfare funds indictable under the RICO statute?*
5. *Would one act of embezzlement of pension or welfare funds constitute a violation of the RICO statute?*

Answers

1 It will be found in the sets of United States Code Annotated or in United States Code Service. Use U.S.C.A., where the titles and section numbers are on the books' spines.

2. Title 18 §§ 1961-1968.

3. "Racketeer Influenced and Corrupt Organizations," also known as "RICO."

4. Yes, in Section (1)(B) we are told that "'racketeering activity' ... means any act which is indictable under any of the following provisions of title 18, United States Code: ...§ 664 (relating to embezzlement from pension and welfare funds)."

5. No, Section (5) of the statute specifies that there must be "a pattern of racketeering activity" (at least two acts).

LIBRARY EXERCISE

Finding a Statute From Citation: Exercise Two

You are reading a case about alimony awarded to a woman who did not finish high school and had not worked outside the home in the 30 years since her marriage. The judge gave her an adequate award but for only five years, citing 29 U.S.C.A. 2301 et seq. You would like to know if the cited statute has anything to do with the judge's decision to terminate the alimony after the specified period of time.

Questions

1. *How do you find the statute?*
2. *In U.S.C.A. or U.S.C.S., look at the volumes that cover Title 29 and choose the one that will have § 2301. Don't forget to look in the Pocket Part for sections that were added since the printing of the hardbound edition. Turn to the section. What is the name of the Act?*
3. *What sections are included in the Act?*
4. *What is the goal of the statute (the Act)?*
5. *Can any woman in the situation described above benefit from this program?*
6. *What might have been the reason for the limited award of alimony, and why did the court refer to the Act?*

Answers

1. Use the sets of U.S.C.A. or U.S.C.S.
2. "Displaced Homemakers Self-Sufficiency Assistance."
3. Title 29 §§ 2301-2314.
4. In § 2301(b) **Purpose**, Congress wrote that the goal was to provide assistance to states to provide services to displaced homemakers and displaced homemaker service providers.
5. No, among other qualifications, § 2302(3)(B) provides that the person must be unemployed or underemployed and experiencing difficulty in obtaining or upgrading employment.
6. Judges sometimes give limited alimony in order to give the divorced spouse a period of support while she gains the skills and experience necessary in order to support herself. The spouse would probably be eligible to apply to training and assistance programs funded by the Act during that year.

3. Using Popular Name Indexes to Find a Federal Statute

You may hear a federal statute referred to by its popular name—for example, the Civil Rights Act, the Taft-Hartley Act or the Marine Mammal Protection Act. You can find such a statute by using:

- the "popular names index" that accompanies the United States Code Annotated (U.S.C.A.)
- the "popular names table" volume that accompanies the United States Code Service, Lawyer's Edition (U.S.C.S.) or
- *Shepard's Acts and Cases By Popular Names: Federal and State*. This publication is particularly useful for finding both state and federal statutes and cases through their popular names. Not all libraries carry it, however.

The U.S.C.A. *Popular Names Index* is included with the U.S.C.A. set of books, directly following it on the shelves. This index gives a citation that refers you to the correct title and section (for example, Title 20 § 607) of the named statute. Below are the popular names index entries for two of the three acts mentioned above. As you can see, the Civil Rights Act of 1964 is contained in Titles 28 and 42, and the Marine Mammal Protection Act is found in Title 16 of the federal code. Section 2, above, explains how to find the actual statute once you've found a citation.

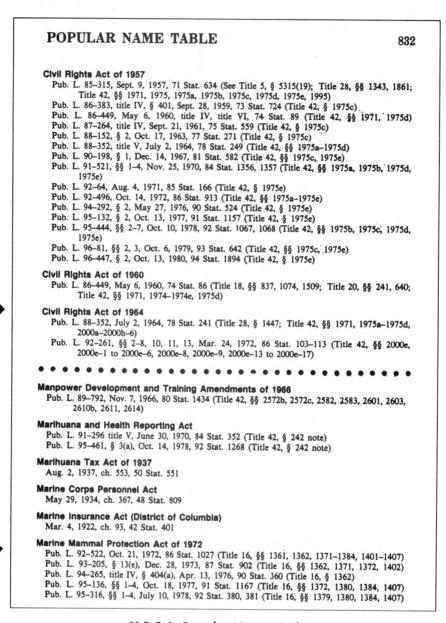

POPULAR NAME TABLE **832**

Civil Rights Act of 1957

Pub. L. 85–315, Sept. 9, 1957, 71 Stat. 634 (See Title 5, § 5315(19); Title 28, §§ 1343, 1861; Title 42, §§ 1971, 1975, 1975a, 1975b, 1975c, 1975d, 1975e, 1995)
Pub. L. 86–383, title IV, § 401, Sept. 28, 1959, 73 Stat. 724 (Title 42, § 1975c)
Pub. L. 86–449, May 6, 1960, title IV, title VI, 74 Stat. 89 (Title 42, §§ 1971, 1975d)
Pub. L. 87–264, title IV, Sept. 21, 1961, 75 Stat. 559 (Title 42, § 1975c)
Pub. L. 88–152, § 2, Oct. 17, 1963, 77 Stat. 271 (Title 42, § 1975c)
Pub. L. 88–352, title V, July 2, 1964, 78 Stat. 249 (Title 42, §§ 1975a–1975d)
Pub. L. 90–198, § 1, Dec. 14, 1967, 81 Stat. 582 (Title 42, §§ 1975c, 1975e)
Pub. L. 91–521, §§ 1–4, Nov. 25, 1970, 84 Stat. 1356, 1357 (Title 42, §§ 1975a, 1975b, 1975d, 1975e)
Pub. L. 92–64, Aug. 4, 1971, 85 Stat. 166 (Title 42, § 1975e)
Pub. L. 92–496, Oct. 14, 1972, 86 Stat. 913 (Title 42, §§ 1975a–1975e)
Pub. L. 94–292, § 2, May 27, 1976, 90 Stat. 524 (Title 42, § 1975e)
Pub. L. 95–132, § 2, Oct. 13, 1977, 91 Stat. 1157 (Title 42, § 1975e)
Pub. L. 95–444, §§ 2–7, Oct. 10, 1978, 92 Stat. 1067, 1068 (Title 42, §§ 1975b, 1975c, 1975d, 1975e)
Pub. L. 96–81, §§ 2, 3, Oct. 6, 1979, 93 Stat. 642 (Title 42, §§ 1975c, 1975e)
Pub. L. 96–447, § 2, Oct. 13, 1980, 94 Stat. 1894 (Title 42, § 1975e)

Civil Rights Act of 1960

Pub. L. 86–449, May 6, 1960, 74 Stat. 86 (Title 18, §§ 837, 1074, 1509; Title 20, §§ 241, 640; Title 42, §§ 1971, 1974–1974e, 1975d)

→ **Civil Rights Act of 1964**

Pub. L. 88–352, July 2, 1964, 78 Stat. 241 (Title 28, § 1447; Title 42, §§ 1971, 1975a–1975d, 2000a–2000h–6)
Pub. L. 92–261, §§ 2–8, 10, 11, 13, Mar. 24, 1972, 86 Stat. 103–113 (Title 42, §§ 2000e, 2000e–1 to 2000e–6, 2000e–8, 2000e–9, 2000e–13 to 2000e–17)

• •

Manpower Development and Training Amendments of 1966

Pub. L. 89–792, Nov. 7, 1966, 80 Stat. 1434 (Title 42, §§ 2572b, 2572c, 2582, 2583, 2601, 2603, 2610b, 2611, 2614)

Marihuana and Health Reporting Act

Pub. L. 91–296 title V, June 30, 1970, 84 Stat. 352 (Title 42, § 242 note)
Pub. L. 95–461, § 3(a), Oct. 14, 1978, 92 Stat. 1268 (Title 42, § 242 note)

Marihuana Tax Act of 1937

Aug. 2, 1937, ch. 553, 50 Stat. 551

Marine Corps Personnel Act

May 29, 1934, ch. 367, 48 Stat. 809

Marine Insurance Act (District of Columbia)

Mar. 4, 1922, ch. 93, 42 Stat. 401

Marine Mammal Protection Act of 1972

→ Pub. L. 92–522, Oct. 21, 1972, 86 Stat. 1027 (Title 16, §§ 1361, 1362, 1371–1384, 1401–1407)
Pub. L. 93–205, § 13(e), Dec. 28, 1973, 87 Stat. 902 (Title 16, §§ 1362, 1371, 1372, 1402)
Pub. L. 94–265, title IV, § 404(a), Apr. 13, 1976, 90 Stat. 360 (Title 16, § 1362)
Pub. L. 95–136, §§ 1–4, Oct. 18, 1977, 91 Stat. 1167 (Title 16, §§ 1372, 1380, 1384, 1407)
Pub. L. 95–316, §§ 1–4, July 10, 1978, 92 Stat. 380, 381 (Title 16, §§ 1379, 1380, 1384, 1407)

U.S.C.A. Popular Names Index

LIBRARY EXERCISE

Finding Statutes by Their Popular Names

Now it's time to use the library to apply what you've just learned. This exercise asks you to find citations to several statutes known only by their popular names. Additional research exercises that include these and other skills are in the Appendix.

Questions

1. *(State Statutes) You are researching the limitations placed by different states on the importation of plants from another state. You come across a reference to a New Mexico law, the "Harmful Plant Act." You want to find the citation to this statute.*
   a. *What nationally applicable index can be used to locate the citation to a state statute by its popular name?*
   b. *Using that resource, what is the citation for the Harmful Plant Act?*
2. *(Federal Statutes) While researching the historic relationship between the United States and the countries of the Middle East, you read about something called the Middle East Peace and Stability Act. Where in the U.S. Code Annotated (U.S.C.A.) can you find the citation for this act?*
3. *(Federal Statutes) You are researching the legal aspects of the introduction of oleomargarine into American culture, and find a mention of the Oleomargarine Acts passed in the early part of the 20th century.*
   a. *What resource provided by U.S.C.S. can you use to find the citation to these Acts? (You want the Oleomargarine Acts specifically, not any other statutes that may affect oleomargarine.)*
   b. *Find the statute in U.S.C.S. Use the material following the statute (which includes sections titled "Cross References," "Research Guide" and "Interpretive Notes and Decisions"). Two references mention colored oleomargarine. What are they?*
4. *(Federal Statutes) While researching laws that protect the environment and wildlife, you come across a reference to the Congaree Swamp National Monument Expansion and Wilderness Act, with a notation that it was passed in the 1988 100th Congress. Use the U.S. Code Congressional and Administrative News to find this statute.*

Answers

1. a. *Shepard's Acts and Cases by Popular Names: Federal and State.* (If you had access to New Mexico statutes, you could find the citation in the popular name index to that annotated code; but *Shepard's* has citations to cases and statutes from all the states.)
   b. By looking in the volume subtitled "ACTS G-Q," under Harmful Plant Act, you find that the citation to the Act is New Mexico Statutes, 1978, §§ 76-7A-1 et seq.
2. By looking in the Popular Name Table at the end (after Z) of the index volumes to the *United States Code Annotated*, you find that the citation to the Act is Title 22, §§ 1961-1965.
3. a. The *United States Code Service* has a Table of Acts by Popular Names in one of the Tables volumes at the end of the set. The Oleomargarine Acts were enacted May 9, 1902 and are now designated as Title 21, § 25. The "ch. 784" means that the Acts were designated as chapter 784 in the Statutes at Large in 1902.
   b. (1) Colored oleomargarine, intrastate sales of, 21 U.S.C.S. § 347 et seq.
   (2) "States may...prohibit manufacture of oleomargarine artificially colored." McCray *v.* *United States*, 195 U.S. 27, 49 L. Ed. 78, 24 S. Ct. 769 (1904).
4. There are several volumes for each session of Congress: one set for 1988, for example, and a set for 1989. The last volume for each year contains Tables and Indexes. Look at the Table of Contents in the front of that volume in the 1988 set, and you will see that the Popular Name Acts is Table 10 on page 416. In Table 10, you find The Congaree Swamp ... Act, and are referred to page 2606. On the spine of each volume for 1988, the included pages are listed. Volume 2 includes page 2606, where you find the Act.

FINDING STATUTES BY CHAPTER, SECTION OR TITLE NUMBER

Sometimes statutes are commonly known by a title, chapter or section number that refers to how the statute itself is organized, not where it can be found. For instance, many people may have heard of Title VII, the statutes that address discrimination in the workplace. However, this Title VII has nothing to do with Title 7 of the *United States Code.* Instead it is the Congressional designation for a group of statutes within the Civil Rights Act of 1964. In fact, the Title VII statutes are located in Title 42 of the *United States Code.*

Where did the "Title VII" come from? When bills are written, they are assigned internal organizing labels for legislative purposes. A bill isn't assigned to a Title of the federal code until it actually passes and becomes a law.

If you are researching a statute that you know only by one of its internal organizing designations—such as Title VII, Chapter 7 (Bankruptcy Code) or Section 8 (Low Income Housing Assistance)—first see whether it is listed that way in a popular names index. If not, focus on the subject of the statute—for instance "civil rights" or "job discrimination"—and use one of the Code indexes discussed in subsection 4, below.

4. Using Annotated Code Indexes to Find a Federal Statute

If you think a federal statute may apply to your situation, but you don't know the name or citation of the statute, start with the index. Each title of the annotated codes has a separate index located at the back of the last book of the title. There is also a general index for all the titles as a whole. If you know what title your statute is in—or likely to be in—start with the index for that title. If you aren't sure which title your statute is in, use the general index.

For example, suppose you are interested in federal statutory restrictions on the use of federal education funds by state schools. If you happen to know that such restrictions are found in Title 20, you can use the index to that title. If you didn't know in advance that Title 20 contains the education statutes, however, you would use the general index at the end of the entire code.

Some titles contain a variety of subject matter. For instance, Title 42 contains statutes relating to water resources, water planning, voting rights, civil rights and the National Science Foundation in addition to its general topic of public health and welfare.

Helpful Hint If you are using the *U.S.C.S.* and don't find what you're looking for in either the title index or the general index, try the *U.S.C.A.* index, or vice versa. The second one you try may have one of the terms you look up. Once you find the correct citation, you can use whichever annotated code suits you best.

LIBRARY EXERCISE

Finding Federal Statutes by Using the Index to the U.S. Codes

The students at Gallaudet University, a university created by federal statute to "provide education and training to deaf individuals and otherwise to further the education of the deaf," are outraged because the Board of Trustees of the University has not even one trustee who is deaf.

You are assigned to research federal statutes to find out how the Board is selected/elected. Find the statute about the University, determine how the Board members are selected/elected, and advise the concerned students.

Questions

1. *Where in U.S.C.A. or U.S.C.S. do you look?*
2. *What words or phrases in the General Index do you look under?*
3. *What do you find under that entry?*
4. *Take down the U.S.C.A. or U.S.C.S. volume for Title 20 that will include § 4301. Turn to the Act and look at the Table of Contents for the Act. Where will you find information abut the Board of Trustees?*
5. *Turn to those sections (don't forget the Pocket Parts) and read them. If a member of the Board other than a public member dies or retires, how is the vacancy filled?*
6. *Does the code section address the issue of deaf members?*
7. *Is there anything in subsection (a)(1)(B) which suggests that your inquiry might not be finished?*

Answers

1. In the General Index to either annotated code, U.S.C.A or U.S.C.S.
2. Try the most specific: Gallaudet University
3. The first entry among the many listed says "Text of Act, 20 § 4301 et seq."
4. Section 4303(a) and (b) address the composition and powers of the Board.
5. By vote of the remaining members of the Board of Trustees.
6. No.
7. Yes, subsection (a)(1)(B) provides that, of the 18 non-public members, "one of whom shall be elected pursuant to the Regulations of the Board of Trustees...." We will need to read the regulations to see whether the Board's own rules require at least one deaf member. If they don't, it might be useful for the students to know how regulations are proposed and passed, in case they want to press for a rule requiring at least one deaf member.

5. Using One Citation to Research Statutory Schemes

It is usually insufficient to just locate one statute when seeking an answer to a legal question. Statutes tend to come in bunches. For instance, if you are doing research to find out whether a particular person is entitled to inherit from a person who died without a will, it might be necessary to skim five or six separate statutes before you would fully understand what the law is on this subject. A group of related statutes is termed a statutory scheme. Fortunately statutes that form part of a statutory scheme usually are all located together, so it's only a question of reading from one to another.

Sometimes an index will alert you to the existence of a statutory scheme. You know you have to look at more than one statute if an index entry to a statute has an "et seq." at the end. ("Et seq." means "and following.")

To better understand the concept of statutory schemes, let's look at the federal Civil Rights Act of 1964, which contains a large number of individual statutes dealing with discrimination in such matters as housing, public accommodations and employment. Some of the statutes prohibit discriminatory acts on the basis of race, creed, national origin, color or sex. Other statutes provide remedies for violations—that is, penalties for discrimination and procedures for enforcement of the law.

The basic Civil Rights Act, of which these various statutes form a part, was originally passed by Congress in 1964. Both the original statutes, and some that were added later, have since been amended from time to time. The statutes together constitute a statutory scheme, passed by a number of different sessions of Congress.

The part of the Civil Rights Act of 1964 that deals with employment discrimination is commonly known as Title VII. You may hear it said that somebody has filed a Title VII complaint about a discriminatory employment practice.

In fact, Title VII is itself a collection of statutes and can be termed a statutory scheme in its own right. If you believe you have been discriminated against and want to read the law, you will need to read the separate statutes that cover (1) what must be alleged in the complaint, (2) what defenses are available to the employer, (3) what kinds of remedies the court is authorized to grant, (4) whether attorneys fees should be paid and so on.

6. Using the Pocket Part to Get the Latest Version

Federal statutes often are amended or replaced by subsequent sessions of Congress. Indeed, many laws are totally changed by amendment and deletion in just a few years. This continuous change has required a method for keeping hardcover federal annotated codes up-to-date. The primary method for doing this, in virtually universal use for all collections of annotated statutes, both state and federal, is called the "pocket part system."

Pocket parts are paper supplements that fit inside each hardcover volume, usually at the back. They are published once a year and contain any statutory changes occurring in the interim. When the pocket parts get too bulky because of legislative changes, either a new hardcover volume is published that incorporates all of the changes since the last hardcover volume was published, or a separate paperback volume is published that sits on the shelf next to the hardcover book.

Always check the pocket part to see if a statute you're reading has been amended or repealed. If you don't, you may find that the statute you discovered in the hardcover volume has long since been amended or even repealed.

LIBRARY EXERCISE

Using Annotated Code Index to Find a Federal Statutory Scheme

You are on a research team working on an Indian reservation. One of the elementary school teachers has asked you whether a traditional children's game played with cards and sticks (where pennies are won and lost) would be considered illegal gambling. He is worried about a law called something like the "Indian Gambling Regulation Act." You have gone to the library and are looking for the Act by using the Popular Name Table in the United States Codes.

Questions

1. *Where in United States Code Annotated (U.S.C.A.) and United States Code Service (U.S.C.S.) is the Popular Name Index?*
2. *Using what the teacher told you about the name of the statute, what do you find in the Popular Name Table?*
3. *There are three notations under the Indian Gaming Regulation Act, showing that the Congress established the Act in 1988 and amended it twice (in 1991 and 1992). Where in the U.S. Code can the Act be found?*
4. *You are looking for a "statutory scheme," which will probably involve a group of Code sections. Title 25 U.S.C. §§ 2701 - 2721 looks like the most likely candidate. Check Title 18 U.S.C. §§ 1166 and 1168 just in case. What is the subject matter of the Title 18 statutes? (Remember to check the Pocket Part.)*
5. *Now turn to Title 25 §§ 2701 - 2721. At the beginning of the scheme, in a part entitled "Chapter 29," is a Table of Contents. Look through the Table of Contents to find the section that will define different gaming activities.*
6. *Read § 2703. In what category (I, II or III) would the children's game most likely fall?*
7. *Go back to the Table of Contents and look for an entry regarding the regulation of Class I gaming. Do you find one?*
8. *Read § 2710(a). What sovereign (the federal, state, or Indian government) regulates Class I gaming?*
9. *How will you answer the teacher's question?*

Answers

1. In the U.S.C.A., it is in the last volume of the soft-backed multi-volume General Index, after Z. In the U.S.C.S., it is in one of the books of tables at the end of the set.
2. There is an entry for "Indian Gaming Regulatory Act."
3. In Title 18 U.S.C. § 1166 and 1168; and in Title 25 §§ 2701 - 2721.
4. Title 18 U.S.C. § 1166 deals with the application of State gambling laws to gaming activities on Indian reservations **except** as to those activities covered by the Indian Gaming Regulatory Act. Section 1168 proscribes the punishment for stealing from a gaming establishment licensed by the National Indian Gaming Commission.
5. Section 2703 is entitled "Definitions."
6. Section 2703(6) defines "Class I gaming" as including, among other activities, social games for prizes of minimal value. The teacher's game would fit within this definition.
7. Yes, § 2710(a) deals with "Exclusive jurisdiction of Class I gaming activity."
8. The section states that Class I gaming on Indian lands is within the exclusive jurisdiction of the Indian tribes and is not subject to the provisions of the Indian Gaming Regulation Act.
9. As long as the game remains a social one played for minimal prizes, it will not be considered "gambling" and he need not apply for permission from the National Indian Gaming Commission.

⚠ If the book you are using does not have a pocket part or a separate paperback pamphlet next to the hardcover volume on the bookshelf, and the book was not published in the year you are doing your research, inform the law librarian and ask if there is a current pocket part available. Never rely on out-of-date codes when doing statutory research unless you know that the statute being sought has not been amended since the publication of the book.

The pocket parts for *U.S.C.A.* reprint the sections of any statutes in the hardcover version that have been amended. Sections of the statute that have not been amended are not reproduced in the pocket part; instead, you are referred to the hardcover volume for the text. The example set out below first shows the portion of the statute as found in the hardcover volume and then shows how amendments appear in the pocket part. Note how the pocket part refers the reader back to the hardcover volume for sections that have not been changed.

The United States Code Service (U.S.C.S.) handles its pocket part in exactly the same way.

Handy Hint When you know the approximate date a statute was passed, you should first check the publication date of the hardcover volume. If this date is prior to your statute, then go right to the pocket part. In fact, many researchers prefer to start with the pocket part and then work backwards to the hardcover. Either way is fine so long as you never, ever, forget to check the pocket part.

⚠ Pocket parts are only published once a year. If you suspect that a statute was passed recently enough to not be included in the current pocket part, use the techniques discussed in Section D, below.

D. How to Find a Recent or Pending Federal Statute

Often you will want to locate a statute or amendment that:

- has just been passed and signed into law but not yet found its way into the pocket part, or
- is pending before Congress.

For instance, if a new statute becomes effective in October of 1995, it may not show up in the pocket part until April or May of 1996. In this situation there are two approaches to finding the legislation. If the statute or amendment is at least three months old, try an advance legislative service (see subsection 1, below). If the bill is brand new or even pending in Congress, get it through your elected representative or use Congressional research materials (subsection 2, below).

1. Statutes at Least Three Months Old

Each federal code has a monthly advance legislative service that prints statutes a month or two after they have been passed by Congress. The one for *U.S.C.A.* is called the *U.S.C.A. Quarterly Supplement*; the one for *U.S.C.S.* is the *U.S.C.S. Advance Legislative Service*.

Ch. 16A ATLANTIC TUNAS CONVENTION 16 § 971a

§ 971a. Commissioners

(a) Appointment and number; selection of Chairman; rules of procedure

The United States shall be represented by not more than three Commissioners who shall serve as delegates of the United States on the Commission, and who may serve on the Council and Panels of the Commission as provided for in the Convention. Such Commissioners shall be appointed by and serve at the pleasure of the President. Not more than one such Commissioner shall be a salaried employee of any State or political subdivision thereof, or the Federal Government. The Commissioners shall be entitled to select a Chairman and to adopt such rules of procedure as they find necessary.

(b) Alternate Commissioners

The Secretary of State, in consultation with the Secretary, may designate from time to time and for periods of time deemed appropriate Alternate United States Commissioners to the Commission. Any Alternate United States Commissioner may exercise at any meeting of the Commission, Council, any Panel, or the advisory committee established pursuant to section 971b of this title, all powers and duties of a United States Commissioner in the absence of any Commissioner appointed pursuant to subsection (a) of this section for whatever reason. The number of such Alternate United States Commissioners that may be designated for any such meeting shall be limited to the number of United States Commissioners appointed pursuant to subsection (a) of this section who will not be present at such meeting.

(c) Compensation

The United States Commissioners or Alternate Commissioners, although officers of the United States while so serving, shall receive no compensation for their services as such Commissioners or Alternate Commissioners.

(Pub.L. 94–70, § 3, Aug. 5, 1975, 89 Stat. 385.)

16 § 971 CONSERVATION

§ 971a. Commissioners

(a) Appointment and number; selection of Chairman; rules of procedure

(1) The United States shall be represented by not more than three Commissioners who shall serve as delegates of the United States on the Commission, and who may serve on the Council and Panels of the Commission as provided for in the Convention. Such Commissioners shall be appointed by and serve at the pleasure of the President. Not more than one such Commissioner shall be a salaried employee of any State or political subdivision thereof, or the Federal Government. The Commissioners shall be entitled to select a Chairman and to adopt such rules of procedure as they find necessary.

(2) Of the Commissioners appointed under paragraph (1) who are not governmental employees—

(A) one shall be appointed from among individuals with knowledge and experience regarding commercial fishing in the Atlantic Ocean, Gulf of Mexico, or Caribbean Sea; and

(B) one shall be appointed from among individuals with knowledge and experience regarding recreational fishing in the Atlantic Ocean, Gulf of Mexico, or Caribbean Sea.

(3)(A) The term of a Commissioner shall be three years.

(B) An individual appointed in accordance with paragraph (2) shall not be eligible to serve more than two consecutive terms as a Commissioner.

[See main volume for text of (b) and (c)]

(d) Travel expenses

(1) The Secretary of State shall pay the necessary travel expenses of United States Commissioners, Alternate United States Commissioners, and authorized advisors in accordance with the Federal Travel Regulations and sections 5701, 5702, 5704 through 5708, and 5731 of Title 5.

(2) The Secretary may reimburse the Secretary of State for amounts expended by the Secretary of State under this subsection.

(As amended Pub.L. 101–627, Title II, §§ 201(a), 203, Nov. 28, 1990, 104 Stat. 4459, 4460.)

How Federal Statutes Are Updated

These advance services are, in one sense, a pocket part to the pocket part and make it possible to find a federal statute shortly after it becomes law. The new or newly-amended statutes are organized in these services by public law number. As explained in Section A, above, this is the number the statute carries when it emerges from Congress. If you don't know the public law number, you can use the subject index in either of the supplements. For example, if you are looking for a new statute concerning conservation, look under "conservation" in the index to determine the page on which the new statute is located. An example of an advance legislative service index is shown below.

INDEX
References are to Pages

COAST GUARD AUTHORIZATION ACT OF 1989
Generally, **103 Stat. 1908, Leg. Hist. 1368**

COINS
Bicentennial of the congress commemorative coin, first strike ceremony, **103 Stat. 69**

COLLEGES AND UNIVERSITIES
Historically Black colleges and universities, executive order, **B15**
National historically Black colleges week,
Joint resolution, **103 Stat. 630**
Proclamation, **A118**
Student Loan Reconciliation Amendments of 1989, **103 Stat. 2111, Leg. Hist. 1906**
Veterans' Education and Employment Amendments of 1989, **103 Stat. 2078, Leg. Hist. 1469**

COLUMBIA
International Narcotics Control Act of 1989, **103 Stat. 1954, Leg. Hist. 1404**

COLUMBUS DAY
Proclamation, **A164**

COMMERCE, DEPARTMENT OF
Appropriations, **103 Stat. 988**
Quarterly financial report program, time, **103 Stat. 1943**

COMMERCE AND BUSINESS
Business and Commerce, generally, this index

COMMISSIONS AND BOARDS
Boards and Commissions, generally, this index

COMMUNITY DEVELOPMENT
Generally, **103 Stat. 1987**

COMMUNITY FOUNDATION WEEK
Joint resolution, **103 Stat. 948**
Proclamation, **A213**

COMMUNITY ORGANIZATIONS
Drug-Free Schools and Communities Act Amendments of 1989 **103 Stat. 1928. Leg. Hist. 1399**

COMPACTS
Marshall Islands and Micronesia, compacts of free association, approval. **103 Stat. 162**
Palau, compact of free association, implementation, **103 Stat. 1870, Leg. Hist. 1322**
South Dakota-Nebraska boundary compact, joint resolution, **103 Stat. 1328**

COMPACTS—Cont'd
Southeast Interstate Low-Level Radioactive Waste Compact Amendments Consent Act of 1989, **103 Stat. 1289**

COMPENSATION AND SALARIES
Congress, this index
Federal Officers and Employees, this index
Judges, this index
Military Forces, this index
Minimum wage, **103 Stat. 938, Leg. Hist. 696**
Performance Management and Recognition System Reauthorization Act of 1989, **103 Stat. 670**
Veterans' Benefits Amendments of 1989, **103 Stat. 2062, Leg. Hist. 1469**

COMPROMISE AND SETTLEMENT
Agent orange payments, exclusion from federal means-tested programs, **103 Stat. 1795**
Attorney general, authority to settle claims for damages, investigative or law enforcement activities, **103 Stat. 1805, Leg. Hist. 1226**
Coquille Restoration Act, **103 Stat. 91**
Puyallup Tribe of Indians Settlement Act of 1989, **103 Stat. 83**

COMPUTER MATCHING AND PRIVACY PROTECTION ACT AMENDMENTS OF 1989
Generally, **103 Stat. 149**

CONDEMNATION
New York City, criminal justice system and federal agencies, **103 Stat. 936**

CONGRESS
Bicentennial of the congress commemorative coin, first strike ceremony, **103 Stat. 69**
Compensation and salaries, **103 Stat. 1768**
Increases, joint resolution, **103 Stat. 3**
Ethics Reform Act of 1989, **103 Stat. 1716**
Legislative Branch Appropriations Act, 1990, **103 Stat. 1041**
One Hundred First Congress, second regular session, convening, **103 Stat. 1945**

CONSERVATION
See, also, **Environmental Protection**, generally, this index
National Oceanic and Atmospheric Administration Ocean and Coastal Programs Authorization Act of 1989, **103 Stat. 1005**
National wilderness preservation system, twenty-fifth anniversary, joint resolution, **103 Stat. 592**
North American Wetlands Conservation Act, **103 Stat. 1968, Leg. Hist. 1437**

I6

Advance Legislative Service Index

Also, if you know the *U.S.C.A.* or *U.S.C.S.* citation to the statute that you know has been amended, you can use a table in the legislative service that converts the citation to the public law number. For example, if you know that Title 26 *U.S.C.* § 32 has been amended and want to find the public law number in order to chase down the amendment, the table shown below (taken from an issue of the *U.S.C.S. Advance Legislative Service*) will do the job.

TABLE OF CODE SECTIONS ADDED, AMENDED, REPEALED, OR OTHERWISE AFFECTED
101st CONGRESS 2nd SESSION
(Public Law 101-508 only)

Section	Effect	Public Law No.	
	TITLE 26 (cont'd)		
29(f)(1)(B)	Amd.	101-508	Sec. 11501(a)(2)
29 nt.	Added	101-508	Secs. 11501(b)(2), (c)(2); 11813(c); 11821
32	Amd.	101-508	Sec. 11111(a)
32(i)(1)(B)	Amd.	101-508	Sec. 11101(d)(1)(B)
32(i)(2)(A)(i)	Amd.	101-508	Sec. 11111(e)(1)
32(i)(2)(A)(ii)	Amd.	101-508	Sec. 11111(e)(2)
32(i)(2)(B)	Amd.	101-508	Sec. 11111(e)(3)
32(j)	Added	101-508	Sec. 11111(b)
32 nt.	Added	101-508	Sec. 11111(f)
prec. 38	Amd.	101-508	Secs. 11511(c)(1); 11611(d)
38(b)(1)	Amd.	101-508	Sec. 11813(b)(2)(A)
38(b)(4)	Amd.	101-508	Sec. 11511(b)(1)
38(b)(5)	Amd.	101-508	Secs. 11511(b)(1); 11611(b)(1)
38(b)(6)	Added	101-508	Secs. 11511(b)(1); 11611(b)(1)
38(b)(7)	Added	101-508	Sec. 11611(b)(1)
38(c)(2)	Rpld.	101-508	Sec. 11813(b)(2)(B)

Advance Legislative Service Conversion Table

New statutes and amendments are also printed in a publication known as the *U.S. Code Congressional and Administrative News*. This publication is found near the *U.S.C.A.* or *U.S.C.S.* in most libraries. The volumes are very thick and are organized by legislative session (for example, 93rd Congress, 94th Congress, etc.). Some volumes contain the verbatim text of statutes, and the others contain the legislative history of the statutes; they are labeled accordingly. (See Section M, below, for a discussion of how to research legislative history.)

SUMMING UP

HOW TO FIND A FEDERAL STATUTE OR AMENDMENT PASSED WITHIN THE PAST YEAR

1. If you have the citation, check the pocket part of the *U.S.C.A.* or *U.S.C.S.* volume. If the new statute or amendment is not in the pocket part, go to the most recent advance legislative service update and check the index of new statutes. If you don't find what you're looking for, work backwards through the indexes of prior paperback volumes published subsequent to the statute's date.
2. If you don't know the citation, check the subject index of the most recent advance legislative service update volume. If you find no reference, work backwards through the subject index of prior volumes.
3. If you still find no reference, check the pocket part for the general index to the *U.S.C.A.* or *U.S.C.S.* under the appropriate subject headings.

2. Pending or Very Recent Legislation

You may want to examine legislation that has been passed very recently (and not yet published in the advance legislative service) or that is currently being considered by Congress. Perhaps a piece of environmental protection legislation or a bill to confer educational benefits on native Americans particularly interests you.

If you wish to see an actual copy of the current bill, you will usually have to obtain one through your elected representative. Call the local office of your senator or representative and request that a copy of the bill and other relevant documents (official "comments" explaining the bill, for example) be sent to you. If for some reason you don't get what you need, you can get a good description of the legislation by following these steps:

1. Locate the *Congressional Index* (published by Commerce Clearing House).
2. If you don't know the bill number (for example, H.R. 1 or S. 687), use the *Congressional Index* subject index to find it.

3. If you already know the bill number, use the status table in the *Congressional Index* to find out the bill's current status.
4. Review the bill's contents in the *Congressional Index* digest section.

If you wish to see legislative history for a statute—such as committee reports—or a specific pending statute, use a publication called *Congressional Information Service/Index* (*CIS*).

You may also consult a publication called *Digest of Public General Bills and Resolutions* for lengthy descriptions of pending legislation.

Library Note These legislative research materials are usually only available in large law libraries and the government document sections of large general purpose libraries.

E. Finding Out-of-Date Statutes

If you are looking for a specific statute that has been amended or deleted and no longer appears in the *United States Code*, you can find it in two publications:

- the *Statutes at Large*
- the *U.S. Code Congressional and Administrative News*.

The *Statutes at Large* series contains statutes organized by their public law numbers (Section B, above) instead of their federal code citations. The *U.S. Code Congressional and Administrative News* publication also carries statutes by their public law number, but is annotated and generally an easier resource to use.

For example, suppose a significant income tax reform bill wins passage in 1992 and is signed by the President. If a new volume of the *United States Code* is published in 1993, the laws for the tax years before passage of the tax reform measure will no longer appear in the code. The annotated codes show the statutes as they currently stand.

If, however, the IRS decides to audit you in 1993 and a dispute arises over your tax return for 1991, you may want to locate the law in effect for that tax year, even though it no longer currently applies. The statutes at large permit you to do this.

First, examine the current version of the statute. Directly beneath it, in parentheses, are listed the citations to every public law that affected the statute. You can use these citations to reconstruct the statutory language that was in effect during the period you are interested in. Here is how.

Assume that in 1993 you want to know what the law on a particular point was in tax year 1991. Your research in the *United States Code* shows you that the latest amendment occurred in 1992. The citation for this amendment is shown as Pub. L. No. 107-678. The next most recent amendment occurred in 1990. The citation for that amendment is Pub. L. No. 104-1289. That is the statute you would want to find to see what the law was before the most recent amendment. To find Pub. L. No. 104-1289 in *Statutes at Large* or *the U.S. Code Congressional and Administrative News*, find the volume that contains the statutes for the 104th Congress (this information appears on the spine), turn to where Pub. L. No. 104-1289 appears—it will be in numerical order within the volume—and *voila*, you have your statute.

LIBRARY EXERCISE

Finding Statutes by Pub. L. No.

Now it's time to use the library to apply what you've just learned. This exercise asks you to use the *U.S. Code Congressional and Administrative News* to find a statute known only by its Public Law number. Additional research exercises that include these and other skills are in the Appendix.

Question

You are researching federal disaster assistance acts, and find a reference to Pub. L. No. 101-82. Using U.S. Code Congressional and Administrative News *only, find the statute and any clues as to where to find its legislative history.*

Answer

The 101 means the statute was passed by the 101st Congress. On the spine of Volume 1 of 101st Congress 1st session 1989, it says Laws Pub. L. No. 101-189.

The statutes are more or less in order by their public law number, and Public Law No. 101-82 is found on page 103 Stat. 564 (Stat = Statutes at Large). The title is Disaster Assistance Act of 1989. Right under the title it says "For Legislative History of Act, see p. 514."

F. Finding State Statutes in Codes and Collections

Many of the principles that apply to researching federal statutes can be used when dealing with state statutes. However, there are some differences in federal and state legislative processes and in the resources that you use to find and interpret state statutes.

1. Overview of Annotated Collections of State Statutes

State statutes are organized by subject and published in two formats:

- annotated volumes that contain explanatory information about each statute and references to court decisions that have interpreted the statutes, and
- non-annotated volumes, which contain only the text of the statutes.

Intensive legal research almost always is done with the annotated volumes. However, many people, lawyers and non-lawyers alike, use the non-annotated version of certain statutes (say, the criminal statutes, or those relating to probate) as a handy desk reference.

Some states organize their statutes in codes according to subject. California, for example, has a separate code for each legal area—the Penal Code for criminal statutes, the Education Code for education statutes and so on. New York organizes its statutes in a similar fashion except that instead of the word "code," the word "law" is used. In New York you find education statutes in the volume called Education Law, the criminal statutes in the volumes labeled Penal Law and so on.

In a number of other states, statutes are collected into annotated volumes organized by title number or by "chapter." In Vermont, for instance, the *Vermont Statutes Annotated* (*Vt. Stat. Ann.*) consists of Title 1 through Title 33, each Title covering a particular subject matter area.

Finally, in still other states, the statutes are simply numbered sequentially without regard to their subject matter and published in collections with such names as *Massachusetts General Laws Annotated* (*Mass. Gen. Laws Ann.*), *Michigan Compiled Laws Annotated* (*Mich. Comp. Law Ann.*) and the *Maine Revised Statutes Annotated* (*Me. Rev. Stat. Ann.*).

2. Using State Statute Indexes

Many collections of state statutes have indexes for each subject (that is, for each title, code or chapter) and for the collection of laws as a whole. In California, a separate index called *Larmac*, published by Parker & Sons, also provides a detailed subject index to California statutes.

If your state's statutes are found in two or more publications, feel free to use either index. For example, the California statutes are published both in *West's Annotated Codes* and in *Deering's Annotated Codes*. If you can't find what you're looking for in the West index, use the Deering index. Since both publications index the same statutes and use the same citations, a citation you find in the Deering index can be looked up in the West code, and vice versa. (For assistance in using legal indexes, see Chapter 4, *Putting Your Questions Into Legal Categories*.)

3. Understanding State Statutory Citations

Citations to state statutes normally refer to the title (or volume) and section numbers. The three examples shown below are typical.

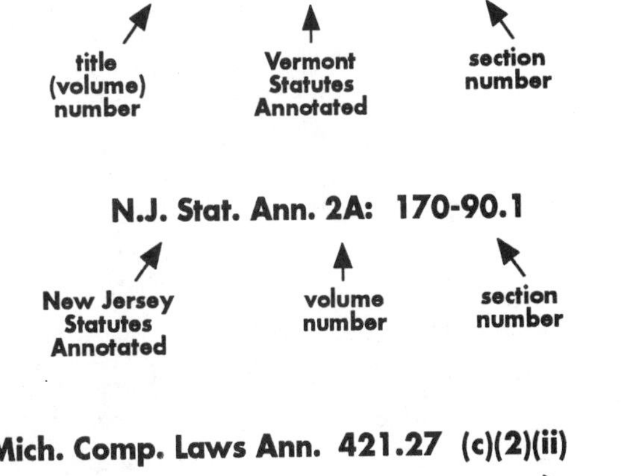

Examples of State Statute Citations

In the states that have codes, like New York and California, citations look like those shown below.

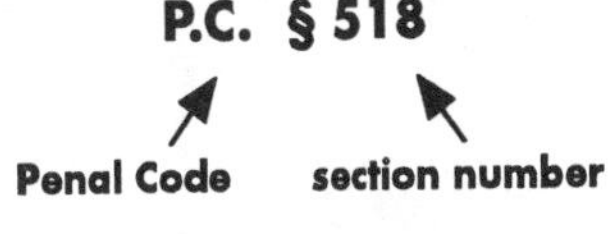

Sample California and New York Citations

USING CITATIONS TO FIND STATUTES

To read a particular statute, first locate the volumes containing your state's statutes. Then find the correct volume or title (the first number of the citation). Finally, turn to the correct section number. Once you have read the statute, make sure you have the current version. We tell you how to do this in subsection 5, below.

4. Reading All Relevant Statutes

State statutes are organized in clumps called "statutory schemes." (See Section C5, above, for more on how statutory schemes work.) If you are interested in a particular area of the law (small claims court, for example) be sure to read all relevant statutes on that subject. You may find that you can sue for up to $2000 in one statute and then learn in another one that a lower limit has been set for cases involving evictions.

5. Using Pocket Parts to Get the Latest Version

In many states, legislatures have a severe case of hyperactivity, continually passing new statutes and amending old ones. It is very important to get the very latest version of the statute you are interested in.

Hardcover volumes of state statutes should have current "pocket parts," paper supplements that fit inside the back cover of each hardbound volume. These update the hardcover portion on an annual basis (unless the hardcover volume you are using has just been published or the legislature only meets every other year). Always check the pocket part to see if a statute you're reading has been amended or repealed. If the pocket part is not current (say you are using the book in 1996 and the pocket part says 1995), ask the law librarian if there is a newer version.

There are two ways that pocket parts show updates. In most states, the part of the statute that has been amended is shown in the pocket part, with additions underlined and deletions marked by asterisks. For example, a California statute in its original form as it appeared in the hardcover volume, and the amended version as it appeared in the pocket part, are both shown below. As you can see, words that have been added to the statute are underlined and words that have been taken out are represented by asterisks.

§ 1942. Repairs by lessee; rent deduction; limit

If within a reasonable time after notice to the lessor, of dilapidations which he ought to repair, he neglects to do so, the lessee may repair the same himself, where the cost of such repairs do not require an expenditure greater than one month's rent of the premises, and deduct the expenses of such repairs from the rent, or the lessee may vacate the premises, in which case he shall be discharged from further payment of rent, or performance of other conditions. (Enacted 1872. As amended Code Am.1873–74, c. 612, p. 246, § 206.)

Main Volume Statute

§ 1942. Repairs by tenant; rent deduction or vacation of premises; presumption; limit; nonavailability of remedy; additional remedy

(a) If within a reasonable time after written or oral notice to the * * * landlord or his agent, as defined in subdivision (a) of Section 1962, of dilapidations rendering the premises untenantable which * * * the landlord ought to repair, * * * the landlord neglects to do so, the * * * tenant may repair the same himself where the cost of such repairs does not require an expenditure * * * more than one month's rent of the premises and deduct the expenses of such repairs from the rent when due, or the * * * tenant may vacate the premises, in which case * * * the tenant shall be discharged from further payment of rent, or performance of other conditions as of the date of vacating the premises.

Pocket Part Statute

In some states, the pocket parts reprint the sections of any statutes that have been amended. Sections of the statute that have not been amended are not reproduced in the pocket part; instead, you are referred to the hardcover volume for the text. For a sample of how this works, see Section C6, above. Note how the pocket part refers the reader back to the hardcover volume for sections that have not been changed.

G. Finding Recently Enacted Statutes

If your research involves a statute that is newly passed, repealed or amended, the changes may not yet be reflected in the pocket parts, which come out only once a year. Fortunately, most states have arranged for newly passed statutes to be published prior to their inclusion in the pocket parts. These legislative update publications have different names in different states. Some examples are *McKinney's Session Law News of New York*, *Vernon's Texas Session Law Services* and *Washington Legislative Services*.

Whatever their names. these publications are organized in pretty much the same way and there are several ways to get to the statutes you seek. First, the statutes appear in numerical order according to the number given them by the state legislature. In many states, statutes appear according to their "chapter" number. (See the example below.) In others they are listed by "Session Law" number. If you already know which number statute you're looking for, you can get to it directly.

Another way to use the Advance Legislative Service is by the annotated code or collection citation. If you know, for example, that Labor Code § 560.5 has been amended, a table at the front or back of each legislative service volume will convert your "code" citation to the appropriate chapter number.

Finally, all advance legislative services have a detailed alphabetical table of contents in the front and a cumulative subject index in the back. The examples below show the subject index of a Texas advance legislative service for 1991.

Advance legislative update services are usually located next to the annotated state statutes. If you can't find them, ask the law librarian.

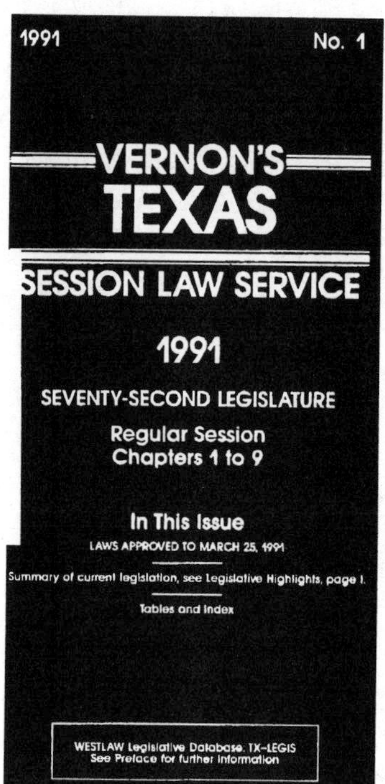

1991 No. 1

VERNON'S TEXAS

SESSION LAW SERVICE

1991

SEVENTY-SECOND LEGISLATURE

Regular Session
Chapters 1 to 9

In This Issue

LAWS APPROVED TO MARCH 25, 1991

Summary of current legislation, see Legislative Highlights, page I.

Tables and Index

WESTLAW Legislative Database: TX-LEGIS
See Preface for further information

INDEX

Vernon's Texas Session Law Service

SUMMING UP

HOW TO FIND A STATE STATUTE OR AMENDMENT PASSED WITHIN THE PAST YEAR

1. If you have the annotated code citation for the statute, check the pocket part of your state's annotated code.
2. If the new statute or amendment is not in the pocket part, go to the most recent volume of the advance legislative service for your state's annotated code.
3. If you already have the chapter or session law number, look it up starting with the most recent advance legislative service volume. If the statute is not there, work backwards through all volumes dated subsequent to the time the statute or amendment was passed.
4. If you don't know the chapter or session law number, find the table that converts the annotated code citations into chapter or session law numbers. Then look up that number in the advance legislative service.
5. If you don't have a citation to the statute or amendment, check the date on any pocket part in your state's annotated code. If the date is after the date the statute or amendment was passed, use the pocket part to the subject index for your state's annotated code.
6. If the date on the pocket part is earlier than the date the statute or amendment was passed, use the cumulative subject index for the most recent advance legislative service update volume.

H. How to Find Pending State Legislation

If you want to examine a piece of legislation that is currently before your state legislature, probably the best way is to call your local elected representative's office and ask for a copy of the bill. If you know what the bill concerns and, if possible, the legislator who is sponsoring it, you probably won't need to know the number of the bill. However, if you want to use your local law library (or your public library if it is large enough to carry state legislative materials) follow these steps:

- Determine the number of the bill—for example, Assembly Bill 27 or Senate Bill 538.
- If you don't know the bill's number, find out whether the legislature prints a subject index to current legislation. If so, use the index. If not, call your elected representative's office and ask for the number.
- Ask the reference librarian whether your legislature publishes a daily or weekly journal summarizing current legislative activity. If it does, locate the listing for the bill by its number and determine its status (for instance, is it still in committee, has it passed both houses?). If there is no journal, ask your elected representative or the bill's sponsor to find out the bill's status.
- Find out whether your local law library receives copies of the bills as they are produced and amended (called "slip laws"). If so, locate the latest version of the bill and read it.
- Increasingly, pending state legislation can be researched through the Internet, and computers can be used to access legal databases such as Lexis and Westlaw. See Chapter 13 for information on using computers to do legal research.

I. How to Read Statutes

Most legal research projects involve finding out what the law "is" in a particular circumstance. This usually involves finding a statute and then deciding how a court would interpret it given the facts in your situation. Courts consider it their responsibility to carry out the legislature's will as expressed in its statutes. If a statute is unclear—and many are—the court will try to figure out what the legislature intended. Only if the legislature exceeded its powers or intended something unconstitutional will courts ignore the dictates of a statute—and that doesn't happen very often.

Trying to determine what the legislature intended is often like trying to predict the roll of dice. Sometimes it seems that statutes are deliberately written to be incomprehensible. Certainly, many of them are almost impenetrable. One simple reason for this is that the lawyers who draft them have often not mastered basic English and disguise the fact by relying on "wherefores," "therefores," "pursuants" and so on.

Also, and perhaps more important, from the time a proposed statute is drafted until it emerges from the legislature in final form, legislators compromise, delete words and add more words in an attempt to get enough votes to pass the bill. What may have begun as straightforward and clear language often becomes so riddled with exceptions and conditions that the result presents serious difficulties to anyone who wants to understand what was intended. In the words of one frustrated judge:

> *I concur in the opinion of the majority because its construction of Code of Civil Procedure Section 660 seems plausible and hence probably correct, although—given the cosmic incomprehensibility of the section—once can never be absolutely sure.*
>
> *It occurs to me that Section 660 illustrates poignantly the maxim so useful in statutory construction—that if the Legislature had known what it meant, it would have said so.*
>
> *It seems to be me shameful, however, that large sums of money should change hands depending upon one's view of what this dismal, opaque statute means.*[1]

When searching for the meaning of a statutory provision, courts employ a number of rules of interpretation that have been developed over the years. These "rules" are often imprecise and sometimes contradictory, but if you are aware of them you should arrive at a more accurate interpretation than if you use only your common sense. Below we provide some guidelines that reflect the approach used by the courts for reading and understanding statutes. For a more detailed analysis of how to interpret statutes and regulations, see Statsky, *Legislative Analysis: How To Use Statutes and Regulations* (West Publishing Co., 1975).

Rule 1: Read the statute at least three times, then read it again

Often a different and hopefully more accurate meaning will emerge from each reading. Never feel that somehow you are inadequate because despite a number of readings you aren't sure what a particular statute means. A great many lawsuits result from the fact that lawyers disagree about confusing statutory language.

Rule 2: Pay close attention to "ands" and "ors"

Many statutes have lots of "ands" and "ors" tucked into different clauses, and the thrust of the statute often depends on which clauses are joined by an "and" and which by an "or." When clauses are joined by an "or," it means that the conditions in at least one of

---

[1] *Bunton v. Arizona Pacific Tanklines*, 141 Cal. App. 3d 210 (1983), 190 Cal. Rptr. 295.

the clauses must be present but not in all. When clauses are joined by an "and," the conditions in all the clauses must be met.

INTERPRETING "ANDS" AND "ORS"

Consider the following provision taken from 42 U.S.C.A. § 416:

"An applicant who is the son or daughter of a fully or currently insured individual, but who is not (and is not deemed to be) the child of such insured individual under paragraph (2) of this subsection, shall nevertheless be deemed to be the child of such insured individual if:

"(A) in the case of an insured individual entitled to old-age insurance benefits (who was not, in the month preceding such entitlement, entitled to disability insurance benefits)—

"(i) such insured individual—

(I) has acknowledged in writing that the applicant is his or her son or daughter

(II) has been decreed by a court to be the mother or father of the applicant, or

(III) has been ordered by a court to contribute to the support of the applicant because the applicant is his or her son or daughter,

"and such acknowledgment, court decree, or court order was made not less than one year before such insured individual became entitled to old-age insurance benefits or attained retirement age (as defined in subsection (l) of this section), whichever is earlier..."

Interpretation: To be considered a child of an insured child, a person must satisfy at least one of the three conditions under section (A)(i)—because of the use of the word "or"—and the condition must be met within one year of when the insured individual became entitled to old age insurance benefits or retained retirement age, because of the "and".

Rule 3: Assume all words and punctuation in the statute have meaning

Often, statutes seem to be internally inconsistent or redundant. Sometimes they are. However, courts presume that every word and comma in a statute means something, and you should do the same. If you're unsure about what a word or phrase means, look it up in a law dictionary or a multi-volume publication titled *Words and Phrases*. (See Section K, below, for a discussion of this resource.)

Rule 4: Interpret a statute so that it is consistent with all other related statutes, if possible

Sometimes it appears that a statute is totally inconsistent with other statutes in the same statutory scheme. It may be, but a judge who examines the statutes will make an attempt to reconcile the meanings so that no conflict exists. It is wise, therefore, to ask yourself whether any interpretation of the statute can be made that will make it consistent rather than inconsistent with other statutes.

Rule 5: Interpret criminal statutes strictly

Over the centuries the courts have applied a doctrine called "strict interpretation" to the criminal law. This reflects the policy that no person should be held accountable for a crime without adequate notice that his behavior was criminal. The only way to provide this type of notice is to insist that criminal laws be interpreted literally. And the defendant must be afforded the benefit of any ambiguities in the language. For example, to convict somebody of "breaking and entering a building belonging to another with the intent to commit theft or a felony therein" (a common definition of burglary), a prosecutor has to prove each element of the crime—that the person broke *and* entered *and* intended to commit a felony inside.

Example A young man in Vermont was charged with breaking and entering into the county courthouse, a felony. He had been found in the morning passed out under the judge's desk with some rare coins in his pocket that had been taken from the desk.

At his trial, the young man testified that he thought the courthouse was a church and that he simply broke in to get some sleep. However, once inside, he decided to look around and ended up stealing the coins. He didn't remember passing out. The trial judge (not the coin collector, but a more disinterested jurist) instructed the jury that unless they found beyond a reasonable doubt that the young man actually intended to commit a felony or the theft at the time he entered the courthouse, they could not convict him of breaking and entering. He was acquitted.

Rule 6: Interpret ambiguities in statutes in ways that seem to best further the purpose of the legislation

Much legislation is designed to either protect the public from ills or to provide various benefits. When ambiguities exist in these types of statutes—commonly called social welfare legislation—the courts tend to interpret them so that the protection or benefit will be provided rather than the other way around.

Example A statute allows welfare recipients to "earn" up to $100 a month without losing any benefits. The purpose of the statute is to provide an incentive for those on welfare to find work. Tom's father gives him $100 a month to stop drinking. Tom reports this to the welfare department, which promptly reduces Tom's monthly grant by $100. Tom goes to court, arguing that he is "earning" the money by not drinking and is therefore entitled to the $100 exemption. The welfare department contends that since the statute was intended to stimulate employment, the term "earns" means income from employment. The welfare department's argument will probably win, since its interpretation is more consistent with the statute's underlying objective.

Rule 7: Interpret the statute so that it makes sense and does not lead to absurd or improbable results

Courts are sometimes called on to interpret statutes that, if taken literally, would lead to a result that the legislature could not (in the court's opinion) have intended. In such an instance, a court will strain to interpret the statute so that it does make sense or lead to a logical result.

Example A California statute literally imposed a $100 daily penalty on landlords who interfered with a tenant's utilities with an intent to evict the tenant. The California Supreme Court ruled that the legislature could not have intended this harsh result, and instead interpreted the statute as allowing a penalty of up to $100 per day.

This rule of interpretation is especially important for non-lawyers to understand. Lawyers are used to the inherent paradoxes and uncertainties in statutory interpretation (indeed, they create them). However, few things are harder for a layperson to take than when the judge rejects a literal interpretation of a statute because "the legislature couldn't have intended it." The moral? When reading a statute, ask whether your interpretation is grounded in common sense and in the way the law was probably intended to work.

Rule 8: Track down all cross-references to other statutes and sections

People who draft statutes are very fond of including references to other statutes and sections of the same statute. When faced with such a statute, the human tendency is to ignore the cross-references and hope that they don't pertain to your situation. Our advice, quite simply, is to track down each and every cross-reference and make sure you understand how it relates to the main body of the statute you are analyzing. If you don't, you could overlook something crucial. An example of what we're talking about is shown below.

§703.520. Making of Claim of Exemption.

(a) The claimant may make a claim of exemption by filing with the levying officer a claim of exemption together with a copy thereof. The claim shall be made within 10 days after the date the notice of levy on the property claimed to be exempt was served on the judgment debtor.

(b) The claim of exemption shall be executed under oath and shall include all of the following:

(1) The name of the claimant and the mailing address where service of a notice of opposition to the claim may be made upon the claimant.

(2) The name and last known address of the judgment debtor if the claimant is not the judgment debtor.

(3) A description of the property claimed to be exempt. If an exemption is claimed pursuant to Section 704.010 or 704.060, the claimant shall describe all other property of the same type (including exempt proceeds of property of the same type) owned by the judgment debtor alone or in combination with others on the date of levy and identify the property, whether or not levied upon, to which the exemption is to be applied. If an exemption is claimed pursuant to subdivision (b) of Section 704.100, the claimant shall state the nature and amount of all other property of the same type owned by the judgment debtor or the spouse of the judgment debtor alone or in combination with others on the date of levy.

(4) A financial statement if required by Section 703.530.

(5) A citation of the provision of this chapter or other statute upon which the claim is based.

(6) A statement of the facts necessary to support the claim. **Leg.H.** 1982 ch. 1364, operative July 1, 1983.

Ref.: Cal. Fms Pl. & Pr., "Attachment," "Executions and Enforcement (Pt I)," "Homesteads," "Judgments."

Statute Containing Cross-References

J. The Importance of Cases That Interpret Statutes

It would be nice if research into the meaning of statutes began and ended with reading the statutes themselves. Unfortunately, statutes are subject to varying interpretations no matter how clearly they are worded or how closely they are studied. Lawyers are paid large sums of money to argue that the word "may" really means "shall," and vice versa. The ability of lawyers to interpret the meanings of common words in new (and often absurd) ways is sometimes breathtaking and often bizarre.

For example, a Nolo Press author was receiving more than his share of parking tickets as a result of a San Mateo, California, ordinance banning overnight parking and his close friendship with a San Mateo resident, whose many wonderful attributes didn't include a driveway. Afraid that the tickets he inevitably received would eventually sour his romance, the author went to court to overturn the ordinance. He argued that the state statute authorizing cities to ban overnight parking on "certain city streets" didn't mean a city could ban such parking on "all" streets, which was how San Mateo interpreted it when it passed the ordinance. Briefs were written and arguments held on the question of whether "certain" could be read to mean "all" or had to mean "less than all." The judges hearing the case on appeal eventually concluded that certain meant "less than all," so the author's romance was saved.

As this story illustrates, the judiciary is charged with the task of interpreting statutes when a dispute over their meaning is presented in a lawsuit. Court interpretations of statutes are every bit as much a part of the statute as the words themselves.

For example, a California statute mentioned earlier provided that landlords were liable to tenants in the amount of $100 for each day the utilities were shut off by the landlord for the purpose of evicting the tenants. When a landlord appealed a judgment against him under this statute, the California Supreme Court decided that it would be unconstitutional to penalize a landlord $100 per day regardless of circumstances.[2] The Court interpreted the statute to allow a penalty of up to $100 per day, depending on circumstances. Immediately after this court decision, the law of utility shutoffs in California could only be determined by reading the statute and the court case together. The California legislature later amended the statute to comply with the Court's ruling.

There are two primary ways to find out what the courts have had to say about a particular statute:

- case notes that accompany the statutes in annotated codes
- a series of books called *Shepard's Citations for Statutes*.

These methods (and others) are covered in Chapter 9, *Finding Cases*.

WHAT SHEPARD'S CITATIONS FOR STATUTES DOES

Shepard's Citations for Statutes *tells you each time a case has mentioned a particular statute and provides a reference (citation) to the case. In addition,* Shepard's *provides references to amendments that have been made to the statute and instances when attorney general opinions and law review articles have mentioned the statute. Serious statute researchers will want to learn how to use this resource.*

[2]*Hale v. Morgan*, 22 Cal. 3d 388 (1978), 149 Cal. Rptr. 375, 584 P.2d 512.

K. Using Words and Phrases To Interpret Statutes

"When I use a word," Humpty Dumpty said, in a rather scornful tone, "it means just what I choose it to mean—no more, no less." "The question is," said Alice, "whether you can make words mean so many different things." "The question is," said Humpty Dumpty, "which is to be master—that's all."[3]

In the Land of the Law, judges are master. To properly interpret a statute you usually need to know how courts have interpreted one or more of the specialized words and phrases it contains. One tool to help you do this is a multi-volume set called *Words and Phrases* (West Publishing Co). It contains one-sentence interpretations of common words and phrases that have been pulled from cases and organized alphabetically. This publication allows you to find out whether courts have interpreted or used any particular word or phrase you are interested in, and if so, how.

In a real sense, *Words and Phrases* is a kind of dictionary that offers contextual definitions instead of the abstract and disconnected entries found in most law dictionaries. Below is part of the *Words and Phrases* entry for "landlords."

As with other hardbound legal resources, don't forget to check the pocket part in the back of each book for the newest entries.

While *Words and Phrases* can be helpful in understanding statutory language, it isn't a substitute for a court's interpretation of the specific statute you are concerned with. If the statute has been interpreted by a court, that interpretation will prevail over another court's interpretation of the same language in a different statute under different facts.

[3]*Alice in Wonderland*, Lewis Carroll.

LANDLORD AND TENANT

In general

The relation of "landlord and tenant" depends upon agreement. Estes v. Gatliff, 163 S.W.2d 273, 275, 291 Ky. 93.

A "landlord and tenant relationship" will be implied from occupancy of premises with owner's consent. Crawford v. Jerry, 11 A.2d 210, 211, 111 Vt. 120.

The relation of "landlord and tenant" arises only where one in possession of land recognizes another as his landlord. Hoffmann v. Chapman, Tex.Civ.App., 170 S.W.2d 496, 498.

A contract establishing "landlord and tenant relationship" does not include principal and agent or master and servant relationships. Butler v. Maney, 200 So. 226, 228, 146 Fla. 33.

The relation of "landlord and tenant" may arise by express or implied contract and on slight evidence. Delay v. Douglas, Mo. App., 164 S.W.2d 154, 156.

Words and Phrases

LIBRARY EXERCISE

Using Words and Phrases

Find the blue set of West's *Words and Phrases*.

Questions

1a. In which book of the set would you look to find a definition of USURER?

1b. There are two definitions under Usurer, from two different courts: Arkansas and New York. By what standard does each state measure usury?

2a. Now use the Pocket Part to find a more recent definition of USURIOUS from a court in Florida. What is the name of the case?

2b. According to the definition, for a transaction to be considered usurious under Florida law, is it enough that the interest exceeds the rate allowed by law?

Answers

1a. In volume 43A ("Unless" to "Vale").

1b. In the Arkansas case, the court says that a usurer is one who lends money at a rate greater than the *limit set by law*. In the New York case, a usurer is defined as one who lends money at an *excessive or inordinate rate*. The New York case uses a subjective standard, whereas the Arkansas case uses an objective one.

2a. *In re Tammey Jewels, Inc.*

2b. No, several conditions must be met: there must be an express or implied loan, an understanding between the parties that the loan is to be repaid, and there must be a corrupt intent to charge more than the legal rate of interest.

L. Using Attorney General Opinions to Interpret Statutes

Attorneys general, the highest legal officers in government, are often asked by government agencies to interpret the meaning of statutes. When they do, it is often in the form of a written opinion. These attorney general opinions are not binding on the courts, but they have influence, especially when there is no precedent to the contrary. And they can be very helpful in deciphering an otherwise hopelessly complicated statute.

Attorney general opinions are collected in publications usually called something like *Opinions of the Attorney General of the State of...* A separate set exists for each state and for the federal government. If a statute is the subject of an attorney general's opinion, the citation to the opinion citing the statute will appear after the case citations in *Shepard's Citations for Statutes*. (See Chapter 9, Section B3, for how to use this valuable tool.)

M. Using Legislative History to Interpret Statutes

You may be uncertain about the meaning of a statute no matter how much you study it. For instance, many statutes provide that certain government employees are entitled to an administrative hearing if they lose their jobs. What such statutes often don't say is whether the hearing must be provided before the discharge or after it.

If you are unable to find a court decision on the question, how should you proceed? One common way (and in many cases the only way) is to find out what the legislators intended at the time they passed the statute. Their intent can be inferred from legislative committee reports, hearings and floor debates—what is called the statute's "legislative history." The general idea underlying doing a legislative history is simple: legislators are presumed to know what they're doing and why.

When you investigate legislative history, keep a couple of points firmly in mind. As mentioned earlier, what the legislature intended in a statute is supposed to be gleaned from the "plain words" of the statute itself. So if a judge believes the words of a statute are reasonably clear, no inquiry into the legislative intent will be considered.

The second point is a bit more cosmic. Legislative intent can be seen as a kind of mass delusion that the judicial community buys into when it doesn't know how to interpret a statute any other way. Why a delusion? Because most of the time there is no one clear legislative intent. Typically, a few legislators know what's intended by the words of any particular statute, while the great majority who haven't even read it vote for or against the bill for reasons unrelated to how it's worded. For that reason, some judges stick to the words of the statute, no matter how difficult it is to understand.

1. Finding Federal Legislative History

Conducting a full investigation of legislative history for a federal statute can be an exhausting and often inconclusive task. You will be probably be glad to know that most of the time it is also unnecessary. Normally, locating the more important federal committee reports is all the legislative history research you need to do.[4]

Most statutes in the annotated federal codes (U.S.C.A. and U.S.C.S.) are followed by a reference to the U.S. *Code Congressional and Administrative News*, which contains federal legislative history. An example of how this works is shown in the federal statute set out below. Examine the small print following the statute. The last paragraph sets out where the legislative history for the original statute and the 1982 amendment can be located in the U.S. *Code Congressional and Administrative News*.

If the federal statute you are investigating does not have a citation to its legislative history, you can check the subject index, popular names table, and statutory reference table in each volume of the U.S. *Code Congressional and Administrative News*. There is one major limitation to the value of these indexes and tables, however: They are not cumulative. In other words, they index only materials from the legislative session covered by that volume.

Suppose, for example, that you are dealing with a statute passed in 1984 but don't know its public law number or its U.S. *Code* citation. You can use the subject index for the U.S. *Code Congressional and Administrative News* for that year to find the legislative history.

If, however, you already have the public law number of a statute, find the volume containing the public laws for the Congress indicated in the public law number. For instance, if the number is 94-584, find the volume containing material for the 94th Congress. Then use the statutory reference table to locate the committee reports.

[4]For more detailed guidance, consult Goehlert, *Congress and Law Making: Researching the Legislative Process* (2d Ed., Clio Books 1989).

16 § 831s **CONSERVATION Ch. 12A**

§ 831s. Possession by Government in time of war; damages to contract holders

The Government of the United States hereby reserves the right, in case of war or national emergency declared by Congress, to take possession of all or any part of the property described or referred to in this chapter for the purpose of manufacturing explosives or for other war purposes; but, if this right is exercised by the Government, it shall pay the reasonable and fair damages that may be suffered by any party whose contract for the purchase of electric power or fixed nitrogen or fertilizer ingredients is hereby violated, after the amount of the damages has been fixed by the United States Claims Court in proceedings instituted and conducted for that purpose under rules prescribed by the court.

(May 18, 1933, c. 32, § 20, 48 Stat. 68; Apr. 2, 1982, Pub.L. 97-164, Title I, § 161(2), 96 Stat. 49.)

Historical Note

1982 Amendment. Pub.L. 97-164 substituted "Claims Court" for "Court of Claims".

Effective Date of 1982 Amendment. Amendment by Pub.L. 97-164 effective Oct. 1, 1982, see section 402 of Pub.L. 97-164, set out as an Effective Date of 1982 Amendment note under section 171 of Title 28, Judiciary and Judicial Procedure.

Termination of War and Emergencies. Joint Res. July 25, 1947, c. 327, § 3, 61 Stat. 451, provided that in the interpretation of this section, the date July 25, 1947, shall be deemed to be the date of termination of any state of war theretofore declared by Congress and of the national emergencies proclaimed by the President on September 8, 1939, and May 27, 1941.

Legislative History. For legislative history and purpose of Pub.L. 97-164, see 1982 U.S. Code Cong. and Adm.News, p. 11. ←

Federal Statute Showing Legislative History Reference

If you don't know the public law number, the *U.S. Code* citation or the approximate year the statute was passed, you will have difficulty finding the appropriate committee reports; your best bet is to search for the *U.S. Code* citation. (See Section C, above.)

It is important to remember that the typical statute is amended many times over its lifespan. Each amendment has its own committee reports. The legislative history of a statute, therefore, generally refers to a collection of legislative histories. Each of these legislative histories must be separately researched, because any given volume of the *U.S. Code Congressional and Administrative News* contains only the committee reports for the session covered by that volume.

In the federal statute set out above, the legislative history of the original statute is contained in an earlier *U.S. Code Congressional and Administrative News*, while the history of the 1992 amendment is in the 1982 *U.S. Code Congressional and Administrative News*. You would need to read both to glean a full legislative history of the statute.

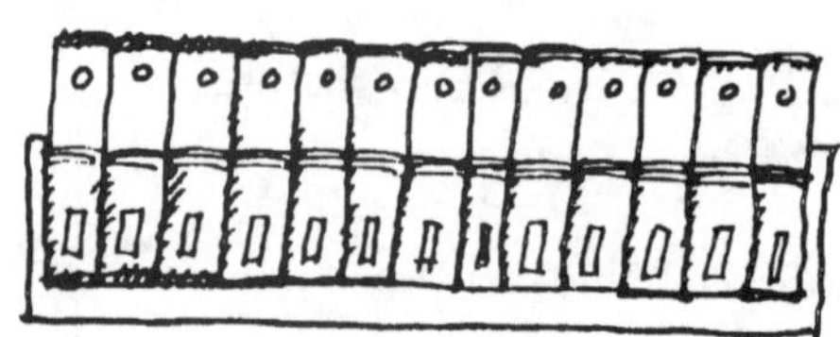

LIBRARY EXERCISE

Finding the Legislative History of Federal Statutes

Now it's time to use the library to apply what you've just learned. This exercise asks you to locate the legislative history of a federal statute. Additional research exercises that include these and other skills are in the Appendix.

Question

Your research involves the custody of Native American children. You are asked to find the legislative history of Title 25, §§ 1911 and 1912—part of the federal Indian Child Welfare Act of 1978.

1. *Find the statutes in the United States Code Annotated (U.S.C.A.). What does the material directly following them tell you about their legislative history?*
2. *Look for the legislative history and describe the documents you find.*

Answers

1. In the "Historical Note" following both sections, it says "For legislative history and purpose of Pub. L. 95-608, see 1978 U.S. Code Cong. and Adm. News, p. 7530."
2. First find the volumes of the 1978 U.S. Code Congressional and Administrative News that contain legislative history (shown on the spine). Select the volume that includes page 7530; this is Volume 6. On pages 7530 and following, you find House Report No. 95-1386, Analysis of the Report, Cost Estimate from the U.S. Budget Office and statements from various cabinet officers, legislators and agencies.

LIBRARY EXERCISE

Using U.S. Code Congressional and Administrative News

Until 1990, the United States Supreme Court had held that the First Amendment Freedom of Religion protects individuals from penalty or prosecution when the individuals' actions are part of their religion.

In 1990, the Supreme Court upheld the states' right to enforce drug laws against Native Americans whose religious practice included ceremonies in which peyote is used.

Your office wants to defend a client in a similar situation and has heard that the U.S. Congress passed a statute overturning the 1990 decision (*Employment Division v. Smith*, 110 S. Ct. 1595 (1990)).

You are assigned to go to U.S.C.A. (not U.S.C.S.) and U.S. Code Congressional and Administrative News and try to find the statute's text and legislative history. It's called something like "Religious Freedom Act 1993."

Questions

1. *Where in U.S.C.A. do you start?*
2. *What do you find under Religious Freedom?*
3. *Where in U.S.C.A. is the "Popular Name Table?"*
4. *Look up the Religious Freedom Restoration Act in the Popular Name table. What information are you given?*
5. *Now that you know the Act's Public Law number, where is the best place to find the federal law by its public law number, along with legislative history?*
6. *How do you find the book with the legislative history in it?*
7. *Open Volume 3. The headings on the right-hand pages list the Acts in bold type and the Public Law numbers directly below. The Religious Freedom Restoration Act of 1993 begins on page 1893. The first words under the title tell you to* "see page 107 Stat. 1488." *Where is that page, and what's there?*
8. *Now, go back to Volume 3. When the Senate Committee on the Judiciary voted on whether to report the bill to the full Senate, how many voted for reporting, and how many against? Where did you find this information?*

Answers

1. The General Index for U.S.C.A. is the set of softbound volumes at the end of the entire set. "Religious Freedom" would be in the Volume P - R.
2. There is an entry entitled: "Religious Freedom Restoration Act of 1993." Under the entry is the notation "Text of Act. See Popular Name Table."
3. The last volume of the General Index (U to Z) also includes the Popular Name Table (after Z), which is noted on the spine of the book.
4. We are given its public law number, the date of enactment, and the statute number: Pub.l. 103-141, Nov. 16, 1993, 107 Stat 1488.
5. In the U.S. Code Congressional and Administrative News.
6. U.S. Code Congressional and Administrative News is arranged by year, with several volumes making up each year. We know that the Act was passed in 1993, so we consult the 1993 volumes. On the bottom of the spine of the third volume ("103rd Congress FIRST SESSION 1993") is the information "LEGISLATIVE HISTORY [P.L. 103 - 66 con't to 103 - 160]." The bottom line of information gives the volume's page numbers. Since we are looking for Pub. L. 103 - 141, we know we have the right book.
7. At the bottom of the spine of Volume 2 of 103rd Congress First Session 1993, the page numbers are 1 - 662. Page 107 is within those pages. We could also have gone directly to 107 Stat 1488 when we found the entry in the Popular Name Table (*see* Question 4).
8. On page 1892, there is a Table of Contents for the Senate Report, showing page numbers of the original report. These page numbers appear in brackets ("[page 2]") at page breaks throughout the Report. Entry VI in the Table of Contents is "Vote of the Committee ...... 14." [Page 14] begins on page 1903 of our Volume. The vote of each member of the Committee is recorded in that section, and 15 voted for it, 1 against.

2. Finding State Legislative History

State legislative history is usually more difficult to uncover than federal legislative history. However, many states have legislative analysts (lawyers who work for the legislature) whose comments on legislation are considered by the state legislators in the same way as committee reports are considered by Congress. These comments are sometimes published in the advance legislative update services (discussed above in Section G) as an introduction to the new statute.

Statutes and accompanying comments that are printed in these advance legislative services are later bound and retained in volumes called Session Laws, according to the year they were passed. It is sometimes possible to discover the legislative history of an older state statute by finding these legislative analyst comments with the statute in the bound Session Laws. To find a statute in the Session Laws, you need the chapter number assigned it by the legislature. That number appears directly after the text of the statute as printed in a code.

It is also common for legislative committees to have their own staff lawyers draft memoranda to guide them in their deliberations. These memoranda are normally not available in law libraries, but they may be kept on file with the legislature. Legislative procedures vary greatly from state to state. In Oregon, for example, committees keep microfilmed minutes of their hearings and records of all exhibits introduced at the hearings. Many other states don't keep such records. The best course for a researcher is probably to ask a law librarian what kinds of legislative history for state laws are available in that state.

For more detailed information about state legislative history, see Fisher, *Guide to State Legislative Materials* (4th Ed., American Association of Law Libraries 1988).

Don't get too carried away researching legislative history. It is often possible and usually preferable to determine the meaning of a statute without resorting to the legislative history. Most statutory provisions have been interpreted by courts, and courts tend not to use legislative history unless an important ambiguity really exists.

N. Using Uniform Law Histories to Interpret Statutes

There is currently an effort to make a number of substantive areas of the law uniform among the states. A group of lawyers, judges and law professors called the National Conference of Commissioners on Uniform State Laws (National Conference) drafts legislation covering certain areas of law and then tries to get as many states as possible to adopt the "uniform" legislation.

The packages drafted by the National Conference are not law and have no effect on our legal system until they are adopted by one or more state legislatures. And the fact that the package is adopted in one or more states does not make it law in any other state that has not adopted it.

This approach to making law uniform has been highly successful in many legal areas. In other areas, the National Conference has met with less success.

UNIFORM LAWS ADOPTED BY MANY STATES

- Uniform Commercial Code
- Uniform Controlled Substances Act
- Uniform Gifts to Minors Act
- Uniform Transfers to Minors Act
- Uniform Partnership Act
- Uniform Child Custody Jurisdiction Act

If the statute you are researching was a uniform law adopted by your state, you can get some help interpreting its meaning by looking at a series of books called the *Uniform Laws Annotated (U.L.A.)*, published by West. It contains all of the uniform laws, the original comments accompanying them, a listing of the states that have adopted them, notations of how states have altered each provision in the course of adopting it, summaries of case opinions that have interpreted each statute, and references to pertinent law review discussions. The *U.L.A.* gives you excellent insight into what any particular part of a uniform law package was originally intended to accomplish and how the states and courts have treated it.

Unfortunately, the *U.L.A.* has neither an overall index nor an overall table of contents. However, the volumes are grouped according to general subject matter. For example, some of the volumes contain uniform laws treating "Estate, Probate and Related Laws," while others contain laws pertaining to "Civil Procedural and Remedial Laws." In addition, each uniform law package carries its own index. So, if you have the reference for a uniform law package, you can find the volume containing this package and use the specific index to find the particular part you are interested in.

How can you tell whether a state statute you are interested in interpreting originally came from a uniform law package? If your annotated state statutes are published by West Publishing Co. (almost all are), the annotation following the statute will tell you. In addition, the annotation will reproduce the National Conference comment that accompanied the statute as it was originally proposed, and will also contain comments about how the state version of the statute differs from the original.

States seldom adopt uniform law packages lock, stock and barrel. Usually they change or delete some of the statutes in the package. Also, in many cases, new sections are added. So by the time uniform laws have been adopted by the various states, they are no longer, strictly speaking, "uniform." Still, for the most part, if you have an overall understanding of the package as it was produced by the National Conference, you will have a good grasp of the final result in any given adopting state.

O. Regulations

Legislatures often pass laws that need active enforcement. For example, a complex series of federal statutes provide for the collection of the federal income tax. However, the federal government wouldn't be solvent very long if it relied on everyone to voluntarily line up and empty their pockets. Accordingly, Congress created the Internal Revenue Service (IRS) to:

- resolve specific questions that arise with respect to how the tax laws should be interpreted
- provide specific guidelines that enable millions to prepare their own tax returns every year, and
- keep a close watch on us all to make sure we pay our fair (or unfair) share.

The IRS is but one of many of the "administrative agencies" created by Congress over the years to implement its programs. State legislatures have created a similar alphabet soup of agencies to carry out their programs.

Legislatures give such agencies the power to make rules and guidelines to carry out the goals of the statutes that authorized the creation of the agency and the programs over which it has authority. These rules and guidelines are collectively termed "regulations." Some are directed at the general public, some at business entities and some at the agency itself. If they are consistent with the parent legislation, they have the force and effect of law. This is a fancy way of saying that regulations are just as binding and enforceable as statutes. Therefore, when regulations are at issue in a dispute, it is often crucial to first determine whether they are valid under the terms of the statutes that govern the agency's activities—and thus have the force and effect of law.

Courts are willing to overturn agency regulations when they conclude that the agency misinterpreted the law or issued a regulation when it didn't have the authority to do so. For example, the U.S. Supreme Court struck down Federal Occupational Safety and Health Administration (OSHA) regulations that allowed industries to balance worker safety against the cost of implementing safeguards.

1. Finding Federal Regulations

Most federal regulations are published in the *Code of Federal Regulations* (C.F.R.), a multi-volume and well-indexed paperbound set organized by subject.

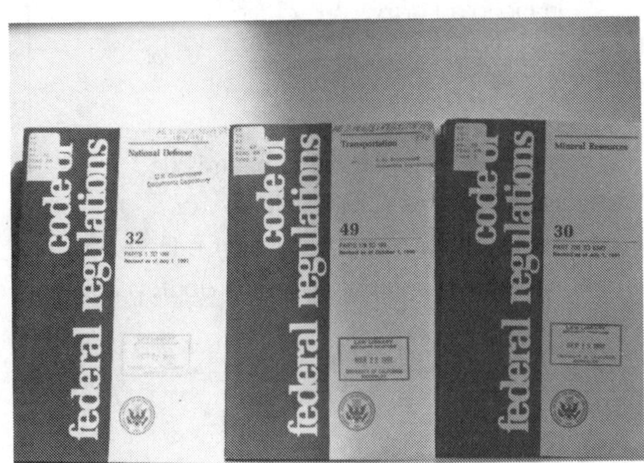

The Code of Federal Regulations (C.F.R.)

The C.F.R. is organized into 50 separate titles. Each title covers a general subject. For instance, Title 7 contains regulations concerning agriculture, Title 10 contains energy regulations, and so on. C.F.R. titles often, but not always, correspond to the U.S.C. titles in terms of their subject matter. For example, Title 7 of the *United States Code* covers statutes relating to agriculture while Title 7 of the C.F.R. contains agriculture regulations. But Title 42 of U.S.C. contains statutes on the Medicaid program while the Medicaid regulations are found in Title 45 of the C.F.R.

Along with each regulation, the C.F.R. provides a reference to the statute that authorizes it and a reference to where (and when) the regulation was published in the *Federal Register*. (All regulations are supposed to be published first in the *Federal Register*, discussed in Section 2, below.) Below is an example of the information provided along with each regulation in the C.F.R.

The best way to find a federal regulation published in C.F.R. if you don't already have the correct citation is to use the Martindale-Hubbell C.F.R. index or start with the general subject index that comes with this series. If you already know which title your regulation is likely to be in, use the Table of Contents at the end of each individual Title.

Once you've found a regulation, you need to be sure it's still current. A new edition of the C.F.R. is published each year on a staggered quarterly basis. Titles 1-16 are published on January 1, Titles 17-27 are published on April 1, titles 28-41 are published on July 1 and titles 42-50 are published on October 1. Each year the C.F.R. covers change colors.

When a new annual edition is published, the regulations in it are current as of that date. What, however, if the C.F.R. volume that contains the regulation you are interested in was published January 1, 1992, and you are doing your research in July 1992? How can you make sure you are up-to-date? Simple. First, consult the latest monthly pamphlet called C.F.R.-L.S.A., which stands for "List of C.F.R. Sections Affected". Find the title and section number of the regulation you are interested in. Then see if there have been any changes between the last published *C.F.R.* volume (January 1 in our example) and the date of the pamphlet (July 1992) Below is a typical page from *C.F.R.-L.S.A.*

Suppose now that you are doing your research on July 15, 1992, and the July version of the *C.F.R.-L.S.A.* has not yet hit the library shelf. You would first use the *C.F.R.-L.S.A.* for June. Then you can use a publication called the *Federal Register,* where all new federal regulations are originally published. The *Federal Register* also contains proposed regulations, schedules of government agency meetings, Presidential documents and lists of bills that have been enacted.

The *Federal Register* can be hard to use because it contains many pages of very small type on newsprint. It is published daily, and a cumulative monthly index is available to help you find the regulation you're after. However, this index is generally organized according to the agency that initiated the action, so unless you know which agency you're dealing with, it's of little help.

If you have a *C.F.R.* citation to the new regulation, or you want to bring your *C.F.R.* search completely up to date (see above), you can consult the *C.F.R.* sections affected list in the latest issue of the *Federal Register.* This will give you a listing of all *C.F.R.* sections that have been affected during the current month of the *Federal Register.*

SUMMING UP

HOW TO FIND FEDERAL REGULATIONS

1. Consult either the general subject index to the Code of Federal Regulations (C.F.R.), the hardcover index to the Code of Federal Regulations published by Martindale-Hubble, or the Index to the Code of Federal Regulations (commercially published by C.I.S.).

2. After you find the regulation, read the latest monthly issue of the C.F.R. List of Sections Affected (C.F.R.-L.S.A.) to see whether changes in the regulation have been made since the C.F.R. volume was published.

3. Consult the List of C.F.R. Sections Affected in the latest daily issue of the Federal Register for the most current status of a regulation.

4. For regulations that have been issued since the latest C.F.R. volume was published, consult the cumulative index to the Federal Register under the appropriate agency.

CHANGES APRIL 1, 1991 THROUGH NOVEMBER 29, 1991

TITLE 19 Chapter I—Con. Page

171.33 (b)(1) and (d) heading revised....40780
(b)(1) and (d) corrected....48823
172.22 (e) added....40780
(e) corrected....48823
172.33 (b)(1) revised....40780
177 Interpretive rule....46372
177.22 (b) introductory text amended....46115
178.2 Table amended....32087
191.10 (e)(1)(i) amended....46115
191.21 (c) and (d) amended....46115
191.27 (c) amended....46115

Chapter II—United States International Trade Commission (Parts 200—299)

200 Authority citation revised....36726
200.735-102 (g) removed....36726
200.735-103 (a) and (c) introductory text amended; (b) and (c)(2) revised....36726
200.735-114 Nomenclature change....36726
200.735-115 Nomenclature change....36726
200.735-116 (b) revised....36726
200.735-121 Nomenclature change....36726

Chapter III—International Trade Administration, Department of Commerce (Parts 300—399)

356 Revised....37804

Title 19—*Proposed Rules:*

4....40283, 48448, 51762
10....48448, 51762
19....22833, 33733
24....31576
101....21111, 22369, 55102, 56179
102....48448, 51762
113....22833, 33733
118....33734
134....48448, 51762
142....42568
141....56608
142....56608
144....22833, 33733
162....25363
177....46134, 48448, 51762

TITLE 20—EMPLOYEES' BENEFITS

Chapter I—Office of Workers' Compensation Programs, Department of Labor (Parts 1—199)

Page

10.305 Revised....47675
10.306 (a) revised....47675
10.311 (c) revised....47675

Chapter II—Railroad Retirement Board (Parts 200—399)

200.8 (b) amended; (d)(1), (2), (3), (f), (g) and (h) redesignated as (d)(2), (3), (4), (g), (h) and (i); (d)(1), (f) and (j) added....50247
216 Revised....28692
236 Removed....55073
240 Removed....55073
323 Added....26328
330 Revised....28702
367 Added....46375

Chapter III—Social Security Administration, Department of Health and Human Services (Parts 400—499)

404.362 (b)(1) revised; (b)(2) removed; (b)(3) redesignated as (b)(2)....24000
404.367 Introductory text and (b) revised....35999
404.401—404.499 (Subpart E) Authority citation revised....41789
404.401 (d) revised....41789
Technical correction....50157
404.402 (d)(1) revised....41789
Technical correction....50157
404.469 Added....41789
Technical correction....50157
404.501—404.515 (Subpart F) Authority citation revised....52468
404.520 Added....52468
404.521 Added....52468
404.522 Added....52469
404.523 Added....52469
404.524 Added....52469
404.525 Added....52469
404.526 Added....52469
404.621 (a)(2)(i) and (ii) removed; (a)(2)(iii) and (iv) redesignated as (a)(2)(i) and (ii)....58846

Note: **Boldface entries indicate November changes.**

List of C.F.R. Sections Affected (C.F.R.-L.S.A.)

LIBRARY EXERCISE

Finding Federal Regulations

Now it's time to use the library to apply what you've just learned. This exercise asks you to locate and update federal regulations that govern the labeling of margarine. Additional research exercises that include these and other skills are in the Appendix.

Question

You are a graphic artist making a new package for Sun Dew Margarine. You are searching for federal regulations that regulate how big the word "margarine" must be on the box.

1. *What indexes can you use to find a federal regulation ?*
2. *What words can you look under to find out how big the word margarine must be on the box?*
3. *What does it say under these entries?*
4. *What does 21 C.F.R. 166 mean?*
5. *Find 21 C.F.R. 166. What subsection is titled "Labeling of margarine"?*
6. *Find all subsections under 166.40 that deal with how tall the letters must be.*
7. *What is the smallest the letters can be?*
8. *Where do you look first to see if there have been any changes to the regulation you are using?*
9. *Do you find any changes to your regulation listed in that publication?*
10. *Do you need to read about the changes to 21 C.F.R. 166?*
11. *Do you have to look in each daily issue of that resource?*
12. *Are there any changes?*

Answer

1. The Index to the Code of Federal Regulations or the U.S.C.S. Index and Finding Aids to Code of Federal Regulations or Martindale-Hubbell's Code of Federal Regulations Index.
2. Oleomargarine or Margarine or Food labeling.
3. In the C.F.R. index or the U.S.C.S. Index: Under Oleomargarine it says: see Margarine and under Margarine it says: Food grades and standards 21 C.F.R. 166. Under Food labeling it says: Margarine standards 21 C.F.R. 166.

   In the Martindale-Hubbard Index: In the Contents at the beginning of Volume 1, you see that there are two Indexes to Food and Drug regulations; in volume 1, there is an index to Title 21 (Food and Drugs), and in the Topical Index there is a category for Food and Drugs, in volume 3 pages FD-1 to FD-174. On page FD-1 is a list of major subject headings for that category; Margarine is listed there, and when you go into the index you find: Margarine 21 C.F.R. 166.40, 116.110. Looking under Food labeling, margarine will get you the same citation to 21 C.F.R. 166.40.
4. Code of Federal Regulations Title 21, Section or Part 166.
5. § 166.40.
6. § 166.40(c)(1); § 166.40(h).
7. 20 points or 20/72 of 1 inch.
8. LSA starting with the month after the date on the front of the volume you are using.
9. No.
10. 21 C.F.R. 166.40 is the subsection concerned with letter size. The changes to the legislation do not deal with that subsection, but they should still be read in case they deal with an important related issue.
11. No; the last day of each month includes all changes recorded that month; each day is cumulative for that month as well (July 15 includes all changes recorded July 1-15).
12. When we looked at this Regulation in December 1994, the last changes had been made on May 25, 1994. When you do the research, what do you find?

2. Finding State Regulations

State regulations are usually more difficult to locate than federal regulations. While at least 30 states have an administrative code containing a portion of the state's regulations, a common practice is for each agency's regulations to be kept in loose-leaf manuals published by the individual agency. This means it is often necessary to know which state agency is responsible for writing a particular regulation before you can find it. Some larger law libraries carry all or most of the regulations for their state, but more often you'll have to call or visit the agency itself to get regulations.

Regulations are constantly being changed by the agencies that issue them, and it is important to always check to make sure that the regulation that you've found is up to date. This can be done by checking with the agency, where you might discover someone who will help you find everything you need.

3. How to Read and Understand Regulations

The general rules of statutory interpretation set out in Section G, above, also apply to interpreting regulations. But there are some additional factors to consider in the interpretation of regulations. The most important are that:

- Agency interpretations of a regulation should either be followed or argued against, but not ignored. Because regulations are often written to implement a general statutory scheme, they tend to be both wordy and hard to understand, even more so than statutes. Increasingly, however, regulations are written so that they can be more clearly understood.
- Regulations should be interpreted in a way that best fulfills the intent of the authorizing statute.

SUMMING UP

HOW TO FIND STATE REGULATIONS

1. If your state's regulations have been collected and published in an "Administrative Code," use the subject index. If there is no index, find the place in the publication that covers the agency issuing the regulations and check the table of contents.
2. If there is no administrative code or analogous publication, find out what agency issued the regulations. Then ask the law librarian whether the library carries that agency's regulations.
3. If the regulations cannot be found in the law library, check with the nearest large public library.

   If the regulations aren't kept there, contact the agency issuing the regulations and ask how you can get a copy of the regulations you're interested in.

A typical regulation consists of the actual rule that is being put forth and a paragraph or two of agency interpretation. Sometimes examples are given on how the regulation is supposed to apply to a specific set of facts. Only the rule part of the regulation acts like a law. The interpretation and examples are designed only to explain its application.

P. Procedural Statutes and Rules

If your research involves procedural issues—such as getting the case into court and keeping it there—there are several types of laws you need to pay special attention to, all of which can usually be found in a law library with the help of the law librarian.

1. Rules of Civil Procedure

Rules of Civil Procedure are usually statutes passed by a legislature or rules issued by a State Supreme Court. They govern such matters as:

- who can sue whom, for what kinds of wrongs, and in which courts
- which kinds of documents must be filed with the court to initiate a lawsuit and respond to it
- time limits for filing various court papers
- what court papers must say to be effective
- what are the ways each side to a lawsuit can find out necessary facts from the other side and from third-party witnesses (discovery)
- how a case is actually brought to trial
- what kind of trial you are entitled to (that is, by judge or jury)
- what kind of judgment and relief you are entitled to if you win
- what happens to you if you lose
- how you can enforce a judgment
- how you can appeal a judgment if you lose, and
- what kind of appeal is available if the court does not comply with the laws in the pre-trial stage of the case.

You must follow these rules exactly. While some procedural mistakes can be fixed, especially if this is done very promptly, many violations mean that your case is lost, just as surely as if you went to trial and the court or jury found against you.

Rules of Civil Procedure for the federal courts are found in Title 28 of *U.S.C.A.* Rules of Civil Procedure for state courts are usually found among the other state statutes in a code, title or chapter entitled "civil procedure" or "court rules."

2. Rules of Court (if any)

Your state may have an additional publication called Rules of Court or something similar. If so, it will contain rules issued by the state's Supreme Court and specify in more detail the procedures that must be followed. For example, a statute might specify that a certain document must be filed with the court, but the Rule of Court would specify the precise form the document must follow.

3. Local Rules (if any)

Many courts have their own local rules that get even more detailed. A local rule might specify the size of the paper that must be used or where an attorney's name must be placed on the page. Although these housekeeping matters may not seem as important as the accuracy of the facts and law in your papers, many lawyers have learned the hard way that you ignore them at your peril. Some judges and clerks love to use deviations from local rules as the basis for returning your papers or even denying your motion.

DESK REFERENCES

It is no secret that legal secretaries and paralegals often know more about the actual techniques involved in getting the right papers to the right courts on time than lawyers do. These details are commonly put into a step-by-step form and published in handbooks and "desk references." You can find information about filing fees, service of process, statutes of limitation, time limits, common motions and similar nitty-gritty matters in these publications, which exist in most larger states. For example, in California you can use The Paralegal's Handbook, *by Mack (Parker & Son). Ask a legal secretary, paralegal or law librarian if this sort of resource is published in your state.*

Q. Local Law—Ordinances

Counties, cities, and special districts (for example, school districts or sanitation districts) have a good deal of power over day-to-day life. The amount of rule-making authority that is afforded these local entities is usually set out in the state constitution and statutes. Subject to these higher forms of law, cities commonly have authority to:

- divide their domain into zones of activity (called the "zoning power")
- set requirements for new buildings and for the refurbishing of old buildings
- pass and enforce local parking and driving rules
- set minimum standards for health and safety in rental properties
- promulgate fire and police regulations.

Local laws are usually called "ordinances." Ordinances are like statutes and regulations in that they have the force and effect of law, assuming they are within the local government's lawful authority. Special districts are usually empowered to pass regulations that are also binding law.

Because of the many different forms of local government, it is difficult to specify the exact way in which you might research these ordinances or specialized regulations. Here are some general suggestions:

- Ordinances are often divided into local codes such as the "traffic code," "planning code," "building code" and the like. These codes are usually available in your local public library or law library, and can also be obtained from the pertinent city office for free or a small sum to cover reproduction costs.
- City and county agencies keep collections of ordinances that pertain to their agency.
- Special districts usually publish their regulations in paperbound pamphlets that can be obtained free or for a low price.

Ordinances, like statutes, are occasionally interpreted by the courts. If you want to find out whether or not an ordinance you're interested in has been considered by a court, use either *Shepard's Citations for Statutes* or a special volume called *Shepard's Ordinance Law Annotations*. This latter tool (not found in many law libraries) is organized by subject and provides references in respect to ordinances from all different parts of the country. (For instructions on how to Shepardize statutes or ordinances, see Chapter 9, *Finding Cases*, Section B2.)

REVIEW

Questions

1. *What's the first step when doing constitutional research?*
2. *What does each element of the citation Pub. L. No. 94-583 mean?*
3. *How many titles does the U.S. Code consist of?*
4. *What are names of the two annotated versions of the U.S. Code?*
5. *In addition to the federal statutes, what else do the annotated codes offer the legal researcher?*
6. *What information is contained in the following federal statute citation mean? 17 U.S.C.A. § 567*
7. *What are the three tools that let you find a federal statute by its popular name if you don't know its citation?*
8. *What is a statutory scheme?*
9. *What is the most common method for keeping state and federal annotated codes up to date?*
10. *What tools help you find recently enacted federal and state statutes that haven't yet been published in a pocket part?*
11. *What are the eight rules of statutory interpretation?*
12. *How does* Words and Phrases *help you interpret statutes?*
13. *What is the most common way to locate legislative history for a federal statute?*
14. *What special tool is available to help you understand a state statute that is based on a "uniform law"?*
15. *What publication contains the federal regulations?*

Answers

1. Find a good constitutional law hornbook written for law school students.
2. The Pub. L. stands for public law. The 94 stands for the Congress that passed the law (the 94th Congress). The 583 is the number that has been assigned to the statute.
3. 50.
4. *United States Code Annotated* (U.S.C.A.) and the *United States Code Service, Lawyer's Edition* (U.S.C.S.)
5. They contain information pertaining to each statute, including:
   - one-sentence summaries of court cases that have interpreted the statute
   - notes about the statute's history (amendments, etc.)
   - cross-references to other relevant statutes
   - cross-references to administrative regulations that may be helpful in interpreting the statute
   - citations to the legislative history of the statute
   - research guides (references to relevant materials by the same publisher).
6. The 17 means Title 17. U.S.C.A. means *United States Code Annotated*. § means section. 567 is the section number.
7.
   - the "popular names index" that follows the *United States Code Annotated* (U.S.C.A.)
   - the "popular names table" volume that accompanies the *United States Code Service, Lawyer's Edition* (U.S.C.S.)
   - the *Shepard's Acts and Cases By Popular Names*.
8. A group of statutes that are related to an overall subject matter. Sometimes an index will alert you to the existence of a statutory scheme by putting an "et seq" at the end of a single statutory reference. ("Et seq." means "and following.)

9. Pocket parts—paper supplements that fit inside each hardcover volume, usually at the back. Pocket parts are published once a year and contain any statutory changes occurring in the interim. When doing legal research in an annotated code, always remember to check the pocket part.

10. Each federal and state annotated code has a monthly advance legislative service that prints statutes a month or two after they have been passed by Congress or the state legislature. The one for U.S.C.A.. is called the U.S.C.A. *Quarterly Supplement* while the one for U.S.C.S. is known as the U.S.C.S. *Advance Legislative Service*. The names very for the state advance legislative services.

11. Rule 1: Read the statute over at least three times. Then read it again.

    Rule 2: Pay close attention to the "ands" and "ors."

    Rule 3: Assume all words and punctuation in the statute have meaning.

    Rule 4: Interpret a statute so that it is consistent with all other related statutes, if possible.

    Rule 5: Interpret criminal statutes strictly.

    Rule 6: Interpret ambiguities in statutes in ways that seem to best further the purpose of the legislation.

    Rule 7: Interpret the statute so that it makes sense and does not lead to absurd or improbable results.

    Rule 8: Track down all cross-references to other statutes and sections.

12. This publication contains one-sentence interpretations of common words and phrases that have been pulled from cases and organized alphabetically. It allows you to find out whether courts have interpreted or used any particular word or phrase you are interested in, and if so, how.

13. Most statutes in the annotated federal codes (U.S.C.A. and U.S.C.S.) are followed by a reference to the *U.S. Code Congressional and Administrative News*, which contains federal legislative history.

14. A series of books called the *Uniform Laws Annotated* (U.L.A.), published by West. It contains all of the uniform laws, the original comments accompanying them, a listing of the states that have adopted them, notations of how states have altered each provision in the course of adopting it, summaries of case opinions that have interpreted each statute, and references to pertinent law review discussions.

15. The *Code of Federal Regulations* (C.F.R).

CHAPTER 7

Understanding Case Law

Finding the right court decision (case) is the heart of the legal research method outlined in Chapter 2, *An Overview of Legal Research.* No matter how clear a statute or regulation may seem on its face—and few fit that description—you need to find out what the courts have done with it in situations like yours. And the best path to that result is first to find one relevant case that, through the cross-reference materials covered in Chapter 10, *Shepard's and Digests: Expand and Update Your Research*, will lead you to others.

This chapter introduces you to cases—what they are and how they influence later disputes. The next chapter (Chapter 8, *How Cases Are Published*) explains where you find cases. Chapter 9, *Finding Cases*, tells you how to find them.

A. What Is a Case?

A case starts in the trial court and may end up being appealed to a higher court—an intermediate appellate court or a supreme court. It is the published opinions of these appellate or supreme courts that make up most of the cases you will find in a law library. The books they are published in are called case reports or reporters.

1. The Nuts and Bolts of a Case

When you look at the beginning of a case in one of the reporters, you will find certain basic information. Look at the beginning of the *Keywell* case, which we have reproduced below, and follow along as we identify the important information contained on the first page.

The Citation The editors of the Federal Reporters make it impossible for you to forget what case you're reading. At the top of each right-hand page, the case name is given and you are told that you should cite the case as, for example, 33 F.3d 159 (2nd Cir. 1994).

The Parties In a civil case, the parties are known as the plaintiff (the one who filed the lawsuit) and the defendant (the one being sued). In a criminal case, the plaintiff is "the People" of the United States Government (if it's a federal case), or the People of one of the states (if it's a state case). The defendant is the person being charged with a crime.

Some reported cases are from the trial level (for example, all of the cases in "F. Supp" are from United States District Courts), and, in that case, the parties are identified as "plaintiff" and "defendant." When a reported case is from one of the appellate courts, the original parties are also identified as the appellant (the one who lost below and is now bringing the appeal) and the appellee (the one who won below and is now having to defend that victory).

In the *Keywell* case, Keywell corporation is identified as the "Plaintiff-Appellant." This label tells you that Keywell initiated the lawsuit at the trial level and was the one to file the present appeal. Weinstein and Boscarino were the defendants at the trial level and are the appellees now.

The Docket Number When a case is filed in the trial court, it is given a number, called the "docket number," by the clerk of the court. While the case remains in the trial court, it is referred to by that number. If the case goes to the appellate level, it will be given a different number by the clerk of the appellate court. If you wanted to examine the court file in either court, you would have to use that number when making your request at the clerk's office. The docket number is also the number that is attached to an opinion when it is first issued (as a "Slip Opinion"), before it goes into the reporter series and gets its permanent cite.

KEYWELL CORP. v. WEINSTEIN 159
Cite as 33 F.3d 159 (2nd Cir. 1994)

KEYWELL CORPORATION, Plaintiff-Appellant,

v.

Daniel C. WEINSTEIN and Anthony Boscarino, Defendants-Appellees.

No. 1208, Docket 93-7994.

United States Court of Appeals, Second Circuit.

Argued March 7, 1994.

Decided Aug. 23, 1994.

Purchaser of metal recycling plant brought suit under CERCLA against two shareholders, officers, and directors of selling corporation to recover environmental cleanup costs. The United States District Court for the Western District of New York, William M. Skretny, J., granted summary judgment for defendants, and purchaser appealed. The Court of Appeals, Jacobs, Circuit Judge, held that: (1) genuine issue of material fact on reasonableness of purchaser's reliance on seller's misrepresentations precluded summary judgment on fraud claims, but (2) purchaser was not entitled to recover cleanup costs under CERCLA, since parties clearly allocated risk of CERCLA liability to purchaser under terms of purchase agreement.

Affirmed in part, and reversed and remanded in part.

1. Federal Courts ⚷766

When reviewing district court's grant of summary judgment, Court of Appeals must determine whether genuine issue of material fact exists and whether district court correctly applied law.

2. Federal Civil Procedure ⚷2470.1

Summary judgment is appropriate only if, resolving all ambiguities and drawing all factual inferences in favor of nonmoving party, there is no genuine issue of material fact to be tried. Fed.Rules Civ.Proc.Rule 56(c), 28 U.S.C.A.

3. Federal Civil Procedure ⚷2544

Party seeking summary judgment bears burden of demonstrating absence of any genuine factual dispute. Fed.Rules Civ.Proc. Rule 56(c), 28 U.S.C.A.

4. Federal Civil Procedure ⚷2504

Purchaser raised genuine questions of fact on reasonableness of its reliance on sellers' misrepresentations regarding release of hazardous substances on property, precluding summary judgment for sellers on its claim of fraudulent misrepresentation under New York law, since reasonable jury could conclude that purchaser, having conducted environmental due diligence and received report that was consistent with sellers' representations that there had been no dumping or other release of hazardous waste on property, had no obligation to investigate further, despite recommendation for additional testing in environmental audit.

5. Contracts ⚷2

New York law applied to claim questioning validity of contract, though parties chose Maryland law to govern their contract, where contract was made in New York.

6. Contracts ⚷2

Questions concerning validity of contract should be determined by law of jurisdiction in which it was made.

7. Fraud ⚷3

In New York, plaintiff claiming fraudulent misrepresentation must prove that defendant made material false representation, defendant intended to defraud plaintiff thereby, plaintiff reasonably relied on representation, and plaintiff suffered damage as result of such reliance.

8. Fraud ⚷22(1)

When party is aware of circumstances that indicate certain representations may be false, that party cannot reasonably rely on those representations, but must make additional inquiry to determine their accuracy.

9. Fraud ⚷31

Defrauded party is permitted to affirm contract and seek relief in damages, rather than choose remedy of rescission.

Opinion in Keywell Corp. v. Weinstein

10. Health and Environment ⚡25.5(5.5)

Purchaser of metal recycling plant was not entitled to recover costs of environmental cleanup from two officers, directors, and majority shareholders of selling corporation as signatories to purchase agreement, where agreement clearly allocated risk of CERCLA liability, which purchaser assumed when indemnity period expired, as shortened by the signing of release. Comprehensive Environmental Response, Compensation, and Liability Act of 1980, §§ 107(a), 113(f), 42 U.S.C.A. §§ 9607(a), 9613(f).

11. Health and Environment ⚡25.5(5.5)

Private parties may contractually allocate among themselves any loss they may suffer by imposition of CERCLA liability. Comprehensive Environmental Response, Compensation, and Liability Act of 1980, § 107(e)(1), 42 U.S.C.A. § 9607(e)(1).

Stuart A. Smith, New York City (Alfred Ferrer III, Piper & Marbury, Joseph G. Finnerty, Jr., Charles P. Scheeler, of counsel) for plaintiff-appellant.

Thomas E. Lippard, Pittsburgh, PA (Craig E. Frischman, Thorp Reed & Armstrong, of counsel) for defendant-appellee Weinstein.

Jeremiah J. McCarthy, Buffalo, NY (Phillips, Lytle, Hitchcock, Blaine & Huber, of counsel) for defendant-appellee Boscarino.

Before: WALKER, JACOBS, Circuit Judges and CARMAN,* Judge.

JACOBS, Circuit Judge:

Keywell Corporation ("Keywell") has incurred costs for environmental cleanup at an industrial facility that it purchased in 1987 from Vac Air Alloys Corporation ("Vac Air"). Defendants–Appellees Daniel C. Weinstein ("Weinstein") and Anthony Boscarino ("Boscarino") were shareholders, officers and directors of Vac Air prior to the purchase and at the time of the transaction, and were signatories to the Purchase Agreement. Keywell has brought suit against Weinstein and Boscarino, (i) alleging that they induced Keywell to buy the property by making misrepresentations bearing upon the environmental risks at the premises, and (ii) alleging that, as owners and operators of Vac Air, they are strictly liable to Keywell for their equitable share of response costs pursuant to §§ 107(a) and 113(f) of the Comprehensive Environmental Response, Compensation, and Liability Act ("CERCLA"). 42 U.S.C. §§ 9607(a) and 9613(f). Following the parties' submission of cross-motions for summary judgment, the district court dismissed Keywell's claims, finding as a matter of law that Keywell could not have reasonably relied on the allegedly fraudulent misrepresentations, and that Keywell had contractually released its right to sue defendants under CERCLA.

We affirm the dismissal of the CERCLA claims on the ground that the parties allocated the risk of CERCLA liability in their Purchase Agreement, the terms of which establish that such risk now falls on Keywell. However, we reverse the dismissal of the diversity fraud claims and remand for further proceedings.

BACKGROUND

The facts, drawing all justifiable inferences in favor of the non-movant Keywell, are as follows. Weinstein founded Vac Air in 1966 and, until the time Keywell purchased certain Vac Air assets in December 1987, was a principal shareholder, president, chief executive officer, and member of the board of directors of the company. Boscarino joined Vac Air in 1971 as an assistant to the secretary/treasurer, and by 1978 he had become a stockholder, director, and vice-president of the company. Both Weinstein and Boscarino took an active part in conducting the business of Vac Air, which included the operation of a metals recycling plant located in Frewsburg, New York (the "Frewsburg plant").

From the time Vac Air was founded in 1966 until Keywell's acquisition of assets in December 1987, the Frewsburg plant recycled scrap metal—a process that entailed the

* Honorable Gregory W. Carman of the United States Court of International Trade, sitting by designation.

Keywell Corp. v. Weinstein (continued)

In the *Keywell* case, the docket number is "No. 1208 Docket Number 93-7994." When this case was first listed in *Shepard's*, the listing would have looked like this: "Dk2 93-7994." The "Dk2" tells you that this is a Slip Opinion from the Second Circuit.

The Court This is the name of the court that wrote the decision. In the *Keywell* case, the decision was written by the United States Court of Appeals for the Second Circuit, which heard the case. In order to find out which trial court had the case originally, you will have to read the **Summary**, discussed below.

The Dates Many opinions include the date that the case was argued and the date the court issued the opinion. If the decision announces a new rule of law, or invalidates a statute, the issue date will be important to know. (But watch out: opinions do not become "final" until the time for granting a rehearing has passed. The local rules for each court will specify how long that time period may be.)

The Summary This is usually a one-paragraph summary of the decision, written by the editors of the reporter series and not part of the decision itself. This text cannot be cited. If the opinion is from a trial court (like one you would read in "F. Supp.," which is the reporter series that contains federal district court cases), it will list the issue and the decision. If the opinion is from an appellate-level court, the summary will describe the trial court's decision and will go on to explain the holding of the appellate court.

The Decision Many Summaries end with a one-line phrase describing the holding of the court. In *Keywell*, we are told that the lower court's decision was "Affirmed in part, and reversed and remanded in part." This means that the decision of the trial court was upheld as to one or more issues, but that they were reversed on other issues and the case was sent back to the trial court for further proceedings as directed by the appellate decision.

LIBRARY EXERCISE

Finding the Nuts and Bolts of a Case

You are reading an employment discrimination case for a meeting of your research team. You will be expected to be familiar with the procedural aspects of the case. The case can be found at 3 F.3d 873. Locate the case and learn about its structural and procedural aspects.

Questions

1. *The name of the case is useful because that is how a case is often referred to by people familiar with it. What is the name of your case?*
2. *The citation of a case is how it is referred to in written materials, as in a memo to the court. What is the citation of your case?*
3. *Knowing the docket number of a case and the date of the decision will help you get information or documents from the court. Also, if the opinion is very recent, you need this information to get a copy of the slip opinion from the court or from Lexis. What are the docket number and date of decision of your case?*
4. *Knowing which Court wrote the opinion tells you what other decisions this court had to follow when deciding this case. It also tells you which courts are bound by this decision. What court heard* Moham *and wrote this opinion? What court decisions were the judges bound by, and who is bound by this opinion?*
5. *A trial is a presentation of evidence (witnesses' testimony and physical evidence) as well as lawyers' arguments linking facts and law. Typically, the judge makes decisions about the application of the law, and the jury makes findings of facts (verdicts). In an appeal, there is no presentation of evidence—the only question to be decided is whether the trial court correctly applied the law. Is* Moham *from a trial or appellate court?*

6a. *It is important to know what happened in the lower court in order to understand what issues are being appealed and what will happen as a result of the decision. Where was the trial held?*

6b. *Who was the plaintiff and who was the defendant?*

6c. *Who won in the trial court?*

6d. *Who appealed to the Fifth Circuit?*

7. *What does the Summary of the case tell you about the appellate court's decision?*

Answers

1. The name of the case is *Moham v. Steego*. In a discussion, people would call it "Moham."
2. *Moham v. Steego Corp.*, 3 F.3d 873 (5th Cir. 1993)
3. The docket number is 92-5165, and the date of the decision is September 27, 1973.
4. The U.S. Court of Appeals for the 5th Circuit heard this case. The three judges on the appellate panel were bound by prior decisions of the 5th Circuit. This decision will be precedent for appellate and trial courts within the Fifth Circuit.
5. *Moham* is a decision from an appellate court, and therefore it will discuss whether the lower court correctly understood and applied the law.

6a. The trial was held in the United States District Court for the Western District of Louisiana.

6b. Mr. Moham was the plaintiff, and Steego Corporation was the defendant.

6c. The trial judge found for the employee, Mr. Moham.

6d. Steego Corporation, who lost below, was the appellant; and Mr. Moham, who won, became the appellee.

7. It seems that everyone got something as a result of this trip to the appellate courthouse. The decision of the lower court was "affirmed in part" (meaning that some of its decision was left intact); it was "reversed and rendered in part" (meaning that a part of the judge's decision was overturned and the correct decision was substituted by the appellate court); and it was "remanded" (meaning that the case was sent back to the trial court to re-do some aspect of it in accordance with the instructions contained in the appellate decision).

2. How the Opinion Itself Is Organized

Normally, every intermediate appellate or supreme court opinion contains four basic elements:

1. A detailed statement of the facts that are accepted by the court as true. These facts are taken from the lower court's determination of the facts, unless the lower court's determinations were clearly in error. For intermediate appellate courts, the lower court is usually the trial court. For supreme courts, the lower court is usually the intermediate appellate court.
2. A statement of the legal issue or issues presented by the appealing parties for resolution.
3. An answer to the issues presented for resolution—this is called the ruling or holding. In appeals, the court always takes some specific action. If it agrees with the lower court's conclusions and the relief it ordered for one or both of the parties, the lower court decision is "affirmed." If the court disagrees with either or both of these aspects of the lower court's decision, the decision is "reversed."

Sometimes lower court decisions are affirmed in part and reversed in part. If the intermediate appellate or supreme court agrees substantially with the lower court, but disagrees with some particular point, it may modify or amend the decision. Usually, in the case of a complete or partial reversal, the case is sent back to the lower court to take further action consistent with the intermediate appellate or supreme court's opinion. This is called a remand.

Courts Where Appeals Are Normally Filed

Courts Cases Appealed from	*U.S. Supreme Court*	*U.S. Court of Appeals*	*State Supreme Court*	*State Court of Appeal*
U.S. Courts of Appeal	X			
U.S. District Courts	if issued by a 3 judge panel OR when the U.S., its agent or employee is a party, and an act of Congress is held unconstitutional on its face (not as applied)	X		
State Supreme Courts	if a federal question is involved			
State Courts of Appeal	if a federal question is involved, and the State Supreme Court has denied relief OR declined to hear the case.		X	
State Trial Courts			if there's no court of appeal OR it is a special case (appeal of death penalty case)	X

4. A discussion of why the ruling was made—the court's reasoning or rationale.

The court's reasoning is usually the longest part of the case and most difficult to understand, for a number of reasons:

- The legal issues are complex and require a complex chain of reasoning to unravel.
- The court doesn't understand the legal issues but has to address them anyway because the legal world expects it.
- The court decides the case contrary to established law and spends a lot of time trying to explain this fact away.
- The judge doesn't know how to write.

A major part of law school training is how to analyze this element of court opinions and apply it to other cases. This book can't replace law school, but most researchers get the hang of legal reasoning after reading a few dozen cases. Also, consider reading Statsky, *Case Analysis and Fundamentals of Legal Writing* (3rd Ed., West Publishing Co. 1989) for a structured introduction to case analysis.

Many court opinions present these four components—facts, issues, decision and reasoning—in this order. Others do not. For instance, one format used by some courts is a summary of the issue and the decision in the first couple of paragraphs, followed by a statement of the facts and the reasoning.

The actual opinion issued in a case called *Deason v. Metropolitan Property & Liability Insurance Co.* is shown below. The four elements described above are labeled.

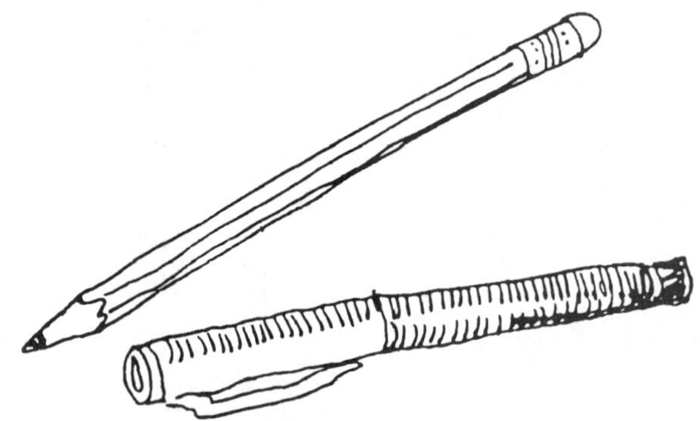

130 Ill.App.3d 620
85 Ill.Dec. 823

Mary Kaye DEASON, Administratrix of the Estate of David A. Deason, Deceased, and Mary Kaye Deason, Plaintiff-Appellee,

and

Florence Petro, Administrator of the Estate of George Petro, deceased; Sherrill Josephson, Administratrix of the Estate of Mathew Josephson, deceased; and Michael Petro, Counter-Plaintiffs-Appellees,

v.

METROPOLITAN PROPERTY & LIABILITY INSURANCE COMPANY, a Corporation, Defendant-Appellant,

and

Auto-Owners Insurance Company, a Corporation, et al., Defendants.

No. 5-84-0073.

Appellate Court of Illinois,
Fifth District.

Jan. 10, 1985.

Action was brought against automobile insurer seeking a judgment declaring that policy issued to driver's parents afforded secondary coverage in connection with an accident which occurred while insureds' son was driving his grandmother's automobile. The Circuit Court, St. Clair County, Richard P. Goldenhersh, J., entered judgment in favor of plaintiffs, and insurer appealed. The Appellate Court, Harrison, J., held that automobile operated by driver was not a "temporary substitute vehicle" under terms of automobile policy issued to parents so as to afford secondary coverage in connection with driver's accident.

Reversed.

1. Declaratory Judgment ⇐168

Case involving question whether coverage existed under terms of automobile insurer's policy was proper subject for declaratory judgment action.

2. Insurance ⇐435.2(4)

Where driver's use of his grandmother's automobile was not to be temporary, but regular and permanent, and the automobile was not intended by driver's parents to be a substitute for either of two automobiles owned by driver's father, under terms of automobile policy issued to parents, the automobile operated by driver was not a "temporary substitute vehicle" so as to afford secondary coverage in connection with driver's accident.

See publication Words and Phrases for other judicial constructions and definitions.

3. Evidence ⇐200

In action brought against automobile insurer seeking a judgment declaring that policy issued to driver's parents afforded secondary coverage in connection with an accident which occurred while insureds' son was driving his grandmother's automobile, trial court correctly noted in its judgment that statements by certain employees of insurer to the effect that they believed driver's parents' policy afforded coverage were merely opinions and were not binding on a court in its consideration of the legal question presented.

Feirich, Schoen, Mager, Green & Associates, Carbondale, for defendant-appellant.

C.E. Heiligenstein, Brad L. Badgley, Belleville, for Mary Kaye Deason.

H. Carl Runge, Jr., Runge & Gumbel, P.C., Collinsville, for Beth Martell, a minor, by her father and next friend, John Martell, John Martell and Patsie Gott, Administratrix of the Estate of Lisa J. Gott, Deceased.

Michael P. Casey, Edward R. Vrdolyak, Ltd., Chicago, for Florence Petro & Sherrill Josephson & Michael Petro.

HARRISON, Justice:

[1] Metropolitan Property & Liability Insurance Company (hereinafter referred to as Metropolitan) appeals from a judgment of the circuit court of St. Clair Coun-

Opinion in Deason v. Metropolitan

Issue

ty declaring that a policy of insurance issued by Metropolitan afforded secondary coverage in connection with a November 30, 1980, accident involving a 1975 Mercury Comet driven by Christopher Warner. The primary issue for our consideration is whether the trial court properly concluded that, under the terms of the policy issued by Metropolitan to Christopher Warner's parents, the Comet operated by Christopher Warner was a "temporary substitute automobile". Because this case involves the question of whether or not coverage exists under the terms of Metropolitan's policy, it is a proper subject for a declaratory judgment action. *Reagor v. Travelers Insurance Co.* (1980), 92 Ill.App.3d 99, 102–03, 47 Ill.Dec. 507, 415 N.E.2d 512.

The policy in question provides coverage to the insured for accidents arising out of the ownership, maintenance or use of an owned or non-owned automobile. The terms "non-owned automobile" and "owned automobile" are defined in the policy as follows:

> " '*[N]on-owned automobile*' means an *automobile* which is neither owned by nor furnished nor available for the regular use of either the *named insured* or any *relative*, other than a *temporary substitute automobile*, and includes a *utility trailer* while used with any such *automobile:*
>
> * * * * * *
>
> '*[O]wned automobile*' means
>
> (a) a *private passenger automobile* or *utility automobile* owned by the *named insured* and described in the Declarations to which the Automobile Liability Coverage of the policy applies and for which a specific premium for such insurance is charged, or
>
> (b) a *private passenger automobile* or *utility automobile* ownership of which is newly acquired by the *named insured*, provided (i) it replaces an *owned automobile* as defined in (a) above, or (ii) METROPOLITAN insures all *automobiles* owned by the *named insured* on the date of such acquisition and the *named insured* notifies METROPOLITAN within thirty (30) days of such acquisition of his election to make this and no other policy issued by METROPOLITAN applicable to such *automobile* and pays any additional premium required therefor, or
>
> (c) a *temporary substitute automobile:*"

The policy defines "temporary substitute automobile" in this manner:

> " '*[T]emporary substitute automobile*' means an *automobile* not owned by the *named insured* or any resident of the same household, while temporarily used with the permission of the owner as a substitute for an *owned automobile* when withdrawn from normal use for servicing or repair or because of breakdown, loss or destruction:"

facts

The facts relevant to a determination of whether the 1975 Comet was a temporary substitute automobile are not in significant dispute. Christopher Warner spent the summer of 1980 in Ohio with his grandmother, Vera Fry. Ms. Fry, an Ohio resident, owned the 1975 Comet, which was insured by a company other than Metropolitan. During that summer, arrangements were made whereby Christopher would take the Comet with him when he returned to his parents' Cobden, Illinois home at the end of the summer. It was further agreed that Christopher would return to Ohio at Christmas time and pay Vera Fry $100 after which she would have the title to the Comet transferred to Christopher and one of his parents. Christopher did in fact bring the Comet back to Cobden in August, 1980, and he and his parents used it regularly. On November 30, 1980, before Christopher had paid any money to Vera Fry, and before title to the Comet had been transferred, the accident in question occurred.

On the date of the accident, Andrew Warner, Christopher's father, owned a 1973 Mercury and a 1974 Dodge pickup truck. Both of these vehicles were insured by Metropolitan. Neither was operable at

Opinion in Deason v. Metropolitan (continued)

the time of the accident; the Mercury had a defective transmission and the Dodge had a twisted drive shaft. Both vehicles were put back into operation shortly after the accident involving the Comet. During his deposition, Andrew Warner testified as follows:

"Q. Did you have any intention if the Comet hadn't been wrecked, did you have any intention to dispose of either of these other two cars just because you got the Comet?

A. Oh, no."

holding

[2] In ruling that Metropolitan's policy afforded secondary coverage in connection with the accident involving the 1975 Comet, the court found that Christopher Warner was "a relative operating a temporary substitute" automobile. Metropolitan contends that this conclusion is incorrect, and we are compelled to agree. Under the terms of the policy, a temporary substitute automobile is defined as one "temporarily used with the permission of the owner as a substitute for an owned automobile when withdrawn from normal use for servicing or repair or because of breakdown, loss, or destruction." Here, the unequivocal deposition testimony of all concerned establishes that Christopher Warner's use of the Comet was not to be temporary, but regular and permanent, as it was the intention of both Vera Fry and Christopher Warner that he would pay $100 for the car at Christmas time, and would not return it to her. Moreover, the Comet was not intended by the Warners to be a substitute for either the Mercury or the Dodge; rather, it was to be kept as a third car, and the fact that the Dodge and Mercury broke down during the Warners' use of the Comet was entirely coincidental. Under these circumstances, the "temporary substitute" provision of the policy issued by Metropolitan did not encompass Christopher Warner's use of the Comet on the date of the accident. (See *Sturgeon v. Automobile Club Inter-Insurance Exchange* (1979), 77 Ill. App.3d 997, 1000, 34 Ill.Dec. 66, 397 N.E.2d 522.) This conclusion is buttressed by the holding of *Nationwide Insurance Company v. Ervin* (1967), 87 Ill.App.2d 432, 436-37, 231 N.E.2d 112, wherein it was recognized that a "temporary substitute" provision of the type under consideration here is to be applied to those situations where an insured automobile is withdrawn from use for a short period, and not where, as here, coverage is sought to be extended to an additional automobile for a significant length of time.

rationale

[3] *Providence Mutual Casualty Company v. Sturms* (1962), 37 Ill.App.2d 304, 185 N.E.2d 366, relied on by appellees, is not on point. *Sturms* addresses the question of whether coverage afforded on a temporary substitute automobile expires immediately upon repair of the insured's regular automobile (37 Ill.App.2d 304, 306, 185 N.E.2d 366), and does not discuss the more fundamental issue of when a vehicle is considered to be a temporary substitute in the first place. While appellees also suggest that portions of Metropolitan's claim file show that certain Metropolitan employees believe that the policy in question afforded coverage, the trial court correctly noted in its judgment that these statements are merely opinions, and are not binding on a court in its consideration of the legal question presented. 31A C.J.S. *Evidence* § 272(b) (1964).

For the foregoing reasons, the judgment of the circuit court of St. Clair County is reversed.

Reversed.

JONES, P.J., and KARNS, J., concur.

Opinion in Deason v. Metropolitan (continued)

HOW APPELLATE COURTS DECIDE CASES

Appellate courts comprise anywhere from three to nine justices. For example, the California Supreme Court and the New York Court of Appeals[1] have seven justices, the Vermont Supreme Court has five, and the U.S. Supreme Court has nine.

Only the actual decision of the majority (or plurality) of justices and the principles of law that are absolutely necessary to that decision serve as precedent for other courts. Other discussion in the opinion may be helpful in understanding the decision, but is not binding on other courts. The court's decision and the law necessary to arrive at it is called the "holding." The rest of the decision is called "dicta." See Section B1, below, for a fuller discussion of precedent.

A justice on an appellate court who disagrees with the decision of the majority on a case may issue a dissenting opinion, which is published along with the majority's opinion. No matter how passionate a dissent happens to be, it has no effect on the particular case. However, it may have a persuasive effect on judges in future court decisions.

A justice who agrees with the majority decision but disagrees with the reasons given for it may issue a "concurring opinion," which is published along with the majority's opinion. A concurring opinion also can have a persuasive influence on future court decisions.

If the main opinion in the case is supported by less than a majority—called a "plurality" opinion—the concurring opinion can in fact operate as a weak type of authority for future cases. For instance, in a 1985 case, the U.S. Supreme Court issued an opinion in which only four justices joined. A fifth justice, Chief Justice Burger, concurred and swung the court's holding to the plurality's view; if Chief Justice Burger had sided with the other four justices, they might have been the majority (or plurality, if he only concurred with and did not join their opinion).

For a fascinating account of how the U.S. Supreme Court decides its cases, read The Brethren: Inside the Supreme Court, *by Woodward and Armstrong (Simon and Schuster, 1979).*

[1]In New York State (and in Texas for criminal cases) the highest state court is called the Court of Appeals rather than the Supreme Court.

3. Using Synopses and Headnotes to Read and Understand a Case

In addition to the court opinions, the publishers of case reports also publish a one paragraph synopsis of the case and some helpful one-sentence summaries of the legal issues discussed in it. The synopsis and "headnotes" come just before the opinion itself. Below are the headnotes from *Deason v. Metropolitan Property & Liability Insurance Co.*

The headnotes are numbered in the order in which the legal issues they summarize appear in the opinion. The part of the opinion covered by each headnote is marked off in the opinion with a number in brackets. See the *Deason* opinion, above, for an example.

Headnotes can be very useful in several ways. They serve as a table of contents to the opinion, so that if you are only interested in one of the many issues raised in a case, you can skim the headnotes, find the relevant issue, and then turn to the corresponding bracketed number in the opinion. Headnotes also allow discussions of legal issues in one case to be cross-indexed to similar discussions in other cases by the use of "digests." (See Chapter 10.) Finally, headnotes are very helpful when you are "Shepardizing" a case. (See Chapter 10.)

Headnotes are prepared by the publisher and are not part of the case as such. Because the editors who prepare the headnotes are human and fallible, don't rely on the headnotes to accurately state the issue or principle of law as it appears in the opinion. You must read the pertinent section of the opinion for yourself. Never quote a headnote in any argument you submit to a court.

DEASON v. METRO. PROP. & LIABILITY INS. CO. Ill. 783
Cite as 474 N.E.2d 783 (Ill.App. 5 Dist. 1985)

130 Ill.App.3d 620
85 Ill.Dec. 823

Mary Kaye DEASON, Administratrix of the Estate of David A. Deason, Deceased, and Mary Kaye Deason, Plaintiff-Appellee,

and

Florence Petro, Administrator of the Estate of George Petro, deceased; Sherrill Josephson, Administratrix of the Estate of Mathew Josephson, deceased; and Michael Petro, Counter-Plaintiffs-Appellees,

v.

METROPOLITAN PROPERTY & LIABILITY INSURANCE COMPANY, a Corporation, Defendant-Appellant,

and

Auto-Owners Insurance Company, a Corporation, et al., Defendants.

No. 5–84–0073.

Appellate Court of Illinois, Fifth District.

Jan. 10, 1985.

Action was brought against automobile insurer seeking a judgment declaring that policy issued to driver's parents afforded secondary coverage in connection with an accident which occurred while insureds' son was driving his grandmother's automobile. The Circuit Court, St. Clair County, Richard P. Goldenhersh, J., entered judgment in favor of plaintiffs, and insurer appealed. The Appellate Court, Harrison, J., held that automobile operated by driver was not a "temporary substitute vehicle" under terms of automobile policy issued to parents so as to afford secondary coverage in connection with driver's accident.

Reversed.

→ **1. Declaratory Judgment ⚷168**

Case involving question whether coverage existed under terms of automobile insurer's policy was proper subject for declaratory judgment action.

2. Insurance ⚷435.2(4) ←

Where driver's use of his grandmother's automobile was not to be temporary, but regular and permanent, and the automobile was not intended by driver's parents to be a substitute for either of two automobiles owned by driver's father, under terms of automobile policy issued to parents, the automobile operated by driver was not a "temporary substitute vehicle" so as to afford secondary coverage in connection with driver's accident.

See publication Words and Phrases for other judicial constructions and definitions.

3. Evidence ⚷200 ←

In action brought against automobile insurer seeking a judgment declaring that policy issued to driver's parents afforded secondary coverage in connection with an accident which occurred while insureds' son was driving his grandmother's automobile, trial court correctly noted in its judgment that statements by certain employees of insurer to the effect that they believed driver's parents' policy afforded coverage were merely opinions and were not binding on a court in its consideration of the legal question presented.

Headnotes from Deason v. Metropolitan Property & Liability Insurance Co.

B. How Cases Affect Later Disputes

Past decisions in appellate cases are powerful predictors of what the courts are likely to do in future cases given a similar set of facts. Most judges try hard to be consistent with decisions that either they or a higher court have made. This consistency is very important to a just legal system and is the essence of the common law tradition. (Common law—the decisions of courts over the years—is discussed in Chapter 3, *An Overview of the Law*.) For this reason, if you can find a previous court decision that rules your way on facts similar to your situation, you have a good shot at persuading a judge to follow that case and decide in your favor.

There are two basic principles to understand when you're reading cases with an eye to using them to persuade a judge to rule your way. One is called "precedent," the other "persuasive authority."

1. Precedent

In the legal sense, a "precedent" is an earlier case that is relevant to a case to be decided. If there is nothing to distinguish the circumstances of the current case from the already-decided one, the earlier holding is considered binding on the court.

The idea of a precedent comes from a basic principle of the American common law system: *stare decisis* (Latin for "Let the decision stand"). Once a high court decides how the law should be applied to a particular set of facts, this decision controls later decisions by that and other courts. For example, a majority of the present U.S. Supreme Court is thought to dislike the common law rule that illegally seized evidence cannot be used in a criminal prosecution. Yet, because this rule was created in past Supreme Court cases, the present court continues to uphold it (while carving out more and more exceptions).

A case is only a precedent as to its particular decision and the law necessary to arrive at that decision. If, in passing, a judge deals with a legal question that is not absolutely essential to the decision, the reasoning and opinion in respect to this tangential question are not precedent, but non-binding "dicta."

Example A Court of Appeals rules that the Lesser Dung Beetle is protected under the Endangered Species Act. As part of his reasoning, the judge writing the opinion states that as he reads the statute, even mosquitoes are entitled to protection. Since the court was asked to rule on the Lesser Dung Beetle, the judge's comments on mosquitoes are dicta—language unnecessary to deciding the case before the court—and not binding as to any future dispute on that point.

It is common for courts to avoid overruling earlier decisions by distinguishing the earlier one from the present one on the basis of some insignificant factual difference or small legal issue. It is much easier to get a court to "distinguish" an old case than openly overrule it. Simply put, it is sometimes difficult to tell whether an earlier case has been overruled (and is clearly no longer precedent) or distinguished (and therefore technically still operative as precedent). (See Chapter 12, *The Legal Research Method: Examples*.)

On the other hand, prior decisions are sometimes expressly overruled as not being consistent with the times. When the U.S. Supreme Court decided *Brown v. Board of Education* in 1954, it held that separate educational facilities for black and white students were unconstitutional. That overruled a 19th century case called *Plessy v. Ferguson*, which had held that such "separate but equal" facilities were constitutional.

A case is only precedent as to a particular set of facts and the precise legal issue decided in light of those facts. The more the facts or legal issues vary between two cases, the less the former operates as precedent in respect to the latter. Teaching the art of distinguishing cases on the basis of the facts and issues decided is what most of law school is all about.

In addition to the degree of similarity between an earlier and a later case, the precedential value of the earlier case is affected by which court decided it. Here are some guidelines for determining the effect that one court's decisions have on another's:

- Appellate court cases (including supreme court cases) operate as precedent with respect to future decisions by the same courts.

  Example In 2020, the Indiana Supreme Court rules that county general relief grants cannot be terminated without first providing the recipient with a hearing. In 2021, a fiscally strapped county cuts everyone off general assistance without hearings. A group of recipients seeks court relief. In 2021, the issue gets to the Indiana Supreme Court, which orders the recipients reinstated on the ground of its earlier ruling.

- U.S. Supreme Court cases are precedent for all courts in respect to decisions involving the U.S. Constitution or any aspect of federal law.

  Example In 2020, the U.S. Supreme Court rules that under the First Amendment to the U.S. Constitution, non-lawyers may help the public use self-help law books without being charged with the unauthorized practice of law. In 2021, the Nebraska Bar Association sues a non-lawyer to stop him from telling people how to use a self-help divorce book. He claims a violation of his First Amendment rights and wins on the basis of the U.S. Supreme Court case.

- U.S. Courts of Appeal cases are precedent for U.S. District Courts within their circuits (that is, the states covered by the circuit) and for state courts in this area with respect to issues concerning the U.S. Constitution and any aspect of federal law. (The country is divided into 12 circuits—see list in Chapter 8, *How Cases Are Published*.)

  Example In 2020, the U.S. Court of Appeal for the First Circuit rules that the Eighth Amendment to the U.S. Constitution requires that bail in a criminal case be set in an amount that the defendant can reasonably afford to raise. In 1999, Perry is charged in the U.S. District Court for New Hampshire with the crime of assault against a federal officer. Since the U.S. District Court for New Hampshire is within the First Circuit, it must follow the rule for bail laid down by the Court of Appeal for that circuit. However, if Perry were charged with the crime in the U.S. District Court in Vermont—which is in the Second Circuit—the First Circuit case would not be binding.

  If Perry were charged with a crime in a New Hampshire state court, he would still be entitled to the new bail rule, since it is based on the U.S.

Constitution and New Hampshire is within the First Circuit.

- U.S. District Court case opinions are never precedent for other courts. (They may be persuasive authority; see subsection 2, below.)

  Example A U.S. District Court in Hawaii rules that the Federal Endangered Species Act applies to mosquitoes. A U.S. District Court in Houston is asked to stop a local development because it threatens an endangered mosquito species. The U.S. District Court in Houston is free to follow the Hawaii case or reach a different conclusion.

- State supreme court cases are precedent with respect to all courts within the state.

  Example The Nevada Supreme Court rules that casinos may not require female employees to wear sexy outfits. This ruling is binding on all Nevada courts that are later faced with this issue.

- State intermediate appellate court cases are precedent with respect to the trial courts in the state. In larger states (for example, California), where the intermediate appellate courts are divided into districts (for instance, the fifth appellate district, the second appellate district) any particular intermediate appellate court's decision is sometimes only regarded as precedent by the trial courts within that district.

  Example In 1996, the intermediate appellate court for the fifth appellate district in California rules that preparing an uncontested divorce petition for another is not the practice of law. As long as this is the only intermediate appellate court ruling on this issue in the state, it is binding on all California trial courts. In 1997, the intermediate appellate court for the second appellate district rules that preparing an uncontested divorce petition is the practice of law and can only be done by attorneys. The first ruling, from the fifth appellate district, is binding on the trial courts located within that district—for example, those in Fresno. The second ruling is binding on trial courts in the second appellate district—for instance, Los Angeles. Trial courts in other appellate districts can follow either precedent, until their intermediate appellate courts issue their own rulings.

2. Persuasive Authority

If a case is not precedent, binding on later courts, but contains an excellent analysis of the legal issues and provides guidance for any court that happens to read it, it is "persuasive authority." For example, the landmark California Supreme Court case of *Marvin v. Marvin*, the first major case establishing the principle of "palimony," was considered persuasive authority by many courts in other states when considering the same issue, though the *Marvin* decision was not binding on courts outside California.

As a general rule, the higher the court, the more persuasive its opinion. Every word (even dicta) of a U.S. Supreme Court opinion is considered important in assessing the state of the law. Opinions written by an intermediate appellate court in a small state, however, are not nearly so influential on other courts.

Example In the case below, a Colorado court used cases from Hawaii, Texas and New York as guidance in arriving at its own decision.

must inevitably result in suppressing protected speech." *Id.* at 526, 528, 78 S.Ct. at 1342, 1343.

Presumptions similar or identical to the one at issue here have been invalidated as unconstitutional by various courts. In *State v. Bumanglag,* 63 Hawaii 596, 634 P.2d 80 (1981), for example, the court held that such a presumption [18] impermissibly inhibited free expression: "Its application would tend to limit public access to protected material because booksellers may then restrict what they offer to works they are familiar with and consider 'safe.' The distribution of protected, as well as obscene, matter may be affected by this self-censorship." [19] 634 P.2d at 96.

In *Davis v. State,* 658 S.W.2d 572 (Tex. Crim.App.1983), the court perceived a similar danger to the guarantees of the first amendment, noting that, especially in the case of a large establishment, "[t]he risk of suppressing freedom of expression is not negligible; ... it rises to astronomical proportions." 658 S.W.2d at 579. In addition to observing that the presumption cannot survive due process analysis, *see Leary v. United States,* 395 U.S. 6, 89 S.Ct. 1532, 23 L.Ed.2d 57 (1969), the Texas court concluded that "[f]reedom of expression is too important a right to allow it to be seriously impeded or impaired by a presumption such as the one implicated in this case." 658 S.W.2d at 580. *See also Grove Press, Inc. v. Evans,* 306 F.Supp. 1084 (E.D.Va.1969); *Skinner v. State,* 647 S.W.2d 686 (Tex.App. 1982) (presumption impermissibly shifts burden of proof and eliminates element of scienter); Model Penal Code § 251.4(2), comment 11 (1980) ("A presumption that one who disseminates or possesses obscene material in the course of his business does so knowingly or recklessly places a severe burden of prior examination and screening on legitimate business. It seems unlikely today that such a presumption would pass constitutional scrutiny."); Note, *The Scienter Requirement in Criminal Obscenity Prosecutions,* 41 N.Y.U.L.Rev. 791, 797–99 (1966) (evidentiary presumptions similar to the one at issue here are invalid after *Smith v. California*).

The Supreme Court has, on one occasion, expressly declined to reach the issue of the constitutionality of such presumptions. *Ginsberg v. New York,* 390 U.S. 629, 632 n. 1, 88 S.Ct. 1274, 1276 n. 1, 20 L.Ed.2d 195 (1968). More recently, however, in a case in which the same issue was raised, the Supreme Court dismissed an appeal for want of a substantial federal question in *People v. Kirkpatrick,* 32 N.Y.2d 17, 343 N.Y.S.2d 70, 295 N.E.2d 753 (1973), *appeal dismissed,* 414 U.S. 948, 94 S.Ct. 283, 38 L.Ed.2d 204 (1973). In *Kirkpatrick,* the state courts upheld the constitutionality of a statutory presumption that the seller of obscene materials knows the contents of that material, and also held that there was sufficient independent evidence of scienter to support the conviction.

[23] This dismissal, in its procedural context, was equivalent to an adjudication of the federal issue on its merits.[20] *Hicks*

18. HRS § 712–1214 provided that:

(1) A person commits the offense of promoting pornography if, knowing its content and character, he:
(a) Disseminates for monetary consideration any pornographic material....

The presumption at issue, contained in HRS § 712–1216, provided that:

(1) The fact that a person engaged in the conduct specified by sections 712–1214 or 712–1215 is prima facie evidence that he engaged in that conduct with knowledge of the character and content of the material disseminated or the performance produced, presented, directed, participated in, exhibited, or to be exhibited....

19. Additionally, the court in *Bumanglag* implied that the challenged presumption violated due process. The court agreed that salespeople generally were less likely than not to know the contents of their entire stock: "We find this difficult to discount, for a conclusion that a person who sold a book also was familiar with its character and content does not comport with what common sense and experience tell us about booksellers, salesclerks and their knowledge of the contents of books." 634 P.2d at 96.

20. We are aware that summary affirmances have sometimes been accorded less than full precedential weight by the Supreme Court. *See Edelman v. Jordan,* 415 U.S. 651, 671, 94 S.Ct. 1347, 1359, 39 L.Ed.2d 662 (1974); *Richardson*

Colorado Case

3. How to Analyze the Effect of an Earlier Case on Your Issue

Reading cases and understanding how they apply to your issue can be vexing. Most law and paralegal schools offer an entire course on case analysis. Obviously this book can't replace that training. The sidebar below offers one possible approach, and a close reading of Statsky's *Case Analysis* will definitely help. But you may have to put in a number of hours of practice before you feel comfortable with the case analysis process.

STEPS TO ANALYZING THE EFFECT OF AN EARLIER CASE

Step 1. Identify the precise issues decided in the case—that is, what issues of law the court had to decide in order to make its ruling.

Step 2. Compare the issues in the case to the issues you are interested in and decide whether the case addresses one or more of them. If so, move to Step 3. If not, the case is probably not helpful.

Step 3. Carefully read and understand the facts underlying the case and compare them to the facts of your situation. Does the case's decision on the relevant issues logically stand up when applied to your facts? If so move to Step 4. If not, go to Step 5

Step 4. Determine whether the court that decided the case you are reading creates precedent for the trial or appellate courts in your area. If so, the case may serve as precedent. If not, move to Step 5.

Step 5. Carefully read and understand the legal reasoning employed by the court when deciding the relevant issues and decide whether it logically would help another court resolve your issues? If so, the case may be persuasive authority.

ARGUING THE LAW

You can often find two attorneys in the same courtroom relying on the same case to support two diametrically opposed positions. This is, at least in part, because lawyers are adept at hairsplitting. Distinguishing one very similar fact situation from another so that the distinguished case will not be used as precedent or persuasive authority in the case you are arguing is a highly developed art. If you want to succeed in the legal world, you must be ready to hairsplit with the best of them. For assistance in learning this valuable legal skill, consult Statsky, Case Analysis and Fundamentals of Legal Writing *(3rd Ed., West Publishing Co. 1989).*

LIBRARY EXERCISE

Anatomy of a U.S. Supreme Court Case

You are reading another employment discrimination case for your research team. This one is a U. S. Supreme Court case and, in addition to understanding the facts and the holding of the case, you will be expected to explain the structural details of the case. The case can be found on page 538 of volume 108 of the Supreme Court Reporter.

Questions

1. *What is the name of the case?*
2. *What is the citation? This is how you will refer to the case in written memos to your boss or to a court. (Note that United States Supreme Court decisions are printed in three reporters. Citations to all of them are included in a complete written citation, with the official reporter (U.S.) listed first.)*
3. *What is the docket number and what is the date of decision?*
4. *What happened in the lower courts? Where do you look for a quick answer to this question?*

5a. *The Supreme Court made a decision that affected the individuals involved (the probation officer and the judge); it also explained or announced a rule of law that others can rely upon and should follow. What happened as far as the individuals were concerned? What does "reversed and remanded" mean?*

5b. *What legal rule did the Supreme Court decide should be used in the case?*

6. *If you wanted to read the opinion of the Court of Appeals which had been vacated by the grant of* certiori *in this case, where would you find it?*
7. *How could you find out what happened to the parties in this case after they returned to the trial court?*
8. *At the end of page 539, there is a syllabus (synopsis of the case). Is this text a part of the opinion, and can it be cited and used as authority?*
9. *Where does the opinion itself start?*
10. *Who wrote the headnotes numbered 1 through 6 on page 539?*
11. *On page 543, about two-thirds of the way down the left column, there is a paragraph with a "[5]" in front of it. What does the "[5]"mean?*

Answers

1. The name of the case is "*Forrester v. White.*"
2. *Forrester v. White*, (1988) 484 U.S. 219; 98 L.Ed.2d 55; 108 S. Ct. 538.
3. The docket number is #86-761, and the decision was issued on January 12, 1988.
4. A quick summary of the decision is found directly after the argument and decision dates. At the trial in the U.S. District Court, the plaintiff, a probation officer, alleged she was demoted and fired by her superior (a judge) because of sexual discrimination. The judge, who was the defendant, claimed that hiring and firing probation officers was a judicial function and that, consequently, he was protected from suit by disgruntled former employees by virtue of his judicial immunity. The jury decided in favor of the plaintiff, but the court granted the defendant's motion for summary judgment on the grounds that he was immune from civil suit. The Court of Appeals affirmed (agreed with) the District Court's decision. Forrester then appealed to the U.S. Supreme Court.

5a. "Reversed" means that the Supreme Court disagreed with the Court of Appeals as to what the rule of law should be. "Remanded" means that, having set the appellate court straight, the Supreme Court sent the case back to the appellate court to decide the issues remaining in the appeal in keeping with the Supreme Court's instruction on the law.

5b. The Supreme Court held that a state court judge was not immune from being sued for sexual discrimination when he dismissed a probation officer because this was an administrative, rather than a judicial, function.

6. The original Court of Appeals opinion would be found at 792 F.2d 647. This citation was included in the summary.
7. The end of the summary notes that the "Opinion on remand" will be found at 846 F.2d 29.
8. No, the "Syllabus" was written by an editor who works for the reporter series (West's), and it may not be cited.
9. The portion of the opinion that may be cited as authority begins at the end of page 540.
10. The editors of the reporter read the opinion and assign headnotes to various sections.
11. This is the part of the opinion which is summarized in headnote 5.

REVIEW

Questions

1. *What is a "case" for the purpose of discussing the law?*
2. *What elements does every intermediate appellate or supreme court opinion contain?*
3. *What is a dissenting opinion and what effect does it have?*
4. *What is a concurring opinion and what effect does it have?*
5. *How are headnotes helpful in legal research?*
6. *What is a precedent?*
7. *What is persuasive authority?*

Answers

1. Cases are the published opinions of appellate or supreme courts.
2. Almost all published cases contain:
   - A detailed statement of the facts that are accepted by the court as true.
   - A statement of the legal issue or issues presented by the appealing parties for resolution.
   - An answer to the issues presented for resolution—this is called the ruling or holding.
   - A discussion of why the ruling was made—the court's reasoning or rationale.
3. A justice on an appellate court who disagrees with the decision of the majority on a case may issue a dissenting opinion, which is published along with the majority's opinion. No matter how passionate a dissent happens to be, it has no effect on the particular case. However, it may have a persuasive effect on judges in future court decisions.
4. A justice who agrees with the majority decision but disagrees with the reasons given for it may issue a concurring opinion, which is published along with the majority's opinion. A concurring opinion can also have a persuasive influence on future court decisions.
5. - They serve as a table of contents to the opinion.
   - They allow discussions of legal issues in one case to be cross-indexed to similar discussions in other cases by the use of "digests."
   - They are very helpful when you are "Shepardizing" a case.
6. An earlier case that is relevant to a case to be decided. If there is nothing to distinguish the circumstances of the current case from the already-decided one, the earlier holding is considered binding on the court. A case is only precedent as to a particular set of facts and the precise legal issue decided in light of those facts.
7. If a case is not precedent, binding on later courts, but contains an excellent analysis of the legal issues and provides guidance for any court that happens to read it, it is "persuasive authority."

CHAPTER 8

How Cases Are Published

Cases are published in volumes called "case reports," "reports" or "reporters." We use the term "reporter" throughout this chapter, except when a particular publication uses a different term. When we refer to a particular publication we also give its citation. We discuss citations in detail in Chapter 9, *Finding Cases*, Section A.

If you are in a law library as you read this, locate the volumes of the *Federal Supplement* —the reporter containing published U.S. District Court cases. You will see almost 800 numbered hardcover volumes; more than 20 volumes a year are added to the collection. If you look around, you will see that some sets of volumes reporting the cases of the other court systems are even larger. All told, there are many thousands of books containing court cases—courts have been cranking out opinions for a long, long time.

There are many separate reports for different courts and for geographical areas; an opinion may be published in more than one. For example, New York Court of Appeal cases are found in a publication titled *New York Appeals* and in a regional reporter called the *Northeastern Reporter*, which contains state court cases from New York, Illinois, Indiana, Massachusetts and Ohio.

California Supreme Court cases are found in three publications:

- California Reports (California Supreme Court cases only)
- California Reporter (all California appellate cases) and
- Pacific Reporter (a regional reporter that collects cases from the appellate courts of 15 Western states)

A. Federal Cases

Federal court cases are published according to the court they are decided by.

1. U.S. District Court Cases

Only a very small percentage—those deemed to be of widespread legal interest—of U.S. District Court cases are published. This means that occasionally a case can be on the front page of your local paper for weeks and never be reported. There is no automatic connection between sensational facts and legal import. All published U.S. District Court cases are collected in the *Federal Supplement* (F. Supp.) or *Federal Rules Decisions* (F.R.D.).

2. Bankruptcy Court Cases

Decisions of the U.S. Bankruptcy Courts are reported in the *Bankruptcy Reporter* (B.R.).

3. U.S. Court of Appeals Cases

All published decisions by U.S. Courts of Appeal are collected in the *Federal Reporter*. This is currently in its second series and is abbreviated as "F." or "F.2d" (*Federal Reporter, Second Series*).

The U.S. Court of Appeals (the intermediate federal appellate court) is divided into 12 circuits and a special court called the Federal Circuit that hears appeals relating to patents and customs. Below is a list of the states in each circuit.

1st Circuit	2nd Circuit	3rd Circuit	4th Circuit	5th Circuit
Maine Massachusetts New Hampshire Puerto Rico Rhode Island	Connecticut New York Vermont	Delaware New Jersey Pennsylvania Virgin Islands	Maryland North Carolina South Carolina Virginia West Virginia	Canal Zone Louisiana Mississippi Texas
6th Circuit	**7th Circuit**	**8th Circuit**	**9th Circuit**	**10th Circuit**
Kentucky Michigan Ohio Tennessee	Illinois Indiana Wisconsin	Arkansas Iowa Minnesota Missouri Nebraska North Dakota South Dakota	Alaska Arizona California Guam Hawaii Idaho Montana Nevada Oregon Washington	Colorado Kansas New Mexico Oklahoma Utah Wyoming
11th Circuit	**District of Columbia Circuit**	**Federal Circuit**		
Alabama Florida Georgia	Washington, D.C.	Patent and Customs Cases		

Circuits of the U.S. Court of Appeals

4. U.S. Supreme Court Cases

Last, but certainly not least, there are three separate reporters for United States Supreme Court cases. Each of them contains the same cases but different editorial enhancements.

You might wonder why it is necessary to have three reporters for a single court. It's really not; many small law libraries only buy one, or two at the most.

a. United States Supreme Court Reports (U.S.)

This reporter is the so-called "official" reporter, commissioned by Congress. Other reports that cover these cases are termed unofficial reports. This doesn't mean the opinions collected in the official reporter are more accurate or authoritative than those in the unofficial reporters; for basic legal research purposes there is little difference between the official and unofficial reporters. However, most courts require a citation to the official reporter when referring to a U.S. Supreme Court case in court documents.

b. Supreme Court Reporter (S. Ct.)

This reporter is part of the West Publishing Company series of reporters, which means it is also part of an elaborate cross-reference system known as the "key system" (explained in Chapter 10, *Shepard's and Digests: Expand and Update Your Research*). If you are using the West research system, it is a good idea to use this reporter.

c. Supreme Court Reports, Lawyer's Edition (L. Ed.)

This reporter is published by Bancroft-Whitney/ Lawyers' Coop and is very handy if you are using that company's research system. (See Chapter 5, Section D1.) This reporter contains not only all of the U.S. Supreme Court cases (as do the other two reports), but also provides considerable editorial comment about the case's impact, including an annotation that relates the case to other cases on the same subject. This reporter is currently in its second series.

Supreme Court Reports

B. State Court Cases

Each state arranges for its appellate court cases to be published in official state reporters. In the larger states, there are usually two official reporters: one for the highest court cases and another for the intermediate appellate court cases. If you are interested in using the official reporters for your state while doing your research, ask your law librarian where the official state reporter is shelved.

In addition to these official reporters, the cases of each state—both supreme court and appellate—are published in a series of reporters called "regional reporters," published by the West Publishing Co. West has divided the country into seven regions, and the cases produced by the courts of each state in a region are published together. For example, cases from Alabama, Florida, Louisiana and Mississippi are all published in the *Southern Reporter.*

West also publishes state-specific versions of its regional reporters. For this reason, the *Southern Reporter* found in an Alabama library might contain only Alabama cases.

THE NATIONAL REPORTER SYSTEM

Full Name of Reporter	*Abbreviation*	*State Courts Included*
Atlantic Reporter (First and Second Series)	A. and A.2d	Supreme & intermediate appellate courts in D.C., Connecticut, Delaware, Maine, Maryland, New Hampshire, New Jersey, Pennsylvania, Rhode Island and Vermont
Northeastern Reporter	N.E. and N.E.2d	Court of Appeals in New York (First and Second Series)and Supreme and intermediate appellate courts in Illinois, Indiana, Massachusetts and Ohio
Northwestern Reporter (First and Second Series)	N.W. and N.W.2d	Supreme and intermediate appellate courts in Iowa, Michigan, Minnesota, Nebraska, North Dakota, South Dakota and Wisconsin
Pacific Reporter (First and Second Series)	P. and P.2d	Supreme and intermediate appellate courts in Alaska, Arizona, California (Sup. Ct. only since 1960), Colorado, Hawaii, Idaho, Kansas, Montana, Nevada, New Mexico, Oklahoma, Oregon, Utah, Washington and Wyoming
Southeastern Reporter (First and Second Series)	S.E. and S.E.2d	Supreme and intermediate appellate courts in Georgia, North Carolina, South Carolina, Virginia and West Virginia
Southern Reporter (First and Second Series)	So. and So.2d	Supreme and intermediate appellate courts in Alabama, Florida, Louisiana and Mississippi
Southwestern Reporter (First and Second Series)	S.W. and S.W.2d	Supreme and intermediate appellate courts in Arkansas, Kentucky, Missouri, Tennessee and Texas
New York Supplement	N.Y.S.	All New York supreme and intermediate appellate courts
California Reporter *(First and Second Series)*	Cal. Rptr. and Cal. Rptr. 2d	All California supreme and intermediate appellate courts

Most academic law libraries carry both the official reporters for their own state and the regional reporters for the entire country. However, when it comes to cases from other states, they probably won't have state-specific reporters. So if you are in New Hampshire and want to look up a New Hampshire case, you will have a choice between the New Hampshire official reports and the *Atlantic Reporter* (the regional reporter for the Northeast). However, if you want to find a Florida case, you will most likely need to use the *Southern Reporter*.

C. Keeping Case Reporters Up-to-Date

A significant lag time usually exists between the date a case is decided and publication of a new hardcover reporter. To make new cases available during the interim, reporters have weekly update pamphlets called "advance sheets." The chances are great that if a case was decided within several months (or even years for some Supreme Court cases) of when you are doing your research, it will be found in an advance sheet rather than in the latest hardcover volumes.

It is important to remember that all appellate opinions (and some at the trial level) are followed by a period of time during which the parties can request and the court can grant a rehearing before the same court. Also, most decisions are appealable by means of a petition for hearing or a writ of *certiori* to the next higher court. Opinions may appear in the advance sheets during this time period. If either a rehearing or a petition for hearing or *certiori* is granted, the underlying opinion is rendered null and void, and it cannot be cited. For this reason, the advance sheets have subsequent case history tables that you should consult whenever you cite to a case that is still in the advance sheets.

Most law libraries shelve advance sheets next to the hardcover volumes. Sometimes, however, they are kept behind the reference desk to avoid theft.

D. The Newest Cases

When an opinion is issued by a judge, it has a life of its own before it appears in the weekly advance sheets. Typically, the opinion is signed by the judge(s) and then sent to the clerk's office for distribution to the public. Copies go to the parties, the general press, the local legal newspapers, the case reporter services (for inclusion in the next advance sheet booklet), and *Shepard's*. Some clerk's offices have a basket on the counter with that day's opinions sitting in it.

During the time that the opinion is simply a bundle of stapled pages, it is referred to as a "slip opinion," and it is identified by its docket number—the court number the case received when it was first filed. When it appears in the next week's advance sheets it will get a regular citation; but before that time, it may be picked up by *Shepard's* if it cites other cases. *Shepard's* will refer to the case by its docket number. If you need to see an opinion that is identified only by its docket number, your best bet is to use one of the computerized research services (Lexis or Westlaw).

It is risky to cite to a slip opinion. As with opinions in the advance sheets, slip opinions can be wiped off the books if a rehearing is ordered or a higher court decides to take the case. Slip opinions do not become "final" and citable until the time for filing these motions has passed. If you cite to a slip opinion, be sure to thereafter track its course through the advance sheets, by checking to see if it appears and whether it shows up in the subsequent case history table.

RESEARCHING CALIFORNIA CASES

In California, unlike most other states, there is a good reason to use the official reporters—*California Reports* for California supreme court cases and *California Appellate Reports* for California court of appeal cases. This is because the California Supreme Court, on occasion, "depublishes" published court of appeal opinions. Depublished opinions can no longer be relied on as a correct statement of California law. When a case is "depublished," its conclusion remains intact as far as the case's parties are concerned, but it is taken out of the official reports and replaced with a notation to that effect. It usually remains in the unofficial reports. By using the unofficial reports, you run a small risk of relying on a case that appears helpful but no longer exists from a legal standpoint.

In California, the advance sheets for the official case reports published by Bancroft-Whitney/Lawyer's Coop contain a section at the back that tells you what has happened to cases since they were published in the reports. Cases are sometimes re-heard, taken for hearing by the Supreme Court or ordered depublished. A table that appears in the Advance Sheets—called the cumulative subsequent history table—informs you when this happens. You may also use *Shepard's Citations for Cases* (discussed in Chapter 10, *Shepard's and Digests: Expand and Update Your Research,* to find out whether a case has been depublished.

Although the concept of depublication appears Orwellian, its purpose is to allow the Supreme Court to administratively weed out misstatements of the law without having to handle the errant case on appeal. Also, it allows a weak or divided Supreme court to render impotent a decision by a lower court that creates new law or is controversial in nature. Depublication allows the appellate court decision to operate as far as the parties to that case are concerned, but its decision does not become a precedent that others can rely upon.

***LAW WEEK* AND OTHER LOOSE-LEAF PUBLICATIONS**

A weekly loose-leaf publication called *United States Law Week* contains the full text of U.S. Supreme Court decisions, often within a week or two of their release by the Court. *Law Week* also publishes opinions from other courts around the country that its editors deem to be of general interest. If you are looking for a recent U.S. Supreme Court case or other cases of interest decided by other courts, try this service. The weekly pamphlets are collected in a large loose-leaf binder and indexed both by subject matter and case name.

If you are looking for a recent case involving a topic that is covered by one of the looseleaf services covered in Chapter 5, Section D7 (such as, family law, environmental law, media law), you might find the case in one of these publications. For example, the CCH tax service regularly publishes all new court cases of significance in the tax field.

While *Law Week* and the other loose-leaf services are good places to read a recent case, you will definitely want to learn the case reporter citation for the case when it becomes available, so you can use the tools discussed in Chapter 10, *Shepard's and Digests: Expand and Update Your Research*, to find your way to other relevant cases.

REVIEW

Questions

1. *What are the books that contain published court opinions called?*
2. *What series publishes decisions by U.S. District Courts?*
3. *What series publishes decisions by the U.S. Court of Appeals?*
4. *What series publishes decisions by the U.S. Supreme Court?*
5. *What series publishes all state court cases, by region?*
6. *How are new cases first published?*
7. *What service does* U.S. Law Week *provide?*

Answers

1. Cases are published in volumes called "case reports," "reports" or "reporters."
2. *Federal Supplement*.
3. *Federal Reporter* (three series).
4. *United States Supreme Court Reports*, *Supreme Court Reporter* and the *Supreme Court Reports*, *Lawyer's Edition*.
5. The "regional reporters," published by the West Publishing Co.
6. Reporters have weekly update pamphlets called "advance sheets."
7. The full text of U.S. Supreme Court decisions, often within a week or two of their release by the Court.

CHAPTER 9

Finding Cases

Every reported (published) case has a unique citation. As long as you have the citation, you can find most any case published in a standard case reporter. This chapter tells you how to interpret these citations and find them when you are looking for a case.

A. Interpreting Case Citations

A case citation consists of five or six items:

- the case name—usually the names of the plaintiff and defendant
- the name of the reporter(s) where the case is published
- the volume number(s) of the reporter(s) where the case is published
- the page number of the volume where the case begins
- the year the case was decided
- for federal Court of Appeal cases, a designation of the circuit; for federal District Court cases, the state and judicial district where the court is located; for state cases, an indication of the state if it's not apparent from the name of the reporter.

Let's take a closer look at each of the elements in a case citation

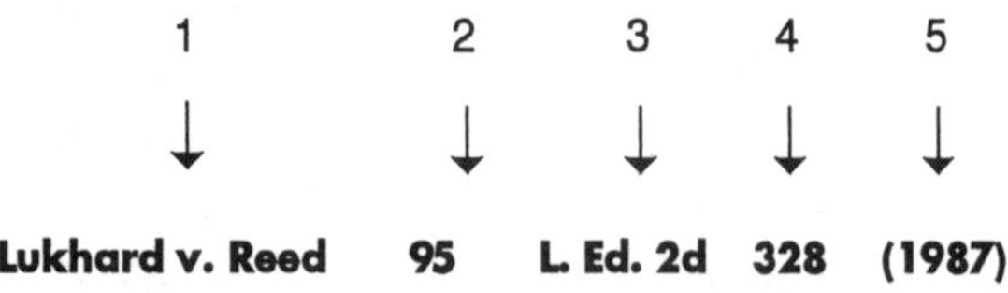

CITATION FORM

Citations often take slightly different forms. For example, it is not uncommon to see the date immediately following the case name or different abbreviations that designate the report. A nationwide system of citations contained in a book titled *A Uniform System of Citation,* 14th ed. (colloquially called the "Harvard Blue Book") has been developed primarily for law school use, but is used in federal courts and most state courts. We follow it here for the most part.

1. Case Name

The first element of a case citation is the case name. *People v. Fields* is a case name. So is *Lukhard v. Reed.* There are usually two names, one on either side of a "v." that stands for versus. This format reflects the adversary aspect of our justice system; one name is the plaintiff's, the other the defendant's. Usually, the first name is the plaintiff's and the second name is the defendant's. But not always. The plaintiff in the *People v. Fields* case was "the people" (this tells us it was probably a criminal case), and the defendant was Fields. In *Lukhard v. Reed,* however, the original plaintiff was Reed, and the defendant was Lukhard. But when Lukhard appealed a lower court decision in favor of Reed, his name was put first.

Sometimes, cases only have one name with some Latin attached. For example, *In re Gault* is the name of a juvenile case; the "in re" means "in the matter of." These types of case names normally appear where the proceeding is brought by the state for the individual's best interest, or where the proceeding is not considered to be an adversary proceeding that warrants the "v."

Finally, cases are sometimes referred to by the subject matter of the dispute. For instance, divorce cases commonly carry such names as *Marriage of Sullivan* (last name of the divorcing couple) or *In the matter of Schmidt*.

2. Volume Number

A case citation provides the volume number of the reporter in which the case is located. The volumes of each separate reporter are numbered consecutively.

3. Name of Reporter

Obviously a citation wouldn't be much help without the name of the reporter. That informatior. comes immediately after the volume number. In the *Lukhard* case, the full name of the reporter is the *Supreme Court Reports: Lawyer's Edition*.

Examples of abbreviations for other reporters:

- "A." (Atlantic Reporter)
- "P." (Pacific Reporter)
- "U.S." (United States Reports)
- "F. Supp." (Federal Supplement)
- "F." (Federal Reporter)

Most reporters have been published in two or more series. For example, the *Lukhard* case is published in the second series of the L. Ed. reporter (L. Ed. 2d). Cases decided in the nineteenth and early twentieth century were published in the first series (L. Ed). In litigious states, like California, the case reporters are up to their third series. For instance, a citation for a recent California case is *Northrop Corp. v. American Motorists Ins. Co.*, 220 Cal. App. 3d 1553 (1990).

Do not worry about memorizing all of these abbreviations. Virtually every legal research tool that you'll be using contains a table of abbreviations for the various case reports. Also, as you do research within your own state, you'll quickly get to know the most commonly used abbreviations. If you are ever in doubt, law librarians will almost always cheerfully come to the rescue.

4. The Page Number

You have undoubtedly already figured out what the next item of a citation is for. It provides the page number the case starts on.

5. Year of the Decision

Citations also carry the year the case was decided. This information can be helpful because old law tends to be bad law. When you're doing research, you usually want to first check the most recent cases relating to your problem.

Now you know that the citation *Lukhard v. Reed*, 95 L. Ed. 2d. 327 (1987), means that a case called *Lukhard v. Reed* was decided in 1987 and can be found in Volume 95 of the *Supreme Court Reports: Lawyer's Edition*, starting on page 327.

6. Federal Cases: The Circuit, State or District

Citations to cases decided by the federal Courts of Appeal usually include the circuit of the court deciding the case. A case decided by the Court of Appeals for the 3rd Circuit might appear as 654 F.2d 925 (3rd Cir. 1984). A U.S. District Court citation should indicate the state and judicial district of the case; for example, in *Peter v. Jones*, 509 F. Supp. 825 (E.D. Pa. 1981), the E.D. Pa means Eastern Judicial District for Pennsylvania.

7. Parallel Citations

As mentioned in Chapter 8, *How Cases Are Published*, cases are often found in more than one reporter. For example, U.S. Supreme Court cases can be found in three separate reporters put out by three separate publishers. When you see a U.S. Supreme Court case referred to (that is, "cited"), you will often see three citations following the case name.

Example

Lukhard v. Reed	481 U.S. 368, First Citation *United States Reports*	95 L. Ed. 2d 328, Second Citation *Lawyer's Edition, 2d Series*	107 S. Ct. 1807 (1987) Third Citation *Supreme Court Reporter*

These three citations are known as *parallel citations* because they parallel each other (that is, refer to the same case).

8. Citations to Advance Sheets

Advance sheets are numbered and paginated in accord with the rest of the report and serve as the report until a new hardcover report is produced. For example, a 1991 U.S. Supreme Court advance sheet (for the *U.S. Supreme Court Reports, Lawyer's Edition*) is labeled Vol. 113 L. Ed. 2d., No. 2. One of the cases reported in this advance sheet is *Columbia v. Omni Outdoor Advertising*, on page 382. The citation for this case (as published in this reporter) is 113 L. Ed. 2d 382 (1991).

When the hardcover book containing the case is published, the volume number for the hardcover is the same as is on the advance sheet and the case is found on the same page. In short, the citation doesn't change.

B. How to Find Cases

Now that you know how to read citations to the publications described in Chapter 8, *How Cases Are Published*, it's time to focus on finding a citation that will get you to the case you need. There are a number of ways to do this depending on where you are coming from in your research.

- If you have found a relevant statute and want to read cases that interpret the provisions you are interested in, you can probably find an appropriate citation in the case notes following the statute (subsection 2, below), or in the listings for that statute in *Shepard's Citations for Statutes* (subsection 3, below).
- If your research involves primarily common law (cases), you might find a helpful citation in a background resource (subsection 1, below) or in the subject index to a case digest (subsection 4, below).
- If you know the name of a case that you want to find but not its citation, you can use the Table of Cases in a case digest (subsection 5, below). If the case is very recent (within the past several months) and not yet listed in the case digest Table of Cases, you can find it by searching the Table of Cases in the advance sheets or recently published hardcover case reporter volumes (subsection 6, below).
- If you have a case citation for one reporter and you need the citation for a second reporter (that

is, the parallel citation), you can find it by using *Shepard's Citations for Cases*. (See Chapter 10, *Shepard's' and Digests: Expand and Up-date Your Research.*)

Below we examine in more detail each of these approaches to finding an appropriate citation to that one good case.

1. Background Resources

Most of the background materials discussed in Chapter 5, *Getting Some Background Information*, are copiously footnoted with citations to cases that discuss specific points of law covered in the main discussion. For example, consider the page from *California Jurisprudence*, a California legal encyclopedia, shown below.

Although we generally recommend that you proceed directly from background reading to any pertinent statutes—and then to cases—it is also common to go directly to any case that appears to be relevant, or to at least note the citation for later reference. For example, if you want to know what your constitutional rights are in the event you are accused of a zoning violation, the case of *Los Angeles v. Gage* (cited in footnote 42 on the page shown below) appears to bear directly on that point. Before you search for a statute related to this issue, you might first read this case to see what light it sheds on your problem. The case itself may discuss relevant statutes.

2. Case Notes That Follow Statutes

If you are searching for a case that has interpreted a relevant statute, check the listings after the text of the statute in an "annotated" version of the code. You should be able to find annotated versions of your state's code and of the *United States Code* in the law library.

In the annotated code, one sentence summaries of court cases that interpret the statute directly follow the notes on the statute's history. These summaries are actually headnotes (see Chapter 7, *Understanding Case Law*, Section B) that have been lifted from the case reporter. Some statutes have been interpreted by the courts so many times that the publisher includes a little index to the case summaries, which are organized by issues raised by the statute. The example below is taken from the *Michigan Compiled Laws Annotated.*

additional time not exceeding a specified number of days as the court may, within the original number of days, allow, but in no event later than a designated number of days after entry of the order, petition the proper reviewing court to review such order by writ of mandate. No such order of vacation is effective, nor may it be recorded in the office any county recorder, until the time within which a petition for writ of mandate may thus be filed has expired.[41]

§ 211. Defenses

Generally speaking, any matter that is germane to a cause of action to enforce a zoning or planning enactment and that presents a legal reason why the plaintiff should not succeed therein may constitute a good defense. It is a good defense, for instance, that the enactment under which complaint is made is unconstitutional or invalid, either in toto or as applied to the defendant's property.[42] In order to plead this defense, however, the defendant must have exhausted the administrative remedies available to him under the enactment.[43] And the partial invalidity of

41. *Deering's Gov C § 65908 subd (b).*

→ **42.** *Los Angeles v Gage, 127 CA2d 442, 274 P2d 34; People v Gottfurcht (2d Dist) 62 CA3d 634, 133 Cal Rptr 270.*

Regarding validity of zoning enactments generally, see §§ 43 et seq., supra.

Practice References: 8 POF2d p. 53, Unreasonableness of Zoning Restriction §§ 1 et seq.; 13 POF2d p. 373, Vested Right in Continuation of Zoning §§ 1 et seq.; 14 POF2d p. 117, Zoning—Nonconforming Use §§ 1 et seq.

43. *San Mateo v Hardy, 64 CA2d 794, 149 P2d 307.*

A church and a member thereof failed to exhaust their administrative remedies before defending on constitutional grounds against the enforcement of an ordinance requiring a use permit as a prerequisite to operation of church on property in a residential zone, where it did not appear that the member even applied for any such permit, and the church dismissed its appeal from the planning commission's decision to the city council before decision by the council. *Chico v First Ave. Baptist Church, 108 CA2d 297, 238 P2d 587.*

Property owners whose auto wrecking yard was found to be a nonconforming use and was ordered terminated by the county board of supervisors on recommendation of the county planning commission were not denied procedural due process, where a public hearing after 15 days' notice was held by the planning commission at which hearing the property owners were represented by counsel and witnesses were

Excerpt from California Jurisprudence

Historical and Statutory Notes

Source:
P.A.1931, No. 328, § 451a, added by P.A. 1969, No. 243, § 1, Eff. March 20, 1970.
C.L.1948, § 750.451a.
C.L.1970, § 750.451a.

750.452. House of ill-fame; keeping, maintaining or operating

statute →

Sec. 452. KEEPING, ETC., A HOUSE OF ILL-FAME—Any person who shall keep, maintain or operate, or aid and abet in keeping, maintaining or operating a house of ill-fame, bawdy house or any house or place resorted to for the purpose of prostitution or lewdness shall be guilty of a felony, punishable by imprisonment in the state prison for not more than 5 years or by a fine of not more than 2,500 dollars.

Historical and Statutory Notes

Source:
P.A.1931, No. 328, § 452, Eff. Sept. 18.
C.L.1948, § 750.452.
C.L.1970, § 750.452.

Prior Laws:
R.S.1846, c. 158, § 10.
C.L.1857, § 5865.
C.L.1871, § 7700.
How. § 9286.
P.A.1887, No. 34.
C.L.1897, § 11697.
C.L.1915, § 15471.
P.A.1927, No. 37, § 1.
P.A.1927, No. 40, § 1.
C.L.1929, §§ 16826, 16860.

Cross References

Disorderly persons, see § 750.167.
Public nuisances, abatement, see § 600.3801.

Library References

Disorderly House ⚷5.
WESTLAW Topic No. 130.
C.J.S. Disorderly Houses § 5.

Notes of Decisions

mini-index →

Conduct or use of house 3
Elements of offense 1
Evidence 6-8
In general 6
Reputation 7
Weight and sufficiency of evidence 8
House, building or place 2
Indictment or information 5
Instructions 10
Jury questions 9
Keeping of house 4
Reputation, evidence 7
Review 12
Sentence and punishment 11
Weight and sufficiency of evidence 8

---

1. Elements of offense

case summary →

Under this section providing that "Any person who shall keep, maintain or operate, or aid and abet in keeping, maintaining or operating a house of ill-fame, bawdy house or any house or place resorted to for the purpose of prostitution * * * shall be guilty of a felony, * * *.", it is only where the operation or maintenance of a house of ill fame is charged that the reputation of the premises is an essential element. People v. Mayes (1973) 205 N.W.2d 212, 44 Mich.App. 482.

A person who solicited a female, who was at the time a prostitute, and inmate of a house of ill fame, to become an inmate of another such house, was not guilty of a violation of How. § 9286, which provided for the punishment of any person who solicited a female to enter such house for the purpose of "becoming" a prostitute. People v. Cook (1893) 55 N.W. 980, 96 Mich. 368.

2. House, building or place

Evidence that defendant kept a house to which men resorted for purposes of prostitution, that frequent acts of prostitution were there committed with her, and that the house

362

Michigan Statute

It is often difficult to tell from such a brief summary whether or not a case is in fact relevant to the problem you are researching. Remember that the editor who wrote these blurbs may not have had her second cup of coffee when she wrote the one you're interested in. Fortunately, the summaries also contain a case citation that allows you to look up the case and read it for yourself. It is essential that you read the case itself and not just rely on what it says in the annotation.

FINDING RECENT CASES THAT HAVE INTERPRETED A STATUTE

Each volume of a case reporter has a "table of statutes" that are mentioned by the cases reported in that volume. The table is usually in the front of the volume. It can be helpful if you know that a statute has been interpreted in some case within a specific period of time.

For example, suppose you hear of a 1992 Illinois court decision that interprets that state's statute governing stock issuances of small corporations. You are familiar with the statute and would like to read the case, but you don't know its name or where to find it. What to do? The most direct approach is to check for the particular statute in the table of statutes in each volume of the *Northeastern Reporter,* 2nd Series, that contains 1992 Illinois cases. If the statute you are interested in was, in fact, interpreted by a case, the table of statutes will tell you precisely which one and provide its citation. Remember to check the advance sheets for the reporter if you think the case was very recent.

3. Shepard's Citations for Statutes

There are several different research tools provided by a service known generically as *Shepard's*. *Shepard's Citations for Statutes* provides a complete listing of each time a particular statute, regulation or constitutional provision has been referred to and perhaps interpreted by a published decision of a federal or state court. In the next chapter, we'll discuss *Shepard's Case Citations*, which tells you every time a particular case has been referred to by a later case. *Shepard's* for both statutes and cases are tools you will definitely want to master.

Before learning how to use *Shepard's Citations for Statutes*, it helps to know the basics:

- *Shepard's Citations for Statutes* are dark red, thick, hardcover volumes with separate update pamphlets that may be gold, red or white, depending on how recently the hardcover volumes were published.
- A separate *Shepard's* exists for the statutes of each state and for federal statutes.
- *Shepard's* hardcover volumes for the statutes of a state or the federal government cover different time periods. For example, one hardcover volume may contain all references made by court decisions before 1980, another may contain all references made between 1980 and 1985, and a third may contain all references made between 1985 and 1990.
- To use *Shepard's*, you need the exact number (citation) of the statute. It is very helpful to know the approximate year it was passed.
- Each *Shepard's* volume is organized in the same way as the statutes being referred to are labeled in the codes of each state or the federal government. So if you want to know whether a particular New York criminal statute has been interpreted by a court, you would first locate the place in the New York *Shepard's Citations for Statutes* that covers the New York criminal laws, and then look for the specific statute by number. In other states, where statutes are not grouped by topic but only by

sequential number, you would only need to find the statute by its number.

- Once you find the statute you are "Shepardizing" in *Shepard's*, you will see whether or not any court decisions have referred to it. If so, the citations tell you the reporter, the volume and the page where the reference occurred.
- *Shepard's Citations for Statutes* are kept in different places in different libraries. Some libraries have their *Shepard's* in a central location, while others have their *Shepard's* at the end of the statutes for each state and at the end of the federal code. Still other libraries have *Shepard's* at the end of the volumes of cases for each state.

Now that you have a general idea of what *Shepard's* is, how it works and where it can be found in the law library, lets Shepardize a statute together.

Example You are in Florida and want to know if stopping payment on a check can be a criminal offense. By using the index to the *Florida Statutes Annotated*, you find the statute shown below:

832.041 Stopping payment with intent to defraud

(1) Whoever, with intent to defraud any person shall, in person or by agent, make, draw, utter, deliver or give any check, draft or written order for the payment of money upon any bank, person or corporation, and secure from such person goods or services for or on account of such check, draft or written order, whether such goods or services be valued at the amount of such check, draft or written order or at a greater or lesser value, and shall, pursuant to and in furtherance of such intent to defraud, stop payment on such check, draft or written order, shall be deemed to be guilty of a felony of the third degree, punishable as provided in § 775.082, § 775.083, or § 775.084, if the value of the goods or services secured for or on account of such check, draft or written order be $50 or more; and if the value of the goods or services secured for or on account of such check, draft or written order be less than $50, shall be guilty of a misdemeanor of the second degree, punishable as provided in § 775.082 or § 775.083.

(2) This section shall be taken to be cumulative and shall not be construed to repeal any other statute now in effect.

Florida Bad Check Statute

This statute was passed in 1965. Checking the pocket part, you find that it was amended in 1986. The amended version made no substantive change except for raising the dollar amount of the check from $50 or more to $130 or more.

To find out how this statute has been interpreted and applied by the courts, you look to *Shepard's*. Your first job is to locate the *Shepard's Citations for Statutes* applicable to the state of Florida. Assume that your research takes place in June 1991. You would find five volumes on the shelf:

- a red hardcover volume, dated 1986
- a red hardcover volume entitled "Supplement 86-90"
- a gold paperback Annual Cumulative Supplement, dated June 1990
- a bright red paperback Cumulative Supplement, dated April 1991
- a skimpy white paper supplement entitled Advance Sheet Edition, dated May 1991.

The white supplement contains, in a circle on the front cover, a list of the hardbound volumes and paperback supplements you should check. Gold supplements come out every six to 12 months, and bright red ones every two months or so. When a new bright red supplement is issued, it incorporates the white supplements and replaces any bright red supplements that have been published since the gold supplement. This means you should never have to check more than one gold supplement, one red supplement and one white supplement.

Look at the hardcover volume dated 1986 first. It is divided by year. You quickly conclude that looking in any year before 1965 is irrelevant. Why? Because the statute you are interested in was first passed in 1965.

Because Florida statutes are organized by number (not by subject), you turn in the 1986 volume of *Shepard's* to where statute number 832.041 (the stop-payment statute) is listed. Below is a page out of *Shepard's Citations for Florida Statutes*.

Sanity Note Don't freak out at all the numbers you encounter on a *Shepard's* page. Almost everyone says "yuck" when they see a *Shepard's* page for the first time. But the rest of us survived the experience, and you will too.

FLORIDA STATUTES—FLORIDA STATUTES ANNOTATED

1983, 827.03

361So2d406
377So2d1158
379So2d422
383So2d713
425So2d189
460So2d492
40FlS103
440F2d339
20MiL591
25MiL418
26MiL318
26MiL601
66CR681
78CR108
1A52n
Subsec. 1
295So2d690
317So2d864
C354So2d867
425So2d188
Subsec. 2
295So2d691
317So2d864
C354So2d867
355So2d130
425So2d188
28MiL375
Subsec. 3
C356So2d314
377So2d1158
383So2d692
430US677
51LE734
97SC1415
827.04
Ad1974C383
A1975C298
A1977C429
346So2d992
361So2d407
379So2d408
385So2d1054
425So2d189
453So2d799
78CR108
Subsec. 1
420So2d919
462So2d833
Subsec. 2
C361So2d406
C376So2d862
388So2d563
425So2d188
33MiL970
33MiL1100
Subsec. 3
Ad1977C73
C370So2d1
C377So2d674
378So2d831
440So2d631
443So2d180
32MiL1108
827.05
A1971C136
A1975C298
A1977C429
U346So2d992
361So2d407
385So2d1054
388So2d563
425So2d189
20MiL591
25MiL418
32MiL1104
33MiL970

827.06
Ad1974C383
517F2d788
Subsec. 1
A1975C298
827.071
Ad1983C75
827.08
A1971C136
16MiL195
827.09
A1979C298
A1980C293
6FSU694
828.02
8So2d392
63So2d508
351So2d749
401So2d1112
150Fla592
torture
310So2d43
828.03
A1975C223
A1976C102
30MiL161
Subsec. 2
A1977C174
828.05
A1980C188
A1984C105
28MiL828
828.073
Ad1975C223
Subsec. 2
A1976C102
A1978C12
A1979C234
Subsec. 3
A1976C102
A1978C12
Subsec. 4
A1979C102
Subsec. 6
Subd. b
A1976C102
828.08
A1971C136
R1974C383
Re-en
[1975C298
828.12 to
828.14
63So2d509
828.12
A1970C50
A1982C116
63So2d508
210So2d443
310So2d43
351So2d749
C401So2d
[1111
451So2d880
4FlS2d108
828.121
Ad1971C12
828.122
Ad1976C59
A1981C224
Subsec. 4
A1982C116

828.13
A1971C136
A1981C17
A1982C116
Subsec. 2
464So2d668
Subd. a
C464So2d668
Subd. b
C464So2d668
828.14
Subsec. 1
A1971C136
828.15
U63So2d508
828.16
A1971C136
828.161
Ad1967C177
Subsec. 4
A1971C136
828.17
A1973C334
828.23
Subsec. 1
A1971C377
828.24
Subsec. 2
A1977C104
828.26
Subsec. 1
A1971C136
Subsec. 2
A1971C136
831.01
et seq.
257So2d92
298So2d551
358So2d889
426So2d79
831.01
A1971C136
A1973C334
9So2d712
46So2d453
74So2d370
75So2d195
76So2d645
107So2d379
111So2d460
114So2d198
117So2d408
117So2d737
118So2d193
118So2d630
123So2d464
133So2d74
192So2d45
200So2d829
227So2d524
243So2d437
256So2d223
257So2d93
267So2d702
298So2d551
312So2d808
330So2d160
341So2d539
345So2d363
351So2d377
355So2d818
366So2d1208
404So2d762
428So2d363
451So2d993
451So2d1048

452So2d957
458So2d423
462So2d1131
151Fla293
423US441
445US270
46LE619
63LE388
96SC836
100SC1137
469F2d1345
580F2d766
631F2d1258
219FS263
17MJ783
10MLQ200
22MiL607
28MiL897
831.02
A1971C136
74So2d370
75So2d195
114So2d198
117So2d408
117So2d737
118So2d193
133So2d74
181So2d231
192So2d45
192So2d293
200So2d829
214So2d516
256So2d223
257So2d93
266So2d695
274So2d18
278So2d643
290So2d77
292So2d72
313So2d432
317So2d853
330So2d160
332So2d354
339So2d172
341So2d539
345So2d363
355So2d818
356So2d347
356So2d870
357So2d491
361So2d826
366So2d1208
367So2d695
368So2d634
397So2d410
402So2d1288
415So2d50
415So2d114
426So2d81
428So2d363
435So2d963
438So2d974
452So2d957
445US270
63LE388
100SC1137
627F2d707
219FS262
17MJ783
22MiL272
22MiL606
28MiL897

831.03
A1971C136
469F2d1345
831.04
Subsec. 1
A1971C136
Subsec. 2
A1971C136
831.05
A1971C136
831.06
266So2d695
28MiL897
831.07
A1971C136
358So2d889
630F2d393
831.08
A1971C136
345So2d363
440So2d507
630F2d393
831.09
A1971C136
358So2d888
831.10
A1971C136
152So2d755
18MiL395
20MiL272
831.11
A1971C136
262So2d457
28MiL897
831.13
A1971C136
440So2d507
831.15
A1971C136
345So2d363
440So2d507
831.16
A1971C136
440So2d507
831.17
152So2d755
18MiL395
20MiL272
831.18
428So2d734
831.20
A1973C334
831.22
A1971C136
831.23
A1971C136
9FLR293
831.24
A1971C136
831.25
A1971C136
831.26
A1971C136
A1977C104
831.27
A1971C136
831.29
A1969C313
A1971C136
A1973C334
C407So2d231
20MiL276

831.30
Ad1971C331
A1972C234
Subsec. 1
A1973C331
831.31
442So2d287
444So2d64
C446So2d
[1185
463So2d1144
469So2d231
469So2d957
Subsec. 2
Subd. b
469So2d231
832.04
et seq.
1975C189
257So2d92
305So2d188
30MiL84
832.04
Subsec. 1
A1971C136
95So2d23
113So2d387
9FLR293
832.041
285So2d428
290So2d123
20MiL245
Subsec. 1
A1971C136
832.05
1965C1503
C95So2d20
105So2d505
113So2d384
123So2d753
126So2d540
145So2d736
153So2d850
193So2d691
193So2d706
255So2d264
301So2d109
C305So2d187
324So2d191
333So2d63
339So2d213
341So2d216
356So2d347
368So2d948
372So2d489
390So2d1199
396So2d1108
403So2d616
404So2d749
433So2d1249
433So2d1336
470So2d88
470So2d835
452US921
69LE426
101SC3060
444F2d235
16BRW212
16MiL234
22MiL258
22MiL606
33MiL870
Subsec. 1
A1984C297
C95So2d20
433So2d1250

444F2d235
Subsec. 2
A1984C297
84So2d42
C95So2d20
113So2d383
113So2d387
115So2d169
123So2d335
123So2d753
128So2d757
136So2d633
153So2d850
161So2d697
188So2d861
203So2d174
235So2d751
239So2d857
325So2d466
326So2d63
370So2d800
393So2d1188
444F2d235
16FLR260
16MiL234
18MiL396
26MiL367
Subd. a
402So2d577
336So2d686
341So2d217
343So2d58
361So2d159
372So2d489
420So2d880
36FlS195
444F2d237
Subd. b
A1971C136
113So2d384
345So2d397
444F2d237
Subsec. 3
Ad1979C98
455So2d1154
Subd. a
444So2d564
Subsec. 4
A1984C297
113So2d384
113So2d387
123So2d335
123So2d752
128So2d757
136So2d633
148So2d261
153So2d849
161So2d696
184So2d698
188So2d861
190So2d621
C196So2d218
203So2d174
231So2d31
235So2d751
239So2d857
264So2d121
305So2d188
305So2d459
337So2d415
345So2d829
356So2d346
356So2d838
C358So2d545
360So2d486
363So2d165

368So2d948
393So2d1188
404So2d792
16MiL234
18MiL395
20MiL245
20MiL275
24MiL258
24MiL350
30MiL670
Subd. a
235So2d752
255So2d264
274So2d18
277So2d310
C358So2d546
393So2d1188
420So2d880
26MiL367
28MiL898
Subd. b
A1971C136
113So2d387
123So2d335
123So2d753
128So2d757
404So2d792
Subsec. 5
360So2d486
Subsec. 7
84So2d42
95So2d20
123So2d464
153So2d849
C287So2d134
305So2d188
335So2d1
339So2d213
341So2d218
30MiL670
832.06
Subsec. 1
A1969C77
A1974C348
A1977C174
A1979C11
832.07
Ad1975C189
A1980C301
360So2d486
368So2d948
444So2d564
461So2d979
30MiL84
34MiL524
35MiL494
Subsec. 1
Subd. a
A1977C174
A1979C345
360So2d487
442So2d1019
444So2d564
461So2d979
34MiL524
832.11
433So2d1344
833.04
17MJ783
836.01
et seq.
448So2d528

Shepard's Citations for Florida Statutes

Now back to work. Look where the arrow is pointing at the number 832.041. Under this number are citations to published cases that refer to § 832.041 of the *Florida Statutes*. If you were doing this research, you would write down these citations, find the cases and read them to see what they said about your statute.

In this example, you can see that in 1983, § 832.041 was referred to in volume 285 of the *Southern Reporter, Second Series*, on page 428.

You're not done yet, however. Now you must repeat the process with each volume that may contain later case references to the statute: the red hardcover Supplement 1986-1990 volume, the gold June 1990 Annual Cumulative Supplement, the bright red April 1991 Cumulative Supplement and the white Advance Sheet Edition. For example, as you are checking through the 1986-90 Supplement, you find it not only contains case citations but also a citation to a statute preceded by a capital "A." This is the 1986 amendment to the statute, which you found in the pocket part.

When you're done, you should have a list of citations. Don't worry about memorizing what all the abbreviations in the citations mean; you don't need to. At the front of each *Shepard's* volume there is a table of abbreviations.

Unfortunately, you can't tell from a list of bare citations whether the cases they refer to say anything meaningful about the statute. *Shepard's* simply lists all cases that mention a particular statute. It's up to you to find out if the case is important to your question. This means that you have to skim the portion of each case where the statute is mentioned. However, because some statutes are organized into numerous subsections, *Shepard's* will tell you which precise subsections of a statute are discussed in the case. This will help focus your search and allow you to eliminate cases that deal with irrelevant subsections. For instance, consider this Shepard's listing for Florida Statute § 832.05

832.05
1965C1503
C95So2d20
105So2d505
113So2d384
123So2d753
126So2d540
145So2d736
153So2d850
193So2d691
193So2d706
255So2d264
301So2d109
C305So2d187
324So2d191
333So2d63
339So2d213
341So2d216
356So2d347
368So2d948
372So2d489
390So2d1199
396So2d1108
403So2d616
404So2d749
433So2d1249
433So2d1336
470So2d88
470So2d835
452US921
69LE426
101SC3060
444F2d235
16BRW212
16MiL234
22MiL258
22MiL606
33MiL870
Subsec. 1
A1984C297
C95So2d20
433So2d1250

444F2d235
Subsec. 2
A1984C297
84So2d42
C95So2d20
113So2d383
113So2d387
115So2d169
123So2d335
123So2d753
128So2d757
136So2d633
153So2d850
161So2d697
188So2d861
203So2d174
235So2d751
239So2d857
325So2d466
326So2d63
370So2d800
393So2d1188
444F2d235
16FLR260
16MiL234
18MiL396
26MiL367
Subd. a
202So2d577
336So2d686
341So2d217
343So2d58
361So2d159
372So2d489
420So2d880
36FlS195
444F2d237
Subd. b
A1971C136
113So2d384
345So2d397
444F2d237
Subsec. 3
Ad1979C98
455So2d1154
Subd. a
444So2d564
Subsec. 4
A1984C297
113So2d384
113So2d387
123So2d335
123So2d752
128So2d757
136So2d633
148So2d261
153So2d849
161So2d696
184So2d698
188So2d861
190So2d621
C196So2d218
203So2d174
231So2d31
235So2d751
239So2d857
264So2d121
305So2d188
305So2d459
337So2d415
345So2d829
356So2d346
356So2d838
C358So2d545
360So2d486
363So2d165

368So2d948
393So2d1188
404So2d792
16MiL234
18MiL395
20MiL245
20MiL275
24MiL258
24MiL350
30MiL670
Subd. a
235So2d752
255So2d264
274So2d18
277So2d310
C358So2d546
393So2d1188
420So2d880
26MiL367
28MiL898
Subd. b
A1971C136
113So2d387
123So2d335
123So2d753
128So2d757
404So2d792
Subsec. 5
360So2d486
Subsec. 7
84So2d42
95So2d20
123So2d464
153So2d849
C287So2d134
305So2d188
335So2d1
339So2d213
341So2d218
30MiL670
832.06
Subsec. 1
A1969C77
A1974C348
A1977C174
A1979C11
832.07
Ad1975C189
A1980C301
360So2d486
368So2d948
444So2d564
461So2d979
30MiL84
34MiL524
35MiL494
Subsec. 1
Subd. a
A1977C174
A1979C345
360So2d487
442So2d1019
444So2d564
461So2d979
34MiL524
832.11
433So2d1344
833.04
17MJ783
836.01
et seq.
448So2d528

Section 832.05

The "832.05" is the number of the statute as found in the *Florida Statutes Annotated.* As you can see from the *Shepard's* citations this statute has many subsections. If you are interested only in an interpretation of subsection 3a, you would only have one citation to check out.

Four Warnings When You're Using *Shepard's*

1. Make sure you use the *Shepard's* that covers the state you are interested in.
2. When you look up a statute in *Shepard's*, make sure you use the part that deals with statutes (marked clearly on the front of the volume and the top of the page), and not with the part that deals with cases, regulations or the constitution.
3. Use the *Shepard's* volumes for the appropriate years. A hardcover volume that contains citations made between 1980 and 1985 will not do you any good for a statute enacted in 1986. You should use only the volumes that contain citations to cases decided after the statute was passed.
4. Look in all hardbound volumes and paperback supplements that may contain citations.

SUMMING UP

HOW TO SHEPARDIZE FEDERAL STATUTES

1. Note the year the statute you wish to Shepardize was passed.
2. Find *Shepard's United States Citations for Statutes.*
3. Select the volumes covering the years since the statute was passed.
4. Find the title number of the citation as it appears in boldface at the top of the page (for example, Title 25 U.S.C.).
5. Under the appropriate title number, find the section number of the statute (for example, Title 25 U.S.C. § 863).
6. Copy the citations listed under the section number. The citations refer to the exact page in the case where the statute is referred to.
7. Follow this procedure for all volumes and pamphlets up to the most recent.

SUMMING UP

HOW TO SHEPARDIZE STATE STATUTES

1. Note the year the statute you wish to Shepardize was passed.
2. Find the *Shepard's* volume for your state's statutes.
3. Select the volumes covering the years since the statute was passed.
4. If your state statutes are organized into codes, find the title of the code in the upper margin in boldface (for example, *Penal Code*). If your state goes by a Title system, find the Title number at the top of the page. If your state's statutes are consecutively numbered without reference to a code or title, find the place in *Shepard's* where the number appears in boldface.
5. If you are dealing with a code or title, find the section number of the statute (for example, Title 19, § 863).
6. Note the citations under the section number. These citations are to the book and pages where the statute is referred to.
7. Follow this process for all volumes and pamphlets up to the most recent.

4. The Case Digest Subject Index

If you haven't found a helpful case through one of the first three methods, you can proceed directly to a case digest. Digests are collections of headnotes from cases, which are organized according to subject and indexed. Digests are fully discussed in Chapter 10, *Shepard's and Digests: Expand and Update Your Research*, as a means of finding additional cases once you find a good relevant case to get you to that phase of your research. But the subject index to a digest may also help you discover "that one good case."

For example, if you want to know whether a father who doesn't support his child because he has lost his job can legally be denied visitation rights, you would be dealing with the topics of "child visitation," "child support" and "child custody." You could use the subject indexes (and tables of contents) in a case digest for your state to find a relevant case that deals with your questions.

5. The Digest Table of Cases

It is common to hear well-known cases referred to by name only. A couple of divorce lawyers might talk about the *Marvin v. Marvin* palimony case, or a politician might rant and rave about the harm that the *Miranda* case is doing to the country. Many people have heard of *New York Times v. Sullivan*, the Supreme Court case that extended First Amendment protection to media that report statements by public officials. If you know the name of a case but need its citation to locate and read it, the West *Digest* system is extremely helpful. Each digest is accompanied by a Table of Cases that lists all the cases referred to in that digest. By using the correct digest and accompanying Table of Cases, you can find the name of any case that was decided long enough ago—usually a year or more—to find its way into the Table of Cases.

LIBRARY EXERCISE

How to Use Shepard's Citations: Statutes

Now it's time to use the library to apply what you've just learned. This exercise asks you to use Shepard's Citations for Statutes to find the cases that have referred to (cited) a particular statute. Additional research exercises that include these and other skills are in the Appendix.

Problem

You are researching the federal law governing custody proceedings involving Native American children living in New Mexico. The statutes involved are Title 25 U.S.C., sections 1901 through 1923. You want to find out how these statutes have been interpreted by the U.S. Supreme Court and by the Tenth Circuit Court of Appeals (the circuit that New Mexico is in). You also want to know whether the statutes have been discussed in an *American Law Reports* (A.L.R.) article.

Questions

1. *Which particular volumes of which Shepard's will tell you every time sections 1911 and 1912 of Title 25 U.S.C. were cited in U.S. Supreme Court and Tenth Circuit Court of Appeals cases?*
2. *What is the citation for a Tenth Circuit Court of Appeals case that cited § 1911?*
3. *What is the citation of a U.S. District Court case that cited subsection b of § 1911?*
4. *What is the Supreme Court Reporter citation to a Supreme Court case that cited § 1912 as a whole?*
5. *Are there any A.L.R. annotations that cite § 1911 or 1912?*

Answers

1. Shepard's United States Citations has volumes for cases and volumes for statutes. In the statute volumes, you find Title 25, sections 1911 and 1912. The first volume, which includes Title 25, is Statute Edition, vol. 3, 1986; there are also supplemental volumes that include Title 25 and the paperbound supplements.
2. Cases decided by federal Courts of Appeal are published in the *Federal Reporter*, first and second series (F. and F.2d). The Tenth Circuit Court of Appeals case that cited Sections 1911 and 1912 is found in 822 F.2d 1501.
3. Cases decided by U.S. District Courts are published in the *Federal Supplement* (F. Supp). The citation for the case that cited subsection b of § 1911 is 624 F. Supp. 133.
4. The *Supreme Court Reporter* is abbreviated in *Shepard's* as SC. The citation you are looking for is 109 SC 1603.
5. In *Shepard's*, *American Law Reports* and other secondary sources are listed at the end of all the cases that cited your case. 80 A.L.R. 3d 1141s cited subsection b of § 1912 (the s means the cite is found in the A.L.R. pocket part); 74 A.L.R. 3d 421s cited subsection d and subsection f of § 1912.

The Table of Cases is organized with the plaintiff's name first. If you don't find your case in the Table of Cases, consult the Defendant-Plaintiff table.

When a case starts out in the trial court, the first name is the plaintiff's and the name after the "*v*," is the defendant's. However, if an appeal is brought by the defendant, sometimes the defendant's name is put first on the appeal. Since most cases are opinions issued by appellate courts, a case name may in fact consist of the defendant's name in front of the "*v*" and the plaintiff's name after. This fact gives rise to an extremely important rule of legal research: if you can't find a case under one name, reverse the names and try again. For instance, if you can't find the case you're looking for under *Jones v. Smith*, try *Smith v. Jones*. It works more often than you might think.

a. Federal Cases

The table of cases that is part of the West *Federal Practice Digest, Third Series*, lists every federal case reported since 1975, alphabetically by case name. The West *Federal Digest, Second Series*, lists cases reported between 1961 and 1975. For pre-1961 cases, the Table of Cases for the West *Modern Federal Practice Digest* should be consulted. Moore's *Federal Practice Digest* Table of Cases can also be used for earlier federal cases.

Assume, for example, that you are interested in the rights of unwed fathers with respect to decisions affecting their children. You have heard that a U.S. Supreme Court case called *Caban v. Mohammed* held that a New York law that allows an unwed mother, but not an unwed father, to object to a child's adoption is unconstitutional. You want to read this case but don't have a citation for it. You could go to the West *Federal Practice Digest* Table of Cases (start with the *Third Series*) and look it up. In the Table of Cases for the *Second Series* you would find what is shown below.

Now you have the citation and can go to the appropriate report and read the case for yourself. Easy.

While you can use the *Federal Digest* Table of Cases for U.S. Supreme Court cases, as we showed in the example, you could also utilize the Table of Cases for the West *Supreme Court Digest*.

SUMMING UP

HOW TO FIND FEDERAL CASES WHEN THE CITATION IS UNKNOWN

1. Locate the Table of Cases for West's *Federal Practice Digest* (*Third Series* for cases reported between 1975 and present, *Second Series* for cases between 1961-1975, and *Modern Federal Practice Digests* for earlier cases).

2. Find the case name in the hardcover volume or pocket part and note the citation.

3. If there is more than one entry for the case name, determine from the information provided with each entry (its date and issues decided) which case is the correct one. If cases involve the same topic, note both citations and read both cases.

4. If you don't find an entry for the case name, reverse the names and look again. If you still don't find it, look in the Defendant-Plaintiff Table of Cases under both names.

82 F P D 2d—61

CALIFANO

References are to Digest Topics and Key Numbers

C., Inc. v. Brookside Drug Store, Inc., Bkrtcy.Conn., 3 B.R. 120. See Brookside Drug Store, Inc., Matter of.

→ **Caban v. Mohammed,** U.S.N.Y., 99 S.Ct. 1760, 441 U.S. 380, 60 L.Ed.2d 297.—Adop 2, 7.2(3), 7.4(1); Const Law 70.-3(1), 70.3(6), 224(1), 224(2).

Caban v. Nelson, D.C.Conn., 475 F.Supp. 865. See Velez v. Nelson.

Caban, U. S. ex rel., v. Rowe, D.C.Ill., 449 F.Supp. 360. See U. S. ex rel. Caban v. Rowe.

Cabezal Supermarket, Inc., Matter of, D.C.N.D., 406 F.Supp. 345.—Bankr 303(6), 441.5, 442, 446(8.1).

Caesars Palace Securities Litigation, D.C.N.Y., 360 F.Supp. 366.—Fed Civ Proc 161, 176.

Cafeteria and Restaurant Workers Union, Local 472, AFL–CIO v. McElroy, U.S.Dist.Col., 81 S.Ct. 1743, 367 U.S. 886, 6 L.Ed.2d 1230.—Const Law 278.-4(3), 278.6(1).

Cafferty v. Trans World Airlines, Inc., D.C.Mo., 488 F.Supp. 1076.—Fed Cts 1145; Labor 416.4, 968.

Cagle's, Inc. v. N. L. R. B., C.A.5, 588 F.2d 943.—Labor 290, 367, 379, 382.2, 388.1, 394, 574, 577, 705.

& Supply, Inc., 98 Idaho 495, 567 P.2d 1246.

Calderon v. McGee, C.A.Tex., 589 F.2d 909.—Elections 12; Fed Cts 922.

Calderon v. McGee, C.A.Tex., 584 F.2d 66, vac in part and reh 589 F.2d 909.—Schools 53(1).

Caldwell v. Board of Ed. of City of St. Louis, C.A.Mo., 620 F.2d 1277. See Adams v. U. S.

Caldwell v. Califano, D.C.Ala., 455 F.Supp. 1069.—Social S 142.30.

Caldwell v. Camp, C.A.Mo., 594 F.2d 705.—Courts 508(1), 508(2), 508(7); Fed Civ

SUMMING UP

HOW TO FIND U.S. SUPREME COURT CASES WHEN THE CITATION IS UNKNOWN

1. Locate the Table of Cases for the U.S. Supreme Court Digest or Federal Practice Digest.
2. Find the case name in the hardcover volume or pocket part and note the citation.
3. If there is more than one entry for the case name, determine from the information provided with each entry (its date and issues decided) which case is the correct one. If cases involve the same topic, note both citations and read both cases.
4. If you don't find an entry for the case name, reverse the names and look again. If you still don't find it, look in the Defendant-Plaintiff Table of Cases under both names.

b. State Cases

If you're looking for a citation for a state case, use the West state or regional digests. For example, suppose you want to read the landmark Oregon Supreme Court case of *Burnette v. Wahl*, which held that children can't sue their parents for abandonment. To find the citation, locate the West *Regional Digest* that covers Oregon (the *Pacific Digest*) or the *Oregon Digest* and get the volume containing the Table of Cases. When you turn to *Burnette*, you would find what's shown below:

References are to Digest Topics and Key Numbers

Burnett v. State Acc. Ins. Fund, Or.App., 563 P.2d 1234, 29 Or.App. 415. See Kelly, Matter of.

Burnett v. Superior Court of Orange County, Cal., 528 P.2d 372, 117 Cal. Rptr. 556.—Courts 26; Crim Law 237, 241; Ind & Inf 15(4), 141; Mand 48, 61.

Burnett v. Tisdell, Okl., 370 P.2d 924.—App & E 717, 854(6), 867(2), 977(3); Cust & U 18; New Tr 6, 163(2).

Burnett v. Western Pac. Ins. Co., Or., 469 P.2d 602, 255 Or. 547.—Decl Judgm 322, 329; Insurance 514.9(2), 514.10(1), 514.12, 616.1, 616.2; Judgm 713(2), 720.

Burnette v. McClearn, Colo., 427 P.2d 331, 162 Colo. 503.—Extrad 34.

→ **Burnette v. Wahl**, Or., 588 P.2d 1105, 284 Or. 705.—Action 3; Const Law 70.-1(11); Parent & C 11.

Burney v. State, Okl.Cr., 594 P.2d 1226. —Crim Law 683(2), 1137(5), 1153(1), 1202(4), 1202(6); Witn 269(1).

Burnford v. Blanning, Colo., 540 P.2d 337, 189 Colo. 292.—App & E 1008.1(3); Contracts 352(6); Frds St of 119(2), 131(1); Spec Perf 44; Ven & Pur 85.

Burnford v. Blanning, Colo.App., 525 P.2d 494, 33 Colo.App. 444, rev 540 P.2d 337, 189 Colo. 292.—Contracts 252; Frds St of 129(1), 129(3), 129(5); Ven & Pur 85.

Burnham v. Bankers Life & Cas. Co., Utah, 470 P.2d 261, 24 Utah 2d 277, appeal after remand 484 P.2d 155, 26 Utah 2d 9.—Insurance 11.1, 255, 256.1, 365.2, 365.3; Judgm 181(2).

Burnham v. Burnham, Wash.App., 567 P.2d 242, 18 Wash.App. 1.—Lim of Act 145(1), 148(1), 149(1).

Burnham v. Calfee, Or.App., 608 P.2d 606. See Woelke v. Calfee.

Burnham v. Eshleman, Or., 479 P.2d 501, 257 Or. 400.—App & E 1050.4; Autos 243(1); Evid 380; Trial 56, 251(1).

Burnham v. Nehren, Wash.App., 503 P.2d 122, 7 Wash.App. 860.—Autos 160(1), 160(3), 160(4), 206, 216, 217(1), 217(2), 217(5), 245(6), 245(72), 246(58); New Tr 38.

Burnham v. Yellow Checker Cab, Inc., N.M., 391 P.2d 413, 74 N.M. 125.—App & E 928(1); Autos 245(91), 246(58); Neglig 83.1, 83.6; Trial 203(1).

Burningham v. Ott, Utah, 525 P.2d 620. —Judgm 178, 181(2), 185(1), 186; Lim of Act 104½.

Burnison v. Fry, Kan., 428 P.2d 809, 199 Kan. 277.—Judgm 524, 660, 668(1), 720, 739; Parties 29.

Burnkrant v. Saggau, Ariz.App., 470 P.2d 115, 12 Ariz.App. 310.—Admin Law 229; App & E 1, 781(7); Mand 79; Schools 177.

Burns, Application of, Hawaii, 407 P.2d 885, 49 Haw. 20.—Atty & C 76(4); Divorce 165(6), 402(1), 402(7); Hab Corp 90, 99(3); Infants 18; Judgm 399, 817, 818(1); Parent & C 2(18).

Burns v. A. G. C., Or., 400 P.2d 2, 240 Or. 95.—Insurance 146.7(1), 169(1), 178.-3(2).

Burns v. Anchorage Funeral Chapel, Alaska, 495 P.2d 70.—Dead Bodies 9; Ex & Ad 426, 438(1); Lim of Act 124; Parties 52, 60, 76(1), 80(1), 84(1), 96(2); Plead 408.

Burns v. Atchison, T. & S. F. Ry. Co., Okl., 372 P.2d 36.—App & E 207, 230, 261, 499(1), 501(1), 1060.1(1), 1072; R R 350(1); Trial 131(3), 133.6(8).

Burns v. Burns, Okl.App., 585 P.2d 1126. See Burns' Estate, Matter of.

Burns v. Burns, Ariz., 526 P.2d 717, 111 Ariz. 178.—Const Law 70.1(11); Divorce 313.

Burns v. Burns, Ariz.App., 519 P.2d 190, 21 Ariz.App. 337, vac 526 P.2d 717, 111 Ariz. 178.—Com Law 14; Courts 90(6); Divorce 313; Hus & W 205(2).

Burns v. Burns, Colo., 454 P.2d 814, 169 Colo. 79.—Atty & C 81; Contracts 143(3); Divorce 287; Evid 397(6), 450(1), 455; Hus & W 279(2).

Burns v. Burns, Colo., 392 P.2d 662, 155 Colo. 96.—Hus & W 279(6).

Burns v. Burns, Mont., 400 P.2d 642, 145 Mont. 1, 13 A.L.R.3d 1355.—Divorce 55, 164, 238, 240(2), 286(1).

Burns v. Denver Post, Inc., Colo.App., 606 P.2d 1310.—Libel 6(1).

Burns v. Dills, Wash., 413 P.2d 370, 68 Wash.2d 377.—Autos 163(1), 169, 219, 242(3), 243(1), 246(19), 246(22), 246(30); Evid 472(1); New Tr 39(6); Statut 223.2(20).

Burns v. Ferguson, Okl.App., 576 P.2d 784.—Guar 6.

Burns v. Hand, Kan., 375 P.2d 637, 190 Kan. 471.—Hab Corp 113(9).

Burns v. Herberger, Ariz.App., 498 P.2d 536, 17 Ariz.App. 462.—Const Law 60; Tax 28, 42(1), 347, 348(3), 348.1(1), 348.-1(3), 362½, 485(1), 485(3).

Burns v. Newell, Or.App., 507 P.2d 414, 12 Or.App. 621.—Hab Corp 92(1); Pardon 14.11, 14.15.

Burns v. Norwesco Marine, Inc., Wash. App., 535 P.2d 860, 13 Wash.App. 414. —Atty & C 20, 21; Corp 1.4(1), 1.4(2), 1.4(4), 1.6(3), 1.6(7); Judges 51(2); Pretrial Proc 724.

Burns v. Ottati, Colo.App., 513 P.2d 469. —Autos 227, 246(58); Evid 553(4), 555; Neglig 83.1, 83.6, 83.8, 141(9).

Burns v. Page, Okl.Cr., 446 P.2d 622.—Crim Law 1216(1); Prisons 15(2).

Burns v. Payne, Wash., 373 P.2d 790, 60 Wash.2d 323.—Judgm 106(1); Pretrial Proc 588.

Burns v. Ramsey, Colo.App., 520 P.2d 137.—Insurance 103, 103.1(2).

Burns v. Sheriff, Carson City, Nev., 569 P.2d 407.—Const Law 250.2(1), 263; Crim Law 224; Hab Corp 85.5(2); Homic 139; Ind & Inf 10.2(12).

Burns v. Sheriff, Clark County, Nev., 554 P.2d 257, 92 Nev. 533.—Crim Law 238(3), 404(4); Drugs & N 46; Hab Corp 25.1(2).

Burns v. Slater, Okl., 559 P.2d 428.—Const Law 208(3); Elections 22; States 200.

Burns v. Sommerfeld 96 Idaho 336, 528 P.2d 680. See Andersen v. Burns.

Burns v. Sommerfeld Agency, Idaho, 528 P.2d 680, 96 Idaho 336. See Andersen v. Burns.

Burns v. Southwestern Preferred Properties, Inc., Okl., 580 P.2d 986.—Work Comp 974, 978.

Burns v. State, Kan., 524 P.2d 737, 215 Kan. 497.—Burg 49; Crim Law 273.-1(1), 273.1(2), 274(3), 986, 991(1), 998(14), 998(16), 1158(1); Larc 88.

Burns v. State, Nev., 495 P.2d 602, 88 Nev. 215.—Crim Law 412.1(1), 412.2(3), 706(3), 763(1), 1159.2(5), 1170½(3), 1170½(6), 1202(1), 1202(4); Larc 65.

Burns v. State, Okl.Cr., 595 P.2d 801.—Arrest 63.1, 68; Crim Law 394.1(3), 814(17), 863(2), 1044.1(1); Searches 7(26).

Burns v. State, Okl.Cr., 547 P.2d 978.—Crim Law 1211.

Burns v. State, Wyo., 574 P.2d 422.—Crim Law 936(4), 942(2), 1043(3), 1114(1), 1137(3); Rob 24.3.

Burns v. State, Bureau of Revenue, Income Tax Division, N.M., 439 P.2d 702, 79 N.M. 53, cert den 89 S.Ct. 119, 393 U.S. 841, 21 L.Ed.2d 111.—Tax 28, 31, 959, 959, 966; U S 3.

Burns v. State Dept. of Social and Health Services, Wash.App., 581 P.2d 1069, 20 Wash.App. 585.—Social S 4.5, 11, 194.1, 194.13, 194.19; States 4.13.

Burns v. Superior Court of Pima County, Ariz., 397 P.2d 448, 97 Ariz. 112, 18 A.L.R.3d 1169.—Ex & Ad 130(1), 314(1), 315.6(1); Mand 10, 12, 24, 42.

Burns v. Transcon Lines, N.M.App., 595 P.2d 761, 92 N.M. 791, cert den 593 P.2d 1078, 92 N.M. 675.—Work Comp 89.

Burns v. U & S Motor Co., Inc., Utah, 562 P.2d 233. See Chrysler Credit Corp. v. Burns.

Burns v. U & S Motor Co., Inc., Utah, 527 P.2d 655. See Chrysler Credit Corp. v. Burns.

Burns v. Wheeler, Ariz., 446 P.2d 925, 103 Ariz. 525.—App & E 1002; Autos 157, 197(7), 245(82), 246(10), 246(28); Costs 203; Pretrial Proc 718; Trial 244(4).

Burns v. Yuba Heat Transfer Corp., Okl.App., 615 P.2d 1029.—Work Comp 545, 597, 1418, 1492, 1506, 1939.11(5).

Burns, City of. See City of Burns.

Burns Const. Co. v. Bilbo, Okl., 370 P.2d 913.—Sales 267, 273(1), 441(3).

Burns' Estate, Matter of, Kan., 608 P.2d 942, 277 Kan. 573.—Courts 202(5); Ex & Ad 256(5); Ven & Pur 199.

Burns' Estate, Matter of, Okl.App., 585 P.2d 1126.—Adv Poss 58; Des & Dist 83; Ex & Ad 85(8); Propty 9; Ten in C 3; Trusts 1, 44(1), 62, 86, 88, 89(1), 89(5), 91, 95, 107, 109, 110.

Burns Realty & Trust Co. v. Mack, Colo., 450 P.2d 75. See D. C. Burns Realty & Trust Co. v. Mack.

Burns, State ex rel., v. Blair, Idaho, 417 P.2d 217, 91 Idaho 137. See State ex rel. Burns v. Blair.

Burns, State ex rel., v. City of Livingston, Mont., 395 P.2d 971, 144 Mont. 248. See State ex rel. Burns v. City of Livingston.

Burns, State ex rel., v. Kelly, Idaho, 403 P.2d 566, 89 Idaho 139. See State ex rel. Burns v. Kelly.

Burns, State ex rel., v. Steely, Okl.Cr., 600 P.2d 367. See State ex rel. Burns v. Steely.

Burnside v. Burnside, N.M., 514 P.2d 36, 85 N.M. 517.—Divorce 223, 226, 231, 235, 239.

Burnside v. Landon, Idaho, 487 P.2d 957. See Brown v. Burnside.

Burnside v. Runstetler, Ariz.App., 504 P.2d 1299, 19 Ariz.App. 76.—App & E 846(5); Divorce 165(2), 386(2).

Burnworth v. Burnworth, N.M., 605 P.2d 222, 93 N.M. 714.—Divorce 287.

Burnworth v. Burnworth, Okl.App., 572 P.2d 301.—Divorce 62(1), 160; Judgm 141, 382, 386(3).

Burr v. Burr, Nev., 611 P.2d 623.—Divorce 151, 223, 286(4), 308, 309.4.

Burr v. Capital Reserve Corp., Cal., 458 P.2d 185, 80 Cal.Rptr. 345, 71 C.2d 983. —Brok 8(3); Princ & A 14(1), 24; Usury 12, 16, 18, 42, 102(1), 102(5), 113, 119, 138.

Burr v. Carey, 407 P.2d 779, 2 Ariz.App. 238. See Burr v. Frey.

Burr v. Department of Revenue, Mont., 575 P.2d 45.—Tax 861, 887.

Burr v. Frey, Ariz.App., 407 P.2d 779, 2 Ariz.App. 238.—Hab Corp 113(8).

Burr v. Green Bros. Sheet Metal, Inc., Colo., 409 P.2d 511, 159 Colo. 25.—Autos 205; Neglig 131; Witn 267, 269(2), 276, 282, 405(2), 406.

Burr v. Lane, Wash.App., 517 P.2d 988, 10 Wash.App. 412, 661.—App & E 731(2), 733; Garn 191; Insurance

Table of Cases in Pacific Digest

SUMMING UP

HOW TO FIND STATE CASES WHEN NO CITATION IS KNOWN

1. Locate the Table of Cases for the state or regional digest that covers your state's cases.
2. Find the case name in the hardcover volume or pocket part and note the citation.
3. If there is more than one entry for the case name, determine from the information provided with each entry (its date and issues decided) which case is the correct one. If two cases involve the same topic, note both citations and read both cases.
4. If you don't find an entry for the case name, reverse the names and look again. If you still don't find it, look in the Defendant-Plaintiff Table of Cases under both names.

6. The Case Reporter Table of Cases

Each case reporter volume has a Table of Cases usually at the front. This table contains a listing of all cases in that volume of the report and their page references. This is a very valuable tool if you are searching for a case that you know only by name and that was decided too recently to be listed in a *Digest* Table of Cases (generally, within the previous six months to one year).

If the case is more recent than the dates of the cases in the latest hardcover case reporter, use the Table of Cases in the Advance Sheets. But remember that there is usually a one- to two-month lag between the decision in a case and its publication in an advance sheet. If the case is old enough to be in the hardcover volumes, start with the table of cases in the latest hardcover volume and work backwards.

7. The Case Reporter Subject Index

Each case reporter volume has a subject index, usually at the back. If the reporter is published by West Publishing Co. (most are), the index is in fact organized according to the key numbers that have been assigned the cases contained in the volume. If you know that a case involving a specific topic was decided during a certain time period, but don't know its name, you may be able to find it by looking in the subject index for each volume containing cases for that time period.

LIBRARY EXERCISE

Finding Cases by Popular Name

Now it's time to use the library to apply what you've just learned. This exercise asks you to find the citation for a case that you know by name only. Additional research exercises that include these and other skills are in the Appendix.

Problem

You are researching famous cases in which several defendants were identified by the public as a group. Your research has yielded two popular case names—the *Chicago Seven* case and the *Scottsboro* case. You have searched the Table of Cases for all digests and have come up empty.

Questions

1.a. *To find the citations to the "Chicago Seven" case, what index will you use?*

1.b. *What do you find under "Chicago Seven"?*

1.c. *Find the case in 472 F.2d and write out its full citation.*

2. *How many cases are known as the "Scottsboro" cases? Is there any way to tell whether they are related without going further than* Shepard's?

Answers

1.a. In *Shepard's Acts and Cases by Popular Names: Federal and State,* in the third volume, are federal and state cases cited by popular names.

1.b. The Chicago Seven case is listed with two cites. The first is 461 F.2d 389; the second one is 472 F.2d 340.

1.c. Going to the *Federal Reporter,* 2d series, volume 472, page 340, you find *United States v. Dellinger*, 472 F.2d 340 (1972), cert. den. 93 S. Ct. 1443.

2. *Shepard's Acts and Cases by Popular Names: Federal and State* seems to show five different cases. Although the *Alabama Reporter* (Ala.) citations are different, they are not very far away from each other; in addition, they each have one Supreme Court citation (U.S.) in common with at least one other.

For example, suppose you want to read a 1992 Illinois court decision that interprets that state's statute governing stock issuances of small corporations. You could find what you were looking for by using the subject index for the volumes containing cases decided in 1992. Simply look under "corporations," "stock" or "business" until you find what you are looking for, and the index would refer you to the proper case. (See Chapter 4 for help in using a legal index.)

Be prepared to look under more than one topic when trying to find a case through this method. Also be aware that the volume may contain the case you're looking for even though it's not described in the subject index.

SUMMING UP

HOW TO FIND THE TEXT OF A U.S. SUPREME COURT CASE DECIDED OVER ONE YEAR

1. If you have the case citation, find the indicated reporter, volume and page.
2. If you don't have a citation but know the name of the case, consult the volume containing the Table of Cases for the *United States Supreme Court Digest* (West Publishing Co.). Check both the hardcover volume and the pocket part.
3. If you don't know the case name, utilize the Digest's subject index, starting with the pocket part. Then, turn to the hardcover volume. Be prepared to look under more than one subject.
4. If you can't find a citation to the case in the digest but you know the approximate year the case was decided, use the Table of Cases or subject index in each case reporter volume for Supreme Court cases decided during that period of time.

SUMMING UP

HOW TO FIND THE TEXT OF A U.S. SUPREME COURT CASE DECIDED WITHIN THE PAST YEAR

If you have the citation, locate the advance sheets of the appropriate report and turn to the indicated page. If you don't have the citation, there are two quick ways to find your case.

U.S. Law Week If you know the name of the case, consult the *U.S. Law Week* volume for the current year. This loose-leaf weekly publication contains a table of cases that tells you which page in *U.S. Law Week* the case appears on.

If you don't know the name of the case, use the *U.S. Law Week* topical index. By searching the correct topic, you should find a reference to one or more cases whose description resembles the case you're looking for.

Advance Sheets If you know the name and approximate date your case was decided, start looking in the appropriate Advance Sheets (the ones dated a month or more after the decision). Descriptions by name and subject of the cases contained in each volume can be found on either the outside or the inside of the cover.

A quick skim will tell you whether a particular advance sheet contains the case you are interested in. Also, if you know the name of your case, each advance sheet contains a cumulative listing of case names and citations to where they can be found. A new cumulative index starts for each new report volume number.

SUMMING UP

HOW TO FIND A STATE SUPREME COURT CASE DECIDED MORE THAN ONE YEAR AGO

1. If you have a citation, find the proper volume and page.
2. If you have no citation but know the name of the case, find its citation by consulting the Table of Cases to either the *West Digest* for your state or the *West Regional Digest* that covers your state (if one exists). Check the pocket part first. If you don't find the case name, go to the hardcover volume.
3. If you don't know the name of the case, use the subject index to the appropriate digest and try to find a summary of the case in the body of the digest. If you do, the citation will be provided.
4. If you can't find a citation to the case in the digest but you know the approximate year the case was decided, use the Table of Cases or subject index in each case reporter volume for cases decided during that period of time.

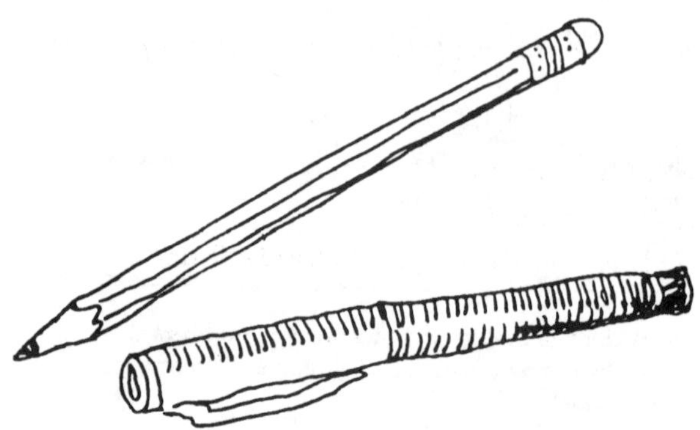

SUMMING UP

HOW TO FIND A STATE SUPREME COURT CASE DECIDED WITHIN THE PAST YEAR

1. If you have a citation, find the proper volume and page.
2. If you have no citation but know the name of the case, locate the advance sheets for a report that publishes the Supreme Court decisions for your state. This will probably be either a regional reporter or the official reporter for your particular state.
3. If you know the approximate date of the case, start browsing through the advance sheets that were published after the case. Each advance sheet should have a case name index to the cases reported in it.
4. If you know the subject that the case addressed but not its name, use the subject index that is included in each advance sheet.

C. The Next Step

Suppose you find a good, relevant case or case; then what? It is at this point that your research efforts can really become productive. Once you have located even one relevant case, you have the key to all other relevant case law. By using two basic tools—*Shepard's Citations for Cases* and the West *Digest* system—you can parlay your case into a notebook full of both helpful and harmful precedent. You can go from the narrowest point of the hourglass research model (Chapter 2) to a broad base of helpful material. These tools are discussed in the following chapter.

REVIEW

Questions

1. *In what year was the case* Ocean v. River, 467 F.2d 208 (5th Cir. 1973), *decided?*
2. *What is the name of the defendant in* Ocean v. River? *The plaintiff?*
3. *What does "5th Cir." mean in the* Ocean v. River *citation?*
4. *What does the F.2d stand for in the* Ocean v. River *citation?*
5. *If the* Ocean v. River *case is in volume 467 of F.2d, what page does it start on?*
6. *How can a background resource lead you to relevant cases?*
7. *If you find a relevant statute and are looking for good cases in the* Notes of Decisions *section following the statute, can you tell for sure from a case note whether a particular case is helpful?*
8. *How does* Shepard's *help you find cases that have interpreted your statute?*
9. *In addition to the hardbound volumes of* Shepard's, *how many gold, bright red and white paper supplements should you have to look in to bring your Shepardizing completely up to date?*
10. *Each* Shepard's *citation has several abbreviations in it. How can you find out what they stand for?*
11. *If you can't find any relevant cases by using background resources, case notes or* Shepard's, *how can the digests help?*
12. *Suppose you are told that a 1990 California case named* Wind v. Rain *is relevant to your problem. You go to the table of cases in the* California Digest *and look under "Wind" but find nothing. What will you try next?*
13. *You are in a digest table of cases looking for* Snow v. Sleet, *and find two cases by that name. How can you tell which is the one you are looking for?*

Answers

1. 1973.
2. River; Ocean.
3. This case was decided by the federal Court of Appeals for the 5th Circuit.
4. This case is published in the *Federal Reporter*, 2d series.
5. Page 208.
6. Most background materials have many footnotes with citations to cases that discuss specific points of law covered in the main discussion.
7. Not really. The case notes are helpful as a weeding-out process, but all possibly relevant cases should be located and read.
8. *Shepard's Citations for Statutes* gives you citations of all cases that have referred to (cited) your statute for any purpose.
9. One of each color.
10. Every *Shepard's* volume, hardbound or paper, has a list of abbreviations in the front.
11. The digests have subject indexes that lead you to the topics and key numbers for your issue.
12. Look under "Rain" in the same table; look under "Wind" in the Defendant-Plaintiff table; look under "Rain" in the Defendant-Plaintiff table.
13. If you know the date of the case, look for that; if that doesn't work, look at the list of topics and key numbers following each entry; look each case up under its topic and key number to see what issues it involves. If you still can't decide, you'll have to read both cases.

CHAPTER 10

Shepard's and Digests: Expand and Update Your Research

Chapter 9, *Finding Cases*, discussed how to find a specific case that might help you answer your research question. This chapter introduces the tools that let you jump from one case to other cases that may shed light on your issues. These may be cases that directly affect the continuing validity of the "one good case" you found (for instance, cases that overrule or reverse the case), or cases that add to your understanding of your issues without affecting the validity of the case you've already found. The tools are:

- *Shepard's Citations for Cases*, and
- the *West* digest system.

A. Shepard's Citations for Cases

Shepard's Citations for Cases is possibly the single most powerful research tool in the law library. Once you have located a case that speaks to your research issues, *Shepard's* gives you a list of every later case that has referred to it. You can use this list to:

- see if the case was affirmed, modified or reversed by a higher court
- see if other cases affect the value of the case as precedent or persuasive authority
- find other cases that may help your argument or give you better answers to your question.

Shepard's works only when the case you are interested in has actually been referred to in the later case by name. If a later case deals with the same subject but doesn't mention your case, *Shepard's* won't help. One of the happy by-products of the adversary system (happy at least for legal researchers) is that attorneys arguing appeals usually dredge up and present to the court every possibly relevant case. These cases, and others located by the court's own clerks, are typically included in the court's opinion. *Shepard's* is therefore an extremely reliable guide to how any given case is used by the courts.

Editor's Note As you read the next several pages, you may feel that the information is so dry and technical that you can't absorb it all at once. Don't try. Just understand the broad outline of how the system works. When you actually need to use *Shepard's*, take this book along. After the first few encounters you will surely get the hang of it.

1. Shepard's Citations for Cases: The Basics

Before learning how to use *Shepard's Citations for Cases* it helps to know the basics:

- *Shepard's Citations for Cases* are dark red, thick, hardcover volumes with separate update pamphlets that may be gold, bright red or white, depending on how recently the hardcover volumes were published. (If you remember from Chapter 6, *Shepard's Citations for Statutes* look the same.)
- Separate *Shepard's Citations for Cases* are published for each state, for federal court cases and for U. S. Supreme Court cases. Sometimes the *Shepard's Citations for Cases* is in a separate volume; sometimes it is combined in the same volume with *Shepard's Citations for Statutes* for that state.
- The outside of each *Shepard's* volume tells whether it covers statutes, cases or both. For example, the *Shepard's Mississippi Citations* has the following on its outside cover:

  "Cases, Constitutions, Statutes, Codes, Laws, Etc."

  Minnesota Shepard's, on the other hand, has case citations in one volume and everything else in another.
- *Shepard's Citations for Cases* is organized according to the case reporters that publish cases. Each

Shepard's volume has a box in the first couple of pages telling you the specific publications covered by that volume. Below is a sample taken from the *Shepard's Citations* for cases contained in the *Northeastern Reporter*.

- To use *Shepard's Citations for Cases*, you need the case citation—the name of the case reporter your case appears in, its volume number and the first page on which the case appears.
- *Shepard's* hardcover volumes for the cases of a particular state's courts, or the federal courts, cover different time periods. For example, one hardcover volume may contain all references made by cases decided before 1980, another may contain all references made by cases decided between 1980 and 1985, and a third may contain all references made by cases decided between 1985 and 1990.

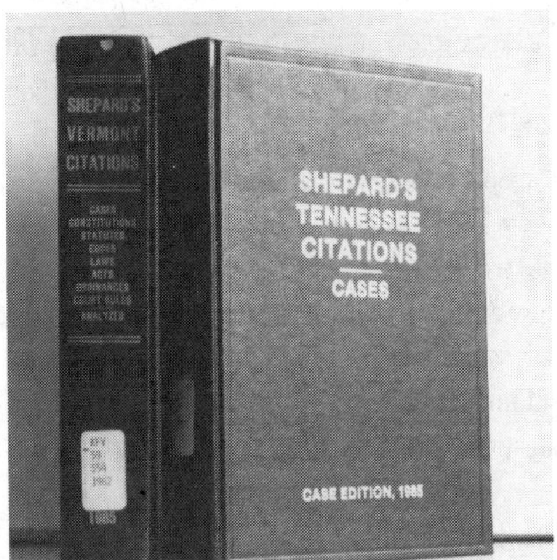

Shepard's Citations for Cases

- *Shepard's Citations for Cases* is kept in different places in different libraries. Some libraries have their *Shepard's* in a central location, while others have their *Shepard's* at the end of the volumes of cases for each state.
- *Shepard's Citations for Cases* uses its own citations system—which is different than the "Blue Book" system, the one used by this book. Every *Shepard's* volume has a table of abbreviations in case you get confused.

SHEPARD'S
NORTHEASTERN REPORTER
CITATIONS

A COMPILATION OF CITATIONS TO
ALL CASES REPORTED IN THE NORTHEASTERN REPORTER

THE CITATIONS
which include affirmances, reversals and dismissals by higher state courts and by the United States Supreme Court

APPEAR IN

NORTHEASTERN REPORTER
UNITED STATES SUPREME COURT REPORTS
LAWYERS' EDITION, UNITED STATES SUPREME COURT REPORTS
SUPREME COURT REPORTER
FEDERAL CASES
FEDERAL REPORTER
FEDERAL SUPPLEMENT
FEDERAL RULES DECISIONS
ATLANTIC REPORTER
CALIFORNIA REPORTER
NEW YORK SUPPLEMENT
NORTHWESTERN REPORTER
PACIFIC REPORTER
SOUTHEASTERN REPORTER
SOUTHERN REPORTER
SOUTHWESTERN REPORTER
AMERICAN BAR ASSOCIATION JOURNAL

and in annotations of

LAWYERS' EDITION, UNITED STATES SUPREME COURT REPORTS
AMERICAN LAW REPORTS

also in Vols. 1–283 Illinois Appellate Court Reports, Vols. 1–19 Ohio Appellate Reports and Vols. 1–101 Pennsylvania Superior Court Reports

SECOND EDITION - - - - - - - - - - - - - - VOLUME 2 (1974)

SHEPARD'S CITATIONS, Inc.
COLORADO SPRINGS
COLORADO 80901

Shepherd's Citations for Cases Published in the Northeastern Reporter

2. How to Use *Shepard's Citations for Cases*

Step 1 Identify the citation of the case you wish to Shepardize. Most cases are published in at least two reporters—the official reporter and a West regional reporter. You may use *Shepard's Citations for Cases* for either. The only parts of the citation you need are the volume, reporter abbreviation and page number—for instance, 112 Cal. Rptr. 456.

Step 2 Find the *Shepard's* volumes that cover the reporter in the citation. If you chose the *Northwestern Reporter* citation, for example, select the *Shepard's* for the *Northwestern Reporter*.

Step 3 If a *Shepard's* volume contains citations for more than one reporter (for example, for both the official reporter and for the West regional reporter), find the part that covers citations for the reporter named in the citation you have selected. For instance, if your citation is for the *Northwestern Reporter*, locate the pages that cover this series rather than the pages that pertain to your state's official reporter.

Step 4 Note the year of the case you are Shepardizing. Select the volume or volumes that contain citations for cases decided after the case you are Shepardizing. Remember to check the update pamphlets—gold, red and white—if you have started with a hardcover volume. Some researchers prefer to work backwards—checking the pamphlets first and then working back to the earliest relevant hardcover volume. Either way is fine.

Step 5 Find the volume number (in boldface) that corresponds to the volume number in the citation to the case being Shepardized. For example, if you are Shepardizing a case with the citation "874 F.2d 1035", search for **Vol. 874** in bold print at the top of or on the page.

Step 6 Under this volume number, find the page number of the citation for the cited case. To continue the example from Step 5, search for the page number (**-1035-**) in bold print.

Step 7 Under the bold page number, review the citations given for the citing cases.

Step 8 Use the letters to the left of the citation to decide whether the case is worth reviewing. (See Sections 3 and 4, below, for a discussion of what these letters mean and when to use them.)

Step 9 Use the numbers to the right of the citation to decide whether the citing case is referring to the cited case for issues you might be interested in. (See Section 5, below, for a discussion of what these numbers mean and how to use them.)

Step 10 After you write down all potentially useful citations, go on to more recent *Shepard's* volumes and update pamphlets and repeat these steps.

HOW SHEPARD'S WORKS: AN EXAMPLE

This example shows how Steps 1 through 7 work. Steps 8 and 9 are covered in subsections 3, 4 and 5, below. We are searching for cases that have referred to *Nationwide Insurance v. Ervin*, 231 N.E.2d 112 (1967). We call *Ervin* the "cited case," and any case that has referred to it is called a "citing " case.

Step 1 Identify the citation for the *Ervin* case. We will use the West regional reporter citation, 231 N.E.2d 112 (1967).

Step 2 Find the volume that contains citations to cases published by the Northeastern Reporter.

Step 3 Use the part of the volume that contains Northeastern Reporter citations. The volume that contains citations for Northeastern Reporter cases also contains citations for the official case reporter (Illinois Appellate Reports).

Step 4 Find the volume for the correct period. We only want to use volumes that have citations for cases decided after 1967, the year *Ervin* was decided. In this example, all volumes of *Shepard's Citations for Cases* that contain Northeastern Reporter citations have at least some citations to cases that have been decided after 1967, so we must check them all, including the pamphlets.

Step 5 Find the volume number appearing in the Northeastern Reporter citation for *Ervin*—Vol. 231.

Step 6 Find the page number. The *Ervin* page number appears as -112-.

Step 7 Review the citations. Under the page number (-112-) appear the citations to every case that has referred to the *Ervin* decision.

See the example on the following page.

That is basically the way you use *Shepard's* to find cases that have referred to the case you're interested. But you often want to know a little bit more about the citing case before you take the time to read it. Does it bear directly on the validity of the cited case? Does it help you understand whether the cited case is precedent or persuasive authority? Does it mention the cited case for the same reasons that interest you?.

Fortunately, Shepard's *provides some guidance on each of these points; subsections 3, 4 and 5, below, explain how.*

3. Was the Cited Case Directly Affected by the Citing Case in an Appeal?

Once you have a case you are interested in, you want to find out whether it has been appealed, and if so, whether the appeal affected the case as a source of law. *Shepard's* uses a code next to its citations that instantly gives you this information.

For example, suppose you read a case called *Jones v. Smith*, which is located at 500 F. Supp. 325. Since the case is published in the *Federal Supplement*, we know it was decided by a U.S. district court. (See Chapter 8, *How Cases Are Published.*) The district court case may not have had the last word, however; the case quite possibly was appealed to a higher court—typically, a U.S. Circuit Court of Appeals, but in rare instances the U.S. Supreme Court.

Once a case is appealed, the published opinion of the lower or intermediate appellate court may or may not continue to be a valid expression of the law. When a higher appellate court reverses a published decision of a lower court, it usually vacates the lower court's opinion. This means that the opinion is not to be considered as law for any purpose. The underlying case may also be affirmed or modified on appeal. In these situations the lower court's opinion will usually remain in existence to provide guidance for future courts, but sometimes also may be ordered vacated and replaced with the higher court's opinion.

NORTHEASTERN REPORTER, 2d SERIES

Vol. 231

323FS[6]344
596FS[6]784
650FS437
64A3506s

—70—
(12OS26)
(41Op159)
231NE[3]332
370NE[3]458
371NE[3]843
381NE[2]972
414NE[4]438
453NE[4]664
454NE[2]1389
488NE927

—71—
(12OA68)
(41Op122)
p166NE808
c484NE220
j484NE221
18A2813s

—81—
(12OA87)
(41Op163)
c432NE[8]212
Cir. 6
577FS[4]1131
Md
513A2d938

—85—
(12OA59)
(41Op117)

—91—
(12OA83)
(41Op160)
521NE[4]1153
521NE[6]1153
31A3585n

—94—
(12OhM127)
(41Op131)

—97—
(87IlA411)
Cert Den
269NE[2]355
269NE[5]356
273NE[1]162
280NE[12]46
283NE[15]43
318NE[12]122
326NE[9]468
363NE[5]625
363NE[12]626
369NE[1]295
369NE[2]295
447NE[6]441
458NE[5]1069
f502NE[6]478
18A2633s

—103—
(87IlA181)
Cert Den
323NE[2]809
323NE[4]809
374NE[4]1140

—107—
(87IlA139)
cc257NE233
317NE[1]631
347NE[1]70
360NE[2]1197
378NE[1]1157

—109—
(87IlA82)
Cert Den
262NE[1]797
281NE[1]388
378NE[3]606
412NE[1]629

—112—
(87IlA432)
241NE[1]120
241NE[3]120
272NE[7]61
274NE[3]879
287NE[1]530
289NE[3]703
293NE[3]704
305NE[3]417
379NE[2]66
d412NE[5]632
d412NE[7]632
e427NE[7]130
474NE[6]785
474NE[7]785
481NE[1]45
497NE[3]479
502NE[2]1295
510NE[2]1183
Ga
221SE482
Iowa
174NW383
N C
198SE56
39A4333n

—115—
(87IlA159)
m243NE225
231NE[13]713
367NE[2]395

—120—
(20NY417)
(284NYS2d
[441)
j437NE1095
437NE[4]1095
287NYS2d
[467
298NYS2d
[645
300NYS2d
[397
f304NYS2d
[263
318NYS2d
[653
335NYS2d
[749
387NYS2d
[718
e388NYS2d
[472
j452NYS2d
[338
452NYS2d[4]
[338

453NYS2d
[597
513NYS2d72
Cir. 2
d282FS[4]73
j282FS[4]82
f292FS[4]115
439FS[4]975
439FS[4]977
Cir. 4
339FS[4]499
Cir. 6
311FS[4]1191
Calif
90CaR921
94CaR604
484P2d580
Colo
509P2d1272
Iowa
247NW271
Mich
164NW37
N H
400A2d53
Wash
496P2d516
W Va
279SE408
34A2155s
65A31069n

—126—
Case 1
(20NY792)
(284NYS2d
[449)
s282NYS2d
[664
242NE395
295NYS2d
[163

—126—
Case 2
(20NY793)
(284NYS2d
[449)
s238NE502
s278NYS2d
[770
s291NYS2d12

—127—
Case 1
(20NY793)
(284NYS2d
[450)
s275NYS2d
[960
s282NYS2d
[973

—127—
Case 2
(20NY794)
(284NYS2d
[450)
s272NYS2d
[446
294NYS2d77

—128—
Case 1
(20NY794)
(284NYS2d
[451)
s274NYS2d
[392
s281NYS2d
[974

—128—
Case 2
(20NY795)
(284NYS2d
[451)
s281NYS2d
[985

—128—
Case 3
(20NY796)
(284NYS2d
[452)
s281NYS2d
[864
468NYS2d
[161

—129—
Case 1
(20NY796)
(284NYS2d
[452)
s282NYS2d
[438

—129—
Case 2
(20NY797)
(284NYS2d
[453)
292NYS2d45
j292NYS2d47
307NYS2d
[191
321NYS2d
[842
426NYS2d
[843
432NYS2d
[156

—130—
Case 1
(20NY798)
(284NYS2d
[454)

—130—
Case 2
(20NY798)
(284NYS2d
[454)
s282NYS2d
[934

—130—
Case 3
(20NY798)
(284NYS2d
[455)
s242NE486
s280NYS2d
[952

—131—
(20NY799)
(284NYS2d
[455)
s232NE652
s234NE840
s261NYS2d
[336
s271NYS2d
[523
s285NYS2d
[621
s287NYS2d
[886
Cir. 2
9BRW824

—132—
Case 1
(20NY801)
(284NYS2d
[456)
s219NE295
s269NYS2d
[368
s272NYS2d
[782
s388US41
s18LE1040
s87SC1873
59LE962n
37A3630n
57A3178n
57A3201n
82A3376n
60ARF710n

—132—
Case 2
(20NY801)
(284NYS2d
[457)
s229NE192
s245NYS2d
[353
s272NYS2d
[974
s282NYS2d
[497
385NYS2d
[681
39A3497n
65A3512n
44A4888n
44A4893n
68ARF957n

—133—
(20NY801)
(284NYS2d
[458)
Cert Den
US cert den
in390US971
s229NE220
s282NYS2d
[538
495NYS2d
[539
33A41132n

—134—
Case 1
(20NY802)
(284NYS2d
[459)
s189NE620
s239NYS2d
[124

—134—
Case 2
(20NY802)
(284NYS2d
[459)

—134—
Case 3
(20NY802)
(284NYS2d
[460)
s205NE879
s257NYS2d
[960
s282NYS2d
[174

—135—
Case 1
(20NY803)
(284NYS2d
[460)
s273NYS2d
[572
s282NYS2d
[639
250NE582
265NE924
288NYS2d
[246
j288NYS2d
[247
303NYS2d
[524
317NYS2d
[629
391NYS2d
[220
392NYS2d28
433NYS2d
[657
434NYS2d
[278
497NYS2d
[530
42A4828n

—135—
Case 2
(20NY804)
(284NYS2d
[461)
s275NYS2d
[674
527NYS2d
[585

—136—
(20NY805)
(284NYS2d
[462)
s274NYS2d
[850
268NE646
j295NYS2d
[970
24A3327n

24A3363n

—138—
(249Ind173)
304NE[4]877
336NE692
339NE97
430NE[1]787
452NE1006
526NE1229

—140—
(249Ind178)
242NE42
f363NE226
e400NE[2]1111

—145—
(249Ind141)
338NE[1]262
j403NE811

—147—
(249Ind144)
360NE604
f408NE620
f408NE[4]621
f408NE[5]621
f408NE[6]621
409NE[6]1272
409NE[4]1274
j437NE113
441NE[5]22
471NE[5]731
471NE[6]731
486NE[1]662
Mass
j440NE776
Calif
140CaR294
Conn
261A2d296
Tex
547SW624
61A31210n
61A31219n
1A475n

—151—
(249Ind168)
241NE[1]368
309NE[2]845
309NE[3]847
316NE[2]689
323NE[1]239
e331NE[1]780
399NE[1]368
Me
318A2d498

—154—
(141InA649)
274NE[5]742
301NE[1]243
310NE[2]279
348NE[1]81
Ala
361So2d9
Minn
222NW80
4COA569§ 3
16A4192n
17A4494n

—157—
(142InA154)
241NE[1]77
Nebr
421NW3

—159—
(141InA669)
d252NE[2]606
d252NE[3]606
254NE[2]219
255NE[1]829
j275NE[1]856
278NE[1]336
278NE[2]336
280NE[2]865
316NE[1]593
316NE[2]593
339NE[1]112
340NE[1]813
357NE[1]256
387NE[2]1339
433NE[2]21

—161—
(141InA655)
233NE[2]805
256NE[3]923
322NE[8]103
323NE[1]238
323NE[8]238
f355NE[7]438
f355NE[8]438
393NE[8]810
417NE[7]338
486NE[8]442
9A21044s

—165—
(141InA672)
231NE[1]863
j235NE[1]99
242NE[4]140
261NE[6]602
308NE878
Okla
541P2d861
40A342n
40A358n
40A375n

—169—
(141InA662)
f239NE[1]173
249NE516
j249NE[3]517
j251NE[3]26
j251NE[4]26
251NE[1]34
269NE[3]767
j269NE[4]770
270NE767
e272NE[4]629
e272NE[3]633
272NE[4]874
f273NE[2]553
f273NE[3]553
277NE606
280NE[3]303
284NE[3]735
286NE[1]698
297NE[1]471
307NE[1]504
383NE1085

Continued

Cases That Cite Nationwide Insurance v. Ervin, 231 N.E.2d 112 (1967)

When a case is directly affected by a higher court on appeal, *Shepard's* places a small letter just before the citation of the case. For instance, if the higher court vacated the cited case's opinion, a "v" will appear next to the citation, as shown below.

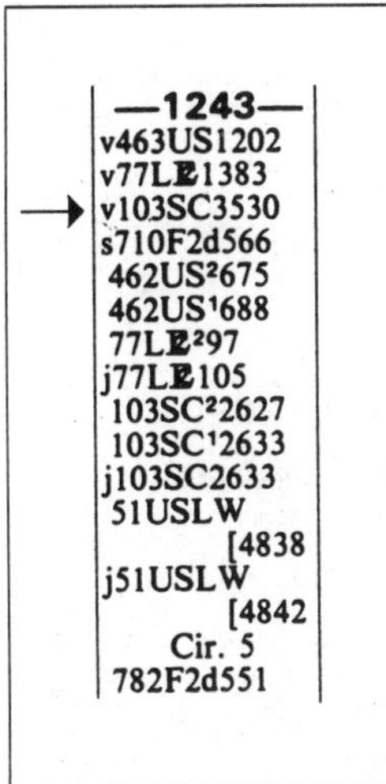

—1243—
v463US1202
v77LE1383
→ v103SC3530
s710F2d566
462US[2]675
462US[1]688
77LE[2]97
j77LE105
103SC[2]2627
103SC[1]2633
j103SC2633
51USLW
[4838
j51USLW
[4842
Cir. 5
782F2d551

Citation Showing Vacating of Lower Court Opinion

Other abbreviations used to indicate information about a case on appeal include those shown below.

SHEPARD'S ABBREVIATIONS: APPEAL OF THE CITED CASE

a affirmed

cc connected case

D dismissed

m modified

r reversed

s same case

v *vacated*

ABBREVIATIONS SHOWING ACTION BY THE SUPREME COURT

When an unsuccessful attempt has been made to take the cited case before the U.S. Supreme Court, *Shepard's* uses certain notations to tells you exactly what happened.

US cert den This means that the U.S. Supreme Court refused to issue a Writ of Certiorari. When this happens, the cited case is considered to be very good law, since the Supreme Court refused to review it.

US cert dis This means that the petition for cert was dismissed, usually for procedural reasons. It's possible that the case may still be taken by the Supreme Court at a later time.

US reh den This only appears when the cited case is a U.S. Supreme Court case and means that the U.S. Supreme Court refused to grant a rehearing in that case.

US reh dis This means that a request for a rehearing was dismissed.

4. Do Other Cases Affect the Value of the Case as Precedent or Persuasive Authority?

The law is constantly changing. New fact situations call for different decisions in order to reach a just result. New social or technological developments (for example, in vitro fertilization, changing racial attitudes, the computer) give rise to entirely new legal theories and cause massive changes in existing legal doctrine. This means that a case you find in your research may or may not represent the way current courts would decide the same issue. Accordingly, each time you find a case that appears relevant, you must find out whether it is still "good law." *Shepard's* helps you do this by using a second set of abbreviations to explain why the citing case referred to the cited case. This set of abbreviations is only used when the citing case is unrelated to the cited case—that is, not reviewing the cited case on appeal.

The most commonly used abbreviations are shown below.

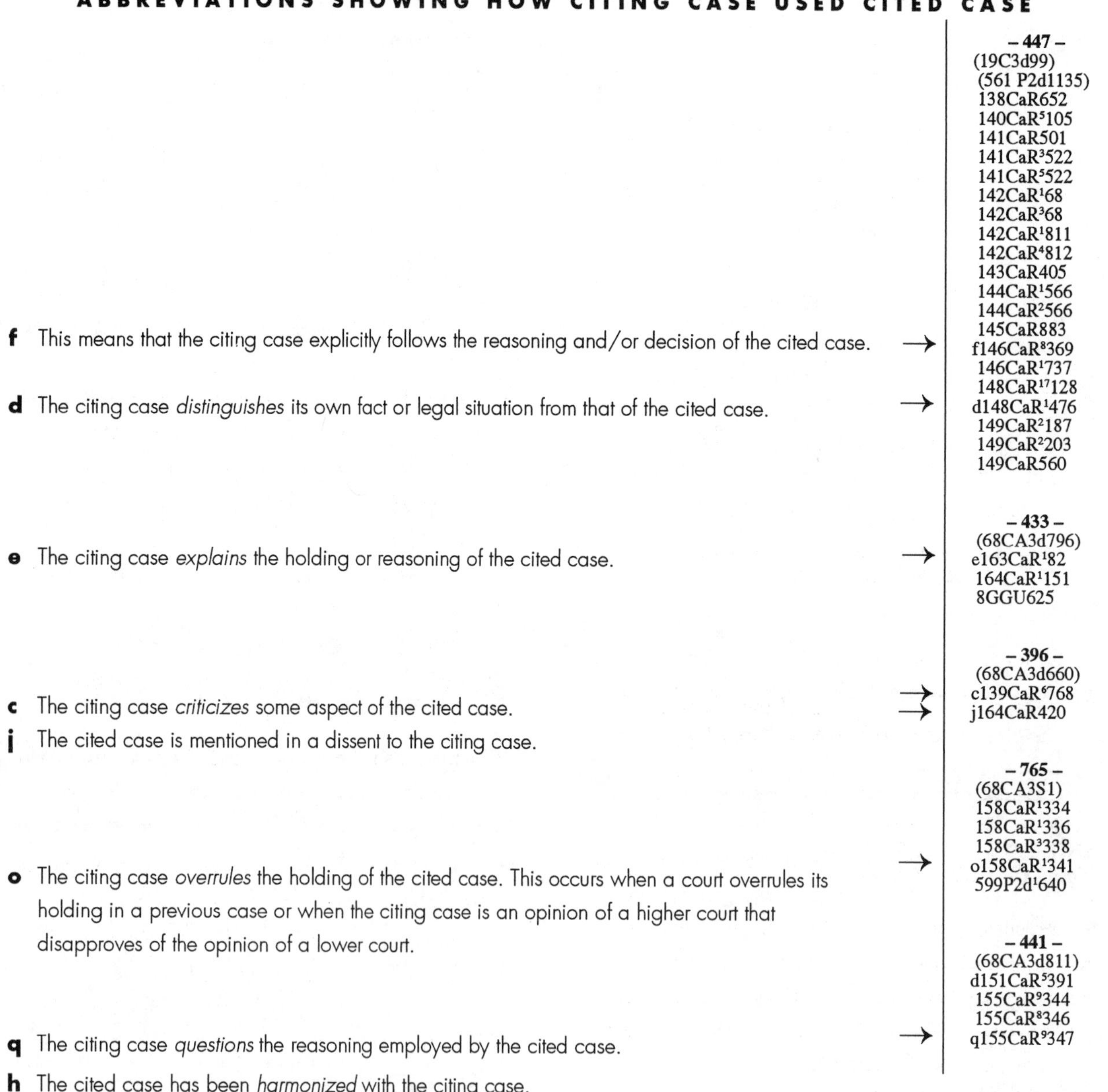

ABBREVIATIONS SHOWING HOW CITING CASE USED CITED CASE
f This means that the citing case explicitly follows the reasoning and/or decision of the cited case.
d The citing case *distinguishes* its own fact or legal situation from that of the cited case.
e The citing case *explains* the holding or reasoning of the cited case.
c The citing case *criticizes* some aspect of the cited case.
j The cited case is mentioned in a dissent to the citing case.
o The citing case *overrules* the holding of the cited case. This occurs when a court overrules its holding in a previous case or when the citing case is an opinion of a higher court that disapproves of the opinion of a lower court.
q The citing case *questions* the reasoning employed by the cited case.
h The cited case has been *harmonized* with the citing case.
p The cited case is almost exactly the same as the citing case.
– 447 –
(19C3d99)
(561 P2d1135)
138CaR652
140CaR[5]105
141CaR501
141CaR[3]522
141CaR[5]522
142CaR[1]68
142CaR[3]68
142CaR[1]811
142CaR[4]812
143CaR405
144CaR[1]566
144CaR[2]566
145CaR883
f146CaR[8]369
146CaR[1]737
148CaR[17]128
d148CaR[1]476
149CaR[2]187
149CaR[2]203
149CaR560
– 433 –
(68CA3d796)
e163CaR[1]82
164CaR[1]151
8GGU625
– 396 –
(68CA3d660)
c139CaR[6]768
j164CaR420
– 765 –
(68CA3S1)
158CaR[1]334
158CaR[1]336
158CaR[3]338
o158CaR[1]341
599P2d[1]640
– 441 –
(68CA3d811)
d151CaR[5]391
155CaR[9]344
155CaR[8]346
q155CaR[9]347

If you are using *Shephero's* primarily as a means of checking a case for its precedential or persuasive value, you can skim down a list of the citations under the cited case and search for these abbreviations. If none appear, or the ones that do appear indicate that your case is still good law, you might stop there (but see our word of caution below). But if the cited case was questioned, criticized or overruled by the citing case, you would definitely want to read that citing case.

If there is no letter to the left of the citation, it usually means that the cited case was mentioned in passing and wasn't important to the decision in the citing case.

If you have the time, it is better to read any case that pertains to your issue (see Section 5, below) and not rely on the abbreviations. The *Shepard's* editors sometimes make mistakes and fail to tag a citation with the proper letter.

The sample page from *Shepard's Citations for Cases*, above, shows how these abbreviations appear next to the citations.

5. Does the Citing Case Discuss the Issue You Are Researching?

Shepard's was designed primarily as an updating tool. However, as we've pointed out, it can be used for much more than updating. Once you've found a case that's relevant, *Shepard's* can be used to find other cases dealing with the same issue. Every citing case is potentially relevant; thus, if you start out with one cited case, you may find any number of useful cases that have referred to it. Then, each of these citing cases can itself be Shepardized.

Suppose, for example, *Shepard's* lists five cases that have referred to your initial case. Then you Shepardize each of these five cases and find an additional two citing cases for each one. In very little time, you have a list of over ten cases that may be relevant to your situation.

There is a catch to this, however. We have seen that *Shephero's* gives you a list of every case that has referred to the cited case. But most cited cases deal with a number of legal issues, and a citing case will usually only mention the cited case in connection with one (or perhaps several) of those issues.

For example, if a cited case touches on 20 different legal issues, a citing case may only refer to it for three of these. If the issues that the citing case is interested in are the same as the issues you are interested in, the citing case may be helpful in your research. However, if the citing case refers to the cited case for issues you aren't interested in, the citing case won't do you any good.

To help you separate the wheat from the chaff and avoid this time trap, *Shepard's* identifies the specific issues that the citing case was interested in when it referred to the cited case. It does this by:

- identifying the issue from the cited case that is being discussed by the citing case
- selecting the headnote in the cited case that most closely states the issue being discussed in the citing case, and
- placing that headnote number just to the right of the citation to the citing case.

Example *Nationwide Insurance v. Ervin*, 231 N.E.2d 112 (1967) is referred to in *Deason v. Metropolitan Property & Liability Insurance* Co., 474 N.E.2d 783 (1985).

the time of the accident; the Mercury had a defective transmission and the Dodge had a twisted drive shaft. Both vehicles were put back into operation shortly after the accident involving the Comet. During his deposition, Andrew Warner testified as follows:

"Q. Did you have any intention if the Comet hadn't been wrecked, did you have any intention to dispose of either of these other two cars just because you got the Comet?

A. Oh, no."

[2] In ruling that Metropolitan's policy afforded secondary coverage in connection with the accident involving the 1975 Comet, the court found that Christopher Warner was "a relative operating a temporary substitute" automobile. Metropolitan contends that this conclusion is incorrect, and we are compelled to agree. Under the terms of the policy, a temporary substitute automobile is defined as one "temporarily used with the permission of the owner as a substitute for an owned automobile when withdrawn from normal use for servicing or repair or because of breakdown, loss, or destruction." Here, the unequivocal deposition testimony of all concerned establishes that Christopher Warner's use of the Comet was not to be temporary, but regular and permanent, as it was the intention of both Vera Fry and Christopher Warner that he would pay $100 for the car at Christmas time, and would not return it to her. Moreover, the Comet was not intended by the Warners to be a substitute for either the Mercury or the Dodge; rather, it was to be kept as a third car, and the fact that the Dodge and Mercury broke down during the Warners' use of the Comet was entirely coincidental. Under these circumstances, the "temporary substitute" provision of the policy issued by Metropolitan did not encompass Christopher Warner's use of the Comet on the date of the accident. (See *Sturgeon v. Automobile Club Inter-Insurance Exchange* (1979), 77 Ill. App.3d 997, 1000, 34 Ill.Dec. 66, 397 N.E.2d 522.) This conclusion is buttressed by the holding of *Nationwide Insurance Company v. Ervin* (1967), 87 Ill.App.2d 432, 436–37, 231 N.E.2d 112, wherein it was recognized that a "temporary substitute" provision of the type under consideration here is to be applied to those situations where an insured automobile is withdrawn from use for a short period, and not where, as here, coverage is sought to be extended to an additional automobile for a significant length of time.

[3] *Providence Mutual Casualty Company v. Sturms* (1962), 37 Ill.App.2d 304, 185 N.E.2d 366, relied on by appellees, is not on point. *Sturms* addresses the question of whether coverage afforded on a temporary substitute automobile expires immediately upon repair of the insured's regular automobile (37 Ill.App.2d 304, 306, 185 N.E.2d 366), and does not discuss the more fundamental issue of when a vehicle is considered to be a temporary substitute in the first place. While appellees also suggest that portions of Metropolitan's claim file show that certain Metropolitan employees believe that the policy in question afforded coverage, the trial court correctly noted in its judgment that these statements are merely opinions, and are not binding on a court in its consideration of the legal question presented. 31A C.J.S. *Evidence* § 272(b) (1964).

For the foregoing reasons, the judgment of the circuit court of St. Clair County is reversed.

Reversed.

JONES, P.J., and KARNS, J., concur.

Page from Deason v. Metropolitan Property & Liability Insurance Co.

In this example, *Ervin* is the cited case and *Deason* is the citing case. *Shepard's* lists the entries for *Ervin* as shown below.

NORTHEASTERN REPORTER, 2d SERIES Vol. 231

323FS[6]344
596FS[6]784
650FS437
64A3506s

—70—
(12OS26)
(41Op159)
231NE[3]332
370NE[3]458
371NE[3]843
381NE[2]972
414NE[4]438
453NE[4]664
454NE[2]1389
488NE927

—71—
(12OA68)
(41Op122)
p166NE808
c484NE220
j484NE221
18A2813s

—81—
(12OA87)
(41Op163)
c432NE[8]212
Cir. 6
577FS[4]1131
Md
513A2d938

—85—
(12OA59)
(41Op117)

—91—
(12OA83)
(41Op160)
521NE[4]1153
521NE[6]1153
31A3585n

—94—
(12OhM127)
(41Op131)

—97—
(87IlA411)
Cert Den
269NE[2]355
269NE[5]356
273NE[1]162
280NE[12]46
283NE[15]43
318NE[12]122
326NE[9]468
363NE[5]625
363NE[12]626
369NE[1]295
369NE[2]295
447NE[6]441
458NE[5]1069
f502NE[6]478
18A2633s

—103—
(87IlA181)
Cert Den
323NE[2]809
323NE[4]809
374NE[4]1140

—107—
(87IlA139)
cc257NE233
317NE[1]631
347NE[1]70
360NE[2]1197
378NE[1]1157

—109—
(87IlA82)
Cert Den
262NE[1]797
281NE[1]388
378NE[3]606
412NE[1]629

—112—
(87IlA432)
241NE[1]120
241NE[3]120
272NE[7]61
274NE[3]879
287NE[1]530
289NE[3]703
293NE[3]704
305NE[3]417
379NE[2]66
d412NE[5]632
d412NE[7]632
e427NE[7]130
474NE[6]785
474NE[7]785
481NE[1]45
497NE[3]479
502NE[2]1295
510NE[2]1183
Ga
221SE482
Iowa
174NW383
N C
198SE56
39A4333n

—115—
(87IlA159)
m243NE225
231NE[13]713
367NE[2]395

—120—
(20NY417)
(284NYS2d
[441)
j437NE1095
437NE[4]1095
287NYS2d
[467
298NYS2d
[645
300NYS2d
[397
f304NYS2d
[263
318NYS2d
[653
335NYS2d
[749
387NYS2d
[718
e388NYS2d
[472
j452NYS2d
[338
452NYS2d[4]
[338

453NYS2d
[597
513NYS2d72
Cir. 2
d282FS[4]73
j282FS[4]82
f292FS[4]115
439FS[4]975
439FS[4]977
Cir. 4
339FS[4]499
Cir. 6
311FS[4]1191
Calif
90CaR921
94CaR604
484P2d580
Colo
509P2d1272
Iowa
247NW271
Mich
164NW37
N H
400A2d53
Wash
496P2d516
W Va
279SE408
34A2155s
65A31069n

—126—
Case 1
(20NY792)
(284NYS2d
[449)
s282NYS2d
[664
242NE395
295NYS2d
[163

—126—
Case 2
(20NY793)
(284NYS2d
[449)
s238NE502
s278NYS2d
[770
s291NYS2d12

—127—
Case 1
(20NY793)
(284NYS2d
[450)
s275NYS2d
[960
s282NYS2d
[973

—127—
Case 2
(20NY794)
(284NYS2d
[450)
s272NYS2d
[446
294NYS2d77

—128—
Case 1
(20NY794)
(284NYS2d
[451)
s274NYS2d
[392
s281NYS2d
[974

—128—
Case 2
(20NY795)
(284NYS2d
[451)
s281NYS2d
[985

—128—
Case 3
(20NY796)
(284NYS2d
[452)
s281NYS2d
[864
468NYS2d
[161

—129—
Case 1
(20NY796)
(284NYS2d
[452)
s282NYS2d
[438

—129—
Case 2
(20NY797)
(284NYS2d
[453)
292NYS2d45
j292NYS2d47
307NYS2d
[191
321NYS2d
[842
426NYS2d
[843
432NYS2d
[156

—130—
Case 1
(20NY798)
(284NYS2d
[454)

—130—
Case 2
(20NY798)
(284NYS2d
[454)
s282NYS2d
[934

—130—
Case 3
(20NY798)
(284NYS2d
[455)
s242NE486
s280NYS2d
[952

—131—
(20NY799)
(284NYS2d
[455)
s232NE652
s234NE840
s261NYS2d
[336
s271NYS2d
[523
s285NYS2d
[621
s287NYS2d
[886
Cir. 2
9BRW824

—132—
Case 1
(20NY801)
(284NYS2d
[456)
s219NE295
s269NYS2d
[368
s272NYS2d
[782
s388US41
s18LE1040
s87SC1873
59LE962n
37A3630n
57A3178n
57A3201n
82A3376n
60ARF710n

—132—
Case 2
(20NY801)
(284NYS2d
[457)
s229NE192
s245NYS2d
[353
s272NYS2d
[974
s282NYS2d
[497
385NYS2d
[681
39A3497n
65A3512n
44A4888n
44A4893n
68ARF957n

—133—
(20NY801)
(284NYS2d
[458)
Cert Den
US cert den
in390US971
s229NE220
s282NYS2d
[538
495NYS2d
[539
33A41132n

—134—
Case 1
(20NY802)
(284NYS2d
[459)
s189NE620
s239NYS2d
[124

—134—
Case 2
(20NY802)
(284NYS2d
[459)

—134—
Case 3
(20NY802)
(284NYS2d
[460)
s205NE879
s257NYS2d
[960
s282NYS2d
[174

—135—
Case 1
(20NY803)
(284NYS2d
[460)
s273NYS2d
[572
s282NYS2d
[639
250NE582
265NE924
288NYS2d
[246
j288NYS2d
[247
303NYS2d
[524
317NYS2d
[629
391NYS2d
[220
392NYS2d28
433NYS2d
[657
434NYS2d
[278
497NYS2d
[530
42A4828n

—135—
Case 2
(20NY804)
(284NYS2d
[461)
s275NYS2d
[674
527NYS2d
[585

—136—
(20NY805)
(284NYS2d
[462)
s274NYS2d
[850
268NE646
j295NYS2d
[970
24A3327n

24A3363n

—138—
(249Ind173)
304NE[4]877
336NE692
339NE97
430NE[1]787
452NE1006
526NE1229

—140—
(249Ind178)
242NE42
f363NE226
e400NE[2]1111

—145—
(249Ind141)
338NE[1]262
j403NE811

—147—
(249Ind144)
360NE604
f408NE620
f408NE[4]621
f408NE[5]621
f408NE[6]621
409NE[6]1272
409NE[4]1274
j437NE113
441NE[5]22
471NE[5]731
471NE[6]731
486NE[1]662
Mass
j440NE776
Calif
140CaR294
Conn
261A2d296
Tex
547SW624
61A31210n
61A31219n
1A475n

—151—
(249Ind168)
241NE[1]368
309NE[2]845
309NE[3]847
316NE[2]689
323NE[1]239
e331NE[1]780
399NE[1]368
Me
318A2d498

—154—
(141InA649)
274NE[5]742
301NE[1]243
310NE[2]279
348NE[1]81
Ala
361So2d9
Minn
222NW80
4COA569§ 3
16A4192n
17A4494n

—157—
(142InA154)
241NE[1]77
Nebr
421NW3

—159—
(141InA669)
d252NE[2]606
d252NE[3]606
254NE[2]219
255NE[1]829
j275NE[1]856
278NE[1]336
278NE[2]336
280NE[2]865
316NE[1]593
316NE[2]593
339NE[1]112
340NE[1]813
357NE[1]256
387NE[2]1339
433NE[2]21

—161—
(141InA655)
233NE[2]805
256NE[3]923
322NE[8]103
323NE[1]238
323NE[8]238
f355NE[7]438
f355NE[8]438
393NE[8]810
417NE[7]338
486NE[8]442
9A21044s

—165—
(141InA672)
231NE[1]863
j235NE[1]99
242NE[4]140
261NE[6]602
308NE878
Okla
541P2d861
40A342n
40A358n
40A375n

—169—
(141InA662)
f239NE[1]173
249NE516
j249NE[3]517
j251NE[3]26
j251NE[4]26
251NE[1]34
269NE[3]767
j269NE[4]770
270NE767
e272NE[4]629
e272NE[3]633
272NE[4]874
f273NE[2]553
f273NE[3]553
277NE606
280NE[3]303
284NE[3]735
286NE[1]698
297NE[1]471
307NE[1]504
383NE1085

Continued

Page from *Shepard's*

The little numbers (6 and 7) between the N.E.2d and the page number (785) are numbers of the headnotes in *Ervin* that, in the opinion of *Shepard's*, best describe the issues which the case is being cited for in *Deason*. These headnotes are shown below.

NATIONWIDE INSURANCE COMPANY v. ERVIN Ill. 113
Cite as 231 N.E.2d 112

1. Insurance ⟹138(1)

Parties to insurance contract are free to incorporate such provisions into it, if not unlawful, as they see fit and it is then the duty of the court to enforce those provisions.

2. Insurance ⟹146.7(8)

Rule that all ambiguities in policy will be construed most strongly against insurance company, as the party that drafted the policy, only has application where ambiguity in fact exists and court may not distort the contract to create the ambiguity itself.

3. Insurance ⟹146.2

Insurance contract should be construed in accordance with the general contract rule of construction that the agreement should be ascertained as a whole to determine intention of parties and purpose which they sought to accomplish.

4. Insurance ⟹435.2(2)

Enumeration in automobile policy of those few situations where coverage is afforded to the insured with reference to other than named automobile serves to limit areas of risk assumed by insurer.

5. Insurance ⟹435.3(1)

Provision of automobile policy limiting coverage for additional owned automobile to 30 days after acquisition by insured permits owner adequate opportunity to acquire necessary additional insurance and is not intended to cover two automobiles for any protracted period.

6. Insurance ⟹435.2(4)

→ Provision in automobile policy granting coverage to insured for temporary substitute automobile, not owned by the insured, applies to those situations where the named automobile is in repair shop or withdrawn from use for short period.

7. Insurance ⟹435.3(1)

Where insured had bought second auto-
→ mobile in July 1964 after transmission "went out" of automobile which was named in policy and which remained inoperable in driveway of his home until repair in spring of 1966, and had accident with second automobile on September 26, 1964, the second automobile was not a "replacement" for the named automobile within policy provision extending coverage to replacement automobile.

231 N.E.2d—8

Barrick, Jackson & Switzer, Rockford, for appellant.

Nordquist & Anderson, Rockford, for appellees.

ABRAHAMSON, Justice.

The Nationwide Insurance Company brings this appeal from a decree of the Circuit Court of the 17th Judicial Circuit, Winnebago County, entered December 29, 1966, that found that an automobile insurance policy issued by it to Douglas Ervin "covered" an accident that had occurred on September 26, 1964, and that a certain automobile operated by Ervin at the time of the accident was a "replacement" as defined in the policy.

On August 16, 1963, Nationwide issued its policy of automobile insurance number 94-441-489 to Ervin for coverage of his 1958 Chevrolet. In July of 1964 the transmission of the Chevrolet, according to Ervin, "went out" and he purchased a 1958 Cadillac. The Chevrolet was retained by Ervin, although inoperable, and left in the driveway of his home.

On September 26, 1964, Ervin was in an automobile accident with the Cadillac that involved a truck owned by the Jones Transfer Company, an Illinois Corporation, and another automobile in which Robert Holmes was a passenger. Holmes subsequently brought suit against Ervin and Jones Transfer for injuries allegedly suffered as a result of that accident. Nationwide was called upon by Ervin to defend him in that suit pursuant to the policy.

Headnotes from Ervin

Thus, *Deason* used *Ervin* when it discussed the issues summarized in these two headnotes. If the issues in these two headnotes were the reason you were Shepardizing *Ervin*, you would want definitely want to read *Deason*. However, if you were not interested in the issues discussed in headnotes 6 and 7, you might wisely choose to not read *Deason*.

If there is no headnote number next to the citation—that is, the citation doesn't identify the issue for which the cited case is being mentioned—it means that the reference to the cited case appeared, to the *Shepard's* editors, to be general rather than in reference to a specific legal issue. The citing case may or may not be of interest, so you should at least skim it.

SUMMING UP

HOW TO SHEPARDIZE STATE COURT CASES

1. Select one of the parallel citations of the case you wish to Shepardize.
2. Note the year of the case you are Shepardizing.
3. Find the *Shepard's* volumes—and if necessary the parts of these volumes—that cover the reporter in the citation.
4. Select the volume or volumes that contain citations for cases decided after the case you are Shepardizing.
5. Find the volume number (in boldface) that corresponds to the volume number of the case being Shepardized.
6. Under this volume number, find the page number (in boldface) of the citation for the cited case.
7. Under this page number, review the citations given for the citing cases.
8. Use the letters to the left of the citation to decide whether the case has been directly affected by a higher court in an appeal.
9. Use the numbers to the right of the citation to decide whether the citing case is referring to the cited case for issues you might be interested in.
10. After you write down all potentially useful citations, repeat these steps with the more recent *Shepard's* volumes and update pamphlets.

SUMMING UP

HOW TO SHEPARDIZE U.S. SUPREME COURT CASES

1. Select one of the three parallel citations for the case you wish to Shepardize.
2. Note the year of the case.
3. Find the *Shepard's* labeled *United States Case Citations.*
4. Select the volume or volumes that contain citations for cases decided after the date of the case you are Shepardizing.
5. Select the part of the *Shepard's* volume that pertains to the citation you are using. For instance, if your citation is for the *U.S. Supreme Court Reporter* (S. Ct.), locate the pages that cover this report rather than the pages that pertain to the *United States Reports* (U.S.) or the *Supreme Court Reports, Lawyer's Edition* (L. Ed.).
6. Find the boldface volume number that corresponds to the volume number of the case being Shepardized.
7. Under this volume number, find the page number of the cited case.
8. Under the page number, review the citations of the citing cases.
9. Use the letters to the left of each citation to decide whether the case has been directly affected by a higher court in an appeal.
10. Use the numbers to the right of the citation to decide whether the citing case is referring to the cited case for issues you might be interested in.
11. After you write down all potentially useful citations, repeat these steps with the more recent *Shepard's* volumes and update pamphlets.

LIBRARY EXERCISE

Using Shepard's Citations: Cases

Now it's time to use the library to apply what you've just learned. This exercise asks you to use Shepard's Citations for Cases to find references to a relevant case that you have discovered in the course of your research. Additional research exercises that include these and other skills are in the Appendix.

Questions

1. *You are researching flag burning cases and have found Street v. New York, 394 U.S. 576 (1969).*
   a. *Only the* Supreme Court Reporter *(West) is available in your law library. Use Shepard's to find the case's citation in the* Supreme Court Reporter.
   b. *Shepardize the* Supreme Court Reporter *citation.*
      1. *Find the citation to the Fourth Circuit case that followed Street on the matter treated in headnote 16.*
      2. *Find a Ninth Circuit case that distinguished itself from Street on the matter covered by headnote 2.*
      3. *Find the references to two American Law Reports annotations that cite Street.*
2. *You are researching the effect of bankruptcy on child support and alimony in New Mexico. You find a helpful case:* Yeates v. Yeates (In re Yeates), *807 F.2d 874 (10th Cir. 1986). You want to use this case to find a case that deals specifically with New Mexico law.*
   a. *Shepardize* Yeates *and find a New Mexico case that has cited* Yeates.
   b. *Find an* American Law Reports *annotation that cites* Yeates.
   c. *What does "GEBL § 15.08" mean?*
3. *You are researching the issue of whether a judge may rule that a* defendant *was not guilty by reason of insanity, even though the jury convicted him. You have a citation to* Douglas v. United States, *239 F.2d 52 (1956) that holds that a judge may do this in an appropriate case, but must do so with caution because of the deference usually given to the jury's resolution of factual issues. This statement could be very helpful to you.*
   a. *Find the case. Which headnote includes the statement you are interested in?*
   b. *Shepardize* Douglas.
      1. *What does the (99 ADC 232) following the case citation mean?*
      2. *Are there any citations listed for cases that followed* Douglas *on the issue dealt with in headnote 3?*
      3. *Are there any cites for cases that distinguished themselves from* Douglas *on the matter dealt with in headnote 3?*
      4. *Are there any citations for cases in which a dissenting opinion cited* Douglas *in support of the statement contained in headnote 3?*

Answers

1. a. Go to *Shepard's United States Citations*. The parallel citation is given only the first time the case is listed in *Shepard's*, so go to the earliest volume that includes 394 U.S. (Volume 5 of Case Edition 1984). When you look under *United States Reports*, volume 394, page 576, the cites in parentheses right after the citation to your case are the parallel citations (citations to the same case published in other reporters). The citation you are looking for is 89 S. Ct. 1354.

   b. Go to *Shepard's United States Citations*; you want to start with the earliest volume that includes 89 S. Ct. (Volume 5, Case Edition 1984), and then continue forward to all other volumes and paper supplements that include 89 S. Ct.

   1. The citation you are looking for is 317 F.Supp. 141 (the reference to *Street* is on page 141, the case starts on some page before that.) You know that this case followed *Street* because of the "f" in the margin to the left of the citation; you know it followed on the matter treated in *Street's* headnote 16 because of the tiny 16 up and to the right of the FS. (FS is the abbreviation used by *Shepard's* for the *Federal Supplement*.)
   2. 462 F.2d 102. You know that this case distinguished itself from *Street* because of the "d" in the left margin. You know it distinguished itself regarding the matter treated in *Street's* headnote 2 because of the tiny 2 above and to the right of the F.2d (*Shepard's* abbreviation for *Federal Reporter*, 2d series.)
   3. 9 A.L.R.3d 462s (the "s" means the citation of *Street* is in the pocket part). 41 A.L.R.3d 505n (the "n" means the citation to *Street* is in a footnote on page 505).

2. a. Go to *Shepard's Federal Citations*, starting with the first volume that includes 807 F.2d (volume 14, 1989) and then proceeding forward to all later volumes and supplements that include 807 F.2d. Looking under all listings for *Federal Reporter*, 2d series, volume 807, page 874, you find, under a subheading "N M", meaning New Mexico, the following citation: 784 P.2d 425.

   b. 74 A.L.R. 2d 758s (the "s" means the citation to *Yeates* was in the pocket part to the annotation).

   c. In the front of the *Shepard's* volume is a list of the sources cited and their abbreviations. GEBL stands for *Guide to Effective Bankruptcy Litigation*, a book by Pollard and Burton, published by *Shepard's* in 1988. 15.08 is the section in the book in which *Yeates* was cited.

3. a. Headnote 3 contains that statement.

   b. Go to *Shepard's Federal Citations*, starting with the first volume that includes 239 F.2d (volume 6, 1989) and then proceeding forward to all later volumes and supplements that include 239 F.2d.

   1. The citation in parentheses means that *Douglas* is also reported in volume 99 of Appeal Cases, *District of Columbia Reports*, on page 232. This is called a parallel citation. Abbreviations are listed in the front of every volume of *Shepard's Citations*.
   2. 251 F.2d 879 and 251 F.2d 880. You know that this case followed *Douglas* because of the "f" in the margin to the left of the citation; you know it followed on the matter treated in *Douglas'* headnote 3 because of the tiny "3" up and to the right of the F.2d. (*Shepard's* abbreviation for *Federal Reporter*, 2d series).
   3. 213 F. Supp. 454. You know that this case distinguished itself from *Douglas* because of the "d" in the left margin. You know it distinguished itself regarding the matter treated in *Douglas'* headnote 3 because of the tiny "3" above and to the right of the FS (*Shepard's* abbreviation for *Federal Supplement*)
   4. 251 F.2d 881; 284 F.2d 254; 325 F.2d 622. You know that *Douglas* was cited in the dissenting opinions of these cases because of the "j" in the margin to the left of each citation. You know that the dissents cited *Douglas* for the matter contained in *Douglas'* headnote 3 because of the tiny "3" up and to the right of the F.2d (*Shepard's* abbreviation for *Federal Reporter*, 2d series).

LIBRARY EXERCISE

Using A.L.R., Case Headnotes and Shepard's

Your employer has taken-on several paid "trainees" for the summer. They are paralegal students. While the regular assistant office administrator is away or busy, they will do work which is regularly done in the office: filing, preparing billings, running to various courts to file documents, and going to law offices around town to pick up or deliver papers.

Your boss thinks that he can pay these "trainees" below the minimum wage required for employees by the Fair Labor Standards Act. He thinks that they are not "employees" because they are in training, will learn how a law office works and will gain "resume value." He has been told that 50 A.L.R. Fed. has an article on this topic and that an important case in your Circuit (the 4th) is *Wirtz v. Wardlaw*.

Questions

1. *Where in the library do you find the* A.L.R. Fed. *article?*
2. *How do you find the case?*
3. *Scan those sections and find* Wirtz*. Where is the case first mentioned, and does this use of the case suggest that it is relevant to your question?*
4. *Find the case.*
5. *Look through the headnotes. This case treats several issues other than the specific one you are concerned with. Which headnote is about the point made in the* A.L.R. *article?*
6. *Shepardize the case: Using the* Federal Shepard's, *find all the volumes which cover Federal Reporter 2d including volume 339. (You will consult the main set, bound supplements and paper supplements.) What cases cited* Wirtz *for the issue covered by that headnote?*
7. *What does the "e" mean in "e473 FS 469"?*

Answers

1. The article will be in A.L.R. Federal, in volume 50. In the front of the volume is an alphabetical list of articles in that volume arranged by subject. Under "Employees," you soon see "When is an individual in training an 'employee' for purposes § 3(e)(1) of the Fair Labor Standards Act (29 U.S.C.S. § 203(e)(1) 50 A.L.R. Fed 632."
2. Turn to page 632. There isn't a list of cases, but there is a Table of Courts and Circuits. Cases from the Fourth Circuit are cited in §§ 2,3,5,6 and 7. On page 638 is *Wirtz v. Wardlaw*.
3. The case is first mentioned on page 635. The text describes the test for determining whether trainees are employees (are their efforts integral to the employer's business?), and cites *Wirtz* as framing this question by asking whether the trainees' efforts actually helped the business of the employer (if they were truly mere trainees, they probably just got in the way!)
4. The cite is to 339 F.2d 785. It is found in volume 339 of Federal Reporter, Second series, on page 785.
5. Headnote 3 concerns the designation of trainees as employees.
6. 406 FS 1307, e473 FS 469, and 992 F.2d 1026. Each of these cites includes a small elevated "3" directly following the "FS" or the "F.2d," which indicates that these cases deal with the issue described in Headnote number 3.
7. It means that the case at 473 Federal Supplement cites *Wirtz* on page 469 and explains *Wirtz* regarding the issue covered by headnote 3.

B. The West Digest System

When researching case law, you're looking for cases with facts that are as close to your facts as possible. The closer the facts, the more authority a case will provide for your position. Obviously, the more cases you examine that have taken up the same legal issue, the better the chance of finding a case with facts like yours.

In Chapter 9, *Finding Cases*, we saw how digests can help you find a good case to open up your research. They can also provide invaluable assistance in finding similar cases.

1. Digests Defined

Digests are collections of headnotes—the one-sentence summaries of how a particular case decided specific legal issues—that are taken from cases as reported in case reports and grouped together by topic. For example, in *Nationwide Insurance Co. v. Ervin*, 231 N.E.2d 112 (1967), one of the issues is classified under "Insurance." The court's holding on that issue is summarized in Headnote 6 shown below.

NATIONWIDE INSURANCE COMPANY v. ERVIN Ill. 113
Cite as 231 N.E.2d 112

1. Insurance ⊂⊃138(1)

Parties to insurance contract are free to incorporate such provisions into it, if not unlawful, as they see fit and it is then the duty of the court to enforce those provisions.

2. Insurance ⊂⊃146.7(8)

Rule that all ambiguities in policy will be construed most strongly against insurance company, as the party that drafted the policy, only has application where ambiguity in fact exists and court may not distort the contract to create the ambiguity itself.

3. Insurance ⊂⊃146.2

Insurance contract should be construed in accordance with the general contract rule of construction that the agreement should be ascertained as a whole to determine intention of parties and purpose which they sought to accomplish.

4. Insurance ⊂⊃435.2(2)

Enumeration in automobile policy of those few situations where coverage is afforded to the insured with reference to other than named automobile serves to limit areas of risk assumed by insurer.

5. Insurance ⊂⊃435.3(1)

Provision of automobile policy limiting coverage for additional owned automobile to 30 days after acquisition by insured permits owner adequate opportunity to acquire necessary additional insurance and is not intended to cover two automobiles for any protracted period.

→ **6. Insurance ⊂⊃435.2(4)**

Provision in automobile policy granting coverage to insured for temporary substitute automobile, not owned by the insured, applies to those situations where the named automobile is in repair shop or withdrawn from use for short period.

7. Insurance ⊂⊃435.3(1)

Where insured had bought second automobile in July 1964 after transmission "went out" of automobile which was named in policy and which remained inoperable in driveway of his home until repair in spring of 1966, and had accident with second automobile on September 26, 1964, the second automobile was not a "replacement" for the named automobile within policy provision extending coverage to replacement automobile.

231 N.E.2d—8

Barrick, Jackson & Switzer, Rockford, for appellant.

Nordquist & Anderson, Rockford, for appellees.

ABRAHAMSON, Justice.

The Nationwide Insurance Company brings this appeal from a decree of the Circuit Court of the 17th Judicial Circuit, Winnebago County, entered December 29, 1966, that found that an automobile insurance policy issued by it to Douglas Ervin "covered" an accident that had occurred on September 26, 1964, and that a certain automobile operated by Ervin at the time of the accident was a "replacement" as defined in the policy.

On August 16, 1963, Nationwide issued its policy of automobile insurance number 94–441–489 to Ervin for coverage of his 1958 Chevrolet. In July of 1964 the transmission of the Chevrolet, according to Ervin, "went out" and he purchased a 1958 Cadillac. The Chevrolet was retained by Ervin, although inoperable, and left in the driveway of his home.

On September 26, 1964, Ervin was in an automobile accident with the Cadillac that involved a truck owned by the Jones Transfer Company, an Illinois Corporation, and another automobile in which Robert Holmes was a passenger. Holmes subsequently brought suit against Ervin and Jones Transfer for injuries allegedly suffered as a result of that accident. Nationwide was called upon by Ervin to defend him in that suit pursuant to the policy.

Headnote from *Ervin*

That headnote has also been published in West's *Northeastern Digest* , with headnotes from other cases that have been assigned the same key topic and key number. (See Section B, below.) The *Ervin* head-note, as it appears in West's *Northeastern Digest,*[1] is shown below and in context on the next page.

> **Ill.App. 1967.** Provision of automobile policy limiting coverage for additional owned automobile to 30 days after acquisition by insured permits owner adequate opportunity to acquire necessary additional insurance and is not intended to cover two automobiles for any protracted period.—Nationwide Ins. Co. v. Ervin, 231 N.E.2d 112, 87 Ill.App.2d 432.

Digest Entry

2. The West Key System

Let's take a closer look at the West Digest system. The most important point to understand about this system is that the West Publishing Co. reports virtually all published cases that emerge from the state and federal courts. This means that West has been able to create a uniform and comprehensive classification scheme for all legal issues raised in these cases. This classification system is called the West Key Number system.

The West Digest Key Number system has 414 key topics and many numbered subtopics. Any given headnote from one case anywhere in the U.S. is grouped with the headnotes from all other cases that deal with that same issue. For example, a particular issue dealing with insurance on replacement automobiles can be assigned a subtopic number and grouped with headnotes from other state and federal court cases that carry the same topic and subtopic number.

This means that all the researcher needs to crack the digest system is one headnote labeled by key topic and number. That key topic and number can then be used to find all other headnotes with the same key topic and number that appear in cases in the geographic area the digest covers. The topic label and subtopic number together constitute the "key" to finding other cases in the digest that have discussed the same or similar issue.

There are a number of different West Digests. There is an overall digest that groups all headnote entries from all parts of the country and from all courts. This is made up of two sub-digests—the *Decennials* and the *General Digest*. West has divided this huge digest into smaller ones:

- The *U.S. Supreme Court Digest* covers only U.S. Supreme Court cases
- The *Federal Practice Digest* covers all federal courts (including the U.S. Supreme Court)
- State digests (for example, the *Illinois Digest* covers only the cases from that state)
- Regional digests (the states have been grouped into four regions: *Atlantic*, *Pacific*, *Northwestern* and *Southeastern*).

[1] Recently West stopped publishing a digest for this region, and for the Southern and Southwestern as well. Consequently, some states are not included in regional digests. They can be found in the *General Digest*, and some of them have their own *Digests*.

18 N E D—53 **INSURANCE ⚷435.3(1)**

Always Consult Cumulative Bound Supplement

Ill.App. 1970. Where automobile liability insurer's policy, by truckmen's endorsement, classified automobiles as (1) automobile owned by named assured, (2) automobile hired on behalf of named assured, with two exceptions, and (3) nonowned automobile defined as "any other automobile", two exceptions to "hired automobile" category fell into classification of "any other automobile" and any automobile falling within either exception was "non-owned automobile."—Kern v. Michigan Mut. Liability Co., 263 N.E.2d 134, 129 Ill.App.2d 423.

Ohio App. 1969. Purpose of provision in automobile liability policy obligating insurer to pay damages arising out of use of nonowned automobile, defined as automobile not owned by or furnished for regular use of either named insured or any relative, was to protect insurer from situation where insured would pay for but one policy and be covered while regularly driving other automobiles owned by members of his family.—Napier v. Banks, 250 N.E.2d 417, 19 Ohio App.2d 152.

Where recently divorced woman stored her furniture and moved temporarily into upstairs room in her parents' home, she and her parents were not members of "same household" within her automobile liability policy, defining covered nonowned automobiles as those not owned by or furnished for regular use of either named insured or any relative, which was defined as relative of insured who is resident of same household, and policy covered accident occurring while woman was driving parents' automobile.—Id.

Ohio App. 1970. Where automobile was delivered to purchaser by dealer with ten-day license cards, she was in possession with dealer's permission and was not, before delivery of certificate of title, owner of automobile within terms of automobile policy held by her father. R.C. § 4505.04.—Oberdier v. Kennedy Ford, Inc., 261 N.E.2d 348.

Ohio Com.Pl. 1967. Where dealer delivered possession of automobile to buyer on October 21 but certificate of title was not issued to buyer until November 4, dealer's policy which excluded from coverage any person other than named insured with respect to automobile possession of which had been transferred to another by named insured pursuant to agreement of sale did not provide coverage to accident which occurred on October 31.—Grange Mut. Cas. Co. v. Clifford, 230 N.E.2d 686, 13 Ohio Misc. 12.

Ohio Com.Pl. 1968. Where divorced daughter was employed in city some 27 to 30 miles away from her parents' home, daughter moved to residence of her parents as a "tentative place to stay," and daughter was driving her father's automobile and had an accident which resulted in a judgment against daughter, and all of the judgment but $10,000 was satisfied by father's insurer, daughter was not a "resident of the same household" of her parents within meaning of daughter's automobile liability policy which excluded coverage of non-owned automobile if insured was a resident of the same household of a relative.—Napier v. Banks, 248 N.E.2d 472, 19 Ohio Misc. 36, affirmed 250 N.E.2d 417, 19 Ohio App.2d 152.

Ohio Com.Pl. 1970. Under automobile liability policy clause defining "non-owned automobile" as an automobile not owned by or furnished for regular use of either named insured or any relative, named insured was not covered while operating automobile titled in the name of his brother who resided in the same household.—Roskin v. Aetna Ins. Co., 263 N.E.2d 923, 25 Ohio Misc. 95.

⚷435.2(6). Hired automobiles.

Ohio App. 1966. Greasing "fifth wheel" (a coupling between tractor and trailer), was not necessary to working condition of tractor and was not part of maintenance which lessor-driver of tractor had agreed to perform but was necessary to use of tractor in combination with lessee's trailer, and collision occurring while lessor-driver was en route to obtain grease to apply to "fifth wheel" of tractor occurred while tractor was being used exclusively in business of lessee for purposes of lessor-driver's liability policy, which was inapplicable while vehicle was being used in lessee's business, and lessee's liability policy, which applied to hired vehicles and persons using them with permission of lessee exclusively in business of lessee.—Hartford Acc. & Indem. Co. v. Allstate Ins. Co., 215 N.E.2d 416, 5 Ohio App.2d 287.

⚷435.2(7). Operator's or nonowner's policy.

Ill.App. 1971. Automobile "operator's policy" insures person or operator while he is in act of operating nonowned vehicles. S.H.A. ch. 95½, §§ 7–315(a), 7–317.—Kenilworth Ins. Co. v. Chamberlain, 269 N.E.2d 317.

Automobile operator's policy did not cover insured while he was driving automobile which he owned, in view of statute providing for both "owner's policy" and "operator's policy," despite contention that purpose of Financial Responsibility Law and public policy required construction in favor of insured, and despite fact that Secretary of State accepted certification of insurance under operator's policy as proof of financial responsibility. S.H.A. ch. 95½, §§ 7–315, 7–317.—Id.

⚷435.3(1). In general.

Ill.App. 1964. Purpose of "automatic insurance clause" or "newly acquired automobile clause" in automobile liability policy is to provide insurance coverage where owned automobile is not described in policy, and once specific insurance is purchased, and automobile becomes described in policy, automobile is no longer "newly acquired automobile" but is then "described automobile," and terms and provisions under "automatic insurance clause" or "newly acquired automobile clause" are no longer applicable.—Cook v. Suburban Cas. Co., 203 N.E.2d 748, 54 Ill.App.2d 190.

Ill.App. 1967. Provision of automobile policy limiting coverage for additional owned automobile to 30 days after acquisition by insured permits owner adequate opportunity to acquire necessary additional insurance and is not intended to cover two automobiles for any protracted period.—Nationwide Ins. Co. v. Ervin, 231 N.E.2d 112, 87 Ill.App.2d 432. ←

Where insured had bought second automobile in July 1964, after transmission "went out" of automobile which was named in policy and which remained inoperable in driveway of his home until repair in spring of 1966, and had accident with second automobile on September 26, 1964, the second automobile was not a "replacement" for the named automobile within policy provision extending coverage to replacement automobile.—Id.

Ill.App. 1968. Automobile which was reacquired by insured after it had been given to insured's son was "newly acquired automobile" within liability policy.—Country Mut. Ins. Co. v. Murray, 239 N.E.2d 498, 97 Ill.App.2d 61.

In order for automobile to be "newly acquired automobile" within provisions of policy its acquisition must occur during policy period.—Id.

"Newly acquired automobile" within terms of policy is not limited to vehicle which had never been previously owned.—Id.

Ohio Com.Pl. 1965. Where insured's nephew purchased automobile when he was living with insured who did not secure coverage on nephew's automobile, and nephew after moving to an apartment permitted his automobile to be driven by insured's wife who permitted

Digest Entry

Each of these digests is discussed below. As you can see, some of these digests overlap. For instance, both the *U.S. Supreme Court Digest* and the *Federal Practice Digest* cover U.S. Supreme Court cases. And both the *Pacific Regional Digest* and the *California Digest* cover California cases. All of these digests duplicate entries in the *Decennial* and *General Digests*. Because all West digests use exactly the same classification system (the key number system) an entry in the *California Digest* (for example) will be found in the *Pacific Digest* under the same key topic and subtopic number.

In the event of an overlap, which digest should you start with? Generally, it pays to start with the specific and move to the more general only if the specific doesn't satisfy your research needs. For example, if you are looking for a California case on a specific point, start with the *California Digest*. Then, if you are not satisfied with what you find, you can consult the *Pacific Digest* for cases decided by the courts of the other states in that region. You won't find any additional California cases under your key topic and number, since they would have been contained in the *California Digest*. And the cases in the *California Digest* will show up in the *Pacific Digest*. If after using the *Pacific Digest* you're still not satisfied, then go to the *Decennial* or *General Digest*.

Always remember to check the pocket part of any digest you use, to get the most recent cases.

Most law libraries do not subscribe to the entire West digest system. However, most medium to large libraries have the West digest for that state, the West digest for the region the state is located in, the West *Federal Practice Digest* and the *Decennials*.

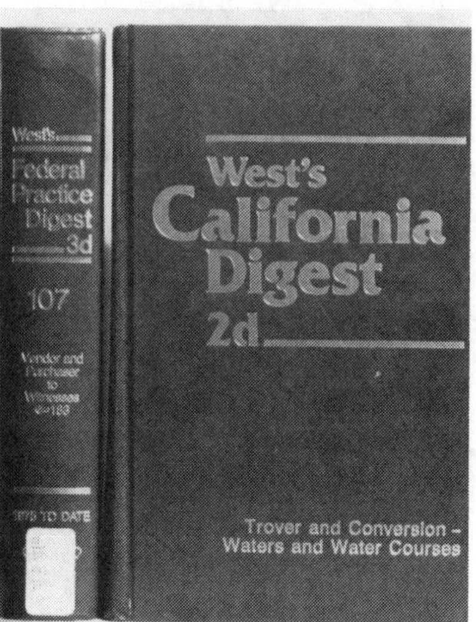

State and Federal Digests Published By West

a. State Digests

West publishes individual digests for every state (and Washington, D.C.) except Nevada, Utah and Delaware. If you are looking for decisions of the courts of your state, it is usually most efficient to start with the West digest for that state. On the other hand, if you live in a small state and are used to using the law produced by courts in adjoining states, you might want to start with the regional digest.

b. Regional Digests

West publishes digests for four regions of the country: Atlantic, Northwestern, Pacific and Southeastern. The regions are the same as those used in the regional reporter system (Chapter 8). Accordingly, if the cases decided by your state's courts are reported in the *Pacific Reporter*, start with the *Pacific Digest*. If they are reported in the *Southeast Reporter*, use the *Southeastern Digest*. If your case has been reported in the *Atlantic Reporter* but you want to locate similar cases from California, you can use either the *California Digest* or the *Pacific Digest*.

c. Federal Court Digests

If you want summaries of federal court decisions, go to the federal case digests in the West system. West publishes the Federal Practice Digest in four series:

- The *Modern Federal Practice Digest* (for cases decided before 1961)
- The *Federal Practice Digest Second Series* (for cases decided between 1961 and 1975)
- The *Federal Practice Digest Third Series* (for cases decided since 1975)
- The *Federal Practice Digest Fourth Series* (for cases decided since 1992).

West also publishes the *Supreme Court Digest* (for all cases decided by the U.S. Supreme Court).

The *Federal Practice Digest* (all four series) contains headnotes from cases reported in:

- the *Supreme Court Reporter (S. Ct.)*
- the *Federal Reporter* (which publishes U.S. Court of Appeal cases), and
- the *Federal Supplement* (which publishes U.S. District court cases).

The *Supreme Court Digest* also contains headnotes from the U.S. Supreme Court cases reported in the *Supreme Court Reporter (S. Ct.)*. So the *Supreme Court Digest* and the *Federal Practice Digest* overlap in respect to U.S. Supreme Court cases.

d. Decennial and General Digests

The *Decennial* and *General Digests* contain all the headnotes from all courts and all parts of the country. Most of the time it is more useful to use a state or regional digest for state cases, and a *Federal Practice Digest* or *Supreme Court Digest* for federal cases, than it is to use the *Decennial or General Digests*. After all, you rarely need to know what courts across the whole country have said about a particular issue. But there may be times when you want to do an extremely thorough research job. In that event, you will find the *Decennial* or *General Digests* a great help.

Initially, *Decennial Digests* were published in editions covering ten years' worth of cases. As of 1976, the *Decennials* are cumulated every five years and issued in two parts. For example, the *Ninth Decennial Digest* Part 1 covers 1976 to 1981, and Part 2 covers cases from 1981 to 1986.

Between publication of each new *Decennial* series, headnotes are collected in a publication called the *General Digest*. About ten of these are published each year, so about fifty will be on the bookshelves before a new *Decennial* emerges. For example, Part 1 of the *Tenth Decennial* will be on the shelves in 1992, covering the period between 1986 and 1991. The *Eleventh Decennial*, however, will not be published until 2001. Until the *Eleventh Decennial* emerges, the *General Digests* must be used for cases decided after 1991. Once the *Eleventh Decennial* is published, the *General Digests* start anew and the *Decennials* can be used for all cases decided before 1991.

A SHORTCUT WHEN USING THE *GENERAL DIGEST*

Each volume of the General Digest *includes all West key topics and numbers. This means that if you are chasing down the key topic and number of a particular headnote, a relevant case summary might appear in any and all volumes. To make your search more efficient, each tenth volume of the* General Digest *contains a Table of Key Numbers that tells you which volumes in the preceding ten volumes have entries under your key topic and subtopic number.*

LIBRARY EXERCISE

Using Digests

This exercise revisits the factual issue discussed in the last Library Exercise, but if you haven't done that one, don't worry.

Your employer has taken on several "trainees" for the summer. They are paralegal students and will do work which is regularly done in the office, such as filing, preparing billings, running to various courts to file documents, and going to law offices around town to pick up or deliver papers.

Your boss thinks that he can pay these "trainees" below the minimum wage required by the Fair Labor Standards Act because, unlike regular employees, they are in training, will learn how a law office works and will gain "resume value." He has been told that an important but old case in your Circuit (the 4th) is *Wirtz v. Wardlaw*, 339 F.2d 785.

Questions

1. *Find* Wirtz *and skim the headnotes following the synopsis. Which headnote appears to deal with minimum wage and employees-in-training, and what is its Key number?*
2. *Which Digest would you use to find other federal cases and, in particular, other 4th Circuit cases on this issue?*
3. *Because you need current law on this issue, go to the latest edition of that Digest. What is it?*
4. *The Volumes' contents are arranged alphabetically, with each book's contents listed on the spine. Find the volume which covers Labor Relations 1178. Which is it?*
5. *In both the main text and the Supplement (pocket part), examine the cases listed under Labor Relations 1178. Are there any 4th Circuit Court of Appeal cases about whether a trainee is entitled to protection under the Fair Labor Standard Act? Where did they arise?*
6. *Are there other cases listed that, although not from the appellate level of the 4th Circuit, might be useful?*

Answers

1. Headnote 3, Key number "Labor Relations 1178" deals with employees in training and minimum wage requirements.
2. Federal Practice Digest.
3. The 4th.
4. Volume 71.
5. Yes, *McLaughlin v. Ensley*, 877 F.2d 1207 (4th Cir. N.C. 1989) is an appellate level case. The information in parentheses tells you that a three-judge panel of the Fourth Circuit Court of Appeals heard a case being appealed from a district court in North Carolina.
6. Yes, a district court sitting in the Western District of North Carolina considered the issue in *McLaughlin v. McGee Bros. Co., Inc.*, 681 F. Supp. 1117 (W.D.N.C. 1988). Although other district courts within the 4th Circuit are not bound by a mere district court holding, some judges might find it persuasive nonetheless. Also, *Reich v. Parker Fire Protection Dist.*, 992 F.2d 1023, rehearing denied (10th Cir. Colo. 1993) was noted in the pocket part.

LIBRARY EXERCISE

Using the American Digest System

Now it's time to use the library to apply what you've just learned. This exercise asks you to use the *American Digest* (West) to find cases that treat the same issue treated by a relevant case you've found in the course of your research. Additional research exercises that include these and other skills are in the Appendix.

Problem

Sylvia Jones lived and died in West Virginia. She left an unwitnessed will that was written, signed and dated by her in her own handwriting. The form on which it was written had "Last Will and Testament" printed at the top and the words "by my hand and seal," "signature" and "date" printed at the bottom.

You are researching the validity of the will. You learn from a background resource that an unwitnessed will that is written, signed and dated entirely in the handwriting of the decedent—called a holographic will—is valid in West Virginia, but that an unwitnessed will on a form containing pre-printed words may not be. As authority for this statement, the background resource cites an Arizona case, *Matter of Estate of Johnson*, 630 P.2d 1039 (Ariz. App. 1981). You need a West Virginia case that speaks to this same issue.

Your first step is to find the *Johnson* case and identify one or more of the headnotes that discuss the issue of printed material on handwritten wills, to find a helpful key topic and number. All the headnotes for *Johnson* are assigned the key topic and number "Wills 132."

Questions

1. *Using the* American (Decennial *and* General) Digest *system, find a 1982 West Virginia case that says: "Under the 'surplusage theory,' non-handwritten material in a holographic will may be stricken with the remainder of the instrument being admitted to probate if the remaining provision makes sense standing alone." What is the citation for this case?*
2. *Continuing in the* Decennial *and* General Digests, *find a 1987 West Virginia case that says "Holographic wills are valid if they are wholly in the handwriting of the testator, if they are signed, and if they evidence testamentary intent."*
3. *Using the General Digests, how do you check to see whether there are any more recent West Virginia cases dealing with your issue?*

Answers

1. The *Ninth Decennial* Part 2 contains cases dated 1981 to 1986. In the volume containing the topic Wills, under key number 132, you find *In re Teubert's Estate*, 298 S.E.2d 456 (1982).
2. The *Tenth Decennial*, Part I, covers cases from 1986 to 1991. Look under Wills 132 to find *Siefert v. Sanders*, 358 S.E.2d. 775 (1987).

   If your law library does not have the *Tenth Decennial* use the *General Digest*. Each volume contains all the topics, from A to Z. To save the time it would take to look in every volume under Wills 132, go to every tenth volume (Volumes 10, 20, 30 etc.) and look for the Table of Key Numbers in the center of the volume—after the case notes arranged by topic and before the table of cases. Find your topic and key number (Wills 132) in the Table and it will tell you which volumes contain case notes under that key number.
3. The General Digests are found directly after the Tenth Decennial, Part I. Each volume contains all the topics from A to Z. To save the time it would take to look in every volume under Wills 132, go to every tenth volume (volumes 10, 20, 30, and so on) and look for the Table of Key Numbers in the center of the volume—after the case notes arranged by topic and before the table of cases. (When we wrote this Exercise, the last volume was number 40. When you do the research, there may be a number 50, 60 and so on.) Find your topic and key number (Wills 132) in the Table and it will tell which volumes contain case notes under that key number. In volume 30, you are referred to volume 25, but the case in that volume is not from West Virginia and does not deal with this issue. In volume 40, you are referred to volumes 32 and 37. Volume 32 cites a Texas case, and volume 37 cites a Montana case.

3. Finding Cases in Your State That Are Similar to Out-of-State Cases

During your research, you may come across a case that was decided just the way you think it should have been. It would be very helpful to your own situation—except that it was decided by another state's court. With the West *Digest* system, you can take a case that has been assigned a West topic and key number (any case in a regional reporter or other report published by West) and discover whether or not a similar case has been decided in your state.

For example, suppose you are a resident of Kansas and want to find out how to dissolve a partnership you formed with a friend. You read an article in the legal encyclopedia *Am. Jur. 2d* (see Chapter 5) about partnerships and come across a helpful statement to the effect that all you have to do is give notice of your intent to dissolve your partnership. The statement is footnoted with an Illinois Court of Appeals case, *Ljo v. Cooper*, 331 N.E.2d 206 (Ill. App. 1975).

Since you are in Kansas, you naturally wonder if this Illinois rule is the law in your state. Fortunately, the West *Regional Digest* system can be used to locate any Kansas case law on this very point.[2] Here's how you do this:

1. Read the citation: 331 N.E.2d 206 (Ill. App. 1975).
2. Locate the *Ljo* case in Volume 331 of the *Northeast Reporter, Second Series* at page 206.
3. Locate the headnote that most closely matches the statement you found in *Am. Jur. 2d.*
4. Note the key topic and number. In this case, the key topic is "Partnerships" and the key number is 259 1/2.
5. Locate the regional digest for Kansas, the *Pacific Reporter.* The regions are listed on a map in the front of each regional reporter.
6. In the *Pacific Digest,* look under Partnerships, key number 259 1/2. There you would find headnotes that resemble the one taken from *Ljo v. Cooper*. Note the one from *Craig v. Hamilton*, 518 P.2d 539 (1974), a Kansas case right on point.
7. Check the pocket part.

Alternatively, you could use the *Decennials* and *General Digest* to more inefficiently accomplish the same result.

Don't rely on digest summaries to tell you the law. The case summaries in digests are written by the editors of the case reports and do not constitute the actual opinion of the court. While digests are good for finding cases that deal with a similar issue, you must read a case itself before you rely on its holding.

Research Tip If you are using the West *Key* system to research the case law from scratch, remember that issues are classified by editors. Thus, two identical cases may be classified differently by two different editors. The result is that the digest doesn't refer to both cases under the same topic and key number. Always look under several key numbers.

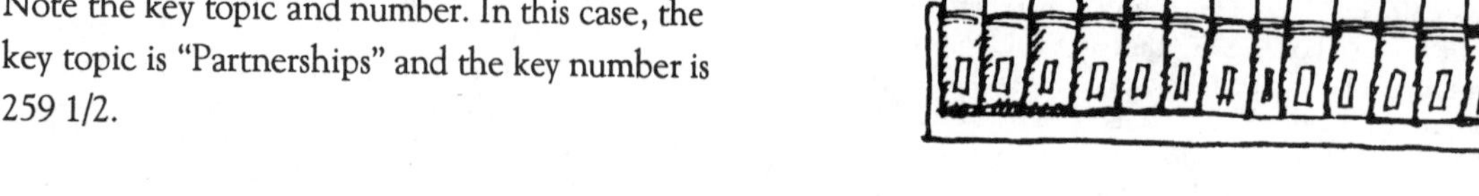

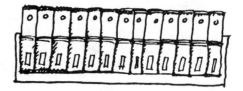

[2] Because most states have adopted the Uniform Partnership Act, you should also check the Kansas version of that Act on this particular point if you are really interested.

SUMMING UP

HOW TO FIND SIMILAR CASES IN DIFFERENT STATES

1. Find the case in your state as it is reported by West Publishing Co. Usually, this will be in the regional reporter.

2. Locate the headnotes that most accurately summarize the issues you are concerned with, and note the key topic and key number.

4. Find the West digest that covers cases decided by the courts you're interested in. If you want to find all similar cases regardless of the state, find the West *Decennial* and *General Digests*.

5. In the digests you are using, locate the topic heading and key number of the relevant headnotes and skim over the case summaries.

6. Find and read any cases that look relevant to your question.

7. Remember to consult the pocket part to the digest if it has one. For the *Decennials*, use the volumes of the *General Digest* to obtain the most up-to-date case summaries.

REVIEW

Questions

1. *When you look up your case in* Shepard's, *what information can you find about your case?*
2. *What information about your case do you need in order to Shepardize it?*
3. *If the case you are Shepardizing is in the Pacific Reporter, Volume 50, what volumes of the Pacific Shepard's do you need to look in?*
4. *How do you know from Shepard's whether the opinion in your case has been made invalid (vacated) by a higher court?*
5. *What does an "f" preceding the citation of the citing case mean?*
6. *What does an "e" mean?*
7. *What does a "q" mean?*
8. *What are digests?*
9. *What digest contains headnotes from all state and federal cases in the United States of America from 1976 to 1981?*
10. *In what digests could you look to find headnotes for cases from California that are reported in California Reporter and in Pacific Reporter?*
11. *If you found a California case that deals with your issue, but you are in Texas and need Texas cases on that topic, what digest would you use?*
12. *If you are using a state digest, where do you look to find the most up-to-date case summaries?*

Answers

1.
   - See if the case was affirmed, modified or reversed by a higher court.
   - See if other cases affect the value of the case as precedent or persuasive authority.
   - Find other cases that may help your argument or give you better answers to your question.
2. To use *Shepard's Citations for Cases*, you need the case citation—the name of the case reporter your case appears in, its volume number and the first page on which the case appears.
3. All volumes that include 50 Pacific Reporter: hardbound volumes and update pamphlets.
4. A "v" will appear in the margin to the left of the citing case citation (the citing case is the one that vacated your case's opinion).
5. The citing case explicitly *follows* the reasoning and/or decision of the cited case.
6. The citing case *explains* the holding or reasoning of the cited case.
7. The citing case *questions* the reasoning employed by the cited case.
8. Collections of the headnotes from cases, arranged according to the specific legal issues.
9. The Ninth Decennial Digest, Part 1.
10. California Digest, Pacific Digest and Decennial and General Digest.
11. The Texas Digest.
12. The pocket part.

CHAPTER 11

How to Write a Legal Memorandum

Do the words "legal memorandum" conjure up images of dusty desks, granny glasses, and massive leatherbound tomes at least two inches thick? If so, your first step is to relax and forget all such notions. A legal memorandum can be a couple of paragraphs long, written in good English, and (trust us on this one) fun to prepare. Whether you are doing research for yourself or for a lawyer, the main purpose of a memo is to force you to put the results of your search in writing.

A. Why Prepare a Legal Memorandum?

Why is this important? For three basic reasons. The first is that you won't really know whether your research is done until you try to write it up. You all have undoubtedly had the experience of thinking you understood something until the moment when you had to put pen to paper. The same is true of legal research. You may think you have answered the question you started out with, but you can't be sure until it plays in black and white. Although you may believe that the formal structure for the memorandum suggested here is unnecessary for this purpose, we think that it serves as a checklist for your research. Later, as you become more proficient, you may wish to adopt a more informal way of checking your results.

The second primary function of a legal memorandum is to provide you with an accessible record of the fruits of your research after time has erased the memories from your mind. It is unfortunately common for people to put in a day or two of research in the law library on a particular issue, neglect to take an extra hour or two to write it up, and later have to spend another day in the library because they are unable to reconstruct what they found from their notes.

The third primary function of a legal memorandum is to communicate the results of your research to someone else. This will be necessary if you are a paralegal doing research for a supervising lawyer, or if you are doing your own case and wish to inform the judge and opposing party of what you've found.

Now that you're convinced of the importance of preparing a legal memorandum, let's take a look at how to do it. For a much more intensive, yet well written, presentation of how to analyze case law and prepare a memorandum, see Statsky and Wernet, *Cases Analysis and Fundamentals of Legal Writing* (3rd Ed., West Publishing Co. 1989).

B. How to Prepare a Legal Memorandum

In this section we tell you how to prepare a legal memorandum. Obviously this is a skill that requires lots of practice. As a follow-up, we suggest that you do at least one of the research hypotheticals in Appendix 2 (if the necessary materials are available in your law library) and prepare a memorandum based on your work. Then compare your memorandum with the one accompanying the hypothetical. If you are able to do all of the exercises, your writing skills will get even better.

1. Overview

In Chapter 9, we stated that judicial opinions almost always have four primary elements:

- a statement of the facts
- a statement of the issue or issues
- a decision or holding on the issue or issues, and
- a discussion of the reasoning underlying the holding.

We also pointed out that these elements don't necessarily appear in any particular order. Like case opinions, legal memoranda should include a statement of the facts, a statement of the issue or issues, a conclusion about what the law is (equivalent to the holding), and a brief discussion of why you reached your conclusion. Also, like judicial opinions, it is not necessary to put these items in any particular order (unless your boss tells you different, of course).[1]

2. Distinguishing Internal From External Memoranda

In this discussion, we are talking about internal memoranda—i.e., memoranda intended solely for your own use or the use of your employer. However, legal memoranda are also prepared for external purposes. Commonly called "briefs" or "memoranda of points and authorities," these documents are ordinarily submitted to the court in the course of a lawsuit to advance a particular position with the utmost vigor (or so the client hopes). The brief submitted for the other side of the case will do the same in respect to that side. A brief presents all the law that is helpful to one's side and downplays from the discussion any law that is harmful.

There is a great difference of opinion among lawyers as to how much you have to acknowledge and deal with cases and authorities that are against you. If the contrary authority is obscure and hard to find, or its bearing on your situation marginal at best, you might decide to gamble and not mention it, hoping that the other side, the judge, and the judge's clerk will either not find it or will consider it inapplicable. On the other hand, if there is authority that is squarely against you, your failure to mention it may undermine your credibility.

[1]It is also a good idea to assign a topic heading to your memo. See the example a little later in this discussion.

Legal memoranda in the sense we are talking about, on the other hand, are not intended to be arguments advancing a particular position. Rather, they are intended to accurately summarize the fruits of the legal research regardless of whether they help or harm one's position. Both sides need to be presented, whether the memorandum is for your own use or is to be turned over to a supervisor. Of course, when you get to court (if you do), you or the attorney you are assisting will want to emphasize the arguments and legal authority that best advances your position.

3. Internal Consistency

The main idea is to structure your legal memorandum so that it is internally consistent. For example, you have to include enough relevant facts in the memo for your statement of the issue to make sense. If your issue is whether a new owner of an apartment house can evict a tenant for having pets even though the prior landlord allowed them, your statement of facts would have to include such items as:

- the kind(s) of pet(s) in question
- the date ownership was transferred
- information about any rental agreement or lease that was executed by the tenant, and so on.

In a similar way, your discussion of the reasoning that you use to arrive at your conclusion has to include cases or statutes that are relevant to the facts that you've listed in the memo. If your law sources and facts don't match up on some level, your reasoning is faulty.

This internal consistency requirement sometimes means that you have to go back and add or subtract a fact or two, or slightly restate the legal issue to square with your conclusion or reasoning. It's very much like fine tuning a television set or car—all of the operating elements have to be adjusted relative to each other.

4. Additional Points for Paralegals

Especially if you are a paralegal and are asked to prepare a legal memorandum for your supervising attorney, three additional points may be useful. The first is, it is usually a good idea to list the resources that you've checked, even if some or many of them didn't pan out. This is because attorneys like to feel secure, and the more thorough your legal research, the more secure they will feel. For example, in any given research project you might check *A.L.R.*, *Am. Jur.*, a local digest or two and some treatises in addition to a local encyclopedia. Even though you only strike pay dirt through the local encyclopedia, the attorney will feel better knowing that you've also checked out the other resources.

The second point is, keep your sentences short and avoid jargon when possible. As we said, one of the three primary purposes of a legal memorandum is to communicate. It is all too easy to get wrapped up in a research project and produce mile-long, convoluted sentences. Don't.

The third point is, all statements about what the law is should be supported by some primary legal authority, such as statutes, regulations, cases or ordinances. Other legal materials generally comprise somebody else's opinion about what the law is. It's okay and even desirable to include references to these secondary or background sources, but they cannot replace primary authority.

C. Sample Legal Memorandum

Now let's look at a sample of a legal memorandum. After each section of the memorandum we provide a comment on what we did and why. While the memoranda that you produce may be different in format, it won't hurt to keep the following checklist in your head:

- Did I put down all facts that are relevant to my legal issue as stated, and to my legal conclusions?
- Did I state the legal issue clearly?
- Did I arrive at a definitive conclusion about the legal issue as applied to my facts?
- Did I state clearly the reasons for my conclusion while presenting all sides of the legal picture?
- Did I support my conclusions with primary legal authority?

Note This particular example involves a paralegal working for a law firm. However, its basic format (except of course for the heading and the list of sources used) and the comments that we provide are generally applicable to all internal memoranda.

SAMPLE MEMORANDUM

Memo From: Terry Paralegal
To: Ruth Lawyer
Topic: Property Tax Exemption For John Ford Commune Project

Facts:

John Ford and his friends want to start an alternative community on some land that they own jointly in upstate New York near New Paltz. They have talked for several years about the deplorable state of the New York City public schools and the need for an alternative school for their children. Although they're all living in New York City and working at a variety of jobs, they wish to move together up to the land in the spring, live in mobile homes at first, and then gradually build their homes and a school for their children.

All together, this group includes 12 adults and 17 children between the ages of 6 and 15. While the primary impetus for making this move is to gain control over their children's education, the adults also share common political and social goals centering around concepts of self-reliance and ecological responsibility. They have ideas of building a demonstration community and producing some income by writing books and selling vegetables. Additional income would come from the adults teaching in local schools.

They have asked us for advice about such questions as what official permission is required to start an alternative school, whether they need to be incorporated, and if so, what that involves, what kind of tax problems they might encounter, whether the land would be exempt from property taxation, and so on. This memorandum focuses on the property tax question.

[Comment: These facts are a very small portion of the universe of facts collected by the researcher in this case. As you can see the facts focus almost exclusively on the intent of the persons settling on the land and on their plans for its utilization. This focus follows from the way the issue is framed in the following portion of the memorandum.]

Issue:

Is property that is owned by a group primarily interested in starting a school for their children, and incidentally interested in developing a demonstration alternative community, exempt from property taxation under New York law?

[COMMENT: As you can see, the issue is consistent with the facts. If the statement of the facts had neglected to mention the secondary interest in developing a demonstration alternative community, for example, the statement of the issue wouldn't make any sense. As it turns out, by stating the issue this way we can draw some fairly definitive conclusions given the state of the law that we've researched.

You may be wondering why the issue was formulated in this precise way. The answer is that the law is structured in a way that makes a group's primary and incidental purposes very important when a decision about tax exemption is to be made (read on). It is common for a legal researcher to begin with one or more tentative legal issues in mind, and then reformulate these issues in the course of the research.]

Conclusion:

So long as the group owning the land is organized predominantly for educational purposes and uses the land predominantly in furtherance of these purposes, the land will be exempt from property taxes even though the group has other purposes and makes other incidental uses of the land.

[COMMENT: Again, we are struggling to maintain an internal consistency. As you can see, the conclusion addresses the precise statement of the issue; otherwise the memorandum would be of little use. Remember, however, that the reality of the law as uncovered in your research ultimately determines how your issues and conclusions are formulated, and which facts are relevant. Now let's take a look at that research.]

Reasoning:

The N.Y. Real Prop. Tax Law §420-a (1)(a) (McKinney Supp. 1984) provides an absolute exemption from real property tax for "real property owned by a corporation or association organized or conducted exclusively for religious, charitable, educational, moral or mental improvement of men, women or children or cemetery purposes, or for two or more such purposes, and used exclusively for carrying out thereupon one or more of such purposes." (Emphasis added.)

By its terms this statute seems to require exclusivity of use and purpose consistent with the exempt categories. However, in Mohonk Trust v. Board of Assessors, 392 N.E.2d 876 (1979), the New York Court of Appeals interpreted these provisions to mean only that the purposes of the landowner and the use to which the land is put must be primarily those provided for in the statute. The court held that incidental or auxiliary non-exempt uses or purposes do not defeat the exemption.

The purpose of the group here is twofold. The primary one is to start a school for their children. The incidental one would be to build an alternative community. While an argument could be made that the incidental purpose is also for educational purposes or for the moral improvement of men, women and children, another court of appeals case seems to rule out such an interpretation.

In Swedenborg Foundation, Inc. v. Lewisohn, 351 N.E.2d 702 (1976), the court was asked to consider whether a foundation that operated to educate the public about the principles of Emanuel Swedenborg, a Swedish theologian, came within the property tax exemption. The court held:

"We think education . . . refers to the development of faculties and powers and the expansion of knowledge by teaching, instruction or schooling. We distinguish the very much broader process of the communication of facts and ideas. While it may be that a small portion of the foundation's activities includes the supplying of lecturers and participation in seminars, it cannot be said that the foundation is itself directly affiliated with any recognized educational institution . . . More significant are the facts that the foundation was not chartered by the Board of Regents and it is not classified as an educational institution by the Department of Education." Swedenborg, 351 N.E.2d at 706

The court went on to rule out the "moral improvement" part of the exemption as well, on the ground that the primary purpose was to disseminate Swedenborg's writings and views rather than to morally improve people.

Clearly, the Swedenborg case interpreted the statute very strictly when it comes to education and moral improvement. It definitely indicates the need for the Ford group to establish some type of formal school arrangement for their children if they are to obtain the property tax exemption.

Another troublesome case is Religious Society of Families v. Assessor, 429 N.Y.S.2d 321, 75 A.D.2d 1004 (1980), a Supreme Court Appellate Division case holding that a group organized around scientific and sociological principles of ecology and land use controls that used the land as its homestead was not qualified for the exemption because it appeared that the homestead was the primary use of the land. (429 N.Y.S.2d at 322.)

On balance, however, assuming an adequate record is made with respect to the educational purpose of this community and assuming that the school is in fact recognized as an acceptable form of education for the children by the appropriate state agencies, the land should be exempt from property taxes.

[COMMENT: Two points. First, the reasoning contains some good news and some bad news. Even though we reached a positive conclusion, there is enough indication of possible trouble to put yourself or a supervising attorney on notice. The memorandum could have drawn the opposite conclusion as well. So long as the full picture is drawn, you or the supervising attorney can take it from there.

Second, the research in this case indicated that the key to obtaining a property tax exemption is to establish the primacy of the education goal and make other purposes and uses incidental. This resulted in the facts, issue and conclusion being framed the way they were. Once again, internal consistency is key to an effective legal memorandum.]

Resources Utilized:

- New York Jurisprudence
- Abbott's Digest
- Corpus Juris Secondum
- A.L.R.
- Powell on Real Property

This example may or may not reflect the current state of New York law on this subject. If you are interested in the issue covered here for New York or any other state, do your own research. However, the cases that we've cited will provide a starting point.

CHAPTER 12

The Legal Research Method: Examples

In Chapter 2, *An Overview of Legal Research,* we showed you an overall method for undertaking a legal research project. And in each of the following chapters we explained an important part of that method. Now it is time to pull it all together in an example.

A. The Facts

Assume the following facts: Laura has enrolled her child Amy in a day care center in California. (Although the law in your state may be different, the method of research would be the same.) Laura came to pick up Amy at the end of the day, but arrived a little early so that she could watch Amy play and could interact with the staff and other parents (a practice that was encouraged by the day care center). Laura stood nearby and chatted with some of the parents as she watched Amy conclude her teeter-totter game.

Amy's joyful play came to a horrific end as, in front of her mother's eyes, she flew off the teeter-totter when the wooden seat detached from the bar. Laura took her immediately to the hospital, where an X-ray disclosed a cranial hemorrhage. Amy was operated upon immediately to relieve the pressure on her brain.

The surgery was a success and the prognosis for Amy was favorable. Laura, however, has suffered extreme anxiety in the form of recurrent nightmares, difficulty in concentrating and fits of uncontrollable crying. She has been unable to forget the awful sight of her daughter flying through the air and landing with a thud on the hard cement of the play yard. Laura's psychological distress has reached the point where she cannot work and has trouble functioning on a daily basis.

Laura has been told by several friends that she ought to see a lawyer. She found out that the wooden play structure that fell apart had been a source of concern to the day care center for some time (they knew that the wood was rotting and had attempted to fix the bolts on the teeter-totter seat). Laura knows that Amy can sue the day care center for her physical injuries, but Laura is less sure whether she herself can recover money damages for her own emotional torment.

Before she sees a lawyer, Laura wants to do a little legal research for herself. As a mother who witnessed her daughter's accident, can she sue for the emotional distress that scene produced? How should she proceed?

B. Classify the Problem

Following the suggestions made in Chapter 4, *Putting Your Questions Into Legal Categories,* Laura must:

- determine whether state or federal law is involved
- determine whether the matter is civil or criminal, and
- determine whether her research will involve procedural or substantive questions.

Since it's apparent that Laura's dispute with the day center involves a personal injury (Laura's emotional distress), and since most personal injury ("tort") cases are controlled by state law (see Chapter 4), Laura would tentatively start with a state law classification. While the day care center might receive some federal money, the receipt of federal funds by an independent or community entity would probably not transform Laura's dispute from a state to a federal question unless her dispute had something to do with the funds themselves.

The next step is to determine that the matter is civil rather than criminal. Criminal matters always directly involve the government and a violation of the criminal law. Although there are times when an act violates both the criminal law and a civil duty owed to another person (failure to pay child support is an example, battery is another), this is not such a case. In any event, if the center had committed any criminal act, the charges would be brought by the government upon Laura's complaint, not by Laura herself.

Now that Laura has tentatively classified the problem as one involving state civil law, she needs to determine whether the question is substantive or procedural. In essence, Laura's question is whether she can recover damages for her torment. This type of question is really at the heart of the substantive law—that is, determining whether someone has done something wrong. But if she decides that the day care center has legally goofed, she would then become interested in state civil procedural law—that is, how Laura's case gets into court and stays there until she recovers.

So Laura's next task is to determine under which civil substantive law category her problem falls. By skimming the list of substantive civil law topics in Chapter 4, she quickly narrows the issue down to "torts." Why? Because Laura suffered an injury—emotional suffering—that was arguably caused by the day care center's failure to properly maintain their equipment. Whether Laura can recover money for her suffering under the law of torts remains to be determined.

C. Select a Background Resource

Now that she has narrowed the issue—a state, civil, substantive, tort—Laura needs to select an appropriate legal background resource to supply an overview of the part of tort law that is relevant to her problem. Basically, Laura wants to find out whether the day care center has wronged her in some way—as opposed to Amy—and if so whether her injury qualifies for damages. Finally, she wants to know what she must show to prove her case. For example, is her testimony enough, or does she need doctors' reports?

Because Laura is in California, a good place to start is with the encyclopedia known as *California Jurisprudence* (*Cal. Jur.*), which we discussed earlier in Chapter 5, *Getting Some Background Information.*[1] In California (and the other states that have state-specific encyclopedias published by one of the major law publishers), this type of publication would be found in any medium to large law library such as the average county library. It is important to note that *Cal. Jur.* is published in three series. The third series, *Cal. Jur. 3d,* is the most up-to-date and the one you want to use.

D. Use the Legal Index

Now that Laura has selected a background resource for her project, she needs to deal with the index. This involves writing down as many words and phrases as she can think of that relate to her specific fact situation. (See Chapter 4, *Putting Your Questions Into Legal Categories*, Section C.) Some of these might be:

- emotional distress
- emotional upset
- emotional suffering
- mental suffering
- negligence
- carelessness
- injury
- child
- parent and child
- anxiety
- damages
- shock
- fright
- sleeplessness
- nightmares

Her next step is to look in the general index of *Cal. Jur. 3d*. While a number of the words and phrases that we listed above would ultimately lead her to the proper discussion, the phrase that will strike pay dirt the fastest is "emotional distress." As you can see from the index entry set out below, this phrase refers you to another entry titled "Pain, Suffering, and Mental Disturbance."

[1]Many California researchers might prefer to start with the appropriate volume in the set called *Witkin's Summary of California Law.* The Witkin series, by California legal scholar Bernard Witkin, is probably the resource of choice for California lawyers who are trying to get a quick fix on any given legal point. There are eight volumes for California substantive law and four volumes covering California procedure. The series is indexed and organized according to general legal categories.

CAL JUR 3d GENERAL INDEX

388

Cal. Jur. 3d General Index

Consulting that heading in the same index, Laura finds a great number of entries. The first one that appears relevant is "intentional infliction of emotional distress," shown below:

CAL JUR 3d GENERAL INDEX

161

Cal. Jur. 3d General Index

While Laura might get confused at this point (it is here that a law school education would probably pay off a little) and start reading some of these discussions, she would soon decide that her case probably does not qualify for "intentional" infliction of emotional distress. While the day-care center may have been impermissibly careless, they in no way "intended" to cause Laura the anxiety or hurt Amy.

THE DIFFERENCE BETWEEN NEGLIGENCE AND INTENTIONAL TORTS

The difference between intentional torts and negligence is not always as clear-cut as this example might suggest. Generally, any action or inaction can be intentional as well as negligent, and cases such as Laura's are usually prosecuted on the basis of both approaches. For the purpose of this chapter, however, let's stick with negligence.

In fact, by again consulting the list of civil law topics in Chapter 4 (see the entry for torts), Laura determines that the day-care center may have been negligent—that is, more careless than a hypothetical "reasonable person" would have been under the circumstances. Once having determined that the emotional distress resulted from negligence rather than from an intentional act, Laura logically follows up on the sub-entry "Negligence," shown below.

CAL JUR 3d GENERAL INDEX

162

Fig. 12-3

Cal. Jur. 3d General Index

Because "negligence, generally" is a subentry to "pain, suffering, and mental disturbance," Laura might well find a discussion of her topic under the indicated sections (§§ 74-76). The other listings do not appear to be of much help.

If Laura had decided to use "negligence" as her first search term instead of "emotional distress," she would have gotten to the same place. Consider the index entry under "Negligence," shown below.

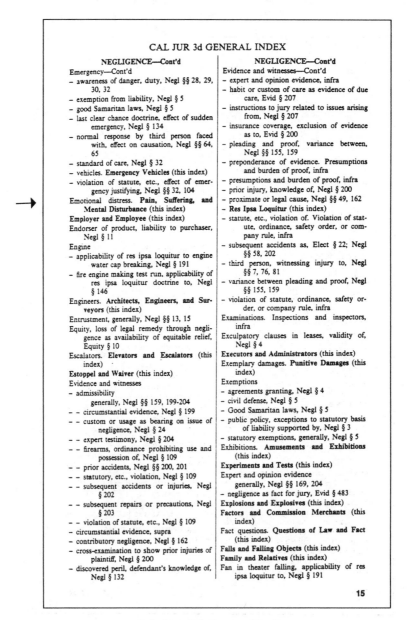

CAL JUR 3d GENERAL INDEX

15

Cal. Jur. 3d General Index

E. Get an Overview of Your Research Topic

The three pages shown below contain the actual discussion in *Cal. Jur. 3d* on negligent infliction of emotional distress. It indicates that a person can recover damages for emotional or mental distress by the negligent acts of another so long as some type of physical injury is associated with the distress. A shock to the nervous system can constitute such a physical injury, according to the discussion in § 75. Read the sections for yourself.

§ 74 NEGLIGENCE

2. Emotional Distress (§§ 74–76]

§ 74. In general

In an action based on negligence, at least where there is a physical impact, the plaintiff may recover for mental anguish or suffering, in addition to any damages he may recover for physical injuries.[27] And damages are recoverable for mental distress caused by tortious infliction of damage to property, unaccompanied by physical injuries.[28] In a personal injury action, however, emotional distress, unaccompanied by a physical impact is not a compensable injury[29] unless such emotional distress results in a physical injury or illness.[30]

in tort actions, generally, see Damages §§ 58 et seq.

27. *Sloane v Southern C. R. Co., 111 C 668, 44 P 320; Merrill v Los Angeles G. & E. Co., 158 C 499, 111 P 534; Easton v United Trade School Contracting Co., 173 C 199, 159 P 597; Deevy v Tassi, 21 C2d 109, 130 P2d 389; Capelouto v Kaiser Foundation Hospitals, 7 C3d 889, 103 Cal Rptr 856, 500 P2d 880.*

Mental suffering is regarded as an aggravation of damage if it ensues naturally from the defendant's wrongful act. *Sloane v Southern C. R. Co., 111 C 668, 44 P 320.*

28. *Crisci v Security Ins. Co., 66 C2d 425, 58 Cal Rptr 13, 426 P2d 173; Windeler v Scheers Jewelers, 8 CA3d 844, 88 Cal Rptr 39.*

A title company insuring real property against liens and encumbrances of record, negligently failing to discover or disclose a recorded lien or encumbrance or failing to exclude a known recorded lien or encumbrance from coverage, and which, on being notified of the existence of the recorded lien or encumbrance, unjustifiably refuses to take legal action to clear the title or eliminate the cloud, is liable to the purchaser in compensatory damages for any emotional distress that results. It was entirely foreseeable that plaintiffs would suffer mental anguish and distress when apprised of defendant's negligence since they relied on the preliminary report. *Jarchow v Transamerica Title Ins. Co., 48 CA3d 917, 122 Cal Rptr 470 (ovrld Quezada v Hart, 67 CA3d 754, 136 Cal Rptr 815* noting that the Jarchow Case involved a willful refusal to take action to clear title, and stating that to the extent that the court in Jarchow purported to allow recovery for emotional suffering in cases involving negligence without bad faith and without physical injury, the extension of prior California law was unwarranted).

Annotations: Recovery for mental shock or distress in connection with injury to or interference with tangible property, 28 ALR2d 1070; Recovery for mental anguish or emotional distress, absent independent physical injury, consequent upon breach of contract in connection with sale of real property, 61 ALR3d 922.

Law Review: 49 CLR 758 (recovery of damages for mental suffering arising from breach of contract).

29. *Sloane v Southern C R. Co.,*

250 46 Cal Jur 3d

Cal. Jur. 3d, Negligent Infliction of Emotional Distress

§ 75. Physical injury without impact

Since California is a "no impact" jurisdiction, it is not necessary in order for plaintiff to recover damages for physical injuries resulting from emotional distress to show that he also suffered a contemporaneous physical impact on his person.[31] Thus, a plaintiff who, as a result of the defendant's negligence, has suffered an emotional trauma resulting in a nervous disturbance or disorder may recover damages. Such shocks to the nervous system are classified as physical injuries.[32]

111 C 668, 44 P 320; Easton v United Trade School Contracting Co., 173 C 199, 159 P 597.

In parents' action based on hospital's negligence in delivering wrong baby, there was no error in instructing the jury that mental suffering alone would not support an action for damages, and that if the only injury suffered was mental suffering, plaintiffs could not recover. *Espinosa v Beverly Hospital, 114 CA2d 232, 249 P2d 843.*

There can be no recovery for emotional distress unaccompanied by physical harm arising from acts solely negligent in nature. *Gautier v General Tel. Co., 234 CA2d 302, 44 Cal Rptr 404.*

Annotation: Right to recover for mental pain and anguish alone, apart from other damages, 23 ALR 361, 44 ALR 438, 56 ALR 657.

Form: Instruction to jury that damages are not recoverable for mental suffering caused by negligence without simultaneous physical impact or injury, 12 Am Jur Pl & Pr Forms (Rev), Fright, Shock, and Mental Disturbance, Form 5.

30. As to recovery for physical injury resulting from emotional trauma but unaccompanied by physical impact, see §§ 75, 76, infra.

As to the measure and elements of compensatory damages for mental anguish and suffering, generally, see DAMAGES §§ 73 et seq.

31. *Dillon v Legg, 68 C2d 728, 69 Cal Rptr 72, 441 P2d 912, 29 ALR3d 1316; Cook v Maier, 33 CA2d 581, 92 P2d 434; Vanoni v Western Airlines, 247 CA2d 793, 56 Cal Rptr 115.*

32. *Lindley v Knowlton, 179 C 298, 176 P 440; Di Mare v Cresci, 58 C2d 292, 23 Cal Rptr 772, 373 P2d 860.*

In an action against the driver of a vehicle which collided with and killed plaintiff's wife, plaintiff's gastric condition constituted sufficient physical injury if it could be fairly said that it was caused by the husband's shock occasioned by his perception of the collision. *Krouse v Graham, 19 C3d 59, 137 Cal Rptr 863, 562 P2d 1022.*

Where plaintiff was shocked at finding a brush which he thought was a spider in his bottle and believed he had swallowed a part of it, the experience caused him such an emotional paroxysm as to result in compensable physical suffering and worry. *Medeiros v Coca-Cola Bottling Co., 57 CA2d 707, 135 P2d 676.*

Shock to the nerves and nervous system sufficed as an allegation of physical manifestation. *Vanoni v Western Airlines, 247 CA2d 793, 56 Cal Rptr 115.*

Cal. Jur. 3d, Negligent Infliction of Emotional Distress (continued)

§ 76. —Witnessing injury to third person

A person may recover damages for physical injuries resulting from emotional trauma upon witnessing the tortious infliction of death or injury on a third party even though the person suffering such damages was not in the zone of danger arising out of the tortious conduct. Recovery in such a situation depends on whether harm to the plaintiff was reasonably foreseeable.[33] In determining whether a defendant should reasonably foresee the injury, the court will take into account such factors as the following: (1) whether plaintiff was located near the scene of the accident as contrasted with one who was a distance from it; (2) whether the shock resulted from a direct emotional impact upon plaintiff from the sensory and contemporaneous observance of the accident, as contrasted with learning of the accident from others after its occurrence; and (3) whether plaintiff and the victim were closely related, as contrasted with an absence of any relationship or the presence of only a distant relationship.[34]

Annotations: Recovery for physical consequences of fright resulting in a physical injury, 11 ALR 1119, 40 ALR 983, 76 ALR 681, 98 ALR 402; Right to recover for emotional disturbance or its physical consequences, in absence of impact or other actionable wrong, 64 ALR2d 100.

Law Review: 24 CLR 229 (recovery of damages for nervous shock without impact).

Forms: Complaint for damages for physical injuries resulting from shock and fright, 12 Am Jur Pl & Pr Forms (Rev), Fright, Shock, and Mental Disturbance, Form 1; Instruction to jury as to damages recoverable for bodily pain and suffering resulting from fright, 12 Am Jur Pl & Pr Forms (Rev), Fright, Shock, and Mental Disturbance, Form 6.

Practice Reference: Liability for injury without impact, 15 Cal Practice, Model Personal Injury Action § 250:12.

33. *Dillon v Legg, 68 C2d 728, 69 Cal Rptr 72, 441 P2d 912, 29 ALR3d 1316* (ovrlg to the extent inconsistent herewith *Amaya v Home Ice, Fuel & Supply Co., 59 C2d 295, 29 Cal Rptr 33, 379 P2d 513).*

34. Obviously, a defendant is more likely to foresee that a mother who observes an accident affecting her child will suffer harm than to foretell that a stranger witness will do so. Similarly, the degree of foreseeability of the third person's injury is far greater in the case of his contemporaneous observation of the accident than that in which he subsequently learns of it. The defendant is more likely to foresee that shock to the nearby, witnessing mother will cause physical harm than to anticipate that someone distant from the accident will suffer more than a temporary emotional reaction. *Dillon v Legg, 68 C2d 728, 69 Cal Rptr 72, 441 P2d 912, 29 ALR3d 1316.*

Cal. Jur. 3d, Negligent Infliction of Emotional Distress (continued)

Laura would then turn to the pocket part to see whether these articles had been updated in any significant way. Assume for a moment that she doesn't find anything.

If she stopped here, she would have to conclude, according to § 75 of the *Cal. Jur. 3d* article on negligence, that California law prohibits her from collecting anything from the day-care center for the distress that she suffered. Why? Because according to this discussion, recovery for personal injuries resulting from negligence requires at least some physical manifestation of the injury, and Laura did not experience any physical symptom or injury.

Remember, however, that background resources provide a start for good legal research, but never a finish. Laura now needs to check out the primary law on which the article is based. If a statute exists, this is the first place to go. But there is no California statute covering this subject (and none is mentioned in the articles), and after some rummaging in the California codes Laura would come to this conclusion. Next Laura should review the cases on which the article is based. Turning back to § 75, Laura notes that the article refers to several cases in footnote 29.

The lead case is *Sloane v. Southern* C.R. *Co.*, but further along *Espinosa v. Beverly Hospital* and *Gautier v. General Tel. Co.* are also cited as authority for the proposition that you can't recover for negligently inflicted emotional distress without a physical injury. The full footnote is shown below.

29. *Sloane v Southern C. R. Co.,*

111 C 668, 44 P 320; Easton v United Trade School Contracting Co., 173 C 199, 159 P 597.

In parents' action based on hospital's negligence in delivering wrong baby, there was no error in instructing the jury that mental suffering alone would not support an action for damages, and that if the only injury suffered was mental suffering, plaintiffs could not recover. *Espinosa v Beverly Hospital, 114 CA2d 232, 249 P2d 843.*

There can be no recovery for emotional distress unaccompanied by physical harm arising from acts solely negligent in nature. *Gautier v General Tel. Co., 234 CA2d 302, 44 Cal Rptr 404.*

Annotation: Right to recover for mental pain and anguish alone, apart from other damages, 23 ALR 361, 44 ALR 438, 56 ALR 657.

Form: Instruction to jury that damages are not recoverable for mental suffering caused by negligence without simultaneous physical impact or injury, 12 Am Jur Pl & Pr Forms (Rev), Fright, Shock, and Mental Disturbance, Form 5.

Footnote from Cal. Jur. 3d Entry

If Laura read these cases, she would learn that they state the law pretty much as the article describes; that is, a person can't recover for emotional distress caused by negligence unless there is a related physical injury. But these cases are quite old. The *Sloane* case, in fact, was decided in the nineteenth century.

Even though the encyclopedia didn't indicate that any changes have occurred—remember, we assumed that for the purposes of this example— Laura can't necessarily rely on that fact. The publishers of background resources like encyclopedias may not be aware of important new cases until a year or two (or even longer) after they are decided. While every attempt is made by the publishers to keep these resources up-to-date, important changes often slip through their fingers.

Therefore, until Laura has determined that the *Sloane* case (and the other cases) are still "good law," her research is not complete. Her next step is accordingly to use *Shepard's* case citations to find out whether these cases are still good law.

F. Use Shepard's Citations for Cases

To begin, Laura would locate the *Sloane* case in *Shepard's*. Looking back to footnote 29, the *Sloane* case is followed by two citations. These are parallel citations (explained in Chapter 9, *Finding Cases*), which means that the *Sloane* case can be found in two different sets of case reports.

Often there are separate *Shepard's* for each separate case report set. In this situation, for example, there is a *Shepard's* for the *Pacific Reporter* (The "P" in 44 P. 320) and a *Shepard's* California Citations for cases located in the *California Reports* (the "C" in 111 C. 668),[2] and California cases cited in the *Pacific Reporter*.

If Laura finds herself getting hazy at this point, she should turn back to Chapter 10, Section A, and review the material there. *Shepard's* is among the most difficult aspects of legal research to learn, but she should take time and regroup before going on.

Let's assume that her law library has both the *Pacific Reporter* and *California Reporter* (obviously, other reports would be relevant if researching this question in another state). We'll use the *Pacific Reporter* citation to Shepardize *Sloane*. Laura would therefore want to locate the volumes of *Shepard's* that are keyed to the *Pacific Reporter*. These will be shelved either in a central location along with all the other *Shepard's* or immediately after the most current volumes of the *Pacific Reporter*.

Upon locating these volumes, she'll find several hardcover volumes and paperbound updates, reflecting the fact that *Shepard's* is updated in paperback every few months. Remember, you have not Shepardized a case until you have checked it through *all* the *Shepard's* volumes that cover the period from the day the case was decided to the most recent monthly update. The most recent update available when this example was prepared was January 1995. By the time you read this, new update pamphlets will be available and you can practice by doing some further updating for yourself.

When we did this research, there were twelve bound *Shepard's* on the shelf. These are Volume 1, Parts 1, 2, 3, 4 and 5, and Volume 2, Parts 1, 2, 3, 4, 5, 6 and 7. These cover all cases through 1994. The hardbound volumes are followed by a red paperback labeled "CUMULATIVE SUPPLEMENT, January 1995," which contains citations to cases decided between the issuance of the hardbound series and January 1995.

To look up the *Pacific Reporter* cite for the *Sloane* case, Laura starts with the book that includes the number 44 (the volume number of the *Pacific Reporter* where *Sloane* is reported), which happens to be Volume 1, Part 1. After pulling this volume, she locates the page in *Shepard's* where this number first appears and flips through to where a -320- appears (the page number where the *Sloane* case starts in the *Pacific Reporter*). There she will find a list of citations to cases that have cited *Sloane* for one reason or another. If she reviewed each of these cases, she would find most resulted in no change in the law. The cases that do represent a change are outlined below.

[2]*Shepard's* uses its own system of abbreviations for reporters instead of following the Harvard bluebook form. If you refer to cases in court documents, you should use the bluebook's system.

Vol. 44 **PACIFIC REPORTER**

101P[2]926
116P754
e124P[2]541
d137P[2]282
236P[1]331
272P[2]1098
4P2d[1]140
34P2d508
51P2d[1]901
51P2d[2]901
59P2d1003
73P2d[1]626
73P2d[2]626
94P2d[1]1061
101P2d[2]1111
116P2d[2]493
128P2d[2]195
128P2d[1]197
144P2d[2]823
j144P2d[1]836
e144P2d842
144P2d[1]843
144P2d[2]843
j207P2d[2]12
98CaR[2]584
Utah
280P[1]737
Ga
49SE315
Iowa
154NW342
154NW354
Minn
108NW481
W Va
96SE943
Wis
107NW463
150ÆR644n
150ÆR645n
150ÆR657n

– 309 –
(111Cal588)
s53P410
128P[4]750
4P2d[4]980
39P2d[1]880
214P2d[4]410
214P2d[1]411
44CaR[3]615
Idaho
241P[4]1016
5ÆR1226n
3Æ2 1316n
3Æ2 1363n

– 312 –
(111Cal648)
50P[3]680
55P[1]990
57P[4]1069
92P[2]499
95P[4]380
117P[3]791
165P[3]563
193P[3]166
214P[3]239
235P[1]660
d242P505
e257P[2]559
260P[4]910
d262P[4]448
263P[4]311
f265P[3]897
d295P[3]906

j8P2d[4]122
94P2d[3]622
262P2d[3]635
276P2d[4]46
d276P2d[3]848
288P2d[3]636
461P2d[3]365
500P2d[3]615
17CaR[3]116
19CaR[4]464
82CaR[3]165
103CaR[3]703
109CaR[3]740
122CaR[3]10
Ariz
136P[3]282
Mont
f77P[2]54
Nev
145P[2]926
Wash
118P[3]922
Mich
81NW925
134NW688
Nebr
212NW611
So C
67SE317
SD
97NW387
234NW624
4Æ3 680n

– 314 –
(111Cal616)
j45P995
54P[5]590
55P[5]1060
57P[5]572
57P[3]771
57P[3]781
75P[5]103
99P[5]201
114P[8]833
115P[8]316
143P[1]1080
147P[3]471
240P518
253P[5]741
286P[5]478
d15P2d540
145P2d[1]595
145P2d[2]596
152P2d[1]245
213P2d[3]115
j245P2d[5]305
287P2d[5]200
j524P2d[5]848
570P2d[8]1052
595P2d[8]95
74CaR[8]23
j115CaR[5]376
141CaR[8]700
f142CaR[3]709
144CaR[8]235
d147CaR[8]221
j147CaR[8]223
147CaR[5]680
153CaR[8]710
155CaR[8]661
157CaR[8]297
157CaR[8]353
175CaR[8]710
d180CaR715
j180CaR717

223CaR[8]739
f229CaR[8]282
Cir. 9
116F[8]486
Idaho
156P105
216P[8]734
Nev
212P2d716
NM
191P[4]454
Wyo
d92P2d[8]556
Ala
100So671
La
129So731
5So2d361
Mo
113SW1065
Nebr
94NW530
ND
149NW357
95Æ2 354n

– 318 –
(112Cal4)
s34P712
52P[2]827
72P351
73P182
73P829
74P701
92P[1]501
d96P[1]910
116P[1]307
124P[2]1001
151P[1]393
169P[2]1001
196P[1]906
217P[1]89
261P520
58P2d[1]190
79P2d198
e289P2d[1]578
298P2d[2]687
58CaR73
Idaho
85P[1]491
90P[1]341
165P2d[1]298
Mont
74P76
Utah
55P[2]382
f84P[2]892
88P[1]671
156ÆR1197n

– 319 –
(111Cal639)
s49P577
cc77P1113
54P532
d57P599
62P58
67P787
67P1056
d70P[1]665
j73P465
74P770
77P660
91P[1]590
100P[1]1083
104P474

151P153
157P15
167P198
171P[1]419
184P25
191P1023
195P[1]273
233P333
240P295
260P350
265P855
60P2d478
75P2d598
Cir. 9
d114F[1]993
260F[1]510
142FS[1]110
206FS[1]442
Idaho
211P536
Mont
124P[1]516
Nev
66P953
Utah
125P[1]869
202P[1]818
Iowa
96NW1082
Va
139SE311
Wis
72NW393
55ÆR1388n

– 320 –
(111Cal668)
p70P118
50P[8]29
53P[1]645
55P[8]327
58P[8]317
61P[8]943
62P[6]307
d63P[2]681
65P479
65P1089
f70P[2]626
83P[1]271
89P[2]851
91P[2]523
92P[1]86
94P[1]854
105P[1]739
108P[1]329
e131P[8]325
137P[6]1087
155P[1]840
159P[1]599
174P[6]308
f176P[3]441
d193P[1]132
d228P738
255P289
261P[6]764
280P[2]166
280P[2]396
13P2d[1]774
67P2d[2]688
77P2d[2]836
92P2d[2]436
107P2d[2]616
130P2d[2]396
f198P2d[2]699
210P2d[2]255
217P2d[1]117

249P2d[2]845
258P2d[2]58
265P2d[2]551
f266P2d[2]819
270P2d[2]945
292P2d[7]83
d319P2d[3]81
353P2d[2]300
373P2d[2]865
d379P2d[2]515
j379P2d[2]531
f441P2d[2]917
f610P2d[1]1334
j610P2d1338
e616P2d[8]817
e616P2d[2]820
5CaR[2]692
17CaR[1]272
17CaR[2]272
17CaR[2]572
23CaR[1]135
23CaR[2]777
d29CaR[2]35
j29CaR[2]51
35CaR[7]330
44CaR[2]407
56CaR117
f69CaR[2]77
88CaR[2]43
136CaR[2]277
f164CaR[1]843
j164CaR847
e167CaR[8]835
e167CaR[2]838
j206CaR6
208CaR[1]533
208CaR[8]533
212CaR856
Cir. 1
396FS1184
Cir. 5
159F[2]7
Cir. 6
237F[3]60
Cir. 8
240F2d[8]756
572FS1204
Cir. 9
100F[3]750
119F404
Cir. 10
244FS[8]315
Idaho
111P[3]1085
Mont
28P2d[2]866
Nev
173P1159
Okla
89P2d[2]778
518P2d[3]59
549P2d[2]396
Ore
51P2d[2]667
Ala
73So208
Ark
45SW352
Fla
42So712
Ga
47SE207
Ind
105NE398

Iowa
73NW1058
80NW678
94NW924
98NW282
126NW781
Md
73At692
98At241
408A2d732
Minn
115NW401
Nebr
203NW648
NY
126NE650
62NYS893
NC
42SE985
69SE635
Ohio
95NE886
193NE749
RI
66At208
So C
29SE909
103SE271
Tenn
194SW902
Tex
54SW945
W Va
95SE800
Wis
123NW626
11ÆR1135n
23ÆR365n
36ÆR1025n
36ÆR1031n
122ÆR1493n
18Æ2 223n
72Æ2 585n

– 325 –
(111Cal662)
d132P[3]775
159P[2]184
288P[2]794
Colo
88P847
Utah
56P2d[1]7
NY
94NE198

– 327 –
Case 1
(5CaU303)
(111Cal xvi)
44P1067

– 327 –
Case 2
(111Cal646)
s27P1094
s28P579
155P625
176P[2]183
f244P[1]331
268P[1]630
61CaR[1]589

– 328 –
(5CaU304)
(111Cal xvii)

cc41P1012
cc53P46

– 330 –
(112Cal42)
49P[1]184
50P[1]399
55P404
59P310
Cir. 9
96F741
96F[2]742

– 331 –
(112Cal91)
61P[1]375
81P129
84P[1]1009
86P[1]985
87P[1]417
88P509
99P[1]397
106P268
152P[1]914
191P[1]969
203P[1]111
238P[1]1104
253P[1]354
284P[1]1049
286P[1]499
f287P[1]152
f287P[1]515
10P2d[1]184
56P2d[1]251
110P2d[1]997
114P2d[1]44
j140P2d[1]391
154P2d[1]380
181P2d75
186P2d[1]680
241P2d[1]1056
302P2d[1]114
136CaR[1]740
Nev
140P2d[1]571

– 332 –
(112Cal14)
s71P171
h51P[1]1080
59P692
92P[1]322
112P300
112P474
e141P[1]927
165P[1]527
182P[1]58
253P782
f264P[1]245
136P2d[1]829
276P2d88
Cir. 9
1FS13
Ariz
318P2d680
Idaho
72P963
Okla
252P[1]849
Iowa
123NW192
59ÆR94n

– 333 –
(112Cal53)
49P[2]201

51P[2]717
61P[2]796
74P[1]852
113P[1]171
136P[1]59
208P329
293P[2]123
d23P2d[2]809
130P2d[2]236
47CaR[2]415
Cir. 9
75FS[1]14
Kan
57P[1]123
154P[2]1023
Utah
50P[1]630
Md
43At813
Mich
153NW721
NJ
59At153
NY
100NE725
NC
138SE432
ND
156NW207
Tex
65SW513
105SW341
11SW565
Wis
26NW150
114ÆR300n
114ÆR314n

– 336 –
(115Cal143)
r46P922
d60P[1]848
78P[1]955
26P2d680
d169P2d[2]448
5ÆR1541n
39Æ2 298n

– 339 –
(112Cal1)
s57P84
152P[1]313
192P[3]537
216P[1]404
282P[2]25
122P2d[1]62
311P2d[2]7
324P2d[1]931
d65CaR[2]779
116CaR592
Cir. 10
69F2d[1]903
Ariz
235P[1]147
Idaho
71P[1]129

– 340 –
Case 1
(112Cal38)
s44P227
cc41P465
300P[1]839
Idaho
f101P[1]598

590

Shepard's Citations for Cases: Citations for 44 P. 320

Laura can tell at once by the number of citations that the *Sloane* case received some judicial attention. Taking a closer look, she learns all of the following:

- A case reported in 610 P.2d cited the *Sloane* case on page 1334 and followed it (the "f" just in front of the citation) in regard to the legal issue summarized in headnote "1" of the *Sloane* case (the "1" just following the "2d" tells you this).
- In the same citing case, *Sloane* was cited in a dissent (the "j" in front of the cite tells you this).
- Another case reported in 616 P.2d cited the *Sloane* case on page 817 and explained (the "e" in front of the cite tells you this) the issue summarized in headnote 9 of the *Sloane* case (the "9" right after the "2d" tells you this).
- This same case also cited *Sloane* on page 820 and explained headnote 2 of the *Sloane* case.
- A case reported in 136 *California Reporter* (this is what the "CaR" means) cited *Sloane* for the issue summarized in headnote 2 of the *Sloane* case (the "2" directly following the "R" tells us this).
- The case reported in 610 P.2d is also reported in 164 CaR, and the case reported in 616 P.2d is also reported in 167 CaR (you can infer this because the clarifying information is identical for the two citations).
- The *Sloane* case is cited by a U.S. District Court case reported in 396 F. Supp. 1184.

The case reported in 616 P.2d and 167 Cal. Rptr. is *Molien v. Kaiser Hospital*, 167 Cal. Rptr. 831, 616 P.2d 813 (1980). This case changed the law on the subject of the negligent infliction of emotional distress. While *Shepard's* indicated that the *Molien* case merely explained *Sloane* (this is what the "e" means), a reading of the case would quickly tell you that the *Sloane* holding on the need for physical injury was actually overruled, and that Laura may now possibly recover damages solely for her non-physical emotional distress.

The excerpts shown below, taken from the *Molien* case as it was published in 167 *California Reporter*, illustrate first how the court deals with the *Sloane* case and then, by its holding, how it changed the law.

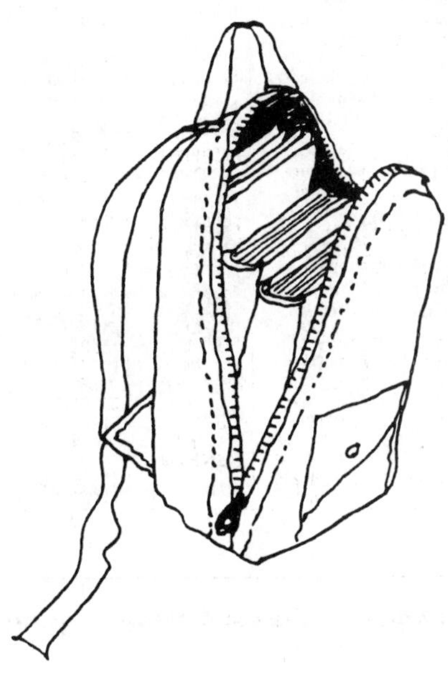

As early as 1896, this court recognized that mental suffering "constitutes an aggravation of damages when it naturally ensues from the act complained of." (*Sloane v. Southern Cal. Ry. Co.* (1896) 111 Cal. 668, 680, 44 P. 320, 322.) But such suffering alone, we said, would not afford a right of action. (*Ibid.*) We pondered the question whether a nervous disorder suffered by the plaintiff after she was wrongfully put off a train was a physical or a mental injury: "The interdependence of the mind and body is in many respects so close that it is impossible to distinguish their respective influence upon each other. It must be conceded that a nervous shock or paroxysm, or a disturbance of the nervous system, is distinct from mental anguish, and falls within the physiological, rather than the psychological, branch of the human organism. It is a matter of general knowledge that an attack of sudden fright, or an exposure to imminent peril, has produced in individuals a complete change in their nervous system, and rendered one who was physically strong and vigorous weak and timid. Such a result must be regarded as an injury to the body rather than to the mind, even though the mind be at the same time injuriously affected." (*Ibid.*)

The foundation was thus laid, nearly a century ago, for two beliefs that have since been frequently reiterated: first, recovery for emotional distress must be relegated to the status of parasitic damages; and second, mental disturbances can be distinctly classified as either psychological or physical injury. That medical science and particularly the field of mental health have made much progress in the 20th century is [925] manifest; yet, despite some noteworthy exceptions, the principles underlying the decision in *Sloane* still pervade the law of negligence.

The present state of the law is articulated in BAJI No. 12.80 (6th ed. 1977): "There can be no recovery of damages for emotional distress unaccompanied by physical injury where such emotional distress arises only from negligent conduct. [¶] However, if a plaintiff has suffered a shock to the nervous system or other physical harm which was proximately caused by negligent conduct of a defendant, then such plaintiff is entitled to recover damages from such a defendant for any resulting physical harm and emotional distress."

The BAJI language appears to be derived mainly from the opinions in *Vanoni v. Western Airlines* (1967) 247 Cal.App.2d 793, 795–797, 56 Cal.Rptr. 115, and *Espinosa v. Beverly Hospital* (1952) 114 Cal.App.2d 232, 234, 249 P.2d 843, both of which relied on *Sloane*. The principle has been reiterated elsewhere, but in each instance is traceable either directly or indirectly to *Sloane*. (See, e. g., *Fuentes v. Perez* (1977) 66 Cal.App.3d 163, 168, 136 Cal.Rptr. 275; *Leasman v. Beech Aircraft Corp.* (1975) 48 Cal.App.3d 376, 381, 121 Cal.Rptr. 768; *Gautier v. General Telephone Co.* (1965) 234 Cal.App.2d 302, 307, 44 Cal.Rptr. 404.) It therefore appears the rule has been immutable since its early origin, with virtually no regard for the factual contexts in which claims arose, or the alleged causes of emotional distress, or the prevailing state of medical knowledge.

Plaintiff urges that we recognize the concept of negligent infliction of emotional distress as an independent tort. In this inquiry we first seek to identify the rationale for the *Sloane* rule. None appears in the opinion, possibly because the court classified the plaintiff's condition, "nervous paroxysm," as a physical injury, and hence had no need to justify a denial of recovery for psychological injury alone. Neither did the *Espinosa* court provide any justification for its rejection of the plaintiff's attempt to "subvert the ancient rule that mental suffering alone will not support an action for damages based upon negligence." (114 Cal. App.2d at p. 234, 249 P.2d at p. 844.) Therefore, we must look elsewhere.

● ● ● ● ● ● ● ● ● ● ● ● ● ● ● ● ●

[6, 7] For all these reasons we hold that a cause of action may be stated for the negligent infliction of serious emotional distress. Applying these principles to the case before us, we conclude that the complaint states such a cause of action. The negligent examination of Mrs. Molien and the conduct flowing therefrom are objectively verifiable actions by the defendants that foreseeably elicited serious emotional responses in the plaintiff and hence serve as a measure of the validity of plaintiff's claim [931] for emotional distress. As yet another corroborating factor, we note the universally accepted gravity of a false imputation of syphilis: by statute it constitutes slander per se. (Civ.Code, § 46, subd. 2; *Schessler v. Keck* (1954) 125 Cal.App.2d 827, 271 P.2d 588.)

It follows that the trial court erred in sustaining the demurrer to the cause of action for emotional distress.

Excerpt from Molien v. Kaiser Hospital

Going further, Laura checks the bound supplement and finds that 246 CaR 538 cited *Sloane* for the issues summarized in headnotes 1 and 2. If she checks this case out, she will find it cites both *Sloane* and *Molien*, but does not change the case law established in *Molien*.

The gold Annual Cumulative Edition lists one case, but for our purposes it is not important.

There are no further references to the *Sloane* case in the red Cumulative Supplement. Laura has now completely Shepardized the *Sloane* case.

G. Check the Pocket Parts

Obviously it's important that your research cover the most recent developments in the law. As we've mentioned, this means checking the pocket parts to whatever resource you are dealing with. In our example, the *Cal. Jur. 3d* pocket part must be checked for recent cases dealing with emotional distress. Earlier we asked you to assume that the pocket part showed no change. However, the pocket part shown below actually shows a considerable change in the law.

As you can see, there are several references to law review articles on negligent infliction of emotional distress, and consulting any of these would yield an in-depth discussion of the *Molien* case. However, if Laura simply skimmed over the case annotations (mostly contained on subsequent pages not reproduced here), she would find no description of the important change that *Molien* made to the law. This means that the *Cal. Jur. 3d* editors failed to expressly account for the case that changed the rules set out in the hardcover discussion, a serious error. The lesson to be drawn from this is clear: Don't rely on the annotations or updates in encyclopedias to bring you up to date. Instead, consult the primary law sources (and update them with *Shepard's*) as we are doing in this example. Moreover, the Shepard's "e" notation preceding the *Molien* cite was quite misleading. Sometimes a court's attempt to say in a later case what the earlier decision "really meant" goes so far as to change the earlier holding in a fundamental way.

§ 74. [Emotional distress] In general

Practice aids:

California's new tort of negligent infliction of serious emotional distress. (1981) 18 Cal West LR 101.

California expands liability for negligently inflicted emotional distress. (1981) 33 Hast LJ 291.

Negligent infliction of emotional distress. (1982) 33 Hast LJ 583.

Negligent infliction of emotional distress: reconciling the bystander and direct victim causes of action. (1983) 18 USF LR 145.

Negligent infliction of mental distress (1981) 8 Western LR 139.

The Dillon dilemma: A closer look at the close relationship [bystander recovery for negligent infliction of emotional distress]. (1984) 11 Western LR 271.

Bystander recovery for negligently

inflicted mental distress. 35 Am Jur Proof of Facts 2d 1.

Recoverability of compensatory damages for mental anguish or emotional distress for tortiously causing another's birth. 74 ALR4th 798.

Case authorities:

In a personal injury action arising from an automobile accident that resulted in plaintiff's injury and his unmarried cohabitant's death, the trial court did not err in sustaining defendants' demurrer to plaintiff's second cause of action for negligent infliction of emotional distress without leave to amend, which cause of action was based on plaintiff's witnessing of his cohabitant's fatal injury. The state has a strong interest in the marriage relationship, and granting unmarried cohabitants the same rights as married persons would inhibit that interest. Allowing such a cause of action would impose on courts the burden of inquiring into relationships to determine whether the emotional attachments of family exist. Further, the number of persons to whom a negligent defendant owes a duty of care must be limited. (Disapproving, insofar as they hold to the contrary, *Ledger* v. *Tippitt* (1985) 164 Cal.App.3d 625 [210 Cal.Rptr. 814], and *Mobaldi* v. *Regents of University of California* (1976) 55 Cal.App.3d 573 [127 Cal.Rptr. 720].) *Elden v Sheldon (1988) 46 Cal 3d 267, 250 Cal Rptr 254, 758 P2d 582, mod (1988) 46 Cal 3d 1003a.*

In an action in which a person seeks to recover from a tortfeasor for emotional shock based on the infliction of injury to or death of another, recovery for such emotional shock may not be had if the shock is caused by hearing of the incident of injury or death from others after occurrence of the incident. However, the fact that a person did not have a visual perception of the incident does not necessarily preclude such recovery. Mental reconstruction of the incident may provide a basis for recovery if such reconstruction occurs

substantially contemporaneously with the incident. *Nazaroff v Superior Court of Santa Cruz County (1978, 1st Dist) 80 CA3d 553, 145 Cal Rptr 657.*

In an action in which the mother of an infant, who died from the effects of near drowning in defendants' swimming pool, sought recovery for physical injuries resulting from her emotional distress at witnessing the infant being pulled from the pool and in participating in attempts to revive the infant, the mother, though she had not witnessed the infant's falling into the pool, was not precluded as a matter of law from recovering for her alleged emotional distress. The mother was alerted to the pool area by a shout, which might have permitted her to reconstruct the scene, and her knowledge of what had occurred was derived from her own senses, rather than from another's recital of an uncontemporaneous event. Furthermore, drowning, or near drowning, though initiated by immersion, is not an instantaneous occurrence. *Nazaroff v Superior Court of Santa Cruz County (1978, 1st Dist) 80 CA3d 553, 145 Cal Rptr 657.*

In a situation in which a child is injured in a swimming pool, or other "attractive nuisance," and in which the child's parent seeks to recover for his or her emotional distress based on the child's injury, an apparent paradox exists in allowing such recovery, because if the parent was present at the time of the child's injury, he or she should have avoided the accident, and if the parent was not present, his or her lack of sensory and contemporaneous observance of the injury would defeat the right to recovery. However, in a rare case, the parent may sense the incident sufficiently contemporaneously with its occurrence, but too late to prevent injury to the child, and recovery for emotional distress would not be barred. *Nazaroff v Superior Court of Santa Cruz County (1978, 1st Dist) 80 CA3d 553, 145 Cal Rptr 657.*

In an action by a husband and wife against a doctor arising out of the

§ 74 Cal. Jur. 3d Pocket Part Entry

H. Use Shepard's and Digests to Find On-Point Cases

The next step is to find cases with fact situations as close as possible to yours. You can use *Shepard's Citations for Cases* and *West Digests* to find cases dealing with the legal issue you are concerned with.

1. Shepard's Citations for Cases

Although the *Molien* case answered a threshold question in Laura's favor (that is, she need not prove physical injury to recover), the facts of that case were not very similar to Laura's. In *Molien*, a hospital was found liable to a husband for falsely diagnosing his wife as having syphilis. In this case, however, Laura wants to recover for distress caused by the day care center's failure to properly maintain play equipment. In other words, Laura is trying to recover for distress caused by the failure to act rather than by an affirmative act. Rather than stopping her research at this point, therefore, Laura should continue to search for a case that presents facts a bit closer to her situation.

Let's first Shepardize the *Molien* case, using its *California Citations*. First check the volume for cases decided in 1985. As it turns out, there is no useful case. But, if Laura perseveres and turns to the Supplement dated 1985-1990, she'll find the entry shown below under 167 Cal. Rptr. 831 (the *Molien* case).

The case referred to by the citation of "208 CaR" which explains and follows the *Molien* case, turns out to involve emotional distress suffered by a mother as a result of the failure of her doctor to diagnose Down's Syndrome in an amniocentesis (a process allowing certain disabilities to be diagnosed in a fetus). In this case, the court indicates that for negligent infliction of emotional distress purposes, there is no difference between the affirmative act of misdiagnosis and the failure to diagnose. Although these facts are still not the same as Laura's, they are at least closer than those in *Molien*.

To be safe, Laura also checks the *Shepard's* gold and red paperback updates—but in this case, there is nothing useful.

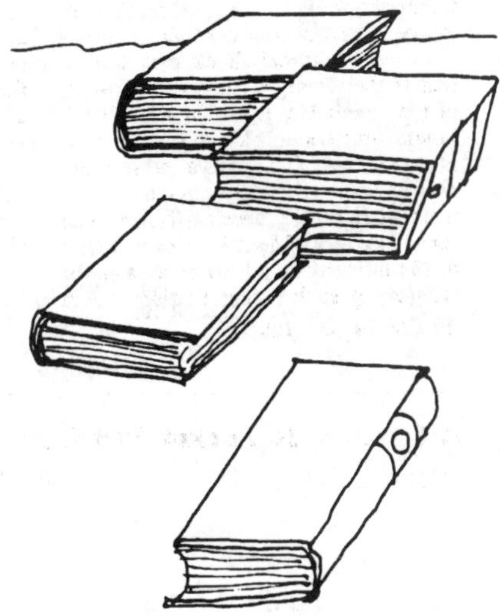

Vol. 167 CALIFORNIA REPORTER

234CaR[2]90
238CaR235
238CaR[1]238

– 292 –
210CaR[1]924
d217CaR[1]275
224CaR[2]54
227CaR[2]826
242CaR[1]722
261CaR[2]609

– 296 –
210CaR[1]839
219CaR[6]110
226CaR721
226CaR[1]722
242CaR729
247CaR640
258CaR58
e258CaR[7]286
d260CaR94
c641FS[1]737

– 303 –
d225CaR[1]574
j225CaR579

– 309 –
190CaR864
221CaR[6]49
238CaR[3]638
f263CaR868

– 320 –
209CaR[1]153
211CaR[2]926
229CaR[2]237
232CaR[1]538
234CaR[2]588

– 326 –
207CaR[2]436
220CaR[4]317
e221CaR[5]302

– 343 –
192CaR715
229CaR[5]81
241CaR866
242CaR[6]660

– 348 –
224CaR[1]794
224CaR[6]795
j224CaR798

– 351 –
238CaR[4]14
238CaR[1]6

– 353 –
215CaR453
230CaR190
245CaR[8]749
249CaR843
263CaR[1]578
f263CaR[2]579
639FS484

– 363 –
259CaR[1]568

– 366 –
207CaR[9]787
208CaR[4]378
219CaR[9]149
227CaR[9]353
250CaR410
f250CaR[1]925
f250CaR[4]926
255CaR[3]520

– 376 –
208CaR696
f208CaR[4]697

– 392 –
209CaR[16]127
d216CaR [17]242
221CaR[4]232
225CaR125
225CaR652
226CaR381
227CaR[1]495
230CaR[11]288
255CaR[27]255
257CaR[25]206
EL§18.01

– 402 –
d215CaR[7]75
215CaR[9]75
234CaR[9]825
236CaR[18]785
239CaR[2]219
244CaR[18]347
244CaR[18]351
f245CaR[15]296
246CaR402
251CaR[9]240
252CaR[15]797
258CaR631
470US[2]78
84LE263
105SC[2]1094
53USLW [4182

– 425 –
d215CaR[6]905
216CaR[5]30
240CaR910

– 429 –
238CaR[11]456

– 436 –
q233CaR[3]99

– 440 –
216CaR[10]43
216CaR[8]44
216CaR[3]45
227CaR[10]498
230CaR[3]632
236CaR[6]349
CLH§22.04

– 447 –
221CaR[1]473
228CaR[1]177

– 461 –
209CaR[1]658
210CaR647
210CaR[3]648

– 463 –
j180CaR411
214CaR[3]585
214CaR[4]585
217CaR[3]171
235CaR329
854F2d[5]1262

– 481 –
s463US1234

– 502 –
232CaR[1]539
259CaR[1]840

– 510 –
213CaR175
219CaR[1]208
243CaR[3]423
244CaR[1]81

– 516 –
214CaR772
222CaR[3]454

– 527 –
219CaR[1]233
222CaR[1]258

– 538 –
e214CaR[2]239
e214CaR[3]239
e214CaR [11]239
214CaR464
753F2d1467
60BRW[12]782

– 545 –
229CaR[2]273

– 549 –
207CaR[6]249
240CaR[1]754
240CaR[3]754
262CaR[5]336

– 552 –
224CaR[5]156
241CaR[3]500

– 557 –
211CaR[12]147
212CaR246
218CaR[16]437
241CaR[11]562

– 571 –
207CaR[3]249
244CaR784
244CaR[1]784
244CaR805
j244CaR809
258CaR80
258CaR86
f820F2d[1]1092

– 573 –
211CaR[20]648
215CaR462
216CaR143
216CaR[17]145
j216CaR155
217CaR[9]222
218CaR[4]834
219CaR[4]864
221CaR72
221CaR[1]176
224CaR853
226CaR[20]897
226CaR[11]898
235CaR[11]198
244CaR[3]888
d244CaR[4]889
d251CaR[3]648
255CaR[20]693
258CaR[20]406
12WSR409
12WSR675

– 584 –
212CaR561
230CaR[7]882
235CaR[1]372
d235CaR373
248CaR[9]120
253CaR[7]505
253CaR[9]505
254CaR84

– 595 –
224CaR733
259CaR[4]786
263CaR687
596FS[4]606

– 603 –
211CaR169
211CaR[2]170
211CaR[3]170
236CaR[2]200
237CaR251

– 610 –
220CaR[4]623
237CaR[4]859
253CaR[18]800
253CaR[19]800
253CaR[20]800

– 629 –
207CaR239
207CaR686

– 636 –
210CaR325
210CaR[18]549
212CaR210
224CaR[18]731
q224CaR [19]731
226CaR[28]183
c227CaR [37]285
f231CaR[27]845
f231CaR[29]845
q234CaR [18]562
234CaR[28]918
c236CaR [27]409
237CaR[29]115
247CaR[30]454
45BRW[34]913

– 666 –
f184CaR[3]627

– 671 –
209CaR[4]364

– 700 –
212CaR[9]333
212CaR[10]695
216CaR[8]536
226CaR741
230CaR760
233CaR[6]702
235CaR[7]622
235CaR[8]623
239CaR[3]420

– 707 –
e207CaR[2]787

– 714 –
216CaR[3]215
221CaR652
230CaR[2]646

– 735 –
211CaR[3]301
222CaR[5]481
222CaR[4]482
257CaR798
262CaR[4]910

– 741 –
217CaR[1]648
217CaR[2]649

– 747 –
209CaR774
209CaR[1]778
d250CaR[1]726
SRI§7.21

– 749 –
221CaR[1]361
221CaR[5]361

– 760 –
209CaR[1]807
238CaR[1]728
256CaR[1]510
c51BRW[1]837

– 762 –
207CaR276
819F2d[2]889

– 768 –
215CaR[2]222
215CaR[2]645
j215CaR879
218CaR498
219CaR[2]287
226CaR[1]397
232CaR[1]219

– 772 –
j207CaR500
j209CaR105
228CaR[3]658
228CaR[2]660
24SAC907

– 778 –
224CaR289

– 796 –
227CaR[1]97
227CaR[1]105

– 801 –
d243CaR[3]250

– 811 –
227CaR[1]808
26SAC87
26SAC100

– 813 –
208CaR[2]622
f208CaR[1]802
221CaR[2]385
226CaR[2]731
233CaR[2]594
236CaR222

– 816 –
225CaR[5]708
225CaR[1]709
234CaR[4]73

– 820 –
f210CaR231
210CaR[6]231
210CaR[2]233
210CaR[5]340
f210CaR[2]495
212CaR[2]561
j217CaR825
220CaR[2]589
229CaR[3]703
229CaR[2]706
231CaR[2]153
235CaR[6]322
235CaR[2]878
248CaR[2]259
253CaR[1]506
253CaR[6]506
253CaR[2]842
254CaR[2]84

– 831 –
d208CaR[2]27
208CaR892
e208CaR[4]896
f208CaR[2]903
f208CaR[7]903
j209CaR153
209CaR[5]197
210CaR419
210CaR[6]588
d210CaR[7]754
210CaR[1]817
211CaR[1]473
212CaR[8]855
212CaR[8]856
212CaR[8]857
216CaR[4]588
216CaR[2]669
216CaR[2]674
j216CaR680
218CaR728
e221CaR[2]378
e221CaR[4]378
e221CaR[8]378
222CaR[4]447
d222CaR[7]448
d222CaR[8]449
223CaR[3]226
225CaR[1]518
228CaR778
e228CaR[7]892
d229CaR[2]199
d229CaR[3]199
229CaR769
230CaR[1]903
d231CaR[2]100
d231CaR[3]100
231CaR185
d231CaR[2]186
231CaR441
e231CaR[7]441
f231CaR460
232CaR[3]531
234CaR[4]480
234CaR[7]609
235CaR[7]846
f236CaR94
236CaR[8]469
d236CaR[7]470
236CaR922
j237CaR879
239CaR[8]744
239CaR[4]746
239CaR[7]768
240CaR328
f242CaR[2]856
243CaR810
245CaR108
245CaR289
f246CaR[4]535
246CaR[2]539
246CaR[6]544
246CaR[5]545
j246CaR549
d250CaR[2]192
d250CaR[3]192
d250CaR[7]192
251CaR[4]70
251CaR[7]70
d252CaR[3]634
d252CaR[4]634
254CaR[8]484
254CaR632
d254CaR[7]843
j256CaR776
257CaR100
f257CaR[2]101
f257CaR[7]101
d257CaR108
257CaR[7]867
j257CaR895
258CaR793
259CaR[3]581
259CaR[4]581
261CaR773
262CaR[1]343
262CaR[1]845
262CaR[4]898
f797F2d[4]737
803F2d1499
804F2d[6]587
f847F2d[6]603
861F2d[7]443
f861F2d[4]444
j861F2d445
876F2d[6]731
885F2d[6]511
885F2d[7]511
638FS1176
665FS986
697FS[6]372
704FS[6]1004
8CoLR81
DTFV §1.28
MMPC§4.04

– 844 –
190CaR[14]485
208CaR[15]254
j209CaR345
209CaR[15]888
209CaR[16]889
210CaR[3]528
210CaR[14]688
212CaR[3]205
d212CaR [11]205
212CaR[4]798
212CaR[5]798
212CaR[6]798
212CaR[7]798
f214CaR[10]560
j214CaR614
214CaR[14]614
215CaR825
216CaR[16]266
223CaR[14]501
226CaR[15]398
228CaR[10]90
q228CaR[8]91
229CaR[3]443
q230CaR[8]480
q230CaR [10]480
233CaR[1]171
233CaR[16]99
j233CaR107
233CaR[4]730
233CaR[8]731
233CaR[10]731
237CaR32
237CaR[4]160
237CaR[6]160
237CaR226
240CaR[14]524
244CaR[11]134
245CaR[9]245
245CaR[10]245
248CaR[3]555
248CaR607
248CaR[14]607
248CaR[15]607
j248CaR619
248CaR[7]826
249CaR[16]605
d250CaR[3]673
d250CaR[4]673
d250CaR[5]673
d250CaR[6]673
d250CaR[7]673
252CaR532
254CaR[2]322
254CaR[3]322
254CaR[6]600
255CaR[11]642
c255CaR [10]874
261CaR[10]602
q261CaR603
q261CaR [16]604
262CaR[14]834
675FS[3]716

– 854 –
207CaR[7]497
209CaR[9]102
209CaR119
212CaR[10]867
212CaR[12]867
221CaR366
229CaR[21]148
229CaR[11]710
229CaR[3]795
229CaR[4]798
237CaR[20]173
243CaR671
246CaR[20]305
246CaR[11]309
246CaR[15]309
251CaR[21]290
252CaR58
f252CaR[19]59
Continued

226

Page from Shepard's Citations for Cases

2. West Digests

Laura's next task is to go on from these cases to find other decisions discussing the same or similar issues. Digests can help Laura determine whether she has a case.

The *Molien* case, as reported in the *California Reporter*, has headnotes that have been prepared in accordance with the West key number system. As discussed in Chapter 10, *Shepard's and Digests: Expand and Update Your Research*, Section B, the key number system takes precise legal issues and classifies them with a topic heading and a sub-category number. The headnote from *Molien* shown below covers the precise legal issue with which Laura started her post-*Molien* research.

> **6. Damages ⇐49.10**
> Cause of action may be stated for negligent infliction of serious emotional distress.

Headnote from Molien v. Kaiser Hospital

The West Key number system has labeled this issue "Damages" and has assigned a sub-category number of 49.10. If you look in any digest prepared by West Publishing Co. (which includes almost all digests) under Damages 49.10, you will find summaries of judicial holdings on the same issue. For example, the page shown below is taken from West's *California Digest*.

First, scan those headnotes and note which court made the decision and when. For example, "D.C. Cal." indicates that the case was decided by the Federal District Court in California, "Cal." refers to the California Supreme Court, and "Cal. App." means that a California Court of Appeal rendered the decision. As discussed in Chapter 9, the higher the court, the more important the decision with regard to the principles of precedent and persuasive authority. (Remember, however, that "D.C. Cal" refers to a federal case, which will not be binding on a state court unless the issue you are researching involves a federal question.) Equally important, though, is the date of the decision. The more current the decision, the more likely it is that the case is still "good law."

In addition to the *California Digest*, she might also wish to investigate the West *Regional Digests*, the *Decennials* and the *General Digest*, all of which contain, under the heading Damages 49.10, summaries of cases that have discussed the relationship between negligence and emotional distress.

Note Although cases from other states might not be of much help in your state, small states often look to the judicial decisions of neighboring states. For example, Vermont and Maine often give serious consideration to the decisions of Massachusetts and New York courts, and California Supreme Court cases have traditionally been given weight throughout the west. Also, if you have found the *Molien* case but live in Arkansas, you would want to find out whether a similar case has been decided in your state. You could do this by locating the regional digest containing Arkansas cases and looking under Damages 49.10.

I. Summary

Because we've covered a lot of ground it might be helpful to summarize what we've done. We have:

- Classified the problem
- Determined the possible words and phrases to look up in a legal index
- Selected a background resource (*Cal. Jur. 3d* in this case)
- Located the article or discussion that most closely covers our topic

18 Cal D 2d—17

DAMAGES ⇐49.10

Law Rev. 1981. Limiting liability for the negligent infliction of emotional distress: the "bystander recovery".—54 So.Cal.L.R. 847.

⇐49.10. Nature of action or wrongful act, in general.

U.S.Cal. 1987. Railway Labor Act did not require that narrow "emotional injury" exception be carved out of the Federal Employers' Liability Act, absent any basis for assuming that allowing FELA actions for emotional injury would wreak havoc with the general scheme of RLA arbitration and absent intolerable conflict between the two statutes. Federal Employers' Liability Act, § 1 et seq., 45 U.S.C.A. § 51 et seq.; Railway Labor Act, § 1 et seq., as amended, 45 U.S.C.A. § 151 et seq.—Atchison, Topeka and Santa Fe Ry. Co. v. Buell, 107 S.Ct. 1410, 480 U.S. 557, 94 L.Ed.2d 563, on remand 818 F.2d 868.

C.A.9 (Cal.) 1989. LMRA preempted employee's claims of negligent and intentional infliction of emotional distress; actions serving as basis of those claims required analysis of collective bargaining agreement. Labor Management Relations Act, 1947, § 301, 29 U.S.C.A. § 185.—Jackson v. Southern California Gas Co., 881 F.2d 638.

C.A.9 (Cal.) 1987. Discharged employee's allegations in complaint, in support of claim of intentional infliction of emotional distress, that she was held in a work area against her will by threat of physical force and asked to commit lewd sexual acts alleged a nonpreempted state claim.—Survival Systems of Whittaker Corp. v. U.S. Dist. Court for Southern Dist. of California, 825 F.2d 1416, certiorari denied 108 S.Ct. 774, 484 U.S. 1042, 98 L.Ed.2d 861.

C.A.9 (Cal.) 1986. Employee could not recover damages for emotional distress suffered upon his termination; distress employee suffered was neither substantial nor enduring, as it must be to recover damages for emotional distress under California law.—Gilchrist v. Jim Slemons Imports, Inc., 803 F.2d 1488.

C.A.9 (Cal.) 1986. Although plaintiffs may not recover emotional distress damages under Title VII claim, Title VII does not supplant independent state remedies; thus, where emotional distress arises in conjunction with Title VII claim, damages may be awarded for harm that is distinct from employment discrimination injury. Civil Rights Act of 1964, § 701 et seq., 42 U.S.C.A. § 2000e et seq.—Miller v. Fairchild Industries, Inc., 797 F.2d 727, appeal after remand 876 F.2d 718, opinion amended and superseded 885 F.2d 498, amended in part on denial of rehearing, appeal after remand 885 F.2d 498, certiorari denied 110 S.Ct. 1524, 108 L.Ed.2d 764.

C.A.9 (Cal.) 1985. Damages for emotional distress accompanying physical injuries are recoverable in traditional Federal Employers' Liability Act [45 U.S.C.A. §§ 51–60] actions. Federal Employers' Liability Act, §§ 1–10, as amended, 45 U.S.C.A. §§ 51–60.—Buell v. Atchison, Topeka and Santa Fe Ry. Co., 771 F.2d 1320, certiorari granted 106 S.Ct. 1946, 476 U.S. 1103, 90 L.Ed.2d 356, affirmed in part, vacated in part 107 S.Ct. 1410, 480 U.S. 557, 94 L.Ed.2d 563, on remand 818 F.2d 868.

C.A.Cal. 1983. Damages for mental or emotional distress accompanied by some physical manifestation are recoverable under the Employee Retirement Income Security Act section governing breach of fiduciary's duties. Employee Retirement Income Security Act of 1974, § 409(a), 29 U.S.C.A. § 1109(a).—Russell v. Massachusetts Mut. Life Ins. Co., 722 F.2d 482, certiorari granted 105 S.Ct. 81, 469 U.S. 816, 83 L.Ed.2d 29, reversed 105 S.Ct. 3085, 473 U.S. 134, 87 L.Ed.2d 96, on remand 778 F.2d 542, vacated 778 F.2d 542.

C.A.Cal. 1982. Claims that employer violated implied covenant of good faith and fair dealing, as applied to situation where former employee alleges no more than long service and existence of personnel policies or oral representations showing implied promise by employer not to act arbitrarily in dealing with its employees, sound in both contract and tort and may give rise to emotional distress damages and punitive damages.—Cancellier v. Federated Dept. Stores, 672 F.2d 1312, certiorari denied 103 S.Ct. 131, 459 U.S. 859, 74 L.Ed.2d 113.

N.D.Cal. 1989. Principal and superintendent who listened patiently to concerns of student's parents about lack of diploma because he had not timely handed in paperwork for independent study in physical education behaved in reasonable manner when they refused to force teacher to change her "no mark" grade or to allow student to participate in graduation ceremony, and they could not be held liable for negligent infliction of emotional distress.—Swany v. San Ramon Valley Unified School Dist., 720 F.Supp. 764.

School official did not behave unreasonably, and could not be held liable for negligent infliction of emotional distress on student who was not permitted to participate in graduation ceremonies, by failing to develop solution to problem of student's failure to timely turn in materials for independent study in physical education prior to the time the graduation ceremonies were held.—Id.

N.D.Cal. 1988. Under California law, federal district judge's former secretary's allegation that she was assigned excessive work with Federal Judges Association failed to state claim against judge and association for negligent infliction of emotional distress; severe emotional distress was not reasonably foreseeable as result of such conduct.—Garcia v. Williams, 704 F.Supp. 984.

N.D.Cal. 1986. Whether recovery for negligent infliction of emotional distress will be allowed in any particular case depends on whether plaintiff's emotional distress was foreseeable result of defendant's conduct.—Safeco Ins. Co. of America v. Simmons, 642 F.Supp. 305.

D.C.Cal. 1985. Swine flu inoculation did not proximately contribute to or cause plaintiff's extended psychological problem of anxiety reaction, in absence of evidence of allergic reaction within 30 minutes of inoculation and in view of plaintiff's psychological vulnerability to anxiety reactions and panic attacks.—Wolfe v. U.S., 604 F.Supp. 726.

D.C.Cal. 1983. Paragraphs of complaint seeking recovery for emotional distress suffered as direct and proximate result of negligent care and treatment given child by defendants, interpreted to mean that parents sought recovery for physical or mental injuries sustained in course of caring for child and responding to his needs, stated a claim upon which relief could be granted.—Cortez v. County of Los Angeles, 96 F.R.D. 427.

Cal. 1988. Threats of divine retribution made by members of church were protected religious speech and could not form basis of a claim of intentional infliction of emotional distress by former members of church. U.S.C.A. Const.Amend. 1; West's Ann.Cal. Const. Art. 1, § 4.—Molko v. Holy Spirit Ass'n for The Unification of World Christianity, 762 P.2d 46, 252 Cal.Rptr. 122, 46 C.3d 1092, rehearing denied and modified, certiorari denied 109 S.Ct. 2110, 104 L.Ed.2d 670.

Cal. 1986. Store's "merchant's privilege" did not preclude customer's recovery for negligent infliction of emotional distress where store reported to police erroneous and unsupported suspicion that customer was tendering counterfeit bill.—Pool v. City of Oakland, 728 P.2d 1163, 232 Cal. Rptr. 528, 42 C.3d 1051.

Cal.App. 1 Dist. 1990. Award of emotional distress damages to employee terminated by school district would be sustained, although decision had held that tort remedies were not available for

Excerpt from West's California Digest

- Read the cases cited by the article as authority for its statements
- Used *Shepard's Citations For Cases* to find out whether the cases cited by the article still represent the state of the law
- Read cases cited in *Shepard's* that seemed appropriate and found the *Molien* case
- Shepardized *Molien* to find a case closer to our facts, and
- Used the *West Digest* system to locate similar cases.

J. Constitutional Research

In 1994 we were asked a question that involved us in a constitutional research project. If you were asked the same question today, your conclusion might be different (depending on the current state of the law), but you could use the same approach that we did. This is what we were asked:

"One of the states has a law from the 1940's that prohibits the handling of poisonous snakes except by trained and licensed medical personnel. May this law be applied to a religious sect who has recently established a presence in the state and would like to use snakes as part of their ritualistic religious practices?"

The process we followed started with a background resource, *American Constitutional Law* by Laurence Tribe, which laid out the history of free exercise claims and analyzed current Supreme Court cases. Tribe led us to read *United States v. Lee*, 455 U.S. 252 (1982), the first case to diminish the requirement of earlier cases that the government show a *compelling* interest in order to justify an encroachment on the free exercise of religion. In *Lee*, the Court held that the government only has to show that its rule is *important* in order to be allowed to apply it to the claimant although it limits or prohibits the claimant's religious practice (such as snake handling). This isn't good news for the snake handlers, but there are a few lines of inquiry that could help us "make a case" for them.

By Shepardizing *Lee*, we found a later important free exercise case, *Employment Division v. Smith*, 110 S. Ct. 1595 (1990), where the claimants were fired and then denied unemployment insurance after they were arrested for using peyote in a religious ceremony in violation of Oregon's anti-drug laws. *Smith* says that a free exercise claim (one that asks that I be exempted from a law of general application, such as drug laws or school attendance laws, because forcing me to comply limits or prohibits my freedom to practice my religion) can only succeed if I can show that another constitutional right is also infringed, such as freedom of speech.

So, one avenue for us to explore was: what other right of the snake handlers is infringed by the prohibition. Freedom of speech is another First Amendment right, so we started looking for Supreme Court cases on the issue of freedom of speech to find factual circumstances and statements of law in the opinions that could help us characterize the snake handlers' activities as "speech." Cases could be found through background resources and the digests (*Supreme Court Digest* or *Federal Practice Digest*). We started with Tribe, and learned that speech doesn't have to be actual words in order to be constitutionally protected, but can also be an act that expresses an idea. In *Stromberg v. California*, 283 U.S. 359 (1931), state law prohibited the display of any red flag as a symbolic act of opposing organized government, and the Court found it to be an unconstitutional restriction of freedom of speech. This prominent case was a good place to start because once we found one good free speech case, we could find others by Shepardizing it or by using the West topic and key numbers assigned to its headnotes to get into the digests.

Another avenue of inquiry is that of questioning whether the statute is really one of "general application" or whether it was passed specifically in order to prohibit religious snake handling. And, even if it was directed specifically at the religious practice, is there any Constitutional prohibition against the government doing that? Initial research in background sources (Tribe and the *Nutshell on Constitutional Law*) yielded two cases that would be a good place to start: *Lemon v. Kurtzman*, 403 U.S. 602 (1971) and *United States v. O'Brien*, 391 U.S. 367 (1968).

Another case, *Church of the Lukimi Babalo Aye, Inc. v City of Hialeah*, 113 S. Ct. 2217 (1993), is relevant but not directly on point. In that case the law was struck-down because the statute had been passed specifically to prohibit the religious practice. In our situation, however, the law was passed decades before the snake handlers had moved to the state. Of course, the Church's lawyer would argue that the original motivation for the law was anti-religious, but that might be hard to prove so long after the fact.

For more ideas, information and insights, we searched for snake handling cases and law review articles. Tribe cited one snake handling case, *Swann v. Pack*, 527 S.W.2d 99 (1975). We Shepardized *Swann* and all the snake cases cited in *Swann*. In the end, it turned out that *Swann* was the latest snake handling case and had cited all the others: *Harden v. State*, 188 Tenn. 17, 216 S.W.2d 708 (1949), *Hill v. State*, 38 Ala. App. 404, 88 So. 880 (1956), *Kirk v. Commonwealth*, 186 Va. 836, 44 S.E.2d 409 (1947), *Lawson v. Commonwealth*, 291 Ky. 437, 164 S.W. 972 (1942), *State v. Massey*, 229 N.C. 734, 51 S.E.2d 179 (1949).

Law review articles can be very helpful in constitutional research because they cite all the primary and secondary sources they can find (saving you a lot of research) and they usually have a point of view that can help you get ideas on how to approach your case.

To find law review articles about snake cases, we searched the *Index to Legal Periodicals* for the few years following *Swann*. In the 197376 volume, under Freedom of Religion, our search through a long list of titles came up with "Religious Snake Handling Abated...," Vand. L. Rev. 29:495-513 (March 1976). Law reviews usually take awhile to respond to cases, so the 1976-1979 volume yielded more articles in: Wash. U. L. Q. 1976:353-67 (Spring 1976); Ky. L. J. 65:195-219 (1976-1977; and Kan. L. Rev. 25: 585-93 (Summer 1977).

These are just the beginning of several roads of inquiry that you could follow to build an argument that has logic and reason within the context of Supreme Court opinions.

CHAPTER 13

Computers and Legal Research

Legal resarch is rapidly becoming automated. Push a button and see a case, flip a switch and read a statute—well, not quite. But certain legal research tasks that might take hours or days in the law library can now be accomplished in minutes with the help of computers.

However, book lovers take heart—it doesn't appear that silicon chips will take the place of well-stocked law libraries, at least for many years to come. For reasons discussed later in the chapter, the computer-assisted legal research systems now available can profitably be used only by persons already skilled in legal analysis and research.

Currently only law schools and large law firms use such systems to any great degree. And even they use them to supplement, and not replace, written materials. The primary reason for this is that using a computer-assisted legal research system requires a way of thinking that is fundamentally different than the one most legal researchers have learned. Access to computerized materials is gained by searching for specific key words actually used in them. The idea of asking a question by anticipating the words in the answer is utterly foreign to most of us.

The other major factors affecting the use of computer-assisted legal research systems are their restricted availability and their cost.

Especially if you are not connected with a large law office or law school, you will have extreme difficulty in obtaining access to either of the two main systems—Westlaw and Lexis. Most public law libraries do not offer these services. Those that do require a sizable advance deposit or a credit card; you pay as you go. If you nonetheless wish to use one of these systems, either ask your law librarian where the nearest publicly accessible terminal is located, or write the companies at the addresses provided below.

If you do find an available service, be prepared for sticker shock. You can end up paying as much as $300 per hour. Although pricing may appear to vary significantly between Lexis and Westlaw, it usually averages out the same because each company measures its "minute" differently.

Much of the following discussion applies to both systems. We do not mean to give the impression that the systems are the same; while broadly similar, each has some unique features. We discuss them together because our primary purpose here is to impart an overall understanding of how computers are used in legal research. For a specialized discussion of how each works, it is best to consult the literature published by each company.

For more information about Westlaw, write to West Publishing Co., 50 W. Kellog Blvd, P.O. Box 3526, St. Paul MN 55165. For Lexis, write Lexis, Mead Data Central, 200 Park Ave., New York, NY 10017.

A. How Westlaw and Lexis Work

When it comes to legal research, a computer can't do anything you couldn't do given enough time. It can only do some things a lot faster.

The legal research computers are great at storing huge amounts of information and retrieving specific items very quickly. That's it—that's all they do. You can't type your legal problem into Lexis or Westlaw and expect an answer. But you can type in specific words that are central to your problem and have the computer find every reference to those words in its huge memory.

This memory contains, among other things, almost all reported cases from state and federal courts, all federal statutes, the statutes of most states, federal regulations, law review articles, commonly used treatises and practice manuals and (in the case of Westlaw) *Black's Law Dictionary*. All the information is stored in central computers; the Lexis and Westlaw terminals found in law libraries and offices are connected to these computers by phone lines. Users of private micro-computers and word processors (for example, IBM P.C., Macintosh, Wang) can also tie into the central computer if they have the proper communication equipment and software, and can pay for the privilege.

The computer's memory is organized into "databases," or electronic files. One database may contain all New York cases, another all federal statutes, and another all IRS regulations. You must therefore specify both where to search (what database) and what to search for (specific words) when you use Westlaw or Lexis. For example, if your legal problem involves the zoning of your New York business, a cement plant, you might ask Westlaw for every New York case that contains the words "zoning" and "cement plant." The computer will search all the information in its database of New York cases and in seconds pull out every case that uses those words. You'll get nothing more, nothing less. You won't get cases that involve zoning and slaughterhouses or smelting plants, even though they may be relevant to your problem. In addition, if you ask for every N.Y. case with the word "zoning," you will get thousands of cases not relevant.

B. How to Use Westlaw or Lexis Economically

Without a doubt, the single biggest impediment to using Lexis or Westlaw is their prohibitive expense. If you're not careful you can easily run up a bill of $100 or more and end up with no more than a few marginally relevant cases. This cost/benefit ratio associated with computerized legal research often has the additional negative effect of making you worry about the "ticking of the meter." Because legal research commonly involves a mixture of concentration on finding materials and reflection on where to go next, anything that disturbs your mental processes (such as incipient bankruptcy due to your inability to pay your Westlaw or Lexis bill) is highly undesirable.

You may be charged as much as $5 each minute, depending on which system you are using and when. (Rates are lower in the middle of the night.) The charges are based on the length of time you're connected with the system and the number of times the words that you're using to access material are used in the database (the more times words appear, the more work the machine has to do to find what you're looking for). In addition, it is necessary to pay subscription fees and sometimes extra fees for special terminals.

Fortunately, you can take steps to minimize the cost of your research and maximize your results. While you may not want to leisurely read a case on the screen at $2 a minute, you may save dozens of hours of work at a cost of just $15 or $20.

1. Learn How to Use the System in Advance

Both Lexis and Westlaw have modules that permit you to self-train at the terminal without charge. You should spend at least five hours going through these modules before even thinking about doing the real thing. The more proficient you are in switching from one database to another, using the commands associated with the particular system and knowing how to formulate your queries, the more efficient your search will be.

2. Plan Your Search

The typical legal research task is most efficiently carried out by making use of both written materials and those in a computer database. First, decide what information you want. In many instances the information may be readily available in written form. For instance, Westlaw contains the full text of a number of law reviews. That's fine if money is no object. However, it will usually make no sense for you to use a computer to read the article if the written volume can be easily obtained. It is often as quick to read the printed words as to call up the same material on the screen, and a whole lot cheaper.

On the other hand, suppose your task involves looking in every West *Decennial Digest* since 1946 for cases relevant to a particular problem. Since this task can take hours, you may be much better off taking the time to construct a search query that will find you the appropriate cases in a manner of minutes. Get the citations from the computer and the books from the library.

Once you decide which type of information you wish to search for with the help of the computer, figure out which database or databases to use. While both Westlaw and Lexis allow you to switch easily from one database to another, a search conducted in the wrong database will be money down the drain. Finally, have your search query written out and in front of you.

C. Choosing a Database

After you "sign on" to Lexis or Westlaw (the law librarian will show you how to do this), the first thing you must do is tell the computer which of its databases you want searched. The computer will give you a "menu" of choices that go from the general to the specific. For example, if you choose "Federal Materials" from the first set of options, you will then be asked to choose from a sub-menu listing "federal cases," "federal statutes," "federal regulations," etc. Or, if you already know your way around the system a little bit and know what database you want, you can issue a direct command (check the manual for the exact way to do this).

Of course, you can go from one database to another and ultimately search every one, but a multi-database search can get quite expensive. Accordingly, if you are doing research for a state law issue, you will usually start with a search of the database for your state. Then, if you want more material, you can branch out to other states that the courts of your state deem influential—for example, Nevada courts might look to California courts for guidance, or vice versa.

Westlaw does offer an option that permits the search of all databases. This can get quite costly since much of your search may be wasted or irrelevant.

D. Formulating Your Query

The key to getting information out of Westlaw or Lexis is knowing what questions to ask. And the key to getting information that you can afford is drafting these questions in advance of asking them—what we call "formulating your query." Here we provide a brief overview of how you do this. More detailed information is available from the database provider.

AN EFFICIENT METHOD FOR FORMULATING QUERIES

Westlaw refers to the best method for query formulation as the TRAC method. This involves:

Terms:	the identification of the key or significant search terms
Roots:	the identification of any potential plural, possessive, or derivative terms in your query that would make a root or universal character appropriate
Alternative terms:	the identification of alternative terms, synonyms and antonyms
Connectors:	the appropriate and logical use of connectors

These concepts are discussed below.

1. Choosing Your Key Words

A well thought-out query is one designed to net just the right amount of relevant cases. This requires the same type of word-finding skill as that discussed in Chapter 4, *Putting Your Questions Into Legal Categories*, where we talked about using legal indexes. Only here, instead of accessing information according to its type or kind, you must figure out what actual words are likely to be used in the particular document you need (for example, case, statute or law review article) and then call it up by these words.

For example, suppose you own a restaurant that specializes in pecan pie made from a recipe developed by your great-great-great-grandmother. One day your baker quits and takes up employment down the street, where she starts producing the same pecan pie that you've always considered your proprietary secret. You want to find out whether you have a right to prevent your competitor from selling pies made from your recipe. If you were using conventional legal research techniques you would find a legal encyclopedia or book specializing in "intellectual property" or "trade secrets" and look in the index under "employees," "injunctions," "recipes" and so on. With a little effort, you would soon find some relevant material.

If you were using Westlaw or Lexis to accomplish the same task, however, you could not use these concepts to find what you were looking for unless these very words were actually used in a case, statute or article. Simply put, you cannot tell the computer to find cases about trade secrets and recipes. Instead, you have to tell the computer to search for cases according to the words the case uses.

If you did tell the computer to search for cases using the terms "trade secret" and "recipes," you would get only cases that use both those exact terms. The computer would not give you an opinion that fails to use these terms but does mention "business know-how" and "culinary information." On the other hand, if your request requires the computer to search for cases containing any of these terms (and more if you can think of them), chances are excellent that you'll find any case on point in the database you're searching. Of course, if you give the computer too many words that individually will produce a reference, then you'll get more material than you can reasonably use. Again, the trick to using Westlaw or Lexis is to pull up just the right amount of relevant material.

2. Using Connectors

Both Westlaw and Lexis use a system of "connectors" that let you design an efficient query. With connectors you can specify that you only want to see cases that have certain key words in the same sentence or paragraph, or you can exclude documents that contain certain other words. How to use specific connectors is explained below.

a. Lexis Connectors

The following connectors are used by Lexis:

W/n This means "within a particular number of words." Thus, "strict w/1 liability" means "strict" within one word of "liability." Given this command, the computer will retrieve documents with either "strict liability" or "liability strict." If the command were W/10, the computer would retrieve all documents in which the two words appeared within 10 words of each other.

AND This means that the item being searched must contain the words on either side of AND. Accordingly, "noise AND nuisance" means the item being searched must contain both the word "noise" and the word "nuisance." Otherwise, Lexis won't produce it.

OR This means that the item being searched must contain either the word that comes before or the word that comes after. Accordingly, "noise OR nuisance" will produce items that contain either the term noise or the term nuisance.

Pre/n This means that the item being searched must contain both the word before the connector and the word after the connector and that the word before the connector must come first. Accordingly, "quiet pre/1 enjoyment" means that the item being searched must contain the term "quiet enjoyment."

AND NOT This means that the term following this connector cannot be in the case. This is used when you don't want to be bothered with a certain type of case. Thus, "child pre/1 custody AND NOT joint" means that you want to see cases on child custody but none that involve joint custody.

Reminder Don't worry about learning these commands and connectors. Our purpose here is to give you an overview of how this all works. When you sit down at a Lexis terminal, you should have the user's manual by your side. A knowledgeable law librarian and an online training module provided by Lexis should also help you get started.

Here are several examples of typical queries with Lexis connectors, just to give you a feel:

Example 1 You want a listing of every case that has used the terms "employment" and "discrimination." If the order in which these terms were used was not important to you, your query would look like this: employment AND discrimination. If you only wanted cases that used the phrase "employment discrimination," your request would read: employment pre/1 discrimination.

Example 2 You want to see every case that has discussed safety standards in low-income housing. Your query might read as follows: moderate or low w/5 income AND safety w/20 housing. This would tend to produce all cases that linked the words "moderate "or "low" with "income" and the word "safety" with "housing."

Example 3 You want to see all cases dealing with decertification of non-agricultural unions. You could use the following query: decertification w/10 union AND NOT agriculture.

b. Westlaw Connectors

The connectors used by Westlaw are slightly different from those used by Lexis, although they perform pretty much the same function.

& This means within the same document. Thus, "limited & partnership" would pick up any document in which both terms appear.

OR This means that either of the terms may appear in the document. Thus "limited OR partnership" would produce documents that have either of these terms.

/P This means the same paragraph. Thus, "limited /P partnership" means that the computer will search for every document (within the specified database) that contains the term "limited" in the same paragraph as "partnership."

/S This means the same sentence. Thus, "limited /S partnership" would require these terms to be in the same sentence.

+S This means the first term precedes the one that follows. Thus "limited +S partnership" would require that the word "limited" precede the word partnership.

/N This means within the number of words. Thus "limited/240 partnership" means that "limited" would have to appear within 240 words of "partnership" to be picked up in the search.

% This means to ignore documents containing terms listed after the sign. For example, "limited & partnership % California" would reject any document that had the term "California "in it.

3. Using Universal Characters and Root Extenders

Part of the art of writing a good query is knowing when and how to use the universal character (the asterisk) and the root extender (the exclamation point).

Let's take the asterisk first. This character serves a function similar to that of a wildcard in poker. When you insert it in a word in a query, it stands for any character occupying that position in the word. Suppose, for example, your search involves women's rights. You would want to include the term women in your search query, but would also want to capture cases that use the term woman. If you only listed "women," you might miss some important cases. By using the asterisk, you can have the computer search for all cases (for example) containing the term "wom*n." This would produce cases with both women and woman.

The exclamation point provides even more flexibility. It must be placed at the end of the word, which instructs the computer to select all documents that contain the string of characters (root) just prior to it. For example, the term "Manag!" would pick up manage, management, manager and managers.

4. Modifying Your Query

It is unusual for even experienced researchers to get their queries right the first time around. Instead, their initial selection of words either produces too many cases or too few. For example, if you asked to see all federal cases with the terms "environmental" and "impact," your search would produce many hundreds of cases, too many for you to reasonably review. You would need to modify your search so that it would provide fewer, but all relevant, cases. If your situation involves a nuclear power plant, you would modify your search to only include federal cases that use environmental and impact and nuclear and power plant.

On the other hand, if your initial query is too restrictive, you may have to drop a term or two to produce any relevant documents. As a general rule, the more words that must be in a case as requested (for example, every case with the words "drunk" and "intoxicated" and "under the influence"), the fewer cases will be found, since any case that doesn't have all the required terms would not be produced. Conversely, the fewer and more general the words in a query that must be in a case to retrieve it (for example, every case with the word "eviction") the more cases will be produced.

5. Doing Segment Searches

As you learned in Chapter 7, a reported case really consists of a number of different elements. The main one, of course, is the written opinion itself. But there are also the case name, the headnotes, a one-paragraph case synopsis, the date the case was decided, the name of the judge who wrote the opinion, the title of the court deciding the case and so on.

Westlaw and Lexis allow you to search documents by reference to these segments. Thus, if you want to retrieve all cases of a specific type decided by a particular judge, you can do so. Or, if you know you are looking for a Ninth Circuit U.S. Court of Appeals case decided between 1972 and 1975, you can specify these dates in your query and the computer will perform the search.

6. Choosing Which Portions of a Document To Review

When you turn up cases during your research, you must sift through them to see if they're useful. When you're looking in books, this sifting generally involves reading the headnotes, finding one or more that looks relevant and reading the portion of the opinion from which the headnote was taken.

When you use Westlaw or Lexis to do legal research, you can do this same type of sifting. Once the computer has responded to your query and located documents containing your search words, you can designate which part of the document you wish to look at. You may choose to see just the portion where your key words appear. Or, you may choose to see the entire page.

MONEY SAVING TIPS

Once you're using the system, there are some techniques that will help you get in and out as quickly as possible.

Change Databases   When you want to change databases, Westlaw gives you a "time out" from being charged while you decide which one to go to next. It is good to use this feature when you want to think about a point, review the progress of your search or reformulate a new query, but don't want to leave the terminal.

Use Field Browsing   Seldom should you read an entire case on the screen. Make liberal use of the option to just view the portion of the document where the key terms appear. If the document looks relevant, note its citation and look up the printed report later. By using this browsing or skimming technique, you can cover a lot of ground in only a few minutes.

Use Your Printer   You can print out any material you discover in your search that looks promising. You are not charged while the printing is being done. Thus, if you find a case that looks relevant, but don't have easy access to it in a library, you can print it for later reference. However, cases are generally much easier to read in the published reports. Accordingly, print only when time is a factor or your access to the published document is limited.

7. Updating a Selected Document and Finding Similar Documents

Among the greatest advantages of Westlaw and Lexis is that their databases are very up-to-date. While it may take several months for a relevant case to show up in *Shepard's*, these computerized services are likely to receive it within a week or two after it is decided, or even sooner. While such timeliness is seldom necessary, it is still comforting to know that your information is completely rather than almost up-to-date.

We saw in earlier chapters that *Shepard's Citations for Cases* and the case digests can be used both to update cases and to find other cases involving similar facts and issues. Because you can search the Westlaw or Lexis databases for any specific character or number, it is extremely easy to find out whether a particular case or statute you are concerned with has been referred to by another case. For example, if the citation to your case is 600 F.2d 679 (4th Cir. 1982), you can check all subsequent cases for that reference and then scan the portion where it occurs to see whether the citing case is relevant. Simply put, by just sitting at your terminal, you can not only find relevant cases (or other material) but can also check for its continued validity and search out other materials that are similar. (See Chapter 10, *Shepherd's and Digests: Expand and Update Your Research*, for how to do this manually.)

COMPUTERIZED LEGAL RESEARCH AT A GLANCE

- Computer-assisted legal research focuses by telling the computer to select only those materials that fit the criteria specified in the search request.
- A computer search request must anticipate which words are used in the document being searched, and their position relative to one another (for example, same sentence, or within 20 words of each other). Connectors and universal characters are used to do this.
- Generally, the fewer and more general the key words the query requires to be in the document being searched, the more material will be produced. The more key words required to be in the document, and the more specific they are, the fewer the materials that will be found.
- The ultimate objective in query formulation is to narrow the search enough, but not too much.

8. The Westlaw Key System

When you use Westlaw, you can search according to the West key system. This in essence puts the entire *American Digest* system at your fingertips. (The West Key system is explained in Chapter 10, *Shepard's and Digests: Expand and Update Your Research*.)

9. The Westlaw Menu System

Westlaw recently introduced an interface that uses a series of menus to get the user to the correct information. While this system of searching takes a little longer than the one described above, the online costs are less. By eliminating a lot of the learning curve that goes with the command approach, this development makes it easier for casual users to get into the system.

10. Natural Language Interface and CD-ROMs

In 1992, Westlaw offered yet another way to extract relevant material from the Westlaw database. Called a "natural language interface," this new approach allows the user to use plain English when asking for information. The computer interprets the words you use and produces a list of cases or other materials in order of their apparent relevance. There is no hard information about whether this approach is more or less efficient than the key word search method described above. But because of the inherent clumsiness of the key word syntax (which uses Boolean logic), the natural language interface will most likely become the preferred way of using Westlaw, once users get used to it.

Another Westlaw innovation involves the new computer storage medium known as CD-ROM. This technology—essentially the same as that used for audio recordings— allows up to 500 times more information to be stored on a CD-ROM disk than is possible on the average floppy disk. This means that entire treatises can be easily distributed on CD-ROM disk and accessed by a means of a player attached to your computer. The advantage here, of course, is that you don't have online charges, except if you wish to update the information on the CD-ROM, which is still handled online. Of course, Westlaw charges a lot for its CD-ROMs and for this reason they usually are only appropriate for firms that use the material a number of times and would otherwise have to buy the books (which cost even more).

NON-LEGAL DATABASES

These days you can gain access to all kinds of computerized databases—not just legal ones. Through Lexis you can get access to Nexis, which contains magazines, newspapers, government reports, proposed legislation and the like. Also available through Lexis is the National Automated Accounting Research System (NAARS), LEXPAT (the full text of all patents issued since 1975), EXCHANGE, an online, in-depth financial look into more than 3000 companies and 100 industries worldwide, and extensive materials on French, British and international trade law. Westlaw provides access to a large non-legal database known as Dialog, which covers areas such as science, business technology, chemistry, medicine and economics. Much of the information is in full text form.

E. Legal Research on the Net

By now everyone has heard of the Internet and such popular commercial online services as CompuServe, America Online and Prodigy. Readers associated in some way with the law industry will want to know whether these and other generally available online resources offer the types of materials needed to conduct old-fashioned legal research.

The short answer is a qualified "No," in the sense that the basic source materials needed for legal research—statutes, archived cases, updating tools and secondary sources prepared by experts—are still only available online through the large expensive proprietary databases, such as Westlaw and Lexis.

However, every day more and more of these basic source materials are finding their way onto far more accessible online sites, referred to collectively here and elsewhere as "the Net." It is probable that by early or mid-1996, the question posed above—that is, whether online resources offer the types of materials needed to conduct old-fashioned legal research—will be answered by a resounding "Yes."

One way to approach online legal research is to think again about what it is that you are doing when you walk into a law library with a legal question. A good definition of legal research is that it involves a search for materials that provide the best possible indication of how a judge would deal with the issue being researched. This definition reflects a fundamental truth about the U.S. legal system: judges are the final arbiters of what the law is in any given context. If you want to know what the law is, find out what a judge has said it is.

For many years, legal researchers have had two fundamental options when searching for materials that a judge would use to decide a case. They could either:

- use print materials in a law library, or
- conduct a computer assisted search by means of Lexis or Westlaw—the two major online legal databases. (See Sections A through D, above.)

While Lexis and Westlaw are rich in legal source materials, and in some situations are more efficient than a law library search, they are both very expensive to use—too expensive for most legal researchers. Fortunately, a third option is now emerging: online research for free or at a nominal cost.

The most important component of this third option is the Internet. The Internet is a world-wide network of computers that share common rules for access to and transfer of data. There are a number of different ways to use the internet to search for relevant material, such as Gopher (a series of nested menus), FTP (a way to connect directly to another computer and download files) and Telenet (a way to actually use programs on remote computers to accomplish a particular task). But by far the most important tool for conducting legal research on the internet is something called the World Wide Web (WWW). This tool offers a point-and-click graphic interface that provides links among documents, and makes it easy to skip from one relevant resource to another. It promises to dominate the Internet for years to come.

A wide variety of legal source materials is also becoming available through the large commercial online services such as CompuServe, America Online and Prodigy. These services not only have their own collections of legal resources, but also provide a gateway to the internet, including the WWW.

Finally, a standardized bulletin board service called PACER is being used by the federal courts to upload recent cases and other information important to those using the courts on a regular basis, such as dockets and local rules.

What follows is a brief description of how to think about these avenues within the traditional legal research framework—that is, how to use what's "out there" to answer specific legal questions. To do this, we will revisit some of our discussions throughout the book concerning the nature of law and the process by which it is made.

⚠ This section will not provide the basic instruction that some readers may need in order to understand and "get into" the services and information available on the Internet. There are several books that serve this purpose. For an exhaustive treatment of the subject, see *Law on the Net*, by James Evans (Nolo Press, 1995).

1. Primary Source Materials

What material does a judge use when deciding what the law is? For starters, the judge looks to see whether a federal, state or local legislative body or agency has spoken to the issue in the form of a *statute, regulation* or *ordinance*. This starting place honors the basic concept that courts are supposed to interpret the law instead of making it. In Section C of Chapter 3, we explained the importance of statutes and regulations, which has increased with the number of federal and state agencies. Chapter 6 provided detailed information on how to find these materials.

If a legislative body or government agency has addressed the issue, the judge's next step is to study all previous *court decisions* that have interpreted the legislative enactment in some way that is relevant to the issue being decided. The judge may or may not follow a previous decision (also known as an "opinion"), depending on which court issued it and how close the relevant facts involved in the earlier case are to the facts in the present case. In Chapter 7, we described the genesis of an opinion; and in Chapter 9, we explained how to find it.

If a legislative body has not addressed the issue—that is, if there is no statute, regulation or ordinance—the judge will conduct a search of reported court cases to see whether the present dispute has been addressed under a similar fact situation. If a previous case is instructive, the judge may or may not follow it, depending again on the court deciding the case and how similar the facts of the previous case are to the current case.

What happens if there is no legislative enactment or previous case that speaks directly to the current situation? In this event the judge will have to break new ground by a process of legal reasoning based on previous cases that are at least similar to the current one.

Statutes, regulations, ordinances and court cases are what we call *primary law sources*. To know "what the law is" in a particular instance means that you need to know what these primary law sources say. It is now possible to find at least some of these primary law sources on the Net, including:

- U.S. Supreme Court cases decided since May 1990
- cases decided by the Federal Circuit Courts of Appeal within the previous several months
- the complete collection of federal statutes (United States Code and recently enacted legislation)
- the complete collection of federal regulations (Code of Federal Regulations and Federal Register)
- the complete collection of California statutes (the California codes)
- specialized collections of primary law sources applicable to areas of federal law such as copyright, patent and trademark, and
- a large assortment of federal and state governmental documents, including treaties, constitutions and historical documents such as the Declaration of Independence.

For a thorough description of the sources available on the Net and how to get to them, see *Law on the Net*, by James Evans (Nolo Press, 1995).

This collection of primary law sources is sure to grow exponentially within the year following the publication of this book (June 1995). To find out which sources have come online after the date this book is published, visit Nolo Press's update service at one of the following Nolo online sites:

- Internet WWW
  (Type: http://gnn.com/gnn/bus/nolo/)
- America Online (Keyword: Nolo)
- eWorld (Go to: Nolo).

2. Secondary or Background Sources

Although relevant primary law sources are the ultimate sources of traditional legal research, it is often helpful to start a legal research task by first finding out what an expert has to say on the matter. Materials that contain comments by experts on particular areas of the law (rather than statutes and cases) are commonly called *secondary* or background sources. In addition to gaining a better understanding of your legal question by reading an expert's commentary on it, you can also use the secondary or background resources to find specific citations to the relevant primary law. Chapter 5 described the various common secondary sources.

The secondary source materials traditionally relied on by legal researchers—such as legal encyclopedias, journal articles and treatises—are not yet widely available online. (At the time of this writing, there are a few journals online, but most of them post only abstracts of their articles.) But there are an increasing number of "alternative" secondary sources on the Net that serve some of the same functions as the traditional secondary sources. Most notably, there are some sources that can help get you oriented and focused on the issue being researched.

Nolo Press is forging the way in putting secondary source material online for the benefit of non-lawyer consumers. This includes sets of "FAQ's" (frequently asked questions) on a wide variety of legal topics and archived articles on legal issues that have appeared in Nolo's quarterly newspaper *The Nolo News*. In the coming months, Nolo expects to make more and more material available online, and by 1996 most Nolo books will hopefully be available for searching online at a very low cost. (See the back of the book for a catalog of Nolo publications.)

In addition to the secondary sources contributed by Nolo Press, a wide variety of secondary sources intended for both lawyers and the general public are being made available on the Net by law schools and law firms. If you are on the World Wide Web ("WWW"), for example, a good way to find these sources is to visit any of the following Web sites, each of which provides links to legal information by specific subject:

- Yahoo (http://www.yahoo.com/Law/)
- Legal Information Institute (http://www.law.cornell.edu/lii.table.html)
- Virtual Law Library (http://www.law.indiana.edu/law/lawindex.html)

One of the most fruitful ways to find information about the law is to visit areas where lawyers answer questions posed to them by people looking for answers. By browsing within the area, you may find material that answers your question as well as the question it was intended to answer.

For example, in a WWW site called "Legal Dot Net"(http://www.legal.net/), you can browse among a series of extensive answers by lawyers to specific legal questions. Or, if you subscribe to the service in question, you can browse within the questions and answers contained in the Legal Information Center on America Online (keyword "legal"), the Nolo Press site on eWorld (keyword "Nolo") or the Legal Research Center on CompuServe (Go legal).

In addition to the legal forums on the WWW and the large service providers, dozens of newsgroups on the UseNet (available over the Internet) focus on specific legal topics, including patent, intellectual property generally, taxes and privacy. There are also a number of list servers (computerized mailing lists) offering material on different topics. (See *Law on the Net*, by James Evans (Nolo Press, 1995).) Reading the conversations on these newsgroups may well get you some valuable information relevant to your research task.

Another good way to get your research off the ground is to pose a question of your own in one of these legal forums, centers or newsgroups. Lots of attorneys cruise these areas, and many are eager to provide long answers or suggestions as to where an answer might be found. In other words, instead of searching for secondary materials that have already been written, you and someone with a helpful response can create secondary source material just for your issue.

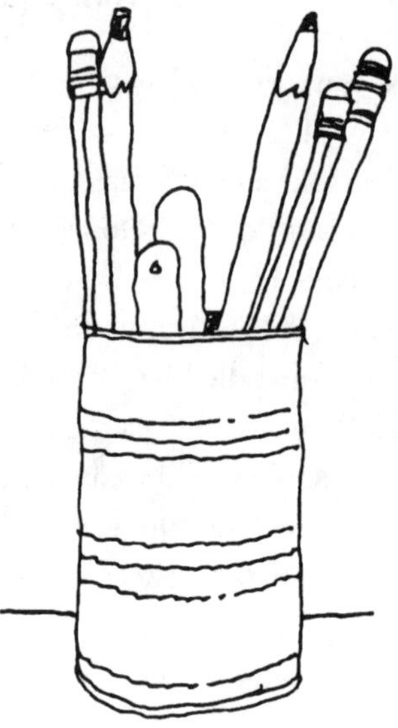

Consider the source It is important that you treat all secondary source material gathered from a person on the Net with circumspection. You have no way of knowing whether the person providing the information knows what he or she is talking about. Don't form any conclusions about the answer until you have found and interpreted the primary law sources.

REVIEW

Questions

1. *Why is the use of computerized legal research systems limited mostly to law schools and large law firms?*
2. *If you select the database for New York cases and ask Westlaw or Lexis to search for the word "bicycle", what will you get?*
3. *What are two ways to use Lexis or Westlaw economically?*
4. *In using Lexis, if you use the connector AND with the words "bicycle" and "accident," what will Lexis produce?*
5. *If using Westlaw, and you ask for "bicycle /S accident" what will Westlaw produce?*
6. *In either system, if you list "bicycl!" what would the system pick up?*
7. *How can you use either system to update your research?*

Answers

1. The primary reason for this is that using a computer-assisted legal research system requires a way of thinking that is fundamentally different than the one most legal researchers have learned. Access to computerized materials is gained by searching for specific key words actually used in them. The idea of asking a question by anticipating the words in the answer is utterly foreign to most of us. The other major factors affecting the use of computer-assisted legal research systems are their restricted availability and their cost.
2. All New York State cases in which the opinion includes the word "bicycle" anywhere in the opinion.
3. First, learn how to use the system in advance. Then, plan your search before you "sign on."
4. Items in which both words appear, in any order.
5. Items in which the two words appear in the same sentence.
6. Bicycle, bicyclist, bicycling.
7. By checking all subsequent cases for references to your case.

Appendix 1

Appendix 1 contains five research hypotheticals. Each hypothetical presents a set of facts and a research question that provides the basis for a research exercise. The exercise consists of a series of questions to be answered in the law library. Answers to the questions are also provided in case you get stuck.

At the beginning of each hypothetical is a list of the resources necessary to answer the question—they should be available in most law libraries. These hypotheticals are intended to sharpen several key research skills that will serve you well time and again. They are not intended as demonstrations of complete legal research tracks. For practice in starting and completing a full legal research task and writing legal memoranda, complete the exercises in Appendix 2.

1. Research Hypothetical

The research for this problem will require that you use the following sources:

- *Federal Reporter*, 2d series
- *Decennial* and *General* digests
- *Shepard's Federal Citations*.

Ms. Sunbeam owns and operates Field and Garden, a well known health food restaurant in Georgia that also sells food nationwide through the mail. A month ago, John Daiken opened a health food restaurant named Field, Garden and Farm, in a different part of the state, and started advertising in the same national vegetarian magazine Ms. Sunbeam uses.

Upon discovering Daiken's ads, Sunbeam sent Daiken a letter demanding that he remove the words "Field" and "Garden" from his restaurant's name to prevent customers from confusing one business with another. Daiken is refusing to comply unless Ms. Sunbeam can prove that customers are actually being confused. Ms. Sunbeam wants to know whether Daiken is right or whether she only need show a *likelihood* of customers being confused.

Questions

A. Using background resources, you have discovered a citation to a case that is relevant to the research question, *Amstar Corporation v. Domino's Pizza, Inc.*, 615 F.2d 252 (5th Cir. 1980). Find this case, choose the headnote that deals most closely with the research question and note its key topic and number.

B. Using the *American (Decennial) Digest* series only, use the topic and key number found in *Amstar* to find a citation for a 1985 5th Circuit case, the headnote for which says "Plaintiff in trademark infringement action was not required to prove confusion by actual customers."

C. The 5th Circuit case is helpful, but since the restaurants are in Georgia, you need a case decided by a Georgia court or by a federal court for the circuit that covers Georgia, the 11th Circuit. Again, use only the *American (Decennial) Digest* series to find the citation to a 1988 Northern District of Georgia case, the headnote for which says "Evidence of actual confusion is not prerequisite to finding likelihood of confusion..."

D. A lawyer friend recalls an earlier Georgia case dealing with your research question, from the 1970s, in which the plaintiff was Blue Bell, Inc. Using the *American (Decennial) Digest* series only, find the citation to that case. Is that case categorized under the same key topic and number that you have been using?

Note Now it is time to Shepardize your three cases to make sure that they are still "good law," that is, to ensure that they have not been overturned or otherwise rendered inoperative by subsequent interpretations. Shepardizing can also lead to additional relevant Georgia and 11th Circuit cases and other sources that may provide even more useful cases.

E. First Shepardize *Amstar*. Remember that *Amstar*'s headnote 11 is the one about your issue, so you will be looking for 11th Circuit cases that have cited *Amstar* for the legal issue summarized in headnote 11.

F. Does *Shepard's* show that *Amstar* has been overturned or criticized by a later case?

G. Was *Amstar* appealed to the U.S. Supreme Court?

H. Have any sources other than later court opinions referred to *Amstar*? If so, which ones? (They would be listed after all the case citations.)

I. Now Shepardize *Marathon* to find any 11th Circuit cases or Georgia cases or other sources that cited it. What does the following citation (226PQ836) mean? What does "Dk" mean?

J. What 11th Circuit or Georgia cases have cited *Marathon*?

K. In 812 F.2d 1353, *Marathon* was cited in regard to the legal issue summarized in headnote 4. Find *Marathon* and determine whether that issue is relevant to your case.

L. What 11th Circuit or Georgia cases have cited *Blue Bell*?

M. What 11th Circuit or Georgia cases have cited *Robarb*?

N. What can you now conclude from your research about Sunbeam's chances?

Note To do a complete research job, you would read the A.L.R. articles and all the cases you turned up, and then use *Shepard's Citations for Cases* and West digests to look for additional cases that address your research question.

Answers

A. Headnote 11 deals specifically with your issue (whether evidence of actual confusion is necessary to determining likelihood of confusion). It is classified under Trade Regulation key 335.

B. The *Ninth Decennial* Part 2 is dated 1981-1986. Looking under Trade Regulation key 335, you find a 5th Circuit [C.A.5(Tex.)1985.] case with the quoted statement, *Marathon Mfg. Co. v. Enerlite Products Corp.*, 767 F.2d 214.

C. Cases after 1986 are included in the *Tenth Decennial Digest* 1986 -1991. In the *Tenth Decennial*, you look under Trade Regulation key 335, and find *Robarb Inc. v. Pool Builders Supply of the Carolinas, Inc.*, 696 F. Supp. 621.

D. To find a case by its name in the *Decennial* digests, you look up *Blue Bell, Inc.* in the Table of Cases for the Digest covering the period of time you are interested in. The *Eighth Decennial* covers 1966-1976; in the Table of Cases A-G, under *Blue Bell, Inc.*, you see several entries, but remember you are looking for a Georgia case, and you find *Blue Bell Inc. v. Reusman*, DC Ga, 335 F. Supp. 236.

Among the many topics and key numbers listed after the citation is yours, Trade Reg 335. So, you could have found the case by going back through each *Decennial* covering the '70s under Trade Regulation 335.

E. By looking in *Shepard's Federal Citations, Federal Reporter*, bound volumes, bound supplements and paper supplements, under 615 Federal Reporter, 2d series, you find many cites to *Amstar* under Cir. 11. Those that cited *Amstar* in regard to the legal issue summarized in headnote 11 are: 711 F.2d 978; 757 F.2d 1185; 805 F.2d 987; 812 F.2d 1355; 812 F.2d 1543 and 852 FS 1552. You know these cases are citing *Amstar* regarding *Amstar*'s headnote 11 because of the small 11 up and to the right of the citing reporter (the F.2d or the FS).

F. There are no citations with o or c in the margin in front of the citation, so *Amstar* has not been overturned or criticized, according to the editors of *Shepard's*.

G. A request for appeal (Petition for Certiorari, commonly called "cert"), was denied. In *Shepard's* it says "U S cert den in 449 US 899." This means that the Supreme Court refused to hear an appeal, so that's the end of the road for the litigants (parties) of *Amstar v. Domino's*.

H. Yes. They are: 76 A.L.R.2d 619s (the s means that the citation is in the pocket part and 89 A.L.R.3d 449s).

I. That the opinion reported at 766 F.2d 214 has also been printed in PQ (*United States Patent Quarterly*) in volume 226, on page 836. To find out what PQ stands for, look in the front of the *Shepard's* volume you are using. We also find a cite that looks like this: "Dk 11 93-4947." This is a cite to a Slip Opinion from the 11th Circuit. The "Dk" means that the citation is to a case that was number 4947 on the 11th Circuit's 1993 docket [list of cases]. A Slip Opinion is the form in which a court decision first appears, before it has made its way into the hardbound reporter series or even the reporters' weekly soft-backed books (called the "advance sheets"). When the *Shepard's* volume that we consulted was printed, this case was brand new and could only be referred to in this manner. When you look at the list in your *Shepard's* book, chances are that enough time has passed for the decision to have become part of a reporter series with a regular reporter (FS or F.2d) cite. You will know whether your reporter cite is to "Dk 11 93-4947" by looking at the reported case itself and finding the docket number at the beginning of the case. (See Chapter 8, Section D, for a more thorough discussion of Slip Opinions.)

J. By looking in *Shepard's Federal Citations, Federal Reporter*, bound volumes, bound supplements and paper supplements, you find that *Marathon* has been cited in 812 F.2d 1353 and 731 FS 486.

K. The words of the *Marathon* court, summarized in headnote 4, say "Test in trademark cases for determining 'likelihood of confusion' involves evaluating a number of factors, including... actual confusion; none of these factors alone is dispositive.... So, the 812 F.2d 1353 citation is relevant to our issue.

L. In *Shepard's Federal Citations, Federal Supplement*, bound volumes and paperbound supplements, you find that *Blue Bell* has been cited by a Georgia District Court in 642 FS 1039.

M. None.

N. Ms. Sunbeam is most likely to win if she can demonstrate the likelihood of customer confusion. The cases consistently hold that a likelihood of confusion is the point to make, and that a showing of actual confusion is not necessary.

2. Research Hypothetical

The research for this problem will require that you use the following sources:

- C.F.R.(*Code of Federal Regulations*)
- an index to C.F.R.
- *Federal Register*
- *Shepard's Code of Federal Regulations Citations*
- *Federal Reporter*, 2d series.

You are self-employed; your office is in your home. During an earthquake a bookcase hung on the wall over your desk falls, breaking your arm and grazing your head. You are unable to work for a week because of your injuries and lose an estimated $500 worth of work. In a newspaper you read that federal regulations provide some disaster assistance in the form of unemployment compensation for people unable to work for a week because of damage from the earthquake. You want to know whether these regulations apply to self-employed people.

Questions

A. Where can you find the text of federal regulations?

B. What research tools can you use to find specific regulations?

C. What terms do you look under to find regulations applicable to your research question?

D. Are there any applicable entries and cites to regulations under these headings?

E. What does 20 C.F.R. 625 stand for?

F. At Title 20 Part 625, is there a section that will tell you whether you are eligible for disaster unemployment assistance?

G. Does § 625.4 say you are eligible? What does it say?

H. § 625.4(e) says the unemployment has to be caused by the disaster as provided in § 625.5; does § 625.5 say anything about your situation?

I. Remember: you are looking at § 625.5 to find out if your unemployment would be considered to be "caused by a major disaster" as required by § 625.4(d). Does § 625.5(b) say that your unemployment was "caused by a major disaster"?

J. Now that you have the applicable regulations, you have to make sure they haven't been changed since the revision date on the front of the volume you are using. Where do you look first?

K. Do you find any changes there?

L. Where do you look to find if there have been any changes in the regulation since the latest C.F.R-L.S.A.?

M. If you were searching from April 1, 1994 to December 31, 1994, what issues of *Federal Register* would you look in?

N. Do you find any changes to your regulation in the C.F.R. List of Sections Affected since the latest L.S.A.?

O. Do the proposed Rules affect the situation you are researching?

P. What tool do you use to find out if there has been any litigation over the regulations you've found?

Q. Have any cases cited 20 C.F.R. 625.4?

R. Have any cases cited other sections of 20 C.F.R. 625?

S. What does the *1985 after the volume and page mean?

T. Find the case. Is it relevant to your issue?

Note In a real research situation, you would look for secondary sources such as *American Law Reports* (A.L.R.) to find relevant cases and perspectives. We are going to end the questions and answers here, but we encourage you to go to a secondary source, continue your research in the digests and *Shepard's*, and write a short memo with your conclusions.

Answers

A. *Code of Federal Regulations* (C.F.R.).

B. Answer: Index to C.F.R., United States Code Service (U.S.C.S.), Index and Finding Aids to Code of Federal Regulations or Martindale-Hubbell's Code of Federal Regulations Index.

C. In Index to C.F.R. and U.S.C.S. Index: Unemployment Compensation or Disaster Assistance.

In Martindale-Hubbell Index: Look in Keyword Index (near the end of Volume 4) under Unemployment compensation or Disaster unemployment.

D. In Index to C.F.R. and U.S.C.S. Index:

- Unemployment compensation: Disaster unemployment assistance 20 C.F.R. 625.
- Disaster assistance: Disaster unemployment assistance 20 C.F.R. 625.

In Martindale-Hubbell Index: Unemployment compensation and Disaster unemployment both refer you to the index for Title 20 and several topical indexes including Employment. In the Employment topical index, you look under Disaster Unemployment Assistance to find:

- Eligibility requirements for: 20 C.F.R. 625.4.
- Unemployment caused by a major disaster: 20 C.F.R. 625.5.

E. *Code of Federal Regulations*, Title 20, Section or Part 625.

F. The little table of contents at the beginning of § 625 says "§ 625.4 Eligibility requirements for Disaster unemployment assistance."

G. Yes. § 625.4(c) says that an individual will be eligible if he/she is an unemployed worker or an unemployed self-employed individual.

H. Yes. § 625.5(b) applies to the unemployed self-employed individual.

I. Yes. § 625.5(b)(4)says that "The unemployment of a self-employed individual is caused by a major disaster if the individual cannot perform services as a self-employed individual because of an injury caused as a direct result of a major disaster."

J. In the L.S.A.'s (List of Sections Affected) starting with the one following the revision date on the cover of your volume.

K. No.

L. Federal Register from the date of the latest L.S.A. to the date of your search.

M. April 29, 1994; May 31, 1994; June 30, 1994; July 29, 1994; August 31, 1994; September 30, 1994; October 31, 1994; November 30, 1994; and December 30, 1994.

N. Yes, there is an entry in the *Federal Register* for 20 C.F.R. 625 : On December 30, 1994, there is a proposed rule change on page 63670.

O. No, they broaden the range of persons who can recover to include those who live outside the disaster area but either work in it or must travel through it to get to work. This does not affect the self-employed person who works at home within the disaster area.

P. *Shepard's Code of Federal Regulations Citations*.

Q. No.

R. Yes, a case has cited 20 C.F.R. 625.2(s) at 826 F.2d 1007. § 625.5 is cited at 633 So. 2d 1176 *1991. This is the opinion of a U.S. District Court in Florida. It is not about disaster relief, but rather about regular unemployment compensation. The judge cited §625.5 because the plaintiff in this case had also filed a disaster relief claim, which was already denied and fully litigated.

S. By consulting the list of abbreviations and symbols at the front of the *Shepard's* volume, you find that *1985 means that the case cited the specific 1985 edition of 20 C.F.R. 625.2(s).

T. No. The case, *Rosa v. Brock*, is not about self-employed people and disaster assistance.

3. Research Hypothetical

The research for this problem will require that you use the following sources:

- *Federal Reporter*, 2d series
- *Decennial* and *General* digests
- *Shepard's Federal Citations*.

You live in Louisiana. Last July you broke your wrist when you tripped on the frayed edge of a braided rug inside the entry way to your local Post Office. You had seen that rug on the Post Office floor for years, and had remarked on its worn and tattered condition. A woman who saw you fall ran over to you and said, "I told the postmaster about that rug two days ago."

You have started to research the issue of whether you can sue the U.S. Post Office for your injury. You have learned that this depends on whether the post office had a duty (responsibility) to prevent the accident, but failed to perform this duty. A background (secondary) source has led you to a 5th Circuit case that discusses this issue, *Salim v. United States of America*, 382 F.2d 240 (1967).

Questions

A. Find the *Salim* case and examine the headnotes. Select the headnote that deals most closely with your issue, and note the key topic and number assigned to that headnote.

B. Using the *American (Decennial) Digest* system only, find a later (after 1967) case from a federal court in Louisiana that 1) held the post office has a duty to use ordinary care to keep the aisles, passageways and floors in reasonably safe condition and (2) involved an accident with a rug.

C. When we did this research in 1994, we used the five-year sets of the *Digest* system up to and including Part 1 of the *Tenth Decennial*. For cases later than 1991, we consulted the *General Digest (Eighth Series)* for yearly information. If you are doing this research after Part 2 of the *Tenth Decennial* has been published (Part 2 will have cases from 1991 to 1996, and will be available in 1997), use Part 2, then use the *General Digests (Ninth Series)* to get the most recent cases. Use the *Digests*, both *Decennial* and *General*, to find a case from your Circuit (the Tenth) that is relevant to your research problem.

D. Read the description of *Kendrick*. How does it relate to our situation?

E. *Kendrick* is from a trial court in Texas, and you are in a trial court in Louisiana. What is the persuasive value for you of a case decided by a trial court in Texas?

Note re Questions F - I Now it is time to Shepardize your cases (*Salim* and *Larson*) to find other relevant Louisiana and 5th Circuit cases and secondary sources that may lead to still more cases. Shepardizing also ensures the continued validity of the cases you want to use as authority.

F. Shepardize *Salim*. What are the cites you find in *Shepard's* for Louisiana cases that have cited *Salim*?

G. Are there any A.L.R. annotations that cited *Salim*?

H. Shepardize *Larson*. Have any cases cited *Larson*?

I. Have any background (secondary) sources cited *Larson*?

Note Remember that U.S. District Court cases like *Larson* and *Gonzalez* are generally not as frequently cited as other cases, because U.S. District Court opinions have little authority as precedent.

However, they can have persuasive authority in both state courts where they are located and in other federal district courts within their circuit.

J. Should you Shepardize *Gonzalez*?

Note In a real research situation, you would eagerly read the A.L.R. annotations to find other relevant cases, practice pointers and perspectives. We are going to end the questions and answers here, but we encourage you to go to A.L.R., continue your research in the digests and *Shepard's*, and write a short memo with your conclusions.

Answers

A. The headnote that deals most closely with your issue is headnote 7. Headnote 3 is also closely related, but you don't have to choose because they are both classified as Post Office key 6.

B. *Salim* is a 1967 case, so start with the *Eighth Decennial*, which covers 1966-1976. Looking under Post Office key 6, you find nothing; in the *Ninth Decennial*, Part 1, 1976-1981, under Post Office key 6, you find *Larson v. U.S.*, 465 F. Supp. 29 (D.C.La. 1978).You know this is in a federal court because the reporter is F. Supp., which reports cases from federal district courts. In the *Ninth Decennial*, Part 2 (1981 - 1986), there are no Louisiana cases cited, nor are there any cases cited in the *Tenth Decennial*, Part 1 (1986 - 1991).

C. We searched through the *Tenth Decennial, Part 1*, and then turned to the *General Digests*. In the *General Digest*, each volume covers all the subjects from A to Z, but every tenth volume has a Table of Key Numbers that tells which of the preceding ten volumes has cases listed under each key number. Volume 10 sends us to Volumes 2 and 4, but our case isn't there; Volume 20 refers us to cases in volume 17, but the case isn't there, either. In Volume 30 (where the heading "Post Office" changes to "Postal Service"), we are referred to Volumes 21 and 26; and in Volume 40, we are sent to Volumes 41 and 42. Our case is in volume 42: *Kendrick v. U.S.*, 854 F. Supp 453 (E.D. Tex 1994). We know it is in the Tenth Circuit because Texas is part of that Circuit. (See the chart in Chapter 8, Section 3.) If you did this research in 1997, you found *Kendrick* in the *Tenth Decennial, Part 2* , but you will still want to check the *General Digest, Ninth Series*, for any newer relevant cases.

D. *Kendrick* notes that a plaintiff's appreciation of the danger is a question of comparative negligence under state law. It does not entirely relieve the government of all liability. I will argue that the government is still partially responsible for my injuries even though I had noticed the worn condition of the rug.

E. Both cases arose in the same Circuit, and although one district court is not bound by a decision of another district court, a trial judge might be persuaded to pay close attention to a decision of a sister court in his or her own Circuit.

F. In *Shepard's Federal Citations, Federal Reporter*, you find cites to *Salim* in volume 8, 1989 and in the hardbound supplement, Part 1. *Salim* was cited in a Louisiana case at 266 Southern Reporter, Second Series on page 509. No particular headnote is indicated, so you would have to read this case to see if it affects the authority of Salim or your research question.

G. A.L.R. 3d series, volume 35, page 248. The n after the page number indicates that *Salim* is cited in a footnote on that page;

A.L.R. Federal, volume 12, page 214n;

91 A.L.R. Fed 41n.

H. No.

I. 64 A.L.R. 2d 335s;

52 A.L.R. 3d 1289s;

48 A.L.R. 4th 241n;

91 A.L.R. Fed. 49n (this is the same annotation that cited *Salim*).

J. No. *Gonzalez* is from a federal district court in New York, so it will have no authority in Louisiana or the 5th Circuit, and you wouldn't even use the case unless it was the only one you could find on your issue, or you might use the headnotes to get a good key topic and number reference for further research in the West digests.

4. Research Hypothetical

The research for this hypothetical will require the following sources:

- *Federal Reporter, 2d series*
- *Decennial* and *General* digests
- *Shepard's Federal Citations.*

Dorothy, a Kansas resident, was divorced five years ago. In addition to other matters, the divorce decree ordered Bob (Dorothy's ex) to "pay the $1000/month mortgage payment, the taxes, insurance and utilities on the house until the mortgage is paid off" as part of the overall property settlement.

A year after the divorce, Bob filed for bankruptcy and listed the mortgage and other house-related payments as debts that he wanted discharged (cancelled). Dorothy's income is only $7,000 per year—including the alimony and child support. She won't be able to provide for her and the children's necessities if she has to make these payments.

Your research has told you that under bankruptcy law, child support and alimony can't be cancelled, but property settlements may be, in some circumstances. Your background (secondary) source cites a U.S. 10th Circuit case, *Yeates v. Yeates (In re Yeates)*, 807 F.2d 874 (10th Cir. 1986), which held that house payments by a Utah debtor should be treated like alimony rather than a property settlement obligation if the payments are necessary to maintain daily necessities. You now want to find a similar case arising in Kansas.

Questions

A. What library tools will help you use the *Yeates* case to find out whether a similar case has been decided by the bankruptcy courts that sit in Kansas?

B. Find *Yeates v Yeates*. What are the key topics and numbers for the headnotes that address your research problem?

C. Using the American Digest System, find a case decided by a court in Kansas that holds that a house payment may be considered "support" (and therefore is not dischargeable in bankruptcy) even though it was included in the "property settlement" section of a divorce decree. Start with the latest *Decennial Digest* (when we did this research in 1995, we used the *Tenth Decennial*, Part 1, 1986 - 1991)

D. The reorganization of the Key numbers has resulted in our having several Key numbers to work with. We could look at cases in every Key number we found, but there is a better way to narrow and speed our search for the right case. The entire Bankruptcy section begins with a table of subjects covered, arranged numerically by Key numbers. Find the new Key numbers and their corresponding subject descriptions. Which Key numbers match our research question?

E. Using Key number 3350(4), which appears to be the most relevant of all the Key numbers, look in the *Tenth Decennial*, Part 1, for a Kansas trial level case that will support Dorothy.

F. A bankruptcy court sitting in Kansas will be bound by the decisions of the federal appellate court that hears cases from Kansas (the 10th

Circuit). Do you find any 10th Circuit cases on point?

G. Using Bankruptcy Key number 3350(4), look in the *Decennial* and *General Digests* to find a 1992 Colorado state case and a 1992 Oklahoma Bankruptcy Court case dealing with the dischargeability of a house payment. (Remember, Dorothy is interested in trial and appellate cases within the 10th Circuit only because her Bankruptcy court is within that circuit. You can refer to the chart in Section A3 in Chapter 8 for a list of the states within the 10th Circuit.)

H. Our research through the *Digests* has yielded one trial level Kansas case *(Rush)*, an appellate level case *(Robinson)*, and two cases from other states within the 10th Circuit (*Wisdom* and *Lane)*. The holdings of the cases are consistent and appear to stand for the rule that an ex-husband's obligation to meet the house mortgage will not be discharged in bankruptcy if, in the context of the entire settlement of the marriage, it is viewed as part of his obligation to support. To be confident that this rule has been applied consistently (and to make sure that the editors of the *Digests* didn't miss a contrary case), it would be a good idea to Shepardize *Yeates* and *Rush*. Start with *Yeates*. Which are the relevant headnotes in *Yeates*?

I. Shepardize *Yeates*. Find the entry with an "e" preceding the citation.

J. Determine the cite and the name for the 10th Circuit case you have just found in *Shepard's*. Read the case. In what way does it amplify the rule announced in *Yeates?*

K. What important lesson have you learned regarding the need to use more than one research tool in the library (for example, the *Digests* plus *Shepard's)?*

Note We are ending the questions and answers here, but we encourage you to read the cases you have found, if necessary to go back to the digests to find as many cases as you can that are relevant and in your jurisdiction, and write a short memo of what you think a bankruptcy court in Kansas would decide in Dorothy's case.

Answers

A. The West Digest system and *Shepard's Citations for Cases*. First we will concentrate on the West Digest system.

B. All the relevant headnotes in *Yeates* are classified under Bankruptcy key 421.5.

C. In the *Tenth Decennial*, under Bankruptcy, the key headings begin with 1000! Surprise: the publisher of the Digests re-organized the Bankruptcy headings. Realizing that many people would be coming to the Digest armed with Key numbers based on the old system (like our Bankruptcy 421.5), the Digest editors provided a translation table at the start of the Bankruptcy section. Table 3 is entitled "KEY NUMBER TRANSLATION TABLE," and lists former Key numbers and their present Key number equivalent. Using this Table, we find that old Key number 421.5 is now covered in new Key numbers 3347 - 3350, 3360, and 3362.

D. Under "X. DISCHARGE" we find the subject descriptions for Key numbers 3347 - 3350, 3360 and 3362. Numbers 3347 ("Alimony, Support, or Maintenance"), 3350(1) ("obligations to 3rd persons") and 3350(4) (dealing with payments to protect a residence) all appear relevant to our inquiry.

E. Under Key number 3350(4), we find *In re Rush*, 100 BR 55 (D. Kan 1989).

F. Yes, *In re Robinson*, 921 F.2d 252 (10 Cir. 1990), discusses the non-dischargeability of an ex-husband's obligation to make house payments despite the ex-wife's re-financing of the mortgage.

G. We looked in the *General Digests* because Part 2 of the *Tenth Decennial* had not been issued. Each volume covers all the subjects from A to Z, but every tenth volume has a Table of Key Numbers that tells you which of the preceding ten volumes has cases listed under each Key topic and number. We looked at that Table under "Bankruptcy 3350(4)" in Volumes 10, 20, 30 and 40 of the *General Digests*, and found many references to cases in other volumes in the *General Digest* set. But since we were interested in cases from the 10th Circuit only, we noted only two: In Volume 15, we found a 1992 case from Colorado (*In re Marriage of Wisdom*, 833 P.2d 844); and in Volume 20, we found *In re Lane*, 147 BR 784 (N.D. Okla 1992).

H. Headnotes 2, 3, 4, 7 and 8.

I. The case listed in Shepard's is "e997 F.2d 721."

J. The case is *In re Sampson*, and its cite is 997 F.2d 721 (10 Cir. 1993). The case explains *Yeates* in light of another 10th Circuit case (*In re Goin*) that was decided a month after *Yeates* but never cited *Yeates*. While *Yeates* seemed to emphasize only the original intention of the parties, *Goin* suggested that both the original intent and the language of the written agreement itself should be consulted when deciding whether a payment is maintenance or a property settlement. The *Sampson* court held that *Goin* merely amplified *Yeates*, and that the entire circumstances of the divorcee should be considered.

K. When we did our research in the *Digests*, we discovered that the Key numbers had been expanded when West's decided to make their bankruptcy section more specific. New Key number 3350(4) (dealing with payments to maintain a residence) seemed to be the most relevant among the options. However, although *Yeates* was listed in that Key number section, neither *Goin* nor *Sampson* were included! We did not discover these cases until we "cross-checked" the completeness of our research by Shepardizing *Yeates*. Had we stopped our research with the *Digests*, we would have missed the important amplification of *Yeates* supplied by *Goin* and *Sampson*.

We went back to the *Digests* and, armed with the cites for *Goin* and *Sampson*, looked at the Table of Cases Cited in the volumes that would have included those cases. Both cases were included in the *Digests* under Key number 3348. A complete search through all of the new Key numbers that were substituted for the single old one would have revealed these cases; however, we found them just as well by Shepardizing our original case.

5. Research Hypothetical

The research for this exercise will require the following sources:

- *Atlantic Reporter*, 2d series
- *Shepard's Atlantic Reporter Citations*
- *American Law Reports* (A.L.R.)

In 1991 John and Susanne purchased a home in Trenton, New Jersey. About a month after they moved in, a heavy rainstorm produced serious flooding in the basement. They called in a local contractor, who informed them that he knew about the problem because it had happened before and he had been paid by the previous owner to analyze it. According to the contractor, the flooding was caused by an improper grade on the lot.

When contacted by John and Susanne, the realtor who had sold them the house said he thought he remembered learning about a flooding problem, but hadn't paid it much mind because it supposedly had occurred during an unusually heavy rainstorm. When John and Susanne questioned the seller, he simply said that he had forgotten to mention it.

John and Susanne discovered that it would take about $20,000 to repair the basement, fix the grade and re-landscape the property. Had they known of the defective grade, they would not have bought the house, at least at the price they paid. However, since they have now moved in, they want to remain living there, but they want the necessary repairs paid for by the broker or seller.

John and Susanne learn from a lawyer friend that they can probably recover their actual damages ($20,000) but that the lawsuit itself is likely to cost more than this amount. The lawyer suggests that they research the possibility of bringing the case against the seller and the broker under the New Jersey Consumer Protection Act, which allows the prevailing party to recover triple damages and attorney's fees.

Approach Statement The issues raised by John and Susanne's research problem are common ones:

- What are the responsibilities of the seller and the broker to the buyer when a major defect in a home is known of but not mentioned? Do the seller and broker have the same or different responsibilities?
- What damages (money) can be collected from the seller and broker if they are held responsible?

When faced with a general question about possible remedies for harm suffered, it is usually best to start with a secondary source to get a feel for the possible sub-issues in the case, and how these sub-issues have been dealt with by legislatures and courts.

After getting this necessary background, and narrowing your question as appropriate, the next step is to find an applicable statute, or a case that discusses the question. Whether you start with a case or statute will depend in part on what references (citations) you find in the secondary source and whether the question is more likely to be answered by the legislature or the courts.

Regardless of where you start, you will want to find a relevant case that gets as close to answering your question as possible. Then, you can use *Shepard's* and digests to update that case and find other similar cases that address the same issue.

We are going to use a nationally available background resource, *American Law Reports* (A.L.R.) because each annotation in A.L.R. has cases from many different states. A relevant New Jersey case is likely to be included.

Questions

1. What do you look under in the "A.L.R. INDEX" (the tan, red and black volumes) to see if A.L.R. has an article (annotation) discussing our main research topic: The broker's or seller's liability to John and Susanne for the defect they know about but did not disclose? Don't forget to check the pocket part at the end of the Index.
2. What is the title and citation for the annotation you find in the index?
3. Does the A.L.R. article discuss New Jersey law?
4. Does the Table of Contents to the A.L.R. article mention liability for a flooding defect and if so, what section is it in? Don't forget to look at the pocket part at the back of the book, where new cases, sections and related new articles are listed for each article in the main text.
5. What section of the A.L.R. article should you probably read first and why?
6. What does the article say about your research question (liability of brokers and sellers in New Jersey)?
7. What authority does the article give for its statement about New Jersey law?
8. Use the 358 A.2d 473 citation to locate the *Neveroski v. Blair* case.
9. Does *Neveroski v. Blair* support the statement in the A.L.R. article? Can the broker escape suit

under the New Jersey Consumer Protection Act for treble damages and attorney's fees for failure to disclose?

10. Does *Neveroski v. Blair* deal with the seller's liability under the New Jersey Consumer Protection Act?
11. Does *Neveroski* provide a "way out" of its holding for real estate transactions conducted after 1975?
12. What court decided *Neveroski*?
13. Now it's time to see whether *Neveroski* has been referred to by later cases. Shepardize *Neveroski* for the issues relevant to our discussion [the issues summarized in headnotes 4 and 6].
14. What court decided the *Arroyo* case and when?
15. Did the *Arroyo* case involve a broker or a seller?
16. How did the *Arroyo* case rule on the question of liability under the New Jersey Consumer Protection Act?
17. Now it's time to Shepardize the *Arroyo* case.

a. What citation do you find for a case that cites *Arroyo*?

b. What does the "f" mean? How do you find out?

c. What does the FS stand for?

18. Find the case that cites *Arroyo* at 761 FS 375. What does that case say about the continuing validity of the Arroyo case?
19. Now it's time to find out whether the *Neveroski* case is still good law as to a seller's liability for non-disclosure under the New Jersey Consumer Protection Act. In the answer to question 13, we saw that the *Arroyo* case was the only case that appeared to cite *Neveroski* in respect to a relevant issue (that is, an issue that *Neveroski* treated in headnotes 4 and 6). But sometimes the *Shepard's* editors make mistakes. Since we already have found one relevant case (*Neveroski*), it is better to continue to use this case as the basis for further research than to strike off in an entirely different direction. This involves skimming the other cases that have cited the *Neveroski* case, even though *Shepard's* doesn't show them as citing *Neveroski* for the relevant issues. As it turns out, one of the other cases listed by *Shepard's* is relevant to this research question. What's the name of that case and on what page did it cite *Neveroski*?
20. What did the *DiBernardo* case say about the *Neveroski* ruling regarding seller liability under the New Jersey Consumer Protection Act?
21. What headnote in *DiBernardo* deals with the holding about sellers under the New Jersey Consumer Protection Act? What is the key topic and number?
22. Using *Shepard's*, find a case that refers to the *DiBernardo* case for the issue summarized in Headnote 3.
23. What does the *Perth Amboy* case say about the *DiBernardo* case's ruling on homesellers under the New Jersey Consumer Protection Act?
24. What could Susanne and John reasonably conclude on the basis of the research they have done so far?

Answers

1. If you look under Brokers, and scan the headings, you come to one that seems promising, "Fraud or misrepresentation" with an annotation listed under it that can be found in 46 A.L.R. 4th starting on page 546. Checking the pocket part, we found two intriguing references: "Fraud or misrepresentation, right to recover for emotional distress, 11 A.L.R. 5th 88," and "financing agency's liability to purchaser of new home or structure for consequences of construction defenses, 20 A.L.R. 5th 499." (The second article may not be relevant since it appears to address the problems of a buyer of a brand new home, but it would be worth checking it out.)

2. 46 A.L.R. 4th 546 Real Estate Broker's Liability To Purchaser for Misrepresentation or Non-Disclosure of Physical Defects in Property Sold.
3. Yes. Directly following the Index (on page 550), the Table of Jurisdictions tells us that a New Jersey case is discussed in § 17(a).
4. Yes. The Table of Contents to the article (page 547) tells us that § 7 discusses flooding defects. The Table of Contents also tells us that § 17(a), where the New Jersey case is found, involves termites. The pocket part had added text for §7 (Flooding), but the cite is not to a New Jersey case. A quick perusal of the pocket part article shows that no New Jersey cases are cited in this update.
5. Probably you should go to § 17(a), the section that contains the New Jersey case. Finding one good case that has been decided by your state's courts is usually a higher priority than finding out what other state's courts have said. However, make sure and write a note to yourself that there are cases in other states that discuss a broker's liability in the context of a flooding defect; these may become important later.
6. § 17(a) says first that a broker may be sued and may be held liable for actual damages in New Jersey for failing to disclose known defects, but it then says that a broker may not be sued under the New Jersey Consumer Protection Act for treble (triple) damages and attorney's fees, since that Act doesn't apply to real estate sales.
7. It refers to *Neveroski v. Blair*, 141 N.J. Super. 365, 358 A.2d 473. The date of the case is 1976.
8. First locate the Atlantic Regional Reporter, 2d Series, then find volume 358 of this series, then turn to page 473. There you will find the first page of the *Neveroski* case.
9. Yes. First scan the headnotes to see what issues are covered in the case. Headnote 4 seems to summarize what was said in the A.L.R. article about brokers. Turn to where [4] appears in the text and read the material. There the court rules that the New Jersey Consumer Protection Act didn't apply to real estate sales by brokers during the period of time at issue in the case
10. Yes. Read the summary for headnote 6. It states that sellers also aren't covered under the New Jersey Consumer Protection Act. Turn to the part of the case where 6 appears. There the court rules that sellers aren't covered for the same reason as brokers aren't covered (real estate sales aren't covered by the Act). Also the court states on page 481: "In the absence of a clear expression of intent to include the normal sale of real estate by a homeowner within the compass of the statute, we find that the act, as articulated, does not cover such a sale."
11. Yes. In footnote 3, *Neveroski* states that the Act was amended effective January 19, 1976 to include real estate sales, but that the amendment doesn't affect the sale at issue in this case, since the sale occurred prior to the amendment.

    Note It is common for the law to change between the time events that lead to a lawsuit occur and the time courts are asked to resolve the dispute. Usually, the courts use the law that was in effect at the time of the events, not the law that is in effect at the time the decision is being made.
12. The New Jersey Supreme Court. This means that this case was the highest source of law when it was decided.
13. Go to *Shepard's Atlantic Reporter Citations*. Find the first volume that includes 358 A.2d (vol. 2, part 4, 1986). Under 358 A.2d and page 473, it has cites for "case 1" and "case 2." If you go back to *Neveroski*, you will see that on page 473, where *Neveroski* starts, there is also another case, very brief, which starts and ends on page 473, and *Neveroski*, ("case 2") starts after it.

Under "case 2" you find cites to three cases that cited *Neveroski* for the issues summarized in *Neveroski*'s headnotes 4 and 6. However, we'll save you the trouble of checking them all and tell you that none of them are relevant to this research exercise.

Look in the hardbound Supplements, 1986-1990, and 1990-1992, and the paper supplements. There you will find the citation for a case that cited *Neveroski* for the issue summarized in *Neveroski*'s headnote 4, in 502 A.2d 107. By looking at the case, you will find that it is *Arroyo v. Arnold Baker & Associates, Inc.*, and starts on page 106.

14. The Superior Court of New Jersey Law Division in 1985 (N.J. Super. 1985).
15. It involved a broker.
16. It ruled that brokers are now subject to the Consumer Protection Act because of the 1976 amendment.
17. Look in all the hardbound volumes and paper supplements of *Shepard's Atlantic Reporter Citations* that include 502 A.2d.
    a. f761FS375.
    b. In the lists of abbreviations in the front of every Shepard's you find that the f means that the citing case (761FS375) followed the decision made by the court in *Arroyo*.
    c. The lists of abbreviations also tell us that FS stands for *Federal Supplement*, the reporter that publishes decisions of federal district courts.
18. The case states that no New Jersey cases have superseded Arroyo, and this case was decided in 1991. This means that as of 1991, the date in question, real estate brokers can be held liable for non-disclosure of important information (possibly, for treble damages and attorney's fees) under the New Jersey Consumer Protection Act.
19. There are a number of cases that you must skim to answer this question. Only *DiBernardo* v. *Mosely* in 502 A.2d at p. 1168 deals with the issue of a homeowner's liability under the New Jersey Consumer Protection Act.
20. On page 1168 it said that because the legislature had not further amended the Consumer Protection Act after the *Neveroski* decision, the law still is, as *Neveroski* held, that "the Act was intended as a response only to the public harm resulting from 'the deception, misrepresentation and unconscionable practices engaged in by professional sellers...and not to the isolated sale of a single family residence by its owner.'"
21. Headnote 3, Consumer Protection 8.
22. There are several cases that refer to *DiBernardo*. The case you are looking for is *Perth Amboy Iron Works v. American Home*, 543 A.2d 1020 (N.J. Super. A.D. 1988)
23. The *Perth Amboy* case explains that the *DiBernardo* case ruled that the Act applies only to commercial practices and that an isolated sale by a homeowner is not a commercial practice.
24. The Consumer Protection Act applies to brokers but doesn't apply to isolated homeowner sales, since the Act only relates to Commercial Practices. Nevertheless, assuming the broker's non-disclosure can be proven, he can be sued for treble damages ($60,000) plus attorney's fees.

Appendix 2

In this Appendix we provide you with three self-teaching Research Problems. Each Research Problem is set in a particular state: Texas, California and West Virginia. The problems emphasize the use of resources that are available in most states, and most of you should be able to complete at least one of the problems, regardless of the state in which you're doing your research.

In each Research Problem, we present you with a legal hypothetical, then lead you through the entire research task with a series of questions that directs you to a variety of resources. Answers are provided for each question in case you get stuck. At the conclusion of the research you are asked to write a memorandum of law, as demonstrated in Chapter 11. A sample memorandum is attached to each Research Problem.

The method we have followed is good for beginning researchers, as it covers all the bases in a methodical way. As you become more experienced, you will develop both your own well organized, inclusive method and your favorite background resources.

At the beginning of each Research Problem we provide an "estimated time" for completion. This is applicable to anyone who has read this book, and completed the library exercises scattered through the text as well as the research exercises in Appendix 1. We recommend doing each problem at one sitting. If you start it one day but don't finish it, you're likely to lose your train of thought and have to go over everything again.

1. Research Problem: Government Tort Liability Hypothetical (Texas)

Estimated time: 4 hours

The research for this problem will require the following skills:

- brainstorming legal terms for using an index (Chapter 4)
- finding a case from its citation (Chapter 9)
- using the case reporters (Chapter 8)
- using *Shepard's Case Citations* (Chapter 10)
- reading a case, including use of headnotes (Chapter 7)
- using West's digests (Chapter 10)
- writing a memorandum of law (Chapter 11).

You will also have to know what common law is (Chapter 3) and if you don't know what a writ of error is, look it up in a legal dictionary.

The following sources will be needed:

- *Texas Annotated Statutes* (Vernon's)
- *South Western Reporter*
- *Shepard's Southwestern Citations*
- *Texas Digest* or *South Western Digest* or *American* (*Decennial* and *General*) digests.

Rachel Pie v. State of Texas

On August 5, 1989, at 2:30 in the afternoon, Robert Roberts, a medical examiner employed by the State of Texas, was driving from Yellow Rose Hospital to Red Ribbon Hospital, for his work. He was driving along Elm Street, the main road between the two towns. The road has one lane in each direction, divided by a solid yellow line, and a wide shoulder that is frequently used by bicyclists and occasionally by pedestrians. It is lined with gas stations and fast food restaurants.

Robert decided to turn in to a Hamburger Queen on his left. He put on his left directional signal and slowed to a stop, waited until there was a long clear stretch of the road with no oncoming cars, then accelerated to cross the oncoming lane and enter the Hamburger Queen lot.

At the same time, Sophie Pie and her daughter Rachel were riding their bicycles along Elm Street on their way from Red Ribbon, where they lived, to Yellow Rose, where they worked in a small factory on the 3-11 shift.

Robert hit Sophie broadside, hurling her and her bicycle through the air in front of Rachel's and many witnesses' horrified eyes. Rachel threw down her bicycle, and sobbing, "no, no, no," ran over to where Sophie lay, in the Hamburger Queen driveway, her body twisted and very bloody. Rachel knelt down at Sophie's side, stroking her mother's forehead and crying. When the police and paramedics arrived, Rachel rode in the ambulance with Sophie. Sophie was unconscious and moaning and Rachel was sobbing, repeating Sophie's name.

"I never saw her," said Robert. "It was as if she materialized out of thin air."

Sophie was in the hospital many weeks and underwent surgery for her head injuries. Despite her doctors' best efforts, she died after suffering considerably. Rachel has suffered from recurrent nightmares in which she relives the moment of impact and the sight of her mother's crumpled body on the pavement.

Everyone agrees that:

- Robert was legally responsible (liable) for Sophie's injuries.
- Had she survived the accident, Sophie's claim against Robert would have been worth approximately $250,000.
- Sophie's claim against Robert can be asserted by her estate as a "survivor's claim." (A survivor's claim is based on the pain and suffering of the deceased up to the point of death, and it is collected by the heirs. A "wrongful death" claim is compensation for being deprived of the companionship and services of the deceased; it is typically brought by the family.)
- As Robert's employer, the State of Texas is also liable to Sophie for her injuries, because Robert was on the job when he hit Sophie.
- Texas law limits the State's liability to $250,000 per accident per victim, and a total of $500,000 per accident.
- Rachel suffered emotional injury as a "bystander" under Texas tort (personal injury) law. (A "bystander" is a person who has witnessed the injury of a close relative and as a result suffers physically and emotionally.)
- Robert's negligence caused this injury to Rachel.
- Texas law allows Rachel to recover (get money damages) for this injury from Robert, and from Texas as Robert's employer.
- Robert has no assets or insurance out of which to pay Rachel's claim, and so Rachel's only chance of recovery is from the State of Texas.

The State of Texas, however, contends that its total liability for the accident is limited to $250,000—which it agrees to pay as a "survivor's claim" to Sophie's estate. This contention is based on these arguments by the State:

- The claims of a bystander-victim (Rachel) are derived from (arise out of) the primary victim's (Sophie's) claim.
- Derivative claims should not be treated as separate claims under the Texas Tort Claims

Act—the law that governs personal injury claims against the state.

- The State of Texas is therefore not liable to pay Rachel's claim.

Remember, Robert has no assets or insurance to pay Rachel's claim, so Rachel's only opportunity for getting money for her injury is to challenge the State's derivative claim argument. If Rachel sues, the case will be brought in the Travis County Court, which is within the Austin Appellate District. Can she win?

Approach Statement This case is basically a personal injury (tort) matter. The only issue that needs to be researched is whether a person who sues as a "bystander" is entitled to a separate recovery under the Texas Tort Claims Act. There are several ways to approach this question.

The most thorough approach is to first find a background resource that discusses the Texas Tort Claims Act. This will give you a feeling for how the Act has been applied in the past to bystander cases. Once you have an overview of this issue, the next step would be to find the Texas Tort Claims Act, read it, and then read one or more cases that interpret the statute in a factual context similar to yours. Finally, as in researching all types of legal issues, you are not finished until you have Shepardized the cases and statutes and checked the digests.

For the purpose of this exercise, assume that initial research in background resources has informed you that (1) the state is immune from suit (governments cannot be held liable by a court) unless the government waives that immunity and allows itself to be sued; (2) the way a government allows itself to be sued is to pass a law called a "government claims act"; and (3) that Texas has a specific law allowing personal injury claims to be filed against the government, called the Texas Tort Claims Act.

The background resources also say that the Texas Tort Claims Act describes in detail the situations in which all levels of government, from municipalities to the State, can be held liable in tort cases. And, the Act specifies maximum amounts that the different levels of government can be required to pay in damages. Nothing is said about bystander cases.

Questions

1. Now that you know what a tort claims act is, that Texas has one, and a little about it, it's time to look at the Tort Claims Act itself. What do you look under in the index to Texas Statutes, and what do you find?
2. How do you find out what CP&R means if you don't already know?
3. Which paragraph numbers are included within the statutory scheme known as the Texas Tort Claims Act?
4. Which section is most likely to be relevant to the issue being researched?
5. According to §§ 101.023(a) and (b), how much is the State liable for if one accident injures two people, as in Rachel's case?
6. Are there any amendments to § 101.023(a) in the pocket part?
7. Check the case summaries in the Notes of Decisions. In the Table of Contents at the beginning of the Notes of Decisions, which entry most likely refers to the issue being researched?
8. Do the cases in the Notes of Decisions say anything about the history of § 101.023?
9. Which of these cases is relevant to Rachel's case? Why?
10. Identify the volume number, West Reporter, and page number for the relevant case. Find the case.

The following questions are based on reading the *City of Austin v. Davis* case and thinking about it in relation to the case of Rachel Pie.

11. Who is the "Davis" in *City of Austin v. Davis*?
12. What is the name of the legal doctrine under which Mr. Davis made his claim?
13. Did the court find that Mr. Davis had bystander injuries?
14. So far, is *Davis* similar to Rachel's case?
15. Did the City of Austin claim that Mr. Davis's bystander injuries were derivative of his son's wrongful death action? What would be the result if the court found them to be derivative?
16. Is this the same claim that the State of Texas is making about Rachel's case?
17. What did the *Davis* court decide about the issue of "derivative injury"?
18. If the claim was not derivative, did the court say that Mr. Davis was therefore a "person injured" for purposes of the Tort Claims Act limitation of liability?
19. According to the *Davis* court, what is the importance of deciding that Mr. Davis was "suing for injuries he personally suffered" (693 S.W.2d at 34), and not for damages a person is entitled to just because she is related to a person who is injured or killed?
20. Is *Davis*, then, a good case for you to rely on as authority?
21. Why is the *Davis* case good authority?
22. Now that you have an authoritative case, *City of Austin v. Davis*, that says what you want it to, how can you make sure that there are no other cases with similar facts and contrary holdings, and that the case is up to date and has not been overturned or otherwise affected by subsequent cases? In other words, how do you determine that it is still "good law"?
23. When you Shepardize *Davis* in *Shepard's Southwestern Citations*, the first entry under the citation is "RNRE"; what does this mean?
24. What is the citation for the case that has cited *Davis* on its page 595?
25. Is the case that cited *Davis* on page 595 a bystander case?
26. Is it about limits of liability?
27. Why was *Davis* cited in this case?
28. Does this case affect Rachel's case in any way?

Note In your notes, write down the citation and your conclusions as to why it is not relevant; that way, if it comes up again, you won't have to look it up again.

29. Locate the case that is cited in *Shepard's* as "872 S.W.2d 766." Note that the case has two entries in *Shepard's*: one with a "c" preceding the cite, and the other with a "j." Locate the case and determine its cite. What do those prefixes mean?
30. What does your legal radar tell you about the need to read *Harris*? Consider the fact that the *Davis* case is cited and disapproved in the majority opinion, and cited in the dissenting opinion.
31. Read *Harris*. How does it affect Rachel's case?

Note The other citations of *Davis* listed in *Shepard's* are no more relevant to Rachel's case than the two discussed above. We will save you the time and trouble; of course, a complete research job would mean looking at every case that cited *Davis* to make sure of not missing any case that might affect your situation.

32. Where would you go next to make sure that there are no other cases that could affect Rachel's case or the authority of *Davis*?
33. How do you choose what topic and key number to look under when you use a West digest?

34. What is the appropriate digest to use to make sure that there are no other cases with similar facts and issues that have contrary holdings?

35. Can you find in the digests reference to any case that might affect the authority of *Davis* on the issue of limitation of liability?

Answers

1. Under "Tort Claims Act", the index says "Generally, CP&R 101.001 et seq."

2. Consult the list of code sections at the front of the index volume. The abbreviation clearly means Civil Practice and Remedies Code.

3. §§ 101.001-101.109.

4. § 101.023. There is a table of contents to chapter 101. Scanning it, we see 101.001 Definitions, 101.021 Governmental liability, and 101.023 Limitation on liability. Because our issue is not about liability (the State agrees it is liable), but only about the limits on liability, go first to § 101.023. You can go back to the definitions section if necessary.

5. Subsection (a) provides that the state government's liability is limited to $250,000 for "each person" and $500,000 for each single occurrence for bodily injury. This would seem to mean that if Rachel and Sophie are each considered a "person injured" then the state's limit for the two of them would be $500,000 , not $250,000, as the State claims. Subsection (b) applies to local governments and is therefore not relevant to our case.

6. No. § 101.023 in the pocket part says "See main volume for text of (a)." This means that no change has been made to (a). There have been some changes to (b), but it still doesn't affect us. There is an additional subsection (c), but this is about municipal government liability, so it doesn't matter to us.

7. The entry of "Per person limitation."

8. Each case description refers to Vernon's Ann. Civ. St. art. 6252-19 and says that that statute has been repealed and is now "this chapter" (the statute we are reading).

9. *City of Austin v. Davis*. The most important reason is that it is the only one of the three cases in the notes that is about limitation of liability in a bystander case (your issue). Secondly, it is from the same appellate jurisdiction in which Rachel would litigate her case (Travis County). Also, it is a recent case.

10. *City of Austin v. Davis*, is in Volume 693 of the South Western Reporter Second Series at page 31. The "ref. n.r.e." means "Application for writ of error refused, no reversible error."

11. The father of a boy who died as a result of the negligence of a City of Austin hospital, and who suffered emotional and physical injuries as a result of coming upon his son's body.

12. The Bystander doctrine.

13. Yes.

14. Yes; and the State of Texas agrees that Rachel has injuries as a bystander.

15. Yes, the City tried to argue that the father's suit was "derivative," which would mean that he would be bound by the recovery limitation imposed on the main, wrongful death, suit of the child's family. In other words, if the father's claim were viewed as "derivative," he and any other wrongful death beneficiaries would have to share in the amount recoverable by "each person."

16. Yes.

17. The *Davis* court decided that the father's injuries were personally suffered by him as a bystander and were not derivative of his son's claim against the City.

18. Yes. In the discussion, the court referred to a $100,000 per person limitation, because that was the limit at that time for municipal (city) governments. The principle is the same for our case; just the numbers are different.
19. The importance of the distinction, the *Davis* court explains, is that if the person's injuries are derivative, then the damages for the other person (Sophie, in our case) and the plaintiff (Rachel, in our case) are lumped together and the total damages are subject to the "each person" limitation. If the plaintiff is found to be a bystander, and is found to have personally suffered the injuries, then he or she has his or her own cause of action (legal claim) and is a separate "person injured" for purposes of the limitation.
20. Yes.
21. The facts and issues are similar to Rachel's case, and the holding favors your client. Also, the court is the appeals court, which has jurisdiction over the Travis County District Court in which Rachel would file her claim.
22. Shepardize and use West's digests.
23. By looking in the front of the *Shepard's* volume, you find that RNRE means "Application for Writ of Error refused, no reversible error." This means that *Davis* has been upheld upon review by the higher court.
24. 731 S.W.2d 590. (The case starts on page 590, *Davis* is cited on page 595.)
25. Yes.
26. No.
27. About bystander issues.
28. No. Our issue is limits of liability; this case is not about that.
29. The case begins on page 759 of Volume 872 of S.W.2d. It is called *Harris County Hospital District v. Estrada* (Tex App.-Houston [1st Dist.] 1993). The "c" means that *Davis* was criticized on page 766, and the "j" means that it was cited in the dissenting opinion on page 770.
30. *Harris* ought definitely to be read, because its interesting use of *Davis* suggests that there may be some new wrinkles on the "derivative" vs. "separate person" analysis of bystander claim status in Texas.
31. The court in *Davis* was concerned solely with whether a bystander's claim was independent or derivative. Once it decided that the claim was independent, it implicitly acknowledged that the father was a "person injured" because it allowed his claim. The claim of the wrongful death beneficiaries was allowed as well.

    In *Harris*, however, the court was not concerned with re-visiting the issue of whether the bystander claim is derivative. Instead, the court focused on the phrase" each person," and decided that the phrase referred only to the first person physically injured by the state (namely, the deceased). The court decided that the state's liability for "each person injured" referred only to that person, and that all claims would have to share in that single award. Whether a claim was derivative or independent was therefore beside the point.

    If *Harris* is applied to Rachel's case, she will not collect as an independent "person injured," despite the fact that her bystander claim is independent and non-derivative, because the only "person injured" will be Sophie. Only one $250,000 award will be available to satisfy both Rachel's and the survivor's claim. Rachel will hope that since *Harris* is from an appellate district (Houston) other than her own (Austin, the home of the *Davis* opinion), her trial court will not follow *Davis*.
32. The digests.

33. If you have an authoritative case like *Davis*, you look at the topic and key number of the headnotes of that case that are most relevant to your research issues. These are headnotes 7 and 8, for which the topics and key numbers are Action key 38(3) and Hospitals key 7. You would also want to pursue *Harris*, whose Headnote 17 (Counties, Key number 141) deals with the issue of several independent claimants having to share a single liability award.

34. Start with the latest edition of *Texas Digest* or *South Western Digest*.

    If you are not in Texas or one of the other states included in the South Western Reporter region, and your library does not have the *South Western Digest*, you will have to use the latest *Decennial Digest* and then all the volumes of the *General Digest* that update the *Decennial* and are cumulated every five years.

35. No. Under Hospitals key 7 "Liability of proprietors, officers and employees" the Texas cases revolve around a hospital's liability under the Texas Tort Claims Act. This was an issue in *Davis* with which we are not concerned.

    Under Action Key 38(3) and Counties Key 141, there are no relevant cases. Given the *Harris* departure from the older rule in *Davis*, however, it would not be surprising to find other appellate districts in Texas beginning to state their own views on the matter.

Legal Memorandum

Okay, you're done with your research. The very final step is to write up what you found in the form of a legal memorandum, using the guidelines set out in Chapter 11. Then compare your result with the sample memo we've prepared for this research (set out below).

Memo From: Terry Paralegal
To: Ruth Lawyer
Topic: Limitation of Liability Under the Texas Tort Claims Act for Rachel Pie

Facts:

In August 1990, Robert Roberts, a state employee, negligently struck with his car and gravely injured Sophie Pie, who was riding a bicycle. Rachel Pie, Sophie's daughter, was riding another bicycle right behind Sophie and witnessed the accident and Sophie's injuries. Sophie died from her injuries. Rachel has nightly nightmares in which she relives the accident.

All the parties, including the State, agree that Sophie's damages exceed $250,000 and that Rachel's damages are $65,000. Sophie's damages are being asserted as a survivor's claim by her estate. Roberts has no assets or insurance, and the parties agree that under the Tort Claims Act, the State of Texas is liable for damages caused by Roberts.

The State accepts liability as Robert's employer as provided by the Tort Claims Act and agrees that Rachel has damages as a bystander under Texas tort law. But it insists that Rachel's bystander damages are derivative of Sophie's, so both Sophie's and Rachel's damages are limited to a total of $250,000.

Issue:

If a person is injured in an accident, and another person who witnesses the accident is considered a "bystander" under Texas law, is she a "separate person" injured under the limits of liability provisions of the Tort Claims Act § 101.023, as interpreted by the courts within this [Austin] Appellate District?

Conclusion:

Yes. Because she is a "bystander," Rachel's injuries are considered to be personally suffered by her, not derivative from Sophie's injuries. However, a recent case from the Court of Appeals in Houston suggests that, in spite of the fact that Rachel has an independent claim, she may be limited in her recovery if the state's liability limitation is read to extend to the limit for each person physically injured by the state.

Reasoning:

At common law, the State is immune from liability. When Texas waives that immunity in certain situations and within certain limits, it is only liable insofar as it has specifically waived the immunity.

The Texas Tort Claims Act (Vernon's Ann. Texas Stat. CP&R §§ 101.001 et seq.), makes the state liable for property damage, personal injury and death negligently caused by an employee of the state while driving a motor vehicle in the scope of his employment if the employee would be held liable under Texas law. § 101.023 limits that liability to $250,000 for each person and $500,000 for each single occurrence for bodily injury or death.

According to Texas case law pursuant to the Texas Tort Claims Act, when a bystander suffers injuries as a result of witnessing the injuries suffered by a close relative, the bystander suffers those injuries personally and is therefore a separate "person injured" for purposes of limits of liability.

In City of Austin v. Davis, 693 S.W.2d 31 (Tex. App. Dist.-Austin 1985), the father of a boy whose death was due to the negligence of a city hospital was found to be a bystander. In Davis, the City claimed that the father's injuries were derivative from the son's claim for the purposes of limitation of liability under the Tort Claims Act. The Davis court held that the bystander injuries sustained by the father were suffered personally by him and were not derivative of the wrongful death of his son. Therefore, the court held, the father was a "person injured" for the purposes of the Tort Claims Act limitation of liability, and he was thus entitled to recover up to the per person limitation for his own injuries.

The issue in Davis is the same as Rachel's: If the bystander's injuries are considered to be derivative of those of the person whose injury they witnessed, then the per person liability limit applies to the total of both persons' injuries. Also the relevant facts of Davis are the same as in Rachel's case: Mr. Davis experienced the death of his son. Rachel witnessed the accident that gravely injured her sister. Both Mr. Davis and Rachel suffered physically and emotionally. The Davis opinion comes out of the Appellate Court for this District so its holding is authoritative. Just as Mr. Davis was found to have suffered his injuries personally, the Court would decide that Rachel is a separate person injured and is thus entitled to recover up to $250,000 for her injuries. Because the parties have agreed that Rachel's injuries amount to $65,000, she will be entitled to collect that full amount from the state, unaffected by the limitation on Sophie's damages.

A worrisome note, however, has been stuck by the Court of Appeals sitting in Houston. In Harris County Hospital District v. Estrada (Tex App.—Houston [1st Dist.] 1993), the majority expressly declined to follow Davis and limited the recovery of two independent, non-derivative types of claims to the single statutory amount specified in the Texas Tort Claim Act. In Harris , the court acknowledged that the bystander claim was non-derivative, but it did not end its inquiry there. Focusing on the "each person injured" language of the statute, the court narrowed that term to refer to the first person physically hurt by the state's negligence. By restricting the definition of the "person injured," the court forced all claimants (regardless of their derivative or non-derivative status) to share in that one recovery limit. If the state raises Harris, our best response will be to note that it is not controlling in our District and that its premise (to deny that the other independent claimants are not also "persons injured") is unwise.

2. Research Problem: Burglary Hypothetical (California)

Estimated Time: 4 hours

The research for this problem will require the following skills:

- finding and reading annotated statutes (Chapter 6)
- using a legal encyclopedia (Chapter 5)
- reading a case, including use of headnotes (Chapter 7)
- using the digests (Chapter 10)
- using *Shepard's Case Citations* (Chapter 10)
- writing a memorandum of law (Chapter 11).

You will also need to know what common law is (Chapter 3).

The following sources will be needed:

- California Annotated Code (West's or Deering's);
- *American Jurisprudence (Am. Jur.)*;
- *California Reporter* or *California Appellate Decisions, 3d*;
- *Shepard's California Citations*;
- *California Digest* or *Pacific Digest* or *American (Decennial* and *General) Digest.*

Charlene owns a house in San Francisco, CA. She lived there until her employer sent her to Los Angeles in January 1989, on a special two-year project at the LA office. The company provided Charlene with a small furnished apartment in LA.

Charlene rented out the house in San Francisco, but in June of 1990 the tenant moved out; Charlene decided to keep the house empty until her return scheduled for January 1991. Charlene hired Sally to maintain the premises, and every week Sally went to the house to clean, change the pattern of the random automatic lighting and otherwise make the house look lived-in.

In October 1990, Alix broke into the house at night to steal whatever she could find and was caught red-handed by the police.

Alix has been charged with first degree burglary, but insists that it should be only second degree because first degree burglary only applies to inhabited premises, and, Alix says, Charlene wasn't living there. You are a paralegal working for the prosecutor's office and have been assigned to research the matter.

Approach Statement Criminal law is almost completely a creature of statute. For a person to be convicted of a criminal act, she or he must have *intended* to do the illegal thing and to have had "notice" that it was illegal. (A person is considered to have notice if the law has been published, as in an annotated code.) So, when researching a criminal law issue, the first thing to do is to find and read the appropriate statutes in an annotated code. Secondly, consult background resources to fill out your understanding of the area of law you are researching. The third step is to find one or more cases that interpret the statute in a factual context as similar to yours as possible. Finally, as in researching all types of legal issues, you are not finished until you have Shepardized the cases and statutes and checked the digests.

Questions

1. What index should you use to locate the appropriate state statute governing your research issue?
2. What topics should you look under for our problem?
3. Where does the index send you?
4. Find Penal Code § 459 and read it. What does § 459 teach you?

5. The first element of the crime of burglary, as defined in § 459, is that the accused must *enter* the house or apartment. In our case, has this element been satisfied?

6. What is the next element of the crime of burglary, as defined in § 459?

7. Has the element of intention to commit a crime been satisfied in our case?

8. How would you find out if Alix's intended crime was of the type required by the statute—grand or petit larceny or a felony?

9. Does § 459 say anything about the issue of "inhabited"? Remember, Alix claims that the burglary is only second degree because Charlene wasn't living there.

10. Now read Penal Code § 460. What is the title of the section?

11. According to § 460, what is the relationship between the question of whether the house is inhabited and the degree of burglary?

Note So now we know, from § 460, that if Alix is to be found guilty of first degree burglary, Charlene's house must have been "inhabited." We also know, from § 459, that inhabited means "currently used for dwelling purposes, whether occupied or not." What we don't know is whether Charlene's house would be considered "currently being used for dwelling purposes" when no one is using the premises to sleep in.

This is the time to go to a background resource to find out how the courts in California have dealt with cases like ours, where the owner of the house is away for a short or long time, and the issue or question is whether the house was occupied when the person accused of burglary did the foul deed.

Unless you are familiar with criminal law and the law of burglary and the issue of "inhabited," we suggest that you wait to look at the Notes of Decisions following the statute until after you have gained some familiarity with the subject from a background resource.

12. Of the general national background resources, we recommend trying *American Jurisprudence*. 2d (*Am. Jur. 2d*), because it gives explanations of the law in language that is not too technical, and also because it will refer you to helpful annotations in the *American Law Reports* (A.L.R.)—because both resources are published by Bancroft-Whitney/Lawyer's Coop.

    a. What word do you look under in the General Index to *Am. Jur. 2d* to find out how a temporarily unoccupied dwelling house affects a burglary conviction?

    b. What helpful entries are there?

    c. In the volume that includes burglary, § 1 is a basic common law definition of burglary. Is this definition similar to the definition in the California statute?

    d. Which section deals with our issue, a temporarily unoccupied dwelling?

    e. What does § 4 say about the owner being temporarily absent?

    f. What does § 4 say about the importance of the length of time the owner is absent?

Now, this is helpful information for us, and gives us a good sense of what factors are important in our case. There is an *A.L.R.* annotation cited, but it is from the first series, which is quite old, and no California case is cited to support the statements made in the text.

    g. What is the next step before leaving *Am. Jur. 2d*?

    h. Where do you look in the pocket part and what do you find there?

    i. From the description in the *Am. Jur.* notes, what does the case seem to hold?

    j. Could this case be important to Charlene's case against Alix?

You will want to write down the citation to *People v. Marquez*, and to the *A.L.R.* article, so that you will be able to find them later without going back to *Am. Jur. 2d.*

The same *A.L.R.* annotation could have been found by looking in the *A.L.R.* index under burglary. It is a helpful annotation because it is an entire article all about the issue of whether a dwelling is "inhabited" in a burglary case if the owner is temporarily absent. If you went to *A.L.R.* first, you would find a discussion of *People v. Marquez* in the pocket part.

Now we need to go back to the annotated code to see how courts in California have dealt with a situation, like ours, where the owner or tenant had been away for a while at the time of the burglary.

13. Go to the annotated code and look at the notes of decisions following § 460 to find any cases with facts and issues similar to ours. There are many cases listed. How do you find the ones about your issue?
14. Looking through the Notes of Decisions, (remember to also look in the pocket part) you find several cases in which the owner or renter was absent for a night or other short period. Do you find any cases that indicate in the notes that the owner was gone for a long time, as in Charlene's situation?
15. Find *People v. Marquez*. Read it, using the headnotes to help you. From reading the case, answer the following questions:
    a. In the case of Charlene and Alix, Charlene had been absent from the house for almost two years. In *Marquez*, had the owner been absent for a similarly lengthy period of time?
    b. Charlene was actually living in another place; was that true in *Marquez* as well?
    c. Was it important to the court in *Marquez* that the owner had not indicated any intent to not return and that the home was being maintained for her by others?
16. If the court in *Marquez* were deciding the case of Alix and Charlene, do you think it would conclude that Charlene's house was "currently used for dwelling purposes" and therefore "inhabited" at the time Alix broke in?

Note The answer to Question 16 means that *Marquez* can be used as authority for the position that Alix is guilty of first degree burglary, as was the defendant in *Marquez*.

17. Now you have an authoritative case that says what you want it to say. How can you make sure that there are not other cases with similar facts and contrary holdings, and that the case is up to date and has not been overturned or otherwise affected by subsequent cases?
18. Shepardize *Marquez* under both the *California Reporter* citation and the *California Appellate Decisions, 3d* citation.
    a. How can you determine whether there are cases that cite *Marquez* about the issue of "inhabited"?
    b. Are there cases that might have cited *Marquez* about the issue of "inhabited"?
19. What is the name of the case that cited *Marquez* at 198 California Reporter 607?
20. Why did the *O'Bryan* court cite *Marquez*? Is this a case about the issue of "inhabited"?
21. What is the name of the case that cites *Marquez* at 259 California Reporter, pages 130 and 131?
22. Is it about the issue of "inhabited"?
23. Is it about whether a house is "inhabited" if the owner is absent?

24. Now go to the digests to find other relevant cases and to make sure that other cases do not affect your determination of the law in our case.
    a. How do you go from the case to the digests?
    b. What is the appropriate digest to use to make sure that there are no other cases with similar facts and issues that have contrary holdings?
    c. Find the case in which, because the renters had moved out and did not intend to return, the burglary of their apartment (despite their *right* to return, and the presence of some of their left-over belongings) could not be classified as first-degree. Do you find any other cases that might affect our case or the authority of *Marquez?*

Answers

1. The index to the annotated collection of California statutes. In California this is *West's Annotated Code* or *Deering's Annotated Code*. California also has *LARMAC*, a separately published index to statutes.
2. Since you know that Alix has been charged with burglary, look under burglary. You also know that the issue is about some difference between first and second degree. "Burglary" is an Index entry, "degrees" is a subheading.
3. It refers you to Pen (the abbreviation for Penal Code) §§ 459 and 460.
4. § 459 is a general description of the crime of burglary. That is, it sets out what factors or elements the State must prove in order for a person to be guilty of the crime.
5. Yes. In our case there is no question that Alix *entered*; she broke a window and climbed in.
6. Intent. The person must enter with the intent or purpose to commit grand or petty larceny or a felony. Actually, this is two elements: (1) the entry must be made with the intention to commit a crime and (2) the intended crime must be grand or petit larceny or a felony.
7. Yes. Alix entered with the intent to "steal whatever she could find." The term "steal" is vernacular for larceny.
8. By looking up the definitions of grand and petit larceny in the statutes in the annotated code; you would start by looking up larceny in the index. To save you the trouble of actually looking this up, we'll tell you that Alix's intention was to commit either grand larceny or petit larceny (which would depend on the value of the property Alix intended to steal).
9. Yes. It says "In this chapter, 'inhabited' means currently being used for dwelling purposes, whether occupied or not."
10. West: "Degrees; construction of section."
    Deering's: "Degrees."
11. "Every burglary of an inhabited dwelling house...is burglary of the first degree." In subsection (b), we are told that all other kinds of burglary are of the second degree.
12. a. Look in the index volume under "burglary"
    b. "Burglary
       "Dwelling house, generally Burgl §§ 1-4
       "Occupancy, generally Burgl sections 4, 27."
    c. Yes, except that the *Am. Jur. 2d* definition includes "in the night time" an element not included in California's statute.
    d. § 4.

e. We are told that the owner must have left with the intention of returning if the house is to be considered "inhabited."

f. The length of time the house is unoccupied seems to be of little importance. "The intention to return is determined mainly from the condition in which the house was left."

g. Time to look in the Pocket Part!

h. Under Burglary § 4 in the pocket part you find a new *A.L.R.* annotation, 20 *A.L.R.* 4th 349, and a California case, *People v. Marquez*, which seems to have facts similar to our case.

i. The case seems to say that the house was "inhabited," and the defendant is therefore guilty of first degree burglary.

j. Yes, if it deals with the issue of "inhabited" in a context of relevant facts similar to ours.

13. At the beginning of the Notes of Decisions following § 460 is a table of contents to the notes. If you are using *West's Annotated California Code*, you'll find:

"Inhabited dwelling or building 4-8

Temporary absence 5."

The numbers represent the Note sections. When you refer to the Pocket Part at the back of the bound volume, you will know to go directly to those section numbers in the Pocket Part's Notes of Decisions.

(The *Deering* set has a similar arrangement.)

14. There is only one case note that indicates that the owner was absent for a long time, and even had "moved to a boarding home..." *People v. Marquez*, (again!) 192 Cal. Rptr. 193, 143 Cal. App. 3d 797 (1983).

15. a. Yes. In *Marquez*, the owner had been absent for several years.

b. Yes; the owner was living in some kind of care facility.

c. Yes. The *Marquez* court said that the important thing in terms of deciding whether premises are inhabited when the owner is absent is whether the owner intends to return. The fact that the home was maintained for her supported the conclusion that she intended to return.

16. Yes. The important (relevant) facts are very similar and the court was deciding the same issue raised by Alix: whether the house was inhabited for the purpose of determining whether the burglary was of the first or second degree pursuant to Penal Code § 460.

17. Shepardize the case and use the appropriate West's case digests.

18. a. Shepard's California Citations shows that a number of cases have cited Marquez, but most of them for points of law dealt with by the Marquez court with which we are not concerned. If you look at the headnotes for the Marquez opinion, you will see that our issue is dealt with in headnotes 2, 3 and 4, and there are several cases that Shepard's says cited Marquez for issues dealt with in other headnotes.

b. Yes: There are three citations that either cited one of the three headnotes we are concerned with or that cited to the case as a whole (no specific headnote). We have to look at these to make sure there is no problem. *Shepard's* also tells us that an *A.L.R.* annotation cited *Marquez* in the pocket part (20 A.L.R. 4th 349s). You will want to make a note of the A.L.R. article in case you need more information or more cases.

19. *People v. O'Bryan.*

20. No. *O'Bryan* cited *Marquez* about an issue regarding burglary (was the place a residence), but NOT about the issue of "inhabited."

    In your research notes, mark this case as not relevant.

21. *People v. Hines.*

22. Yes it is.

23. No. It's about whether a guest house that was broken into was a part of the "inhabited dwelling house." Therefore, it is not a matter of concern to us, because it would not affect the authority of *Marquez*. Make your notes specific on this point.

24. a. By using the key topic and number assigned to the headnotes relevant to your issue.

    b. Taking the key topic and number from the relevant headnotes of *Marquez*, Burglary key 10, go to the latest edition of the *California Digest*.

    c. In *California Digest 2d* under Burglary key 10, we see that the section is titled "degrees," and after looking at the notes for a few cases, we see that this section contains cases about many issues other than "inhabited." Just keep plugging, and you'll pick out cases about "inhabited" in this section. And don't forget the pocket part.

       One of the cases you will find is *People v. Cardona*. You may recall that this was one of the cases noted in the Notes of Decisions following Penal Code § 460, and we told you not to bother looking these up as they were about very short-term absences. This is also true of *People v. Lewis* and *People v. Stewart*. Eventually, you will find *Marquez* again, but no other relevant cases. So, after all the looking, you can conclude there is nothing here that would affect our case or the authority of *Marquez*.

Legal Memorandum

Okay, you're done with your research. Now the very final step is to write up what you found in the form of a legal memorandum. After giving it a good try, using the general approach outlined in Chapter 11, compare your result with the following memo.

Memo from: Terry Paralegal

To: Ruth Lawyer

Topic: Whether Charlene's house was inhabited at the time Alix entered for the purpose of larceny, so as to make Alix guilty of first degree burglary.

Facts:

In October 1990, Alix broke into a house in San Francisco owned by Charlene with the intent to steal. At the time, Charlene was not occupying the house as she had been sent to Los Angeles by her employer for a temporary assignment; she planned to return in January 1991. In her absence the house was maintained by Sally, whom Charlene had hired for that purpose. Alix was seen entering the premises and was arrested there by the police.

Issue:

For purposes of deciding whether a person is guilty of first degree burglary under Penal Code §§ 459 and 460, was the house "inhabited" under the following circumstances?

- No one was actually living in the house when it was broken into.
- The owner/resident was absent from the house for an extended period but intended to return.
- The house was maintained for the owner/resident in her absence.

Conclusion:

The issue of whether a house is inhabited if the owner/resident is absent from the premises depends on the intent of the owner/resident to return. The length of the absence is relevant only insofar as a factor in determining the intent. Charlene showed intent to return, so her house was "inhabited," and Alix is guilty of first degree burglary.

Reasoning:

California Penal Code defines burglary as the entering of a building for certain criminal purposes(Pen. Code sec. 459). It then goes on to set up a distinction between first and second degree burglary (Pen. Code sec. 460). First degree is when the building entered is an "inhabited dwelling house." In our case, there is no doubt that the act of Alix was burglary and that the building entered was a dwelling house. Regarding the issue of whether the house was inhabited, case law indicates that only the owner's intent is determinative. In People v. Marquez, 192 Cal. Rptr. 193, 143 Cal. App. 3d 797 (1983), the elderly owner had moved to a care facility for several years and friends and relatives maintained the house, expecting her to return. The Marquez court held that the length of absence from a person's home is relevant only insofar as it may bear on the determination of whether she intends to return, that the residence was inhabited and the defendant was guilty of first degree burglary.

In our case, Charlene was gone for a long time (almost two years), but she left for a temporary job with a specific two-year duration and a specific return date of January 1991, and employed Sally to create the appearance that the house was occupied. There were no indications that Charlene did not intend to return.

Therefore, based on the holding in People v. Marquez, the court should find that Charlene's house was "inhabited" and that Alix is guilty of burglary in the first degree.

3. Research Problem: Alimony Hypothetical (West Virginia)

Estimated Time: 2 and 1/2 hours

The research for this problem will require the following skills:

- using background resources (Chapter 5)
- finding a case from its citation (Chapter 9)
- using the case reporters (Chapter 8)
- Using *Shepard's Case Citations* (Chapter 10)
- using West's digests (Chapter 10)
- reading a case, including use of headnotes (Chapter 7)
- writing a memorandum of law (Chapter 11).

The sources required to fully research this problem are:

- *American Law Reports* (A.L.R.)
- *Southeastern Reporter*
- a law dictionary
- *Shepard's Southeastern Citations*
- *Virginia and West Virginia Digest* or *Southeastern Digest* or the *Decennial/General* digest.

Joan and Michael Hamish were married in 1952. Joan filed for divorce in early 1981 in the circuit court near their home in West Virginia. Their three children were grown and independent. Michael (55 years old in 1982) was a successful surgeon. Joan (50 years old in 1982) had been a teacher before the children were born and in 1980 had gone back to school for a Ph.D. in psychology with the plan to become a psychotherapist. At the time of the divorce she was working part time in a clinic as part of her school program and earning $6,000 per year.

They made the following agreement, which was approved by the court in a decree dated June 1, 1982.

1. Joan to keep the family home and the car she used in her name.
2. Michael to keep the family boat and the car he used in his name.
3. All other property and debts to be divided equally.
4. Michael to pay Joan alimony as follows: $3000 per month for 5 years (60 months) starting June 1, 1982; then $2000 per month for 3 years (36 months); then $1000 per month for 10 years (120 months). The purpose of the payments is to support Joan while she finishes her degree and becomes self-supporting through her psychotherapy practice, but she may use the funds for any purpose. In any event, the payments will cease on May 1, 2000.

On October 1, 1990, Michael died of a heart attack. His estate was worth over $2 million, but his will made no provision for Joan. The executor was his best friend, Jose Nunez, M.D. Michael had made the October alimony payment which at that time was down to $1000, and Joan was well on the way to being self-supporting, although she was relying on the $1000 monthly payment for ten more years.

Joan called Jose after the funeral and asked him when she might expect the next payment. Jose talked to his lawyer and then told Joan, "Alimony payments terminate when the paying spouse dies. Too bad, Joan, but I can't do anything about it." Joan wants to know whether Jose is right.

Approach Statement Family law (divorce, child support, alimony, adoption, etc.) is a mixture of common law and statutes, with many cases interpreting the statutes, and then more statutes putting the cases into effect (called "codifying the cases").

For this type of research problem, start with a background resource that will help you gain an overview of the issues. Then study the cases and statutes that are mentioned by the resource as bearing on your research question. Finally,

Shepardize the cases and statutes on which you plan to rely and check the digests.

General national background resources include *A.L.R.*, *Am. Jur.*, *C.J.S.* and law review articles. We suggest starting with *A.L.R.* to learn about alimony in West Virginia and the issue of termination of alimony payments on the death of the payor (paying spouse). We recommend trying *A.L.R.* first if you can find a recent annotation about your issue, because it gathers all the cases on a single issue into an easy to use, well-organized form and discusses cases from all states.

Questions

1. Does *A.L.R.* have an annotation (article) about your issue? What topic do you look under in the index?
2. Go to the annotation. Does the *A.L.R.* 9th article discuss West Virginia cases? If so, in which sections?
3. The "Summary and Comment" at the beginning of the article first discusses whether unpaid and overdue alimony payments may be recovered from the estate of a deceased payor spouse. Is this an issue in our case?
4. What does the Summary tell us about what happens to regular periodic alimony payments upon the death of the obligor (paying spouse)?
5. Now it is time to look at the sections that contain West Virginia cases. What West Virginia case is cited in § 2[b]?
6. Make a note of the name and citation of the case and the section you found it in for easy reference later. What does this case seem to say about our problem?
7. What West Virginia case is discussed (not just cited, but discussed) in § 4[a]?
8. What does this case, as summarized in *A.L.R.*, tell us about our question?
9. Do the discussions in §§ 5[a] and 6[a] concern the issue in our case?
10. What is the West Virginia case cited in § 29[a]?
11. Is this case also discussed in § 29[b]?
12. Does § 29[a] refer to the case for the same reason that 29[b] does?
13. § 29 is titled "Alimony in Gross." In order to understand what is meant by this in West Virginia, you will need to read *Weller*. Where do you find the *Weller* case?
14. Read the *Weller* case. What situation does the court define as "alimony in gross"?
15. Was the alimony "in gross" in the *Weller* case? What facts were relevant to that determination?
16. Following the rule of *Weller* for determining whether alimony is "in gross," is the alimony in our case "in gross"?
17. Concerning our issue of whether the payments to Joan are payable to her by Michael's estate, what does the *Weller* court say is the importance of the alimony being "in gross"?
18. What does "vested" mean? The *Weller* court doesn't define it, so where would be the best place to look?
19. What does the *Weller* Court say is the relationship between the alimony being vested and it being "in gross"?
20. Applying the reasoning of the *Weller* court, will Joan's alimony payments survive Michael's death and be payable to her by Michael's estate?
21. In *Weller*, did the court say when Mrs. Weller was to receive the money?
22. Are there difference between the facts of *Weller* and our case?

23. Are these differences relevant? That is, would these differences affect the reasoning and conclusion of the *Weller* court if it were examining our case?

24. Which statutes does the court discuss that might be relevant to your issue?

25. What is the rule of § 48-2-15(f)?

26. Does 48-2-15(f) affect Joan's case? Why?

27. According to *Weller*, what is the court supposed to do in cases where 48-2-15(f) does not apply?

28. Now that you have an authoritative case that says what you want it to, and have determined that the alimony statute does not affect our case, what do you have to do to make sure that there are no other cases with similar facts and contrary holdings, and that the case is up to date and has not been overturned or otherwise affected by subsequent cases (in other words, how do you make sure that *Weller* is still "good law")?

29. Shepardize *Weller*. Are there any cases that have cited *Weller*?

30. a. The first citation, 385 S.E.2d 389, has a "j" in front of it in *Shepard's*. What does the "j" mean?

    b. Read the citing case. Does it affect the holding of *Weller* as it relates to Joan's situation?

31. a. The second citing case is shown in Shepard's as citing *Weller* twice. The first one has a "d" in front of it, one has a small "1" after the S.E.2d and the other has a small "2" after the S.E.2d. What do these notations mean?

    b. Could *Weller* headnotes 1 or 2 be relevant to our case?

    c. Read the case, especially the part on page 479. Does the case in any way change the effect of *Weller* on our case?

32. The third citing case also cites to *Weller's* headnote 1. Find the case and read it. Does it change the effect of *Weller* on our case?

33. Well, that's it for *Shepard's*. Now, what is the appropriate digest to use to make sure that there are no other cases with similar facts and issues that have contrary holdings to *Weller*?

34. What do you look under in that digest?

35. Did you find anything that disturbs the authority of *Weller*?

36. How would you calculate the amount owed by Michael's estate to Joan?

Answers

1. If you look in the *A.L.R. Index* under the heading "ALIMONY" and the subheading "Death" (don't forget the pocket part in the back of the Index volume you are using), you will find a reference to "obligor spouse's death as affecting alimony," 79 A.L.R.4th 10. You're in luck; this seems to be exactly what you're looking for. There is also a reference to "husband's death as affecting alimony 39 A.L.R.2d 406," but this is a much older article (A.L.R 2d), so go first to the newer article and if that one doesn't address your issue, go to the older one.

2. The Table of Jurisdictions represented at the beginning of the annotation shows that there are West Virginia cases in §§ 2[b], 4[a], 5[a], 6[a], 29[a] and 29[b].

3. No. Michael wasn't in arrears at the time of his death—that is, he didn't owe any back support; his payments were up to date.

4. The Summary tells us that the rule of most courts is that an award for regular periodic alimony payments (as in our case) ends on the death of the obligor (payor, paying) spouse, but

that the courts of varying jurisdictions hold widely diverging views on this issue.

5. *Re Estate of Hereford*, 162 W. Va. 477, 250 S.E.2d 45 (1978).

6. Because *Hereford* is cited in footnote 7, read the text preceding the "7." From the text, *Hereford* seems to concern issues about the daily ability of the obligee spouse (the receiver of alimony) to support her/himself and the sufficient size of the obligor's estate to pay the alimony claim. This might be helpful if we don't find anything better.

7. *In Re Estate of Weller*, 374 S.E.2d 712 (W. Va. 1988), on page 30 of the article.

8. This section is about whether a court may order that periodic alimony continue after the death of the obligor spouse. The West Virginia court seems to say that a court may order the obligation to be paid out of the obligor's estate.

9. No. The issue treated in § 5[a] is whether parties getting divorced may provide in their agreement that the payments will survive the death of the payor spouse. This is not our issue: the parties in our case did not so provide and now it is too late. The issue discussed in § 6[a] concerns whether, if the divorce decree says the payments are to continue until the death of the payee spouse, this shows an intent that they would continue after the death of the payor spouse. This is not our issue: in our case there was no such provision.

10. *In Re Estate of Weller*, 374 S.E.2d 712 (1988).

11. Yes.

12. No. § 29[a] says that the cases referred to in that section stand for the proposition that alimony may survive the death of the obligor spouse, whereas § 29[b] says just the opposite.

13. The citation is 374 S.E.2d 712. This case is in volume 374 of the Southeastern Reporter 2nd series, starting on page 712.

14. On page 716, the *Weller* court says an alimony award will be characterized as alimony in gross when the total amount of the alimony payments and the date the payments will cease can be determined from the divorce decree.

15. Yes. In *Weller*, the amount of each payment was designated in the decree, and the exact number of payments could be determined from the decree. Therefore, by simple arithmetic, the total amount of money that the payor spouse was to pay the payee spouse could have been calculated on the date of the divorce decree.

16. Yes. On the date of the Hamish's divorce decree, it would have been possible to determine the total amount Michael was to pay Joan because the exact number of payments and the amount of each payment are stated in the decree.

17. The *Weller* court says that if alimony is "in gross," it is vested as of the date of the divorce decree.

18. The best place to look it up is in a law dictionary, another type of background resource. Two widely used law dictionaries are Black's *Law Dictionary* and Oran's *Dictionary of Legal Terms*, where you will find that vested means the vested thing is absolutely yours and will come to you without your having to do anything except, perhaps, wait.

19. On pages 715-716, the *Weller* court says "Mrs. Weller had a vested right to receive a total sum of $9,000 ... and her award may therefore be properly characterized as 'alimony in gross ....'" Therefore, the obligation of the payor spouse survived his death and was payable to the payee spouse by the payor's estate.

20. Yes. Once it is determined that the alimony is "in gross," it follows that it is also "vested." Alimony that has vested survives the death of the payor spouse, and must be paid to the payee spouse out of the payor's estate.

21. The *Weller* court states on page 716, in the last paragraph of the case, "...Mrs. Weller is entitled to the $6,600.00 she stood to receive from Dr. Weller had he lived, such amount now being payable from Dr. Weller's estate."

22. There are differences in facts between the *Weller* case and ours: the length of time payments were to be made, the amount of the individual payments, and the total amount to be paid.

23. No. The court never attaches any significance to the number of payments or their amount, except to calculate the amount owed.

24. West Virginia Code § 48-2-15(f) and § 48-2-36.

25. The code section states that a divorce agreement or decree must state whether or not alimony is to survive the death of the payor party.

26. No. The *Weller* court held that § 48-2-6 provides that 48-2-15 (enacted in 1984) does not have retroactive effect on alimony payments. Joan and Michael's decree was dated June 1, 1982, so it would not be affected by 48-2-15(f).

27. The court writes that: "We believe the better result will be reached in this case by examining the plain language of the divorce decree..."

28. Use digests and Shepardize.

29. In *Shepard's Southeastern Citations*, under 374 Southeastern Report, 2d Series, page 12, we learn that there are three cases in the Southeastern Reporter that cited *Weller*. There are also other cites, but these only show that *Weller* was cited in 79 A.L.R.4th (the A.L.R article we found it in)!

30. a. By looking in the front of the volume you will find a list of abbreviations. The j means that *Weller* was cited in that case in a dissenting opinion.

    b No. This case is about a completely different issue. The dissenting judge cited *Weller* in support of the statement that the Court's decisions in recent years, including *Weller*, have been requiring fair and just treatment for married women.

31. a. The "d" means that the case on page 749 in volume 424 of S.E.2d distinguished the facts of that case from *Weller*. The little "1" means that the issue for which it cited *Weller* was described in *Weller* in headnote "1." The little "2" means that the court also cited *Weller* for the issue described in *Weller's* headnote "2."

    b. Maybe. Headnote 1 says the court has the power to say that alimony will survive the death of the payor. Headnote 2 states the general rule that alimony ends when a spouse dies unless the decree specifically states that it is binding on the payor's estate.

    c. No. The case offers no legal principles that would change the rule of *Weller* about alimony in gross surviving the death of the payor spouse.

32. No. The court cites *Weller* and makes a finding consistent with *Weller* and other similar cases. It has no effect on *Weller* or our case.

33. Go to the latest edition of the *Virginia and West Virginia Digest*, or the *Southeastern Digest* or, if your library has neither of these, then the *American (Decennial* and *General) Digest*. Don't

forget the pocket parts and don't forget you are looking for West Virginia cases only.

34. Taking the "key number" from the relevant headnotes of *Weller*, you look under Divorce keys 241 and 247.

35. Not as of February, 1995.

36. The amount due is calculated as follows:

Payments to be made:

$3000 per month for 60 months	$180,000
2000 per month for 36 months	$72,000
1000 per month for 120 months	$120,000
TOTAL	$372,000

Michael paid:

at $3000 per month 6/1/82-5/1/87	$180,000
at $2000 per month 6/1/87-5/1/90	$72,000
at $1000 per month 6/1/90-10/1/90	$5,000
TOTAL	$257,000

$372,000-257,000 = $115,000

Legal Memorandum

Okay, you're done with your research. The very final step is to write up what you found in the form of a legal memorandum, using the guidelines set out in Chapter 11. Then compare your result with the sample memo we've prepared for this research (set out below).

Memo from: Terry Paralegal
To: Ruth Lawyer
Topic: The liability of Michael Hamisch's estate for alimony payments to Joan Hamisch

<u>Facts</u>:

Joan and Michael Hamisch were divorced in 1982. Among other terms, the divorce decree, dated June 1, 1982, provided that Michael was to pay Joan alimony starting June 1, 1982 and ending May 1, 2000. The amounts of the payments were specific: $3000 per month for 60 months; then $2000 per month for 36 months; then $1000 per month for 120 months. On October 1, 1990 Michael died; he had made the October 1 payment. Joan is planning to file a claim against Michael's estate for the remaining payments, a total of $114,000. Michael's executor resists Joan's demand on the basis that alimony payments terminate on the death of the payor spouse.

<u>Issue</u>:

Do alimony payments that are for specified amounts and for a specified number of payments terminate on the death of the payor spouse before all payments have been made?

<u>Conclusion</u>:

Because the total amount of the alimony payments could have been calculated on the date of the divorce decree, they vested as of that date. Therefore the balance of payments due to Joan as of the date of Michael's death are owed to Joan by Michael's estate.

<u>Reasoning</u>:

West Virginia Code § 48-2-15(f) provides that in all divorce decrees containing alimony payments, there must be a statement as to whether the payments survive the death of the payor spouse. The Hamish's decree contained no such provision. However, in our case as well as in <u>Re Estate of Weller,</u> 374 S.E.2d 712 (W.Va. 1988), the statute is not applicable because as the <u>Weller</u> court stated, § 48-2-36 provides that the statute, enacted in 1984, is not applied retroactively to prior divorce decrees.

<u>Re Estate of Weller</u> is a case similar to ours in that in <u>Weller</u>, as in our case, the alimony payments were for specified amounts and a specified number of payments and the payor spouse died before all payments were made. In <u>Weller</u>, the Supreme Court stated that whether alimony payments survive the death of the payor spouse, where the statute is not applicable, depends on whether the payments are in "in gross" and therefore vested as of the date of the divorce decree. The court said that, although in general alimony payments terminate on the death of the payor spouse, if the total amount of the payments could be determined as of the date of the decree, then the alimony was in gross; this was possible in both our case and <u>Weller</u>. If the alimony is in gross, and therefore vested as of the date of the decree, the Court said, and the payor spouse dies before all the payments are made, the estate of the deceased payor has to pay to the surviving spouse now, the amount she stood to receive had the paying spouse lived.

Therefore, based on the holding in <u>Weller,</u> a West Virginia court should award to Joan the sum of $114,000, payable to her now by Michael's estate.

Index

A

B

C

D

E

F

G

H

I

J

K

L

M

N

O

P

R

S

T

U

V

W

Y

	EDITION	PRICE	CODE
BUSINESS			
Business Plans to Game Plans	1st	$29.95	GAME
Getting Started as an Independent Paralegal—Audio	2nd	$44.95	GSIP
How to Finance a Growing Business	4th	$24.95	GROW
💾 How to Form a CA Nonprofit Corp.—w/Corp. Records Binder & Disk (PC & Mac)	1st	$49.95	CNP
💾 How to Form a Nonprofit Corp., Book w/Disk (PC)—National Edition	2nd	$39.95	NNP
💾 How to Form Your Own Calif. Corp.—w/Corp. Records Binder & Disk—PC	1st	$39.95	CACI
How to Form Your Own California Corporation	8th	$29.95	CCOR
💾 How to Form Your Own Florida Corporation, (Book w/Disk—PC)	3rd	$39.95	FLCO
💾 How to Form Your Own New York Corporation, (Book w/Disk—PC)	3rd	$39.95	NYCO
💾 How to Form Your Own Texas Corporation, (Book w/Disk—PC)	4th	$39.95	TCI
How to Start Your Own Business: Small Business Law—Audio	1st	$14.95	TBUS
How to Write a Business Plan	4th	$21.95	SBS
Make Up Your Mind: Entrepreneurs Talk About Decision Making	1st	$19.95	MIND
Marketing Without Advertising	1st	$14.00	MWAD
Mastering Diversity	1st	$29.95	MAST
Small Business Legal Pro—Windows	2nd	$27.96	SBW1
💾 Taking Care of Your Corporation, Vol. 1, (Book w/Disk—PC)	1st	$26.95	CORK
💾 Taking Care of Your Corporation, Vol 2, (Book w/Disk—PC)	1st	$39.95	CORK2
Tax Savvy for Small Business	1st	$26.95	SAVVY
The California Nonprofit Corporation Handbook	6th	$29.95	NON
The California Professional Corporation Handbook	5th	$34.95	PROF
The Employer's Legal Handbook	1st	$29.95	EMPL
The Independent Paralegal's Handbook	3rd	$29.95	PARA
The Legal Guide for Starting & Running a Small Business	2nd	$24.95	RUNS
The Partnership Book: How to Write a Partnership Agreement	4th	$24.95	PART
Trademark: How to Name Your Business & Product	1st	$29.95	TRD
CONSUMER			
Fed Up With the Legal System: What's Wrong & How to Fix It	2nd	$9.95	LEG
Glossary of Insurance Terms	5th	$14.95	GLINT
How to Win Your Personal Injury Claim	1st	$24.95	PICL
Nolo's Law Form Kit: Hiring Child Care & Household Help	1st	$14.95	KCHLD

💾 Book with disk

	EDITION	PRICE	CODE
Nolo's Pocket Guide to California Law	3rd	$10.95	CLAW
Nolo's Pocket Guide to California Law on Disk—Windows	3.0	$17.46	CLW3
Nolo's Pocket Guide to Consumer Rights (California Edition)	2nd	$12.95	CAG
The Over 50 Insurance Survival Guide	1st	$16.95	OVER50
What Do You Mean It's Not Covered?	1st	$19.95	COVER
ESTATE PLANNING & PROBATE			
5 Ways to Avoid Probate—Audio	1st	$14.95	TPRO
How to Probate an Estate (California Edition)	8th	$34.95	PAE
Make Your Own Living Trust	1st	$19.95	LITR
Nolo's Law Form Kit: Wills	1st	$14.95	KWL
Nolo's Simple Will Book	2nd	$17.95	SWIL
Plan Your Estate	3rd	$24.95	NEST
Write Your Will—Audio	1st	$14.95	TWYW
FAMILY MATTERS			
A Legal Guide for Lesbian and Gay Couples	8th	$24.95	LG
Child Custody: Building Agreements that Work	1st	$24.95	CUST
Divorce & Money: How to Make the Best Financial Decisions During Divorce	2nd	$21.95	DIMO
How to Adopt Your Stepchild in California	4th	$22.95	ADOP
How to Do Your Own Divorce in California	20th	$21.95	CDIV
How to Do Your Own Divorce in Texas	5th	$17.95	TDIV
How to Raise or Lower Child Support in California	3rd	$18.95	CHLD
Nolo's Pocket Guide to Family Law	3rd	$14.95	FLD
Practical Divorce Solutions	1st	$14.95	PDS
The Guardianship Book (California Edition)	2nd	$24.95	GB
The Living Together Kit	7th	$24.95	LTK
GOING TO COURT			
Collect Your Court Judgment (California Edition)	2nd	$19.95	JUDG
Everybody's Guide to Municipal Court (California Edition)	1st	$29.95	MUNI
Everybody's Guide to Small Claims Court (California Edition)	11th	$18.95	CSCC
Everybody's Guide to Small Claims Court (National Edition)	5th	$18.95	NSCC
Fight Your Ticket ... and Win! (California Edition)	6th	$19.95	FYT
How to Change Your Name (California Edition)	6th	$24.95	NAME
Represent Yourself in Court: How to Prepare & Try a Winning Case	1st	$29.95	RYC
The Criminal Records Book (California Edition)	4th	$21.95	CRIM
Winning in Small Claims Court—Audio	1st	$14.95	TWIN
HOMEOWNERS, LANDLORDS & TENANTS			
Dog Law	2nd	$12.95	DOG
For Sale by Owner (California Edition)	2nd	$24.95	FSBO

Book with disk

TO ORDER CALL 800-992-6656

	EDITION	PRICE	CODE
Homestead Your House (California Edition)	8th	$9.95	HOME
How to Buy a House in California	3rd	$24.95	BHCA
Neighbor Law: Fences, Trees, Boundaries & Noise	2nd	$16.95	NEI
Nolo's Law Form Kit: Leases & Rental Agreements (California Edition)	1st	$14.95	KLEAS
Safe Homes, Safe Neighborhoods: Stopping Crime Where You Live	1st	$14.95	SAFE
Tenants' Rights (California Edition)	12th	$18.95	CTEN
The Deeds Book (California Edition)	3rd	$16.95	DEED
The Landlord's Law Book, Vol. 1: Rights & Responsibilities (California Edition)	4th	$32.95	LBRT
The Landlord's Law Book, Vol. 2: Evictions (California Edition)	5th	$34.95	LBEV

HUMOR

29 Reasons Not to Go to Law School	4th	$9.95	29R
Devil's Advocates: The Unnatural History of Lawyers	1st	$12.95	DA
Nolo's Favorite Lawyer Jokes On Disk—DOS	1.0	$9.95	JODI
Nolo's Favorite Lawyer Jokes On Disk—Macintosh	1.0	$9.95	JODM
Nolo's Favorite Lawyer Jokes On Disk—Windows	1st	$9.95	JODWI
Poetic Justice: The Funniest, Meanest Things Ever Said About Lawyers	1st	$9.95	PJ

IMMIGRATION

Como Obtener La Tarjeta Verde: Maneras Legitimas de Permanecer en los EE.UU.	1st	$24.95	VERDE
How to Become a United States Citizen	5th	$14.95	CIT
How to Get a Green Card: Legal Ways to Stay in the U.S.A.	1st	$22.95	GRN

MONEY MATTERS

Chapter 13 Bankruptcy: Repay Your Debts	1st	$29.95	CH13
How to File for Bankruptcy	5th	$25.95	HFB
Money Troubles: Legal Strategies to Cope With Your Debts	3rd	$18.95	MT
Nolo's Law Form Kit: Buy & Sell Contracts	1st	$9.95	KCONT
Nolo's Law Form Kit: Loan Agreements	1st	$14.95	KLOAN
Nolo's Law Form Kit: Personal Bankruptcy	1st	$14.95	KBNK
Nolo's Law Form Kit: Power of Attorney	1st	$14.95	KPA
Nolo's Law Form Kit: Rebuild Your Credit	1st	$14.95	KCRD
Simple Contracts for Personal Use	2nd	$16.95	CONT
Smart Ways to Save Money During and After Divorce	1st	$14.95	SAVMO
Stand Up to the IRS	2nd	$21.95	SIRS

PATENTS AND COPYRIGHTS

Copyright Your Software	1st	$39.95	CYS
Patent It Yourself	3rd	$39.95	PAT
Software Development: A Legal Guide (Book with disk—PC)	1st	$44.95	SFT
The Copyright Handbook: How to Protect and Use Written Works	2nd	$24.95	COHA
The Inventor's Notebook	1st	$19.95	INOT

Book with disk

TO ORDER CALL 800-992-6656

	EDITION	PRICE	CODE
RESEARCH & REFERENCE			
Law on the Net	1st	$39.95	LAWN
Legal Research: How to Find & Understand the Law	4th	$19.95	LRES
Legal Research Made Easy: A Roadmap through the Law Library Maze—Video	1st	$89.95	LRME
SENIORS			
Beat the Nursing Home Trap: A Consumer's Guide	2nd	$18.95	ELD
Social Security, Medicare & Pensions: The Sourcebook for Older Americans	5th	$18.95	SOA
The Conservatorship Book (California Edition)	2nd	$29.95	CNSV
SOFTWARE			
California Incorporator 1.0—DOS	1.0	$90.30	INCI
Living Trust Maker 2.0—Macintosh	2.0	$55.96	LTM2
Living Trust Maker 2.0—Windows	2.0	$55.96	LTWI2
Nolo's Partnership Maker 1.0—DOS	1.0	$90.96	PAGI1
Nolo's Personal RecordKeeper 3.0—Macintosh	3.0	$34.96	FRM3
Patent It Yourself 1.0—Windows	1.0	$160.96	PYW1
WillMaker 5.0—DOS	5.0	$48.96	WI5
WillMaker 5.0—Macintosh	5.0	$48.96	WM5
WillMaker 5.0—Windows	5.0	$48.96	WIW5
WORKPLACE			
How to Handle Your Workers' Compensation Claim (California Edition)	1st	$29.95	WORK
Rightful Termination	1st	$29.95	RITE
Sexual Harassment on the Job	2nd	$18.95	HARS
Workers' Comp for Employers	2nd	$29.95	CNTRL
Your Rights in the Workplace	2nd	$15.95	YRW

GET 25% OFF YOUR NEXT PURCHASE

RECYCLE YOUR OUT-OF-DATE BOOKS

It's important to have the most current legal information. Because laws and legal procedures change often, we update our books regularly. To help keep you up-to-date we are extending this special offer. Cut out and mail the title portion of the cover of any old Nolo book with your next order and we'll give you a 25% discount off the retail price of ANY new Nolo book you purchase directly from us. For current prices and editions call us at 1-800-992-6656. This offer is to individuals only.

TO ORDER CALL 800-992-6656

ORDER FORM

Code	Quantity	Title	Unit price	Total
			Subtotal	
			California residents add Sales Tax	
			Shipping & Handling ($4 for 1st item; $1 each additional)	
			2nd day UPS (additional $5; $8 in Alaska and Hawaii)	
			TOTAL	

Name

Address

(UPS to street address, Priority Mail to P.O. boxes)

FOR FASTER SERVICE, USE YOUR CREDIT CARD AND OUR TOLL-FREE NUMBERS

Monday-Friday, 7 a.m. to 6 p.m. Pacific Time

Order Line	1 (800) 992-6656 (in the 510 area code, call 549-1976)
General Information	1 (510) 549-1976
Fax your order	1 (800) 645-0895 (in the 510 area code, call 548-5902)

METHOD OF PAYMENT

☐ Check enclosed

☐ VISA ☐ MasterCard ☐ Discover Card ☐ American Express

Account # Expiration Date

Authorizing Signature

Daytime Phone

Allow 2-3 weeks for delivery. Prices subject to change.

LRES 4.0

NOLO PRESS, 950 PARKER ST., BERKELEY, CA 94710

Educators, *you can teach from these books.*

Law on the Net
ISBN 0-87337-282-4, $39.95

Represent Yourself in Court
ISBN 0-87337-222-0, $29.95

Take advantage of Nolo's 25 years of experience in simplifying complex legal material and consider one or more of these Nolo Press titles for your primary or supplementary text(s).

Nolo's Paperbacks for the Classroom

- Comprehensive
- Easy-to-Read
- Affordable

Everybody's Guide to Small Claims Court, National Edition
ISBN 0-87337-161-5, $18.95

Everybody's Guide to Municipal Court
ISBN 0-87337-156-9
Calif. only, $29.95

Collect Your Court Judgement
ISBN 0-87337-151-8
Calif. only, $19.95

To request a complimentary copy for course adoption consideration, please write us or FAX us on your school letterhead. LIMIT: 3 BOOKS. Ask us to send you our complete catalog, too.

The Legal Guide for Starting & Running a Small Business
ISBN 0-87337-287-5, $24.95

The Employers Legal Handbook
ISBN 0-87337-235-2, $29.95

Sexual Harassment on the Job
ISBN 0-87337-265-4, $18.95

How to File for Bankruptcy
ISBN 0-87337-285-9, $25.95

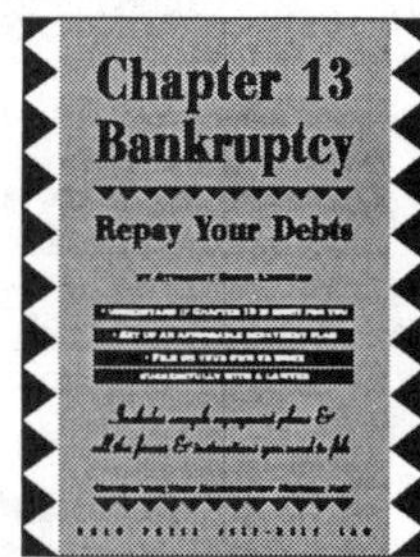

Chapter 13 Bankruptcy
ISBN 0-87337-263-8, $29.95

Software Developement: A Legal Guide
ISBN 0-87337-209-3, $44.95

Nolo's Pocket Guide to CA Law
ISBN 0-87337-292-1, $10.95

Nolo's Pocket Guide to Family Law
ISBN 0-87337-217-4, $14.95

The Independent Paralegal's Guide
ISBN 0-87337-268-9, $29.95

Fed Up With the Legal System
ISBN 0-87337-242-5, $9.95

Nolo Press, 950 Parker St., Berkeley, CA 94710
Attn: Academic Sales • FAX 510-548-5902

NOLO IN THE NEWS

"Nolo helps lay people perform legal tasks without the aid—or fees—of lawyers."

—USA TODAY

[Nolo books are ..."written in plain language, free of legal mumbo jumbo, and spiced with witty personal observations."

—ASSOCIATED PRESS

"...Nolo publications...guide people simply through the how, when, where and why of law."

—WASHINGTON POST

"Increasingly, people who are not lawyers are performing tasks usually regarded as legal work... And consumers, using books like Nolo's, do routine legal work themselves."

—NEW YORK TIMES

"...All of [Nolo's] books are easy-to-understand, are updated regularly, provide pull-out forms...and are often quite moving in their sense of compassion for the struggles of the lay reader."

—SAN FRANCISCO CHRONICLE

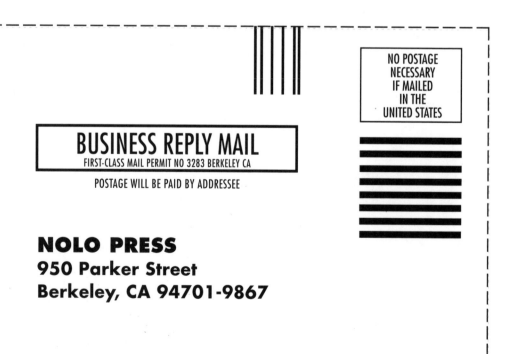

NO POSTAGE NECESSARY IF MAILED IN THE UNITED STATES

BUSINESS REPLY MAIL

FIRST-CLASS MAIL PERMIT NO 3283 BERKELEY CA

POSTAGE WILL BE PAID BY ADDRESSEE

NOLO PRESS
950 Parker Street
Berkeley, CA 94701-9867